THE
INTERNATIONAL
OPERA
GUIDE

THE
INTERNATIONAL
OPERA
GUIDE

♦

F. M. STOCKDALE
M. R. DREYER

Trafalgar Square Publishing

NORTH POMFRET, VERMONT

First published in the United States of America in 1990
by Trafalgar Square Publishing, North Pomfret, Vermont 05053

This book was created and produced by
Roxby General Books Limited
126 Victoria Rise
London SW4 0NW
United Kingdom

Editor: Elizabeth Drury
Design: Eric Drewery
Illustration: Jeff Edwards, Jeremy Ford, Rodney Paull
Typesetting and Origination: Elite Typesetting Techniques, Southampton

Library of Congress Cataloging-in-Publication Data
90-70038

ISBN: 0-943955-27-0

Printed and bound in Yugoslavia by
Mladinska Knjiga, Ljubljana

CONTENTS

Acknowledgements

In preparing this book, my greatest debt is to my mother for the hundreds of opera tickets she bought me. Joe Young and Louise Stein researched and wrote the biographies; Liz Drury, Bryan Evans and Rosalind Hanbury advised on the synopses; and Christine Baxter worked many days, and some nights, to encourage, type and correct the finished product.

Freddie Stockdale

Thanks to Rodney Milnes and Deidre Tilley of *Opera* magazine, the Goethe Institute, York, Valerie Tongue at Roxby Press, many friends and relatives, especially my long-suffering wife, and all the Opera Houses without whom this book would not have been possible.

Martin Dryer

Roxby Press would like to thank the following for their help in providing recordings: B.M.G. Records (U.K.) Limited, E.M.I. Records, Polygram Record Operations and R.C.A. Records. We would also like to thank the following public libraries for their help: Westminster Central Music Library, Battersea Music Library, and Kensington and Chelsea Central Library. Our thanks also to J.M.B. Travel Consultants Ltd.

COMPLETE LIST OF OPERA HOUSES, COMPANIES AND FESTIVALS

KEY TO FACTUAL INFORMATION FOLLOWING ENTRIES:-

☎	Telephone number	💧	Refreshment facilities
TX	Telex number	PT	Public transport
FX	Facsimile number	Ⓟ	Parking facilities
♬	Season dates		
B	Box office address and details	**KEY TO MAPS**	
CC	Credit cards accepted	O	Opera house
⋯	Seating capacity	⊙	Underground

STATE OPERA OF SOUTH AUSTRALIA

Adelaide is home to both the State Opera of South Australia (SOSA) and to Australia's most prestigious festival, which takes place in March in even-numbered years.

The first recorded production in the city is of Auber's *Masaniello* in 1840. A season lasting over three months was provided by the touring Bianchi Italian Opera Company in 1865 with *Lucia, Norma, Traviata* and *Rigoletto* included in the repertory. The Melbourne impresario William Saurin Lyster staged productions of *Aida, Carmen* and *Lohengrin* in 1879. The building of the Tivoli Theatre in 1913 was to have a far-reaching effect: it was reopened as Her Majesty's Theatre in 1962 before being refurbished again in 1979, this time in 1920s style with opulent decor and huge chandeliers. It is now known as the Opera Theatre and has a capacity of 1009.

But it is not the city's only opera facility. The 1978-seat Festival Theatre was completed in 1973, a few months ahead of Sydney Opera House. Its stage is twice the size of Sydney's Opera Theatre, and the wing space is equally capacious. The Festival Centre also includes the 612-seat Playhouse primarily intended for theatre and chamber opera. Between the Theatre and the Playhouse lies the open-air Amphitheatre.

The Festival created a new appetite for opera, which was satisfied by the creation of New Opera South Australia in 1974. Its first musical director was Myer Fredman (1975–80), fresh from a distinguished career on the Glyndebourne staff. Its first general manager was Ian D. Campbell (1976–82). Together they provided a diet of uninhibited productions, introducing young talent and largely steering clear of mainstream works. Changing the company's name to SOSA, they contrived the Australian premiere of *The Midsummer Marriage* for the 1978 Festival.

Ian Johnston took over as general manager in 1984 and oversaw SOSA's most successful contemporary undertaking, Richard Meale's *Voss* (1985). The current musical director is David Kram.

Festival Centre, King William St., Adelaide 5000 ☎ 08-233 4811 TX 82827 FX 08-231 7646 ♬ Jun–Oct B As above ☎ 08-213 4777. Discounts for groups of 12 + ☎ 08–213 4666 CC Amex, Bankcard, Diners, MC, Visa ♿ Wheelchair space, restrooms, ramp ⛲ 1837 🍷 2 restaurants – Lyric ☎ 08-216 8720, Bistro ☎ 08-216 8744 PT Train – North Terrace Station. Bus – King William St. Ⓟ Under theatre.

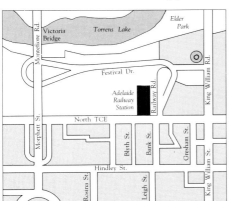

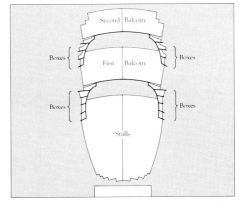

DE NEDERLANDSE OPERA

There is evidence of operatic activity in Amsterdam as early as 1634, when a society modelled on the Florentine Camerata – the Musijck Kamer – was founded to concentrate upon musical drama. The city's first opera house was opened on the Leidse Gracht on New Year's Eve 1680 with Pietro Ziani's *Le Fatiche d'Ercole per Deianira*. The nearest equivalent to the first opera in Dutch was Carolus Hacquart's *De Triomfeerende Min*, written to celebrate the Peace of Nijmegen in 1678, but in fact it is only incidental music created for a play by Dirk Buysero and belongs to the realm of melodrama. By the end of the 17th century sporadic attempts by Hendrik Anders and Servaas de Kunink to develop opera in Dutch petered out, when the French and Italian repertory took hold. Much of it was presented at the Stadsschouwburg theatre (erected in 1638) on the Keizersgracht. The theatre burned down during a performance of Pierre-Alexandre Monsigny's *Le Déserteur* in 1772: its replacement in the Leidse Plein opened three years later.

A pivotal figure in Amsterdam's musical life was the composer-conductor Bartholomeus Ruloffs (1741–1801), who translated several of Grétry's *opéras comiques* into Dutch, often inserting some of his own music. The city had a permanent French

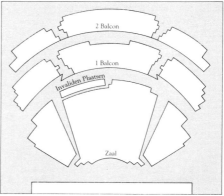

theatre company between 1788 and 1855, with its own small chorus and orchestra: it was inspired by the new Collège Dramatique et Lyrique, where singers were trained from 1781.

A parallel development took place at the Stadsschouwburg during the 19th century, where the facilities were upgraded and Jacob Neyts produced Italian and other operas in Dutch translation. But it was the founding of the Wagner-Vereeniging (Wagner Association) by the conductor Henri Viotta in 1883 which was the most fruitful: a chronological cycle of Wagner's works was mounted, including the first European performance of *Parsifal* (1905) outside Bayreuth. Viotta also conducted works by Strauss and Humperdinck. After his retirement in 1919 the repertory was broadened to include all the major French composers, Willem Pijper (the father of Dutch 20th-century music) and Britten. The origins of the first Nederlandse Opera lay in the Municipal Opera Enterprise, formed in 1941 under German occupation: it became the NO in 1946, giving some 200 performances a year throughout Holland until 1964.

In that year it was reorganized as the Nieuwe Nederlandse Opera under the direction of Maurice Huismann. A pioneering series of baroque operas were presented in the early 1970s and set an international fashion. A Monteverdi cycle followed in 1974. Morale declined at the end of the decade, but was revived by the announcement of a new opera house to replace the small Stadsschouwburg. After five years of construction, the much larger Muziektheater was opened in 1986 to a double bill of ballet and Otto Ketting's one-act opera *Ithaka*.

The Muziektheater has a very large stage – a full semicircle complementing the wide sweep of the auditorium itself, which is comfortable and spacious, and boasts lively acoustics. DNO's progressive policies throughout the 1980s have included Dario Fo's first venture into operatic production, *Barbiere*, and a hi-tech production of *Salome* by Harry Kupfer, as well as an average of one new Dutch work a year: Theo Loevendie's *Naima* (1985) was a particular success. The world premiere of Philip Glass' *Satyagraha* was staged in 1980. This policy seems likely to be enhanced with the appointment as artistic director in 1988 of Pierre Audi, founder of London's enterprising Almeida Theatre. DNO is usually accompanied by the Netherlands Philharmonic Orchestra, whose chief conductor is Hartmut Haenchen. The company travels throughout Holland: regularly to Rotterdam, Scheveningen and Utrecht, less often to Eindhoven, Nijmegen, The Hague and Tilburg.

Muziektheater, Waterlooplein 22, 1011 PG Amsterdam ☎ 020-551 8922 TX 13108 NEDOP FX 020-832 350 ♫ Sep – Jun B P.O. Box 16822, 1001 RH Amsterdam ☎ 020-255455. Mon – Fri 10am – 6pm, Sun, Bank Hol 11.30am – 6pm. For groups ☎ 020-551 8199 CC None ♿ Special seating, access, restrooms, hearing aids ⠿ 1594 ♣ Buffet Fri, Sat, Sun ☎ 020-551 8054 PT Tram – 9, 14. Underground – Waterlooplein ℗ Under theatre.

GREEK NATIONAL OPERA

Athens is not in the front line of international opera, but Greece has produced a number of first-class singers and the prospects look good. The San Giacomo Theatre, financed by Venice, was opened in Corfu in 1691, and Italian companies visited it regularly throughout the 18th century. Pupils of Nicolaos Mantzaros, father of the Ionian School of composers, were responsible for the earliest stirrings of Greek opera: Spyridon Xyndas composed the first opera to a Greek libretto, the satirical O Ypopsifios Vouleftis (The Parliamentary Candidate), premiered in Corfu in 1867; Paulos Karreres wrote two operas about the War of Independence (1821–29).

The first opera performed in Athens was Rossini's Barbiere in 1837, sponsored by the state and intended mainly for foreigners living in Greece. Professional Greek touring companies were founded in the 1880s but it was only in 1900, with the founding of the Athenian Helleniko Melodhrama (Greek Opera) by Dionyssios Lavrangas, that a permanent company took hold: it opened with Bohème at the Demotikon Theatre. By 1935, it had staged 38 foreign and 13 Greek operas, including several by Lavrangas. Manolis Kalomiris, a nationalist composer, founded the Ethnikos Melodhramatikos Omilos (National Opera Company) in 1933;

it was forced to close two years later. He was also the inspiration behind the establishment of a national company at the Ethnikon Theatre in 1939, which moved to the Olympia Theatre a year later. In 1944 it became the Ethniki Lyriki Skini (Greek National Opera) with Kalomiris as director, starting with the verismo opera Rhea by Spyridon Samaras, another native of Corfu.

Maria Callas was the most outstanding singer to emerge from the company, making her debut there as Tosca in 1941. Kostas Paskalis made his debut as Rigoletto in 1951, remaining in Athens for seven years. After an international career, he returned in 1988 as intendant of the company. Though still based at the Olympia, the GNO will move into the Rex-Kotopouli Theatre in the early 1990s. The operatic part of the Athens Festival is usually staged at the 5000-seat Herodes Atticus Theatre, an open-air arena carved into the hillside below the Acropolis.

Olympia Theatre, 59–61 Akadimias St., Athinai ☎ 1-3600180 ♬ Nov – May Ⓑ 18 Har. Trikoupi St, T.T. 143 Athens ☎ As above. Mon – Fri 9am – 1pm, 5 – 8pm CC None ♿ None ♿ 950 ♀ Bar ☎ 1-3600180 PT Bus – 24. Trolley bus – 6, 3 Ⓟ Corner of Ch. Trikoupi and Akadimias Sts.

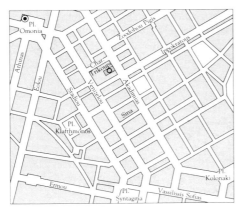

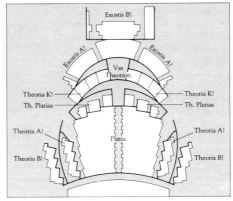

GRAN TEATRE DEL LICEU

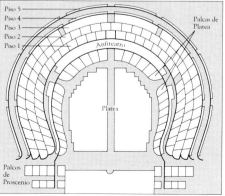

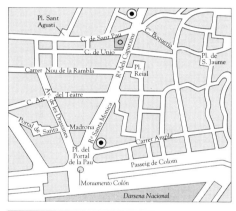

Gran Teatre del Liceu is the correct (Catalan) name for what the rest of Spain knows as El Gran Teatro Liceu, Barcelona's first true opera house. It was built in 1847, not as a shrine to Spanish opera, but as an attempt by Barcelona's new commercial class to put the city on the world map. They were successful, but not immediately. The Liceu's predecessor had been the Teatro de Santa Cruz, which opened in 1708 with Caldara's *Il Più Bel Nome*. Probably the first Italian opera to be produced in Spain, it was written for the marriage festivities of Charles III, Habsburg pretender to the Spanish throne. It was there, too, that the first opera by a Catalan composer, José Durán's *Antigona*, was performed in 1760. Apart from Italian opera, the works of Spanish composer Vicente Martín y Soler were staples of the repertory, notably *Una Cosa Rara* (1786). Soler's collaboration with Lorenzo da Ponte overshadowed even Mozart's in his day.

The first Liceu opened in April 1847 with a magnificent torch-lit gala and a programme of Spanish ballet and theatre. But it burned down 14 years later to the month. There was an instant decision to rebuild even more luxuriously: money was raised through 1000 shares, which still confer the right to a seat. Designed by José Oriel Mestres in the ornate Isabelline style, the present splendid building was opened in April 1862, barely a year after the devastating fire.

The Liceu's rebirth coincided with the revival in fortunes of the *zarzuela*, which had enjoyed a considerable vogue for 150 years until the 1790s. A type of national operetta often compared to Gilbert and Sullivan, its most famous example in current repertory is *Doña Francisquita* (1923), by the Barcelona-born Amadeo Vives. The development of the most distinctively Spanish opera, in the strict sense, rested with the Catalan composer Isaac Albéniz, whose masterpiece, first produced at the Liceu in 1896, was *Pepita Jiménez*. Its libretto is by Francis Money-Coutts (Lord Latymer), whose financial support Albéniz received in exchange for a promise to set his indifferent literary outpourings to music. The original statutes of the Liceu compel it to produce at least one Spanish opera each year. Few of these have survived outside Spain, but extracts from Falla's *Atlántida* were heard in Barcelona in 1961, in advance of its Milan premiere.

The theatre closed during the Spanish Civil War, and only reopened in 1942. Since then it has regained its position as Spain's leading opera house, one of the most beautiful in Europe. With a capacity of nearly 3000, it has stunningly clear acoustics even in its furthest reaches. Its most famous protégée has been Victoria de los Angeles: born in the city, she sang Mimi there while still a student in 1941, making her formal debut as the Countess in *Figaro* at the Liceu in January 1945 when barely 21. Over the last two decades her mantle has been worn by Montserrat Caballé, also a Barcelona native, who won the Liceu's gold medal in 1954 although her debut there was not until 1962 in the title role of Strauss' *Arabella*.

Towards the end of the 1970s company finances began to decline. A new board, or *consorci*, was formed by an alliance between the owners of the Liceu and the city and state councillors, with Lluis Portabella as general manager. There was a noticeable improvement in standards: both orchestra and chorus were reorganized, the latter's ensemble enhanced by an increase from 60 to 94 singers, while stage equipment was updated and rehearsal hours increased. Three outstanding tenors owe their earliest training to Barcelona, José Carreras and Giacomo Aragall, who were both born there, and Alfredo Kraus who came from Las Palmas. At the start of his career Carreras, encouraged by Caballé, sang Gennaro opposite her Lucrezia Borgia at the Liceu. More recently, the soprano Enedina Lloris and the tenor Jesús Pinto appear likely to achieve similar fame.

The company has tended to rely on bringing in productions which have already proved their merit elsewhere, rather than originate its own. Similarly, it has usually been able to afford one or two stars of international repute. From being a Wagnerian powerhouse in the late 19th century, it entered the next as a centre for Strauss, Debussy, and the Russian/Slavonic repertory. There has never been much emphasis on the mainstream classics. Each season includes some Spanish content: Josep Soler's *Oedipus et Iocasta*, which has a Latin libretto, received its stage premiere in 1986, and Lleonard Balada's *Cristóbal Colón* its world premiere in 1989. A typical offering in 1989 brought together Domingo and Baltsa in *Samson et Dalila*, a production imported from Nice. Uwe Mund is the musical director.

Rambla dels Caputxins 65, Barcelona 08002 ☎ 03-318 9122 ⊤Ⓧ 99750 ♫ Sep – Jul Ⓑ Sant Pau 1, Barcelona 08001 ☎ 03-318 9277 ⒸⒸ None ♿ Special parking, elevators, tickets ☎ 03-318 9277 ⸬ 2700 ♣ Snack bar ⓟⓣ Bus – 14, 18, 38, 59, 91. Underground – 3, Liceu Ⓟ nearby.

STADTTHEATER

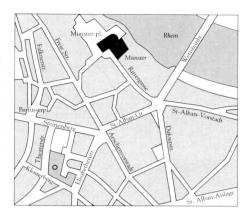

Basel's operatic beginnings were in 1734, when a travelling company played in the former Ballenhaus. Its first proper Stadt-theater (City Theatre), the Theater auf dem Blömlein, opened exactly a century later: lessees staged some 70 operas and plays there every year until 1892, when its shareholders took control. The theatre was redesigned in 1875 to satisfy city planning requirements; it was completely rebuilt in 1909 to the design of Felix Schwarz and Rolf Gutmann after a fire, and was thoroughly renovated in 1975 to bring it into line with the latest tech-nological developments.

Landmarks in Basel's operatic history are the productions of *Rheingold* and *Walküre* by Oskar Wälterlin in 1924–25, with designs by Adolphe Appia so extravagant that the full *Ring* could not be completed. Walter Felsenstein was stage director there (1926–29) at the start of his operatic career. There was also a close and long-standing collaboration with Felix Weingartner.

Several singers made Basel their first pro-fessional base at the beginning of interna-tional careers, notably Montserrat Caballé (1956–58) and Grace Bumbry (1960–64). Swiss composers have found Basel a useful springboard: Honegger's *Jeanne d'Arc au Bûcher* was premiered there in 1938, as was Rolf Liebermann's *Das Neue Land* (1946) and Heinrich Sutermeister's *Titus Feuerfuchs* (1958). *The Consul* had its European premiere there in 1951. Patronage by the conductor Paul Sacher led to the premieres of two instrumental works by Bartók. Con-sistently high standards were sustained dur-ing Silvio Varviso's regime as principal conductor (1950–62).

Basel has never quite sustained the momentum which it achieved in the immediate postwar years, partly because the Stadttheater provides a judicious balance of opera, ballet and straight theatre, rather than concentrating upon opera alone. The com-pany's outstanding feature is its chorus which, under Werner Nitzer, is the equal of

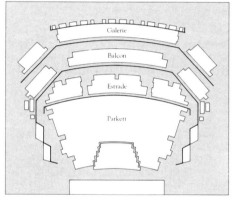

any. There is a resident ballet company under Heinz Spoerli. The Basel Symphony Orchestra and the Basel Radio-Symphony Orchestra share the duties of accompani-ment, and also give concerts at the theatre. The intendant since 1988 has been Frank Baumbauer, the musical director since 1989, Michael Boder.

Elisabethenstr. 16, 4010 Basel
☎ 061-22 11 30   FX 061-22 19 90
♬ Sep – Jun   B As above. Mon – Sat 10am – 1pm, 3.30 – 6.45pm, 45 mins before perf.   CC None   ♿ Wheelchair space, hearing aids ☎ As above   ☷ 1000
♐ Bar   PT Tram – 6, 16, 17 Theatre stop and 1, 3, 8, 14, 15 Barfusserplatz stop. Train – Basel station   ℗ Under theatre.

BAYREUTH FESTSPIELHAUS

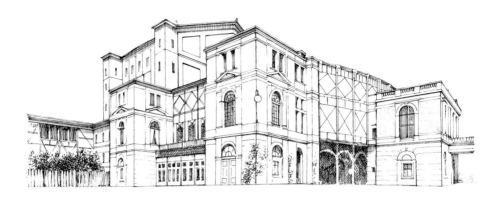

Bayreuth resounds with but a single name – Wagner. His spirit breathes from every corner of the theatre he built, the audience are died-in-the-wool Wagnerians, and the Bayreuth 'style' is imitated in Wagner productions the world over.

But there was operatic life in Bayreuth before Wagner. Siegmund von Birken's *Sophia* celebrated the wedding of Princess Sophie of Saxony in 1661. Margrave Friedrich's wife, Wilhelmine, Frederick the Great's sister, set out to replicate the Prussian court's musical standards: she commissioned the Galli-Bibiena family to design a splendid new theatre, the Markgräfliches Opernhaus, which opened in 1748 with Hasse's *Ezio*. Visiting companies brought productions there intermittently for another century. The Bavarian State Opera still presents an annual spring season. However, it was the theatre's reputation for having one of Germany's largest stages, which first attracted Wagner to Bayreuth, in his search for the ideal venue for a *Gesamtkunstwerk*, a unified work of art.

Finding the theatre unsuitable in other ways, but enjoying Bayreuth's rural, relaxed atmosphere, he persuaded the local burghers to release a hillside site outside the town for a new opera house. He also acquired from Ludwig II a site for his private home, Wahn-

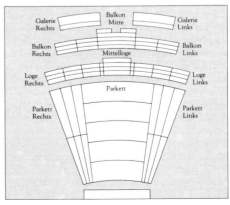

8

fried (where the Wagner archives are presently housed). In 1872, he conducted Beethoven's Ninth Symphony (still the only non-Wagnerian work to be allowed at the Festival) in the old theatre and then laid the foundation stone for the new one. Shortage of funds forced him to plan for a 'one-off' festival and to erect a 'temporary' Festspielhaus, mainly of wood and brick.

Wagner was much influenced by the size and shape of Riga's Vitinghoff Theatre, where he had been music director (1837–39). He commissioned Otto Brückwald to imitate its main features: a single-level auditorium in the shape of a classical amphitheatre, with boxes at the back, a deep orchestra pit and lights which could be dimmed. Pillared buttresses flank the wide auditorium, continuing the effect of a double proscenium arch, while the wooden ceiling gives the impression of an awning. The orchestra lies invisible, in what Wagner called the 'mystical abyss', separating the real from the ideal'; a curved hood behind the conductor blocks him and the players from view, directing the sound towards the singers. This, allied to a reverberation time of $1\frac{1}{2}$ seconds, gives Bayreuth its uniquely blended and spacious acoustics.

The first festival saw the inaugural *Ring* cycle, 13–17 August 1876, which included the premieres of *Siegfried* and *Götterdämmerung*, conducted by Hans Richter. A large financial deficit delayed the prospect of future festivals. The theatre finally reopened in 1882 with the premiere of *Parsifal*, the only work Wagner wrote expressly for Bayreuth: the last scene of the last 1882 performance was the only occasion he conducted there. He died the following year.

Wagner's widow Cosima succeeded him as festival director and gradually introduced all his major works in rigidly prescribed productions. It was 1896 before a complete *Ring* was staged again: Richter returned, and Wagner's son Siegfried also conducted one of the five cycles.

In 1906, ill-health forced Cosima to yield control to Siegfried. Conservative at first, he introduced gradual reforms after 1924: a deeper stage, sets instead of painted backdrops, and more gestural freedom for his singers. His production of *Tannhäuser* in 1930, the year he died, was the first consciously to depart from Wagner's instructions, which were previously treated as graven in stone; it was also the first to be conducted by a non-German – Toscanini.

Siegfried's British-born widow Winifred took charge between 1931 and 1944, attracting criticism for her loyalty to Hitler (who responded with financial help) and encouraging luxuriant new productions under Heinz Tietjen. Lighting techniques were evolved to suggest depth and atmosphere, but political trends also elevated Bayreuth almost to the status of a Teutonic shrine. A seven-year postwar break ended in 1951 with her sons, Wieland and Wolfgang, assuming joint control. The stark simplicity of Wieland's new *Parsifal* played down its purely German qualities and emphasized its universal symbolism – a characteristic which set the trend still largely in evidence today.

Wieland's death in 1966 left Wolfgang as sole director. He has modernized the backstage equipment, increased seating capacity (now 1925) and enlarged the rehearsal areas. Recent new productions under his aegis – by Götz Friedrich (1972), Patrice Chéreau (1976), Peter Hall (1983) and Harry Kupfer (1988) in particular – have reinvigorated Bayreuth's search for the Wagnerian holy grail. Bayreuth continues to be the high altar for Wagnerians, but intending worshippers may first have to spend several years on its waiting-list.

Bayreuth Festspielhaus, D8580 Bayreuth, W. Germany ☎ 0921-20221 ♬ Jul – Aug B As above CC None ♿ Space for 2 wheelchairs ⚬ 1925 ♨ Restaurant and cafe PT Bus – 7, from the market place in city centre Ⓟ Nearby.

NATIONAL THEATRE

Belgrade's National Theatre is more than an opera house, since it combines theatre, opera and ballet companies under one roof. The theatre was built in 1868, and has been renovated frequently since: a three-year programme of modernization is in progress. The auditorium is comfortable and air-conditioned. The company also plays at Zemun.

Ticket prices are extremely low by Western standards, rising slightly when guest (non-Yugoslav) singers are involved. The director is Božidar Radović, the chief conductor Nikolaj Zličar. The theatre maintains its own orchestra, a choir of 80, an ensemble of 40 soloists, and a ballet company of 90. A full international repertory is sustained together with Slavonic works rarely performed outside Yugoslavia.

Mid-19th-century nationalism led to the formation of numerous choirs in Yugoslavia, many of which indulged in a special type of Serbian *Singspiel* (the musical numbers connected by spoken dialogue), fostered by the Slovenian composer Davorin Jenko (1835–1914): his *Vračara* (*The Sorceress*, 1882) was the first Serbian operetta.

In 1894 the first true opera was staged in Belgrade, Vilém Blodek's *V Studni* (*In the Well*), which bears a marked resemblance to *The Bartered Bride*. In 1904 the first Serbian national opera was performed in Belgrade, Stanislav Binički's *Na Uranku* (*At Dawn*), in the *verismo* (realistic) style. A visit by the Zagreb Opera in 1911 revived interest in the establishment of a permanent company. It was founded in 1920 and Binički was chosen as director. His successor was Stevan Hristić (1924–34), who broadened the company's scope by engaging foreign, especially Russian emigré, singers such as Chaliapin and also by training new Serbian talent. His expressionist opera *Suton* (*Twilight*) was staged in 1925. An international perspective was developed through visits by La Scala and the Paris Opéra.

The theatre was bombed in 1941. After

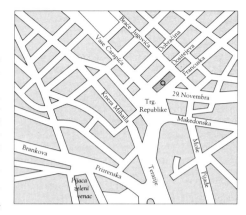

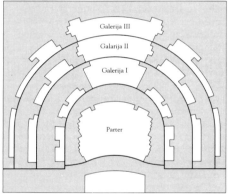

liberation, the first opera staged was *Eugene Onegin* under Oskar Danon. He became director in 1945 and put the company on the map, notably with *Prince Igor* in Lausanne and Paris (1958). He also conducted its *Love for Three Oranges* in Wiesbaden (1959) and Edinburgh (1962). Belgrade's excellence in Russian repertory has been an invaluable window to the West: its *Boris*, *Igor*, *Onegin*, *Khovanshchina* and *Queen of Spades* have all been recorded by Decca.

Narodno pozorište, 11000 Beograd, Francuska 3 ☎ 11-626 566
♫ Sep – Jun B As above CC None
♿ None ﹏ 700 and 40 standing
♨ 2 restaurants PT Bus and trolley bus – Trg Republike Ⓟ Nearby.

KOMISCHE OPER

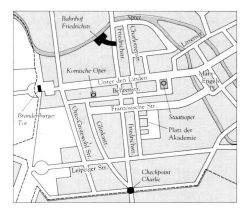

One of East Berlin's most singular attractions is the Komische Oper, a company without an equivalent in western or eastern Europe. It was the brainchild of Viennese-born Walter Felsenstein, who launched it in December 1947 with *Die Fledermaus*. He had spent 20 years before the war as actor and producer in a variety of opera houses, including Mannheim, Basel, Cologne and Frankfurt. His production of *Figaro* at the 1942 Salzburg Festival broke away from convention and he began to probe ways of delivering 'realistic' music-theatre. So, after the war, when the authorities in the Soviet military sector handed over the old Metropoltheater, he saw it as an opportunity to develop his aesthetic concepts of opera.

Over the next 28 years, until his death in 1975, he was responsible for 29 productions, whose impact has reached beyond Berlin and even Germany. His personality and that of the company became synonomous, so all-embracing was his control. The 'dialectical realism' underpinning all his work was founded on the theory of alienation, developed by Brecht during the 1920s, whereby historical happenings could be 'released' from their original context to speak with a contemporary voice, even though in the 'alien' world of the historical.

The effect in Felsenstein's productions, still seen through his disciples Götz Friedrich and Joachim Herz, was that the clichés of opera – music, melody, beautiful voices – were subordinated to the demands of the drama, making them an indispensable means of human expression.

He was succeeded by Herz, who had been his assistant in Berlin (1953–56) before moving to Cologne and Leipzig. He delivered a provocative *Lulu* in 1979. Harry Kupfer, the present director of productions, took over in 1981 after significant periods as director at Weimar and Dresden. He is also much in the Felsenstein mould. Infinitely painstaking in rehearsal, he invests his productions with enormous, occasionally exces-

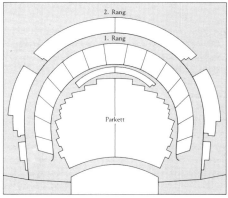

sive, detail so that the music sometimes runs a poor second to the theatre. Big stars are not invited here; performers are chosen rather for their theatrical than their vocal ability. Rolf Reuter is the musical director, Werner Rackwitz the intendant of this challenging company.

Behrenstr. 55-57, Berlin 1086
☎ 02-220 2761 ♪ Sep – Jul Ⓑ As above ☎ 02-229 2555. Tue – Sat 12–6pm and 1 hr before performance, Mon 11–7pm at the Tourist Office, Unter den Linden 41 ☎ 02-2292603 CC None
& ☎ 02-220 2761 ⋙ 1208 ⬤ Bar
PT Local train (S-Bahn) – Friedrichstr. Tram 46, 49, 22. Bus 57, 59. Underground - Stadtmitte Ⓟ Multistorey opposite opera.

DEUTSCHE STAATSOPER

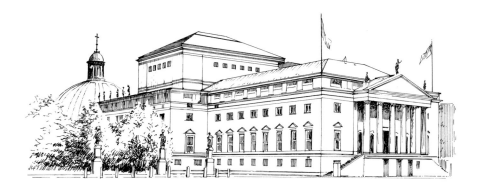

The German State Opera is East Germany's leading company. Its operatic history has a distinguished lineage.

Ariosti's *La Festa del Hymeneo* was the first full-scale work to be seen in Berlin, in 1700, in what is now the Charlottenburg Palace, completed the previous year. But the monarchy was not sympathetic to the genre – until the appearance of Frederick the Great. He instructed Georg Wenzeslaus von Knobelsdorff to design an opera house, and the new Italian Court Opera (often referred to as the Lindenoper) opened in 1742 with Graun's *Cleopatra e Cesare*.

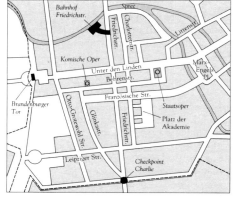

As court *Kapellmeister*, Graun wrote two new works each year until his death in 1759, always in Italian *opera seria* style, which he conducted personally. Frederick contributed six of Graun's librettos and supervised all aspects of the productions. The ensemble dispersed during the Seven Years' War (1756–63). Only *Achille in Sciro* by one of Bach's pupils, Agricola, who was appointed *Kapellmeister* after the war, achieved the grandeur of earlier times. Elisabeth Mara, Germany's first *prima donna*, was given a life contract by Frederick in 1771, but left in 1779.

It was only in 1798 that an opera written and sung in German was first performed at the Lindenoper, *Brennus* by Johann

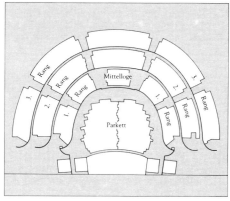

Reichardt, who had been appointed Frederick's *Kapellmeister* in late 1775. Meanwhile the Nationaltheater had begun operations in 1786, and under B.A. Weber keenly fostered opera in German, especially works by Mozart and Gluck: Berlin's first Mozart was *Entführung* in 1788. The Court Opera and the Nationaltheater merged in 1814 to become the Königliche Schauspiele (Royal Playhouse) under August Iffland. Spontini's *La Vestale* had been one of Iffland's first productions (1811), followed by Weber's *Silvana* and *Abu Hassan*. His successor was Karl von Brühl, who brought in Berlin's first *Fidelio* (1815) and premiered Hoffman's *Undine* (1816) as part of the drive to promote German opera.

It was Spontini, former conductor of Napoleon's court orchestra, however, who won the contest between them to become Berlin's first chief conductor (1820–42). The successful world premiere of *Der Freischütz*, conducted by Weber himself on 18 June 1821 at the newly opened Neues Schauspielhaus designed by Karl Schinkel, heralded the popularity of German opera. Marschner's *Hans Heiling* was given its premiere there in 1833. Spontini left under a cloud in 1842, to be succeeded by his arch enemy Meyerbeer.

The royal opera house burned down in 1843. It reopened a year later, enlarged and modernized by Carl von Langhans, with a new Meyerbeer work in which Jenny Lind made her Berlin debut. Nicolai conducted the premiere of his *Merry Wives of Windsor* there in March 1849, two months before his death. After a prolonged dearth of good conductors, the company was revived by Weingartner (1891–98) and Richard Strauss (1898–1918), who refused to have the premieres of his own operas staged there.

After World War I the company became known as Staatsoper Unter den Linden, reopening three days after the armistice with *Meistersinger*. A glorious era began with Kleiber's reign as chief conductor (1923–34): 12 premieres were staged, including *Wozzeck* (1925) after nearly 100 rehearsals. The repertory was also much enlarged:

during renovations in the 1926/27 season – given at the Kroll Theater, where Klemperer later conducted a starburst of influential productions (1927–31) – 66 different operas were presented. Hitler's rise to power in 1933 provoked a considerable exodus of talent, though Furtwängler and Karajan continued reluctantly until the stage was destroyed by bombs in February 1945.

The company was reborn two months later as the Deutsche Staatsoper, now based in the Admiralspalast. Its first world premiere was Paul Dessau's *Die Verurteilung des Lukullus* in 1951, still in the repertory. Not until 1955 was Knobelsdorff's old theatre, rebuilt to his original plans, able to reopen with *Meistersinger* under Konwitschny. The redoubtable Theo Adam, who sang Pogner in that production, is still with the company. With Hans Pischner as intendant (1963–84), it expanded considerably, adding a ballet group and an orchestral series. Otmar Suitner, whom he appointed chief conductor in 1964, is still there. The present intendant is Günter Rimkus.

Since the division of Berlin, the Staatsoper has been unable to attract the same calibre of singer as before. But it maintains a full repertory of German and eastern European as well as mainstream Italian works: five new productions and 35 revivals in 1988/89. Major renovations in 1986 have underlined its sober elegance tinged with rococo flair, although its productions tend to be more staid than those at the Komische Oper.

1086 Berlin, Unter den Linden
☎ 02-200 0491 ♪ Sep – Jul Ⓑ As above ☎ 02-207 1362 Evenings ☎ 02-205 4577. Mon – Sat 12–6pm, Sun and hols 4–6pm CC None ♿ Wheelchair space, restrooms ⋮⋮ 1354 ♨ Refreshments PT Train – Fredrichstrasse station. Bus – 57, August-Bebel Platz. Underground – Hausvogteiplatz ℗ August-Bebel Platz next to theatre.

DEUTSCHE OPER

The postwar political division of Berlin has left one of its three opera houses in the West. The earlier history of opera in Berlin is considered under Staatsoper, East Berlin.

Deutsche Oper's site on the Bismarck-strasse was originally occupied by the Deutsches Opernhaus, which opened in 1912. Its seating capacity was nearly 2100. Georg Hartmann, its first intendant, was a staunch Wagnerian and took pride in organizing the first *Parsifal* in Germany outside Bayreuth in 1914. It failed to recover from financial troubles arising from World War I, and was taken over by the Berlin city authorities in 1925 to become the Städtische Oper.

The appointments of Bruno Walter as conductor (1925–29) and Heinz Tietjen as director (1925–30) thrust the company into serious rivalry with the Staatsoper. Fritz Stiedry (1929–33) conducted the first performances of Weill's *Die Bürgschaft* and Schreker's *Der Schmied von Gent* in 1932. He also collaborated with Carl Ebert on renowned productions of *Macbeth* and *Simon Boccanegra*, then seldom produced. Maria Ivogün and Alexander Kipnis were regular stars between the wars.

Under the Nazi regime, productions became more simplistic: for example, a new *Ring* was specially staged for the 1936 Olympic Games. When the theatre was bombed out in 1943, the company moved to the Admiralspalast, and again in 1945 to the Theater des Westens. Tietjen returned as intendant in 1948, followed by Ebert in 1955.

On 24 September 1961 the company opened with *Don Giovanni* in its present newly constructed house and became the Deutsche Oper. Under Fricsay (1958–62) the orchestral staff was enlarged to 140. Maazel had a notable period as artistic director (1965–71), staging the premiere of Dallapiccola's *Ulisse* (1968).

The house is a product of its era, a giant concrete box, strictly functional, though with lively acoustics. Under Götz Friedrich,

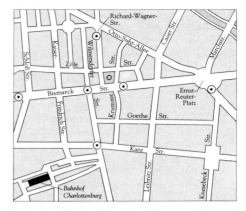

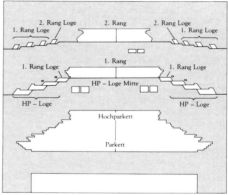

intendant since 1981, with Jesús López-Cobos as musical director since 1978 (to be succeeded by Giuseppe Sinopoli in 1990), the company has pursued an aggressively enterprising stance towards 20th-century pieces, often in startling productions. With more than 75 works, it is reputed to have the largest repertory in the world.

Bismarckstr 35, 1000 Berlin 10
☎ 030-34 38 1   TX 186791 DOLB
FX 030-34 38 232   ♫ Aug – Jul
B Richard-Wagner-Str. 10, 1000 Berlin 10   ☎ 030-34 38 1. Mon – Fri 2 – 8pm, Sat – Sun 10am – 2pm   CC None
♿ Special seats, hearing aids   ⟨⟨⟩⟩ 1885
♉ Bars   PT Bus – 1. Underground – Deutsche Oper   ℗ Krumme Str.

TEATRO COMUNALE

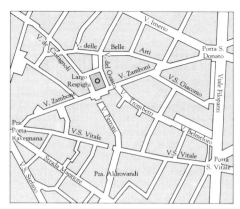

The first properly documented public performance of opera in Bologna – Girolamo Giacobbi's *L'Andromeda* – took place during the Carnevale (pre-Lenten festivities) at the Teatro del Pubblico in February 1610. This was an auspicious beginning. The tradition continued powerfully in the Teatro Formagliari (1636–1802) and then at the Teatro Malvezzi, which opened in 1653. The Malvezzi was enlarged and renovated in 1697 by the members of the famous Galli-Bibiena dynasty of architects and stage designers. When the Malvezzi burned down in 1745, Antonio Galli - Bibiena was asked to design a replacement. The Teatro Comunale opened on 14 May 1763, with Gluck conducting the premiere of his own *Il Trionfo di Clelia*, with Galli-Bibiena's elaborate sets.

Repertory during the mid – 19th century was largely Italian, particularly Rossini and Donizetti, with up to 40 performances of each production. The success of Angelo Mariani's debut conducting *Ballo* in 1860 led to his appointment as musical director, and ushered in a new Wagnerian era in Italy. He conducted the Italian premieres of *Lohengrin* (1871) and *Tannhäuser* (1872), and enjoyed an influential relationship with Verdi, whose *Don Carlos* he introduced to Italy in 1867. Luigi Mancinelli succeeded him and even conducted at Bayreuth. Bologna's Wagner tradition was inherited by the broad – minded Giuseppe Martucci, who conducted the first Italian *Tristan* in 1888.

Toscanini, often credited with creating the Wagner following in Italy, conducted at the Comunale for several years before leaving for the USA in 1908. In the 20th century Bologna has continued in what is, for Italy, a relatively adventurous style. Rossini and the German repertory are the main fare these days. The company's unofficial *primo basso* is the local – born Ruggiero Raimondi. Another favourite is Mirella Freni, who studied in Bologna – and returned in 1988 to sing her first Adriana Lecouvreur there. The Wagner tradition has been revived with a

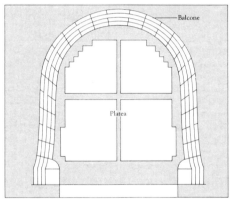

new *Ring* cycle produced by Pier'Alli, which began in 1987, the year when Luigi Ferrari became artistic director. The permanent conductor is Riccardo Chailly. With the Bologna forces, he has recently released *Manon Lescaut* on CD, starring Kiri Te Kanawa and José Carreras. *Sovrintendente* at the Comunale is Carlo Fontana.

Largo Respighi 1, 40126 Bologna
☎ 051-52 90 11   TX 226386 ENLIBO
FX 051-52 99 05   ♬ Sep – Jun   B As above ☎ 051-52 99 99. Mon – Fri 3.30–7pm, Sat, Sun, and festival days 9.30am–12.30pm and 3.30–7pm. For group discounts ☎ 051-52 99 81
CC None   ♿ None   ⚬ 1034   ☎ None
PT Train – Central Station. Bus – 50.

GRAND-THEATRE DE BORDEAUX

Francoeur's *Pirame et Thysbé* was staged in 1729, but Bordeaux is thought to have experienced opera as early as 1688. An opera house was built in 1735 by Mlle Dujardin in the Municipal Gardens. It burned down in 1756 and a temporary building was set up near the Rohan Palace. This provided a base for the Académie Royale de Musique, founded in 1752 with ten soloists.

The Grand-Théâtre came about through the initiative of the Maréchal-Duc de Richelieu, a descendant of the Cardinal. Having chosen a site at the foot of the slope leading to Bordeaux's fort (Château Trompette), he imposed his choice of architect, Victor Louis, upon a reluctant town council. Opened on 7 April 1780, the Grand is an ambitious mixture of styles. Its façade is neoclassical, with a Muses Terrace above the entablature lined by statues of Juno, Venus, Minerva and the nine Muses. The magnificent central Y-shaped staircase inside was used by Garnier as a model for the Paris Opéra. The auditorium, made entirely of wood, is dominated by a chandelier constructed of 14,000 pieces of Bohemian crystal, weighing 3.5 tonnes. Its ceiling, painted by Robin, is an allegory of the city of Bordeaux. There are boxes with special grilles behind the stalls (*parterre*) – to see without being seen. The theatre is small and

relatively uncomfortable. The Bordeaux red of the interior was imposed on it during a Second Empire restoration in 1853.

The Bordelais have sometimes shown perverse taste: in the 19th century *Traviata* was considered inferior to Meyerbeer and *Tosca* criticized for its lack of a ballet. Since then the Grand has maintained a consistent standard, relying more on ensemble than big names, although Caruso, Chaliapin, Pons and Schwarzkopf have all appeared there. It featured the French premieres of Hindemith's *Mathis der Maler* (1963) and Salieri's *Falstaff* (1987). The repertory is fairly conservative, mainly French and German. Accompaniment is provided by L'Orchestre National de Bordeaux-Aquitaine (artistic director Alain Lombard). Gérard Boireau has been director general since 1971. The Bordeaux Mai Musical, founded in 1950, includes opera.

Pl. de la Comédie, 33074 Bordeaux Cedex
☎ 56-90 91 60   TX 560994 OPERMAI
♫ Oct – Jun   B Service Location and as above Tue – Fri 11am – 4pm Sat 9am – 4pm Tue – Sat 9 – 11am   ☎ 56-48 58 54 Discounts for groups of 10 +   CC None
♿ None   ∷ 1205 and 150 standing
♟ Bar   PT Bus – 5, 13, 14, 16, 17, 19, 20, 21, 27, 28   Ⓟ 3 mins walk away.

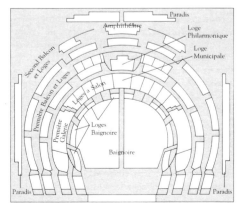

OPERA COMPANY OF BOSTON

Boston has a long and noble operatic tradition, dating back to the presentation of over 150 ballad operas in the 18th century. Touring companies began to appear there from the 1820s onwards. The grand Boston Theater on Washington Street opened in 1854 and was the city's opera house for the next half-century. Here Patti sang her first Rosina in 1860, and her brother-in-law Maurice Strakosch brought his touring company, as did Colonel Mapleson and Maurice Grau. It was the venue for the US premiere of *H.M.S. Pinafore* in 1878, and host to the Metropolitan Opera Company's many visits from 1883.

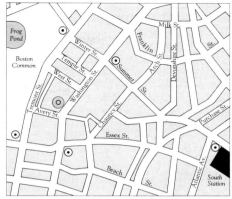

It was superseded in 1909 by the Boston Opera House, erected on Huntington Avenue by Eben D. Jordan, Jr. to house his new Boston Opera Company. The company opened with *La Gioconda*: in the title role was Lillian Nordica, the first American to be engaged at Bayreuth (1894). A disastrous tour to Paris in 1914 led to bankruptcy a year later. In 1917, after two short seasons by the makeshift Boston Grand Opera Company, the Chicago Opera began 15 years of regular visits organized by the Boston Opera Association. The Metropolitan Opera staged annual seasons from 1934 to 1986.

The city's modern operatic era has its true roots in Boris Goldovsky's New England Opera Theater, founded in 1946. One of his protégées, Sarah Caldwell, spearheaded the first attempt to establish a permanent, resident opera company in Boston. The Boston Opera Group (renamed the Opera Company of Boston in 1965) opened in June 1958 with the American premiere of Offenbach's *Le Voyage dans la Lune*. Miss Caldwell remains the company's presiding genius, as conductor, producer and administrator with equal emphasis on theatre and on music.

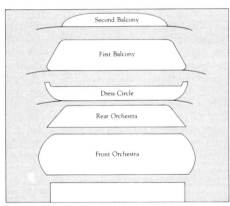

After the original Boston Opera House was mysteriously demolished in 1958, the company performed in a variety of rented venues, including the Donnelly Memorial Theatre (1959–68) and the Orpheum Theatre (1971–78). OCB acquired its own home in November 1978 with the purchase of the old Savoy Theater. Restored to its former elegance, it is one of America's most broad-minded operatic venues.

Opera House, 539 Washington St., Boston, MA 02111 ☎ 617-426 5300 ⊤⊠ 6817551 SCCULCOL ⨍⨯ 617-426 3297 ♬ Jan – Jun Ⓑ As above. Discounts for groups of 20+ ⊂⊂ Amex, MC, Visa ♿ Wheelchair access, seating, restroom facilities ⁙ 2605 ⌷ Bar ☎ 617-426 5300 ⊓⊤ Underground – Park St., Boylston and Washington Ⓟ Lafayette Pl. Garage.

JANACEK THEATRE

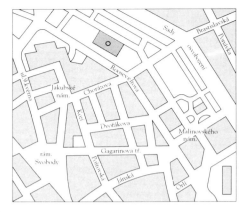

Brno is the capital of Moravia and its opera company is Czechoslovakia's most important after the National Theatre Company in Prague. Theatrically it was five years ahead, erecting its first theatre, the Theater in der Taffern, in Vegetable Market Square, in 1732 before Prague's Kotzen theatre (1737). Here the Mingotti brothers brought their travelling company for four successive seasons. This theatre burned down in 1785. Its successor was the Königlich-Städtisches Nationaltheater (1786) which now survives as the Reduta, reduced in size by an 1870 fire.

Czech plays with songs, in the style of German *Singspiel*, began to appear at Brno in the 1760s and Karel Loos' *Opera Bohemica de Camino* was staged in 1772. *Orfeo, Fidelio* and *Freischütz*, together with several Mozart works, were all seen in Brno soon after their premieres. The first work to be produced in Czech was Méhul's *Joseph* (1839). It encouraged the Brno premiere of František Škroup's *Dráteník* (*The Tinker*, 1840), which in turn stimulated the first new opera by a Brno composer, František Kott's *Žižkův Dub* (Žižka's Oak, 1841).

The opening of the Provisional Theatre in 1884 began a new era. It was enlarged with a second gallery in 1894, and became the National Theatre.

A small permanent ensemble was gradually assembled, its outstanding success being Janáček's *Jenůfa*, premiered on 21 January 1904. The work was carefully prepared but the orchestra of only 29 players was under strength, which prompted Janáček to offer all his subsequent operas to Prague. In the event, all but one (*Výlety Páně Broučkovy, The Excursions of Mr Brouček*) were given their premieres in Brno.

The German Stadttheater (City Theatre), opened in 1882 with a capacity of 1185. This building became accessible to the Czechs after Czechoslovakian independence in 1918. It was here that František Neumann, as head of opera (1919 – 29), introduced most of Janáček's output.

After World War II, the German population was expelled and the City Theatre (now

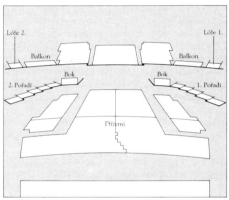

the Mahen) came under Czech ownership. The new, slightly clinical Janáček Theatre, the country's largest and best-equipped opera house, opened in 1965. Here the works of Smetana, Dvořák, Martinů and Janáček are staples of the repertory.

Janáčkovo Divadlo, c/o Státní Divadlo v Brně, Dvořákova 11, 65770 Brno 1
☎ 05-26 311   ♫ Sep – Jun   Ⓑ As above
☎ 05-26 311 183/246. Mon – Fri, 9.30am – 5.30pm; Sat 9am –12pm
CC None ♿ None ⬓ 1317 🍴 Restaurant Bohema   ☎ 05-26 311 313/248 29
PT Tram – 1, 3, 7, 11. Bus – 41, 42, 46a stop opposite theatre   Ⓟ Nearby.

THEATRE ROYAL DE LA MONNAIE

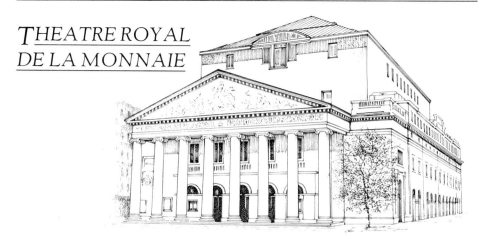

Opera in Brussels has a distinguished history stretching back over 300 years. Its first opera house was the Opéra du Quai du Foin, which opened in 1681. Built to plans by Bezzi on orders from Gian Carlo Bombarda, the Elector of Bavaria's personal treasurer, it stood on the site of an *atelier monétaire* where coins had been minted. It was to become the Théâtre de la Monnaie, where on 19 November 1700 it opened with a production of Lully's *Atys*.

Lully's tragic operas dominated the repertory during the 18th century, with Gluck, Rameau, and Grétry – the nearest thing to a native composer, since he was born at Liège – also enjoying considerable success. One of the earliest producers was the librettist and impresario Charles Favart, appointed in 1745.

La Monnaie survived the end of the *ancien régime*. However, after a performance of Auber's *La Muette de Portici* in 1830 it was the scene of a riot which sparked the revolution leading to the foundation of modern Belgium. A fire on stage in January 1855 devastated the interior of the building, which led to a reconstruction under the architect Poelaert. The present building, modelled on the Paris Opéra, was inaugurated on 24 March 1856 with Halévy's comic opera *Jaguarita l'Indienne*.

Thereafter La Monnaie enjoyed a golden age. For a while, works which had enjoyed success in Paris were usually transferred to

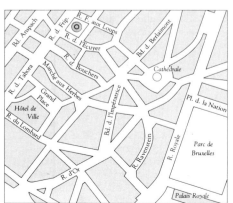

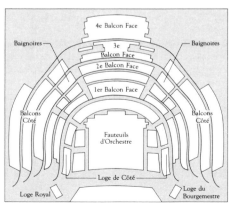

Brussels a few months later. But eventually La Monnaie boasted a string of world premieres of its own: Massenet's *Hérodiade* (1881), Chabrier's *Gwendoline* (1886), Godard's *Jocelyn* (1888) with its famous *Berceuse*, and Chausson's *Le Roi Arthus* (1903). *Carmen*, disdainfully received in Paris, was a triumph in Brussels. Melba made her debut here in 1887 as Gilda. The prestige by now surrounding La Monnaie was further enhanced under the administration of Maurice Kufferath (1900–14).

After the war the pianist and conductor Corneil de Thoran began a long reign which lasted until 1953. In the interwar years, there were several further world premieres: Milhaud's *Les Malheurs d'Orphée* (1925), Honegger's *Antigone* (1927) and Prokofiev's *The Gambler* (1929). Confirmation of La Monnaie's status on the international circuit came with the appearances of Caruso and Chaliapin. Brussels was also the scene of first performances in French of *Prince Igor*, *The Golden Cockerel*, *Turandot*, *Ariadne auf Naxos*, Wolf-Ferrari's *I Quattro Rusteghi*, *Wozzeck*, *The Rape of Lucretia*, *Albert Herring*, *The Rake's Progress* and *The Consul*.

The tenor Joseph Rogatchewsky, director from 1953 to 1959, enlisted singers such as Rita Gorr and Gabriel Bacquier into the company. He was followed in 1959 by Maurice Huisman, who dispensed with the large ensemble originally formed by Kufferath, and invited foreign companies to stage productions at La Monnaie. He was also instrumental in founding the Ballet du XXème Siècle in 1960, under the direction of Maurice Béjart. In 1963 he engaged André Vandernoot as musical director, and the company was renamed the Opéra National. A highlight of his administration was the farewell performance of Elizabeth Schwarzkopf in 1972, singing the Marschallin in *Der Rosenkavalier*. She was to return with the same opera nine years later, this time making her debut as a producer.

Gérard Mortier took over as director on Huisman's retirement in 1981. Declaring that he wanted Glyndebourne standards in Brussels, he increased the orchestra by 40 players and added new voices to the main chorus. He insisted on four or five weeks rehearsal for each opera and stated that the company's main diet would be Mozart and Verdi with some attention given to the French repertory. John Pritchard was appointed musical director, Sylvain Cambreling permanent conductor and Gilbert Deflo chief producer.

Standards improved at once. The new regime's first opera, *Don Carlos* that November, was unanimously acclaimed, with Brussels-born José van Dam singing the role of King Philip. Long needed major structural alterations and 'improvements' from 1986–88 left La Monnaie with an extraordinary excrescence on its roof – a new foyer and rehearsal room which are seriously out of scale and style with the theatre's balanced classical façade. Repainting inside has been crudely done, and there is widespread disquiet that the auditorium's acoustics have been tinkered with at the expense of balance between pit and stage.

Despite being restricted to four new productions a year, Mortier's high standards have not slipped. His Mozart cycle is almost complete, and he has overseen two successful commissions: Philippe Boesmans' *La Passion de Gilles* (1983) and André Laporte's *Das Schloss* (1986) after Kafka. His collaboration with producer Karl-Ernst Herrmann has been particularly fruitful. La Monnaie remains an important opera house, but its risk-taking makes it vulnerable to greater peaks and troughs than elsewhere. André Delvaux's film *Babel Opera*, released in 1985, was shot around a Monnaie production of *Don Giovanni* and is an excellent introduction to the theatre and to Brussels itself.

Rue Leopold 4, 1000 Bruxelles ☎ 02-217 22 11 TX 24575 FX 02-218 35 27 ♫ Sep – Jul B rue de la Reine, 1000 Bruxelles ☎ 02-218 12 11/ 12 02. Mon – Sat 11am–6pm. Discounts for groups of 15 + ☎ 02-217 22 11 CC Amex, Diners, MC, ♿ Elevator ⠿ 1170 ♐ Bar PT Bus – 60, 71. Underground – 1 Ⓟ Nearby.

OPERA ROMANA

Romania and its language have Latin origins, so it is hardly surprising that an Italian opera company was the first to visit Bucharest in 1787. The city's first opera house, the Theatrum Vlahicum Bucharestini, was erected in 1814 but it was used by a variety of foreign companies, including Angelica Catalani's, rather than by native ensembles. In the middle of the century a number of local composers were spurred on by the building of the National Theatre in 1852, which resulted in a number of operettas and vaudevilles in the style of Romberg and Strauss, both of whom visited at various times. A lone exception was Ion Wachmann's *Braconierul* (*The Poacher*, 1833), probably the first Romanian opera, which enjoyed 60 performances in its first season.

The foundation of the Romanian Opera in 1877 established a fountainhead of vocal music, fostering sopranos like Hariclea Darclée, who created Tosca, and Elena Teodorini, the first Romanian to sing at La Scala. Both were pupils of George Stephănescu, the theatre's first musical director (until 1890), who also wrote several operas. His groundwork was built upon by Romania's most revered musician, George Enescu.

Although Enescu wrote only one opera, *Oedipe* (Paris, 1936), he stimulated performances and encouraged the setting up of a national school of composition. He also conducted the performance of *Lohengrin* in 1921 which inaugurated the Opera Romănă as a state institution: it had been founded two years earlier, with royal patronage, as the Asociatia Lirică Romîna Opera, under the conductor Ion Otescu and the composer Tiberiu Brediceanu. A significant figure between the wars was conductor George Georgescu: despite recurring discontent among the singers and a shortage of state subsidy, he encouraged new Romanian works. Sabin Drăgoi contributed several, including *Năpasta* (*The Plague*, 1927), which are now the basis of the native repertory.

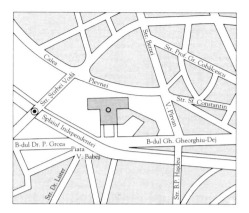

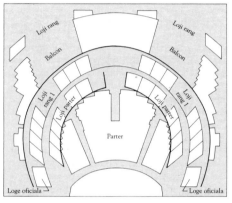

Constantin Silvestri also conducted there regularly between 1935 and 1956.

Weakened by an earthquake in 1940, the ageing theatre was destroyed by bombs in 1944. A new theatre, designed by O. Doicescu and known, like the company, as the Opera Romănă, was opened in 1953. The new theatre, which stands amid gardens in the city's western suburbs, houses the national ballet as well as the opera.

Bd. Gheorghe Gheorghiu-Dej nr. 70–72, sector 5, cod 70609, Bucuresti
☎ 0-15 79 39/0-14 69 80/152 ♬ Sep – Jun Ⓑ As above ⒸⒸ None ♿ None
⛲ 610 🍴 Buffet ☎ 0-13 1857/ 0-14 6980/143 Ⓟ Bus – 168, 368, 126. Trolley bus – 69, 89, 90, 71, 93, 85, 88.

HUNGARIAN STATE OPERA

Opera is a relatively recent phenomenon in Budapest. Performances in German began in the 1780s, but the first opera in Hungarian was *Prince Pikkó* (1793) by József Chudy, conductor of László Kelemen's drama company (1790–96). Hungarian opera was effectively relegated to the provinces by the success in Pest's Town Theatre (opened in 1812) of the German Opera. Then in 1837 the arrival of Ferenc Erkel, conducting a Hungarian company, found a base at the National Theatre. He remained there until 1874, the only 19th-century Hungarian whose operas – notably *Bánk Bán* (1861) – are regularly performed today.

After the unification of Buda and Pest (1872), and Erkel's considerable improvement of standards and repertory, the state agreed the need for an independent opera house. Miklós Ybl's designs in late renaissance style took nine years to fulfil: the Royal Hungarian Opera House opened on 27 September 1884 with acts from *Lohengrin* and *Bánk Bán*. Mahler was music director from 1888 to 1891. He introduced more German opera, especially Wagner, enhancing Budapest's international reputation.

Budapest's golden age was between the world wars, when the works of Bartók, Kodály and Dohnányi came into their own: Bartók's A *Kékszakállú herceg vára* (*Duke Bluebeard's Castle*) had its premiere under Egisto Tango in 1918, Kodály's *Háry János* in 1926, and Dohnányi's *Der Tenor* – a rare comic opera for this period – in 1929. Sergio Failoni, who modelled himself on Toscanini, worked for two decades as principal conductor (1928–47), championing Hungarian music but also extending the Italian and Wagnerian repertory.

After World War II, the theatre adopted its present name – Hungarian State Opera House (Magyar Allami Operaház). Klemperer was chief conductor (1947–50), but it was under János Ferencsik (1957–84) that the company really developed its present style. Still an ensemble company, it is gradually inviting more big-name stars. Several local singers with international reputations are now returning: Eva Marton and Sylvia Sass are recent examples. The Bolshoi are regular visitors. Emil Petrovics has been general manager since 1987.

Magyar Allami Operaház, 1061 Budapest VI, Népköztársaság utja 22 ☎ 01-312 550
♫ Sep – Jun Ⓑ As above ☎ 01-530 170. Tue – Sat 10am – 1pm, 4 – 7pm. For groups write to above address or ☎ 01-119 017 CC None ♿ None ♨ 1261 and 82 standing ♀ 2 Bars PT Bus – 1, 4. Underground – 1, Opera ℗ Difficult.

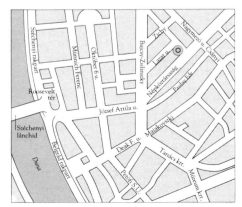

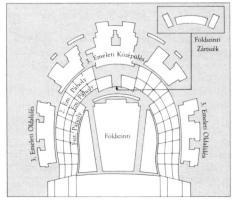

TEATRO COLON

Argentina's capital is home to South America's major centre of operatic activity, El Teatro Colón. Its recent turbulent fortunes to some extent reflect the country's volatile politics of the last four decades. This has scarcely undermined its international reputation, which is solidly grounded.

For two centuries under colonial rule, the Spanish *tonadilla*, a short comic opera, was the only lyric theatre available in Argentina. At the collapse of the colonial regime in 1810, Buenos Aires had but one small theatre, the Coliseo. Here Italian repertory predominated for four decades: *Il Barbiere* was the first complete opera to be presented (1825) and eight more by Rossini followed within five years. European immigration further whetted operatic appetites and by 1854 there were 34 new productions in that year. To satisfy this demand, the first Teatro Colón eventually opened in 1857 with *La Traviata*. It remained Argentina's operatic hub until demolished in 1889.

The present theatre opened in 1908 with *Aida* – a splendid building worthy of comparison with the great European opera houses. Its huge auditorium, sumptuously furnished, has excellent acoustics.

The first season saw 77 performances of 17 operas, including one by a native composer: Ettore Panizza's *Aurora*. Saint-Saëns conducted his own *Samson et Dalila* in 1916, the theatre's first production in French; Weingartner conducted a *Ring* cycle in 1922. Both were brought in by Walter Mocchi, whose decade as director (1915–25) established the theatre's reputation. A chorus, a ballet company and two orchestras became part of the operation.

The early 1970s saw a total change of administration and a lowering of standards. Gradually things improved. Crespin and Dimitrova appeared in 1976, and there was an acclaimed *Peter Grimes* in 1979, revived in 1986. After a slight hiatus over the Falklands war, international stars now appear regularly. Under the current artistic director, Carlos Montero, the repertory is wide without being unduly adventurous, but does include good Argentinian works like Ginastera's *Bomarzo* and the national patriotic opera *par excellence*, Felipe Boero's *El Matrero*, first performed at the Colón in 1929.

Cerrito 618, Buenos Aires 1010
☎ 1-35 66 32   TX 25-593 Colón
FX 1-11-12 32   ♫ May – Dec   B As above ☎ 1-35 54 14   CC Amex, Argencard, Diners, Visa   ♿ Elevator   🚻 2467 and 1000 standing   ♟ Bar   PT Bus – 100, 75, 140, 23, 109, 6, 67. Underground – Tribunales and Diagonal Norte.

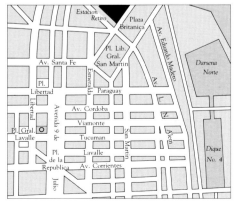

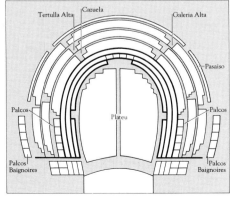

EGYPTIAN OPERA HOUSE

Until tragedy struck in 1971, Cairo had an opera house to rival any Western capital. 'Not even all the tears of the gathered artists of Egypt' could put out the fire which engulfed the old opera house on 28 October that year. However, a new house has replaced the old and Cairo is set to recapture its former glory as a world centre for opera.

The original Cairo Opera House was the idea of the khedive, Ismail Pasha. In 1869 he commissioned two Italian architects, Avoscani and Rossi, to design and build a house in time to coincide with the grand opening of the Suez Canal. On 1 November – a mere six months later – with Napoleon III's wife, Empress Eugénie, as his guest of honour and amid crowned heads from all over Europe, the khedive opened the new, mainly wooden building, with a performance of *Rigoletto* by an Italian company. He further established Cairo upon the operatic map by commissioning *Aida*, the one opera indissolubly associated with Egypt. It was premiered there on Christmas Eve 1871. Most of the musicians were European, but Abou El Kheir Affendi led the brass section of the Egyptian army band on stage.

A number of prominent composers worked in or for Cairo. Bizet wrote three organ pieces for the Opera House, Leoncavallo had a strong influence on Egyptian military music, and Puccini personally supervised productions of his own works in Cairo and Alexandria, as did Mascagni. From 1937 onwards, the directorate was entrusted to Egyptians, particularly Soliman Naguib, whose 16 years until 1954 are widely considered as some of the most important in the flowering of modern Egyptian culture. Until 1961, opera was performed by visiting companies, with Egyptians providing only chorus and orchestra. That year, however, *The Merry Widow* was presented in Arabic, as was *La Traviata* in 1964 and Gluck's *Orfeo* four years later.

A glorious era ended with the 1971 fire. But there was a determination to restore Cairo to its former prominence on the international scene. A state visit to Japan by President Hosni Mubarak in 1983 resulted in an offer by the Japanese government to donate a new opera house. The cornerstone was laid on 31 March 1985 and the building opened three years later to the day.

Geziro, Cairo   ☎ 03-42 05 95/42 06 03/ 41 29 26/ 41 29 27/ 42 05 94   ♫ Oct – Jun ⓑ As above. Booking 10 days in advance ⓒⓒ None   ⑁ Wheelchair access, restrooms, discounts   ⁂ 1200 ⓅⓉ Buses available but not advisable ⓟ Room for 900 cars.

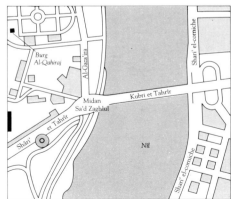

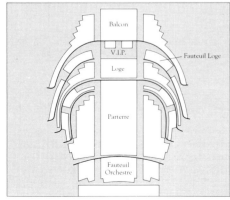

WELSH NATIONAL OPERA

The first Welsh National Opera was formed in 1890 to tour with Joseph Parry's two operas but went bankrupt. The Cardiff Grand Opera Society flourished briefly in the late 1920s and early 1930s. Otherwise, amateurs apart, Wales before World War II had to rely on visiting English companies.

The present Welsh National Opera was formed in 1943 with Idloes Owen as musical director. After several concert performances, the company was launched properly in 1946 with *Cavalleria Rusticana* and *Pagliacci* alternating with *Faust* at Cardiff's Prince of Wales Theatre. WNO was soon lifted to a higher plane by the vision and ruthlessness of business manager William (Bill) Smith, who ensured there was at least one new production every year until 1953, after which two annually (except 1961) until his retirement in 1968. These included the premiere of Arwel Hughes' nationalistic *Menna* (1953), at the National Eisteddfod in 1954.

Verdi's *Vêpres Siciliennes* (1954) marked WNO's move to the New Theatre. The excellence of the chorus, still a strong feature, persuaded WNO to choose a mainly Italian repertory: a German work was not staged until 1962 with *Figaro*. Growing professionalism forced a move in 1965 to a larger HQ, a converted warehouse near the New Theatre. Margaret Price (1962), Stuart Burrows (1963) and Thomas Allen (1969) made their debuts with WNO at this time. In 1968 a professional chorus, the WNO Chorale, came into being, while in 1970 the company formed its own orchestra, the Welsh Philharmonia. These changes coincided with the era of James Lockhart as musical director (1968–73) and Michael Geliot as artistic director (1969–77): the repertory became more adventurous and standards improved. Together they staged the first British performance of *Lulu* in 1971.

Richard Armstrong became musical director (1973–86). He was joined in 1976 by Brian McMaster as general administrator.

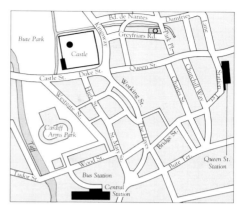

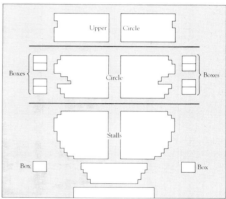

They reinforced WNO's standing, achieved largely through British singers working with foreign theatre directors such as Harry Kupfer and Andrei Serban. The present musical director is Sir Charles Mackerras.

New Theatre, Park Pl., Cardiff CF1 3LN
☎ 0222-489515 ♬ Feb – Mar, May – Jun 🅱 As above ☎ 0222-394 844
CC Amex, Diners, MC, Visa.
♿ Wheelchair space, hearing aids
▦ 1140 ♀ 3 bars PT Train – Central Station. Local trains – Queen St and Cathays stations. Bus – Greyfriars Rd.
Ⓟ Opposite theatre in Greyfriars Rd.

TEATRO MASSIMO BELLINI

Vincenzo Bellini was born in Catania on 3 November 1801. Both his father and grandfather held the position of *maestro di capella* there. So there was a certain inevitability that the child of such a well-known musical family should follow the same profession, even that the city should have a theatre named after its most famous son.

In 1812 plans were drawn up for a public arena. Marauding Algerian pirates forced the abandonment of construction, but in 1821 the Teatro Comunale Provvisorio was opened as a stopgap with a production of Rossini's *L'Aureliano in Palmira*. It was not until 1874 that Carlo Sada was chosen to design a permanent theatre for the original site. The Teatro Massimo Bellini was finally inaugurated in 1890 with Bellini's *Norma*.

The auditorium, painted in red, white and gold, gives an impression of spaciousness but holds only 1300. Each of its 103 boxes, which are arranged in four tiers and decorated in bold red velvet, has its own anteroom. The magnificent ceiling is an integral part of the overall scheme. The city's heraldic symbol, an elephant, is amusingly featured in gold on the velvet covering of the prompter's box. A bronze statue of Bellini by Salvo Giordano adorns the marble foyer.

The theatre closed during World War II and escaped damage. When British forces occupied Catania on 5 August 1943, the commanding officer instructed the mayor to reopen the theatre at once: opera resumed with scenery flown in from Palermo by the American Air Force.

Naturally Catania has spearheaded the Bellini revival since the war: the 150th anniversary of his birth was celebrated in 1951 with all-star casts in *Norma*, *La Sonnambula*, *Il Pirata* and *I Puritani*.

Today the company is making a determined effort to regain national attention by going outside the Bellini canon: the Sicilian premieres of Strauss' *Arabella* and Mozart's *La Clemenza di Tito* were part of the 1989 season. The special commissioner is Francesco Busalacchi, the artistic director Cesare Orselli. The final word on the Teatro Massimo Bellini must go to Gigli, who declared in his memoirs that it was acoustically more perfect than the San Carlo in Naples and even more beautiful than La Fenice in Venice.

Via Perrotta 12, 95100 Catania
☎ 095-312 020   FX 095-321 830
♫ Jan – Jun   B As above. For group discounts contact   ☎ As above
CC None   & ☎ As above
▦ Approx. 1300   ♀ Bar   PT Bus – various   ℗ Nearby.

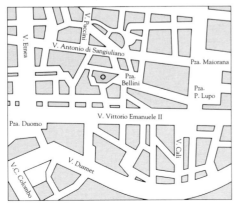

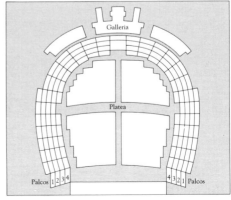

LYRIC OPERA OF CHICAGO

Chicago stands as one of the four most important opera houses in the USA, its reputation firmly built upon productions of Italian repertory, often with singers imported from Europe. A recent example is the Teatro San Carlo (Naples) production of *Sonnambula* which opened the 1988/89 season with Cecilia Gasdia in the title role. It is fair to say that in recent years it has begun to shed some of its earlier conservatism, though without an abiding interest in the opera of our century. The present company was founded in 1954; in the previous century opera had enjoyed a less settled existence in Chicago.

A week of performances of *Sonnambula* was scheduled for July 1850, but only the first took place after the second was disrupted by fire. There was a second season in 1853, and from 1858 to 1871 there were regular visits of up to a fortnight each by touring companies. Meanwhile, Crosby's Opera House had been opened in 1865, but burned down six years later in the great fire which destroyed much of the city centre. Rebuilt in 1873, it catered mainly for touring operetta and musical comedy. The city's first operatic landmark was the Met's touring production of Wagner's *Ring* cycle in 1889. The Chicago Auditorium (capacity 4200) opened in December of that year, with the

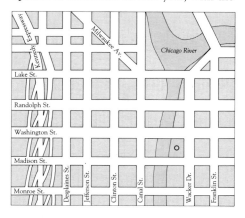

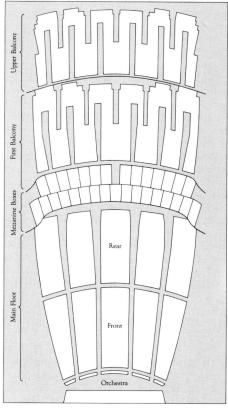

Italian Grand Opera Company of New York in *Roméo et Juliette*. All the important touring companies followed suit in the years up to 1910, when the city's first resident opera company was formed.

The outcome of a struggle between the two rival operatic factions in New York was an enormous gain for Chicago. When Oscar Hammerstein closed down his Manhattan Opera, the company became the backbone of the new Chicago Grand Opera Company, with Andreas Dippel (formerly of the Met) as director and Cleofonte Campanini as chief conductor. Mary Garden, who had grown up in Chicago, sang Mélisande there (1910) and became its prima donna for the next 20 years. The company went bankrupt in 1915, recovered, and appointed Garden as director for the 1921/22 season: she mounted the highly successful world premiere of *The Love for Three Oranges*, with Prokofiev himself conducting, but also accumulated a deficit of over $1 million, a staggering amount in so short a time.

The company lurched forward again in 1924 under the chairmanship of British-born public utilities financier Samuel Insull. One of the company's original backers in 1910, he had grandiose ideas, renamed it the Chicago Civic Opera and moved it into a 45-storey skyscraper, reserving the penthouse for his own use, while creating the present Civic Opera House in the bottom of the building. In the immediate wake of the Wall Street crash of 1929, the house opened with *Aida*. Insull succumbed to the Depression and fled the country: the company folded in 1932, but not before Lotte Lehmann, Jennie Tourel and Dame Eva Turner had all made their US debuts with it. Recreated in 1933 under its original name, the CGOC only intermittently recaptured its former glory, enough to see Björling (1937) and Tagliavini (1946) make their first American appearances there.

Eventually an eight-year operatic drought ended in 1954, two years after Carol Fox, conductor Nicola Rescigno and businessman Lawrence Kelly had formed the Lyric Theatre of Chicago. There were two performances of *Don Giovanni* in February, followed by an autumn season which featured the American debut of Callas – as Norma, perhaps her single most successful role. The company had begun as it intended to continue. The founding triumvirate broke up in 1956, the company given its present name and Fox left in sole control as general manager. A succession of glittering stars adorned those early years: Tebaldi, Birgit Nilsson (as Brünnhilde in *Die Walküre*), Christoff and, especially, Gobbi, who sang 17 different roles there up to 1974, including the title role of *Simon Boccanegra*, which was also his debut as a producer (1965).

A Center for American Artists was begun in 1973 as a training-ground for aspiring singers and a source of new talent for the company. Penderecki was commissioned to write an opera for the 1976 American Bicentennial: *Paradise Lost* was eventually premiered in Chicago in November 1978. It was later taken to La Scala and performed before Pope John Paul II at the Vatican. An era came to an end when Fox retired in 1981, shortly before her death. She was succeeded by Ardis Krainik, a lady of equally formidable personality who had been her assistant since 1960. Top-line stars are not quite so much in evidence these days, but high ticket prices have ensured equally high production standards. The Chicago Opera Theater also gives three productions a year, but in English – unlike the Lyric Opera whose eight annual productions are invariably given in the original language, with English surtitles. The artistic director is Bruno Bartoletti, who made his American conducting debut with the company in 1956.

Civic Opera House, 20 N. Wacker Drive, Chicago, IL60606 ☎ 312-332 2244 TX 190252 FX 312-419 8345 ♬ Sep – Feb B As above. Mon – Fri 10am – 5pm CC Amex, Diners, Discover, MC, Visa ♿ Wheelchair access, restrooms ⸭ 3563 ♟ Bars PT Train – Northwestern Station ☎ 312-836 7801, Union Station ☎ 312-558 1075. Bus and underground – CTA ☎ 312-836 7000 Ⓟ Nearby.

CINCINNATI OPERA

No longer as active as some American companies, the Cincinnati Opera is the second oldest in the country (after the Met). Its summer opera festival, started in 1920, is the oldest. Performances are given in the city's Music Hall.

The city has long enjoyed an active cultural life, perhaps because fully half of its early population were native Europeans, a third being of German origin. As a result a strong choral tradition, first heard in *Sängerfests* throughout the Midwest, was converted in 1873 into a biennial May Festival held at Cincinnati. So successful were the first two festivals that the Music Hall was erected by public subscription. The May Festival, which became an annual affair in 1967, continues to this day. It has had several distinguished directors, including Eugene Goossens (1931–46) and James Levine (1974–78), a native of the city.

Opera was slower in coming to the city. Touring groups began to appear only late in the last century. It was not until the formation of the Cincinnati Summer Opera Association in 1920 that an annual outdoor season was presented in a bandstand at the Zoological Gardens, sometimes to a peacock or penguin accompaniment.

In 1972, after a major conversion of the building, opera was transferred to the Music Hall. James de Blasis, whose first engagement with the company was as stage director in a 1968 'Wild West' version of *L'Elisir d'Amore*, was appointed its general (now artistic) director in 1974. In the following year it adopted its present name. His has been an adventurous regime, given the relatively limited span of the company's season. He conducted Douglas Moore's *The Ballad of Baby Doe* in 1976, Floyd's *Susannah* (1979), and Alfano's *Risurrezione* (1983).

From a peak of eight productions annually in a year-round schedule between 1980 and 1984, usually including two musicals or operettas, CO's 1989 programme reverted to four productions

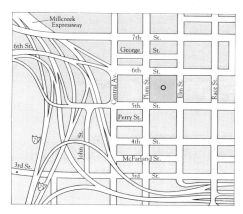

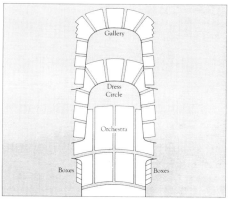

confined to June and July. Touring, however, has continued through its Ensemble Company (ECCO), with 200 performances throughout the year.

The Music Hall, which is renowned for its acoustics, is also home to the Cincinnati Symphony Orchestra and the Cincinnati Ballet, in addition to the May Festival.

Music Hall, 1241 Elm St., Cincinnati, Ohio 45210 ☎ 513-621 1919 ♫ Jun – Jul, Festival in May Ⓑ As above ☎ 513-721 8222. Discounts for groups of 10+ ☎ 513-621 1919 CC Amex, MC, Visa ♿ Wheelchair space, hearing aids ⣿ 3630 ♟ Private club only PT Bus – Queen City Metro Ⓟ Adjacent to Music Hall and connected by covered walkway.

THE DALLAS OPERA

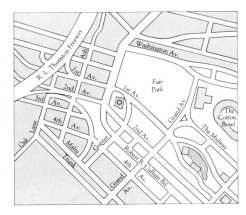

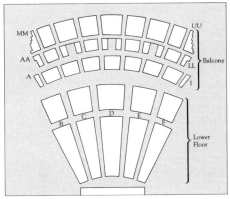

The first Dallas Opera House opened in 1883 with Sullivan's *Iolanthe*. It provided a useful base in southwest USA for touring companies. For 20 years, from 1913, the Chicago Opera Company visited with singers of the calibre of Garden, Tetrazzini and Chaliapin. Fortune Gallo, who pioneered the production of operatic sound films, brought his San Carlo Touring Company during the 1930s. Since 1939 (with the exception of 1941–43 and 1961) the Metropolitan Opera has included Dallas in its annual tour each spring.

Following the break up of the Chicago Lyric Theatre's triumvirate in 1956, manager Lawrence Kelly left for New York, conductor Nicola Rescigno for Europe; both had a long-term vision of together founding a new company in the USA. It was soon to be realized: Dallas Civic Opera was incorporated in March 1957, with Kelly as general manager and Rescigno as musical director. A mere eight months later, the company opened with a Zeffirelli production of *L'Italiana in Algeri* with Giulietta Simionato in the lead. The following year Callas was engaged as Medea. Thereafter four productions were presented each autumn, a total of some 61 works over the next 25 seasons. These included several US premieres, among them Handel's *Alcina*, in which Sutherland made her American debut, *L'Incoronazione di Poppea* and Vivaldi's *Orlando Furioso*. Other international stars whose first American appearances were in Dallas include Alva, Caballé, Vickers and Domingo.

After Kelly's death in 1974 Rescigno assumed his duties for two years, until Plato Karayanis was appointed general manager in 1977. The company's name was changed to The Dallas Opera (TDO) in 1981. With a budget of over $3 million by 1983, it continued to perform in the State Fair Park Music Hall which lacks the cohesive ambience ideally required for opera.

Plans are now being laid for a new purpose-built opera house, to be opened in the late 1990s. Meanwhile, the company's forward-looking policy saw the commissioning and world premiere in November 1988 of Dominick Argento's *The Aspern Papers*, based upon Henry James' novella.

The Music Hall, Fairpark, Dallas, Tx 75201 ☎ 214-979 0123 TX 203941 ACTD UR ♬ Oct – Dec B 3400 Carlisle St., Suite 100, Dallas, Tx 75201. Discounts for groups of 10 + ☎ 214-871 0090 CC Amex, MC, Neiman – Marcus, Visa ♿ Reserved area for parking, restrooms ♨ 3420 ♪ Crystal Terrace Restaurant and Bar ☎ 214-421 3904 PT Dallas Area Rapid Transport ☎ 214-979 1111 taxi Ⓟ Nearby with shuttle service to the Music Hall.

STAATSOPER

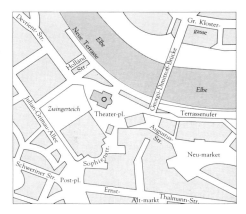

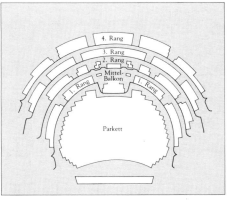

Dresden State Opera is the official name of the company often referred to as the Semper Oper, after its famous opera house.

The earliest opera created in Germany was Schütz's *Dafne*, first staged in 1627 at Hartenfels Castle. For two centuries, however, the main tradition was Italian. The first opera house, the Kurfürstliche Hoftheater (Electoral Court-theatre), was inaugurated in 1667 with Bontempi's *Teseo*.

King Friedrich August I opened the larger Grosses Opernhaus on the Zwinger in 1719 – one of the largest in Europe with a capacity of 2000. It was altered by the celebrated stage designer Galli-Bibiena in 1750. Hasse was music director there (1731–60) creating several works for his wife, the soprano Faustina Bordoni.

The establishment of a German Opera in 1817 was belated recognition of the popularity of opera in the vernacular. Weber became its music director, instituting far-reaching reforms: *Freischütz*, premiered in Berlin (1821), became Dresden's trademark opera.

Dresden's modern era began in 1841 with the building of the Royal Saxon Opera House, designed by Gottfried Semper. A year later Wagner staged the premiere of his *Rienzi* there. At once appointed its director, he went on to give the first performances of *Der Fliegende Holländer* (1843) and *Tannhäuser* (1845) there. When it burned down in 1869, Semper designed its replacement in 1878.

In 1918 the theatre became the Staatsoper. Three new Strauss works were performed under Busch (1922–33), two under Böhm (1934–43). The theatre was bombed out in 1945, and the company moved temporarily to the state theatre complex. Rebuilding of the Semper house was finally announced in 1976 and it opened on 13 February 1985, the fortieth anniversary of the bombing, with *Freischütz*. A stately auditorium, without excessive decoration, it has excellent acoustics. The intendant is now Gerd Schönfelder, the music director Hans Vonk, and the artistic director Joachim Herz, a Felsenstein protégé. Accompaniment is provided by the excellent Dresden Staatskapelle Orchestra. The city stages a festival in late May and early June with a heavy operatic component.

Theaterplatz 2, Dresden 8010
☎ 051-48420 [TX] 26315 OPERDN
♫ Aug – Jul [B] International Travel Agencies and The Hotel Bellevue for foreign visitors [CC] Amex, MC, Visa
♿ Wheelchair space ☷ 1323
🍴 Two buffets and restaurant
[PT] Train – Dresden main station or Neustadter station. Local train – 4, Theaterplatz; 1, 2, 8, 7, 11, 14, 17, Postplatz Ⓟ At theatre.

DEUTSCHE OPER AM RHEIN

Deutsche Oper am Rhein is the company formed in 1956 to provide opera and ballet in the industrial cities of Düsseldorf and Duisburg. The first significant operatic occasion in Düsseldorf was the premiere in 1709 of Agostino Steffani's last opera, *Il Tassilone*, in which the renowned castrato, Benedetto Baldassari, sang the role of Charlemagne's daughter. Mendelssohn became city conductor in 1833, and began a series of Handel oratorios with *tableaux vivants*. But he fell out with the director of the theatre and left in 1835.

The city's first true opera house was built in 1875. It was badly bombed during World War II. The reconstructed Opernhaus Düsseldorf was opened in 1958. Meanwhile Duisburg, whose 1912 house had been similarly damaged, had inaugurated its new Stadttheater in 1950. Alberto Erede was musical director (1958–61), the first Italian to hold such a post in Germany this century.

He was succeeded by Günter Wich, who made a name with modern German operas, notably those of Berg and Schoenberg, but also Zimmermann's *Die Soldaten*, at whose British premiere he conducted the company at the 1972 Edinburgh Festival. Grisch Barfuss was intendant from 1964 and commissioned Alexander Goehr's *Behold the Sun* in celebration of the company's twenty-fifth

anniversary: its first performance was in Duisburg in April 1985. Kurt Horres succeeded Barfuss in 1986 and immediately reinforced the company's earlier vigorous advocacy of unusual, especially German, repertory. Schoeck's *Penthesilea*, Fortner's *Bluthochzeit*, Korngold's *Die Tote Stadt* and Schreker's *Die Gezeichneten* have all been successfully staged in the late 1980s. The company collaborated with Cologne Opera in late 1989 on a *Ring* cycle, produced by Horres and conducted by the present musical director, Hans Wallat.

Opernhaus Düsseldorf, Heinrich – Heine–Allee 16a ☎ 0211-890 81. Theater der Stadt Duisburg, Neckerstrasse 1, 4100 Duisburg 1 ☎ 0203-390 41 ♫ Aug – May Ⓑ As above ☎ 0211-133 940/133 949 – Düsseldorf ☎ 0203-39041 – Duisburg. Discounts for groups of 30 + CC None ♿ Wheelchair space ⚏ OD – 1342, TSD – 1118 ♟ OD – Restaurant ☎ 0211-375 549, TSD – Buffet PT Düsseldorf: U-Bahn – Heinrich–Heine–Allee. Tram – Heinrich–Heine–Allee and Jan–Wellem–Platz. Duisburg: Tram – 901, 904, 909, König–Heinrich–Platz. Bus – 934, 944, Mercatorhalle Ⓟ Nearby.

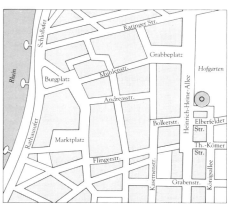

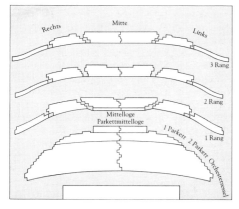

TEATRO COMUNALE

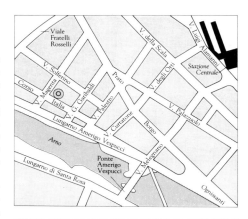

Opera was born in Florence. Between about 1573 and 1587 poets, musicians, dramatists and other assorted intellectuals met regularly as members of Giovanni de'Bardi's Camerata to exchange ideas on blending music with classical drama. They influenced a later group under Jacopo Corsi, who promoted what is generally considered to be the first opera, Jacopo Peri's *Dafne*, presented in Florence during the Carnival of 1598.

During the second half of the 17th century operas were produced by academies – descendants of the Camerata. One of the most notable, the Accademia degli Immobili, founded in 1648, built a large wooden theatre at Via della Pergola which opened in 1656 with Jacopo Melani's *La Tancia*. In 1718 the Pergola was opened to the public with the premiere of Vivaldi's *Scanderbeg*.

Mozart – not a composer much revered in Italian opera houses – first appeared on the Pergola hoardings with *Figaro* in 1788, its Italian premiere. Cherubini, a Florentine, had three operas staged there between 1782 and 1784, before leaving to make his real reputation outside Italy.

After the advent of the Teatro Politeama in 1864 the Pergola might have fallen into total disuse. Instead, it has experienced annual revivals during the Maggio Musicale, when it has been largely given over to recitals.

The first Politeama Fiorentino Vittorio Emanuele was an open-air arena, erected in 1862. It promptly burned down and was just as quickly re-erected in 1864. A roof was added in 1883. In 1932 it was handed over to the city authorities and renamed Teatro Comunale.

The Maggio Musicale, which sometimes starts in late April and often runs until late June, has an international reputation for the range and quality of its operatic output. Besides accompanying the opera the Orchestra del Maggio gives a complete concert season outside the festival. Bruno Bartoletti,

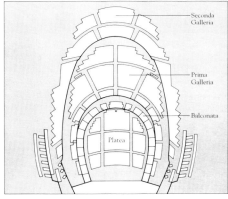

the Comunale's present artistic director, was its chief conductor (1957–64), a position held by Muti (1969–73) and currently (since 1984) by Zubin Mehta. The chief guest conductor, recently appointed chief conductor at the Paris Bastille, is Myung-Whun Chung. The Maggio is now regarded as Italy's foremost festival.

Corso Italia 16, Firenze 50123
☎ 055-27791 TX 574117 MAGMUS
FX 055-29 69 54 ♫ Oct – Dec; May –
Jun B As above ☎ 055-27 7 92 36.
Tue – Sat 9am – 1pm and 1 hr before perf.
Discounts for groups and the disabled
CC None & None ⛲ 1890 ♟ Bar,
sometimes with food PT Train –
Florence Station. Bus – 13, 16 Ⓟ Nearby.

OPER FRANKFURT

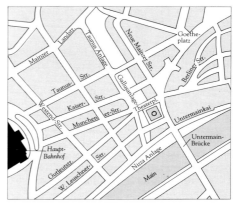

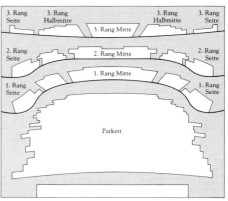

A fire started by a deranged East German refugee virtually destroyed the Frankfurt opera house in November 1987. The stage machinery and newly renovated auditorium were wrecked, and the fly-tower and roof collapsed – not an auspicious start for the new director, Gary Bertini. The company intends to reconstruct the theatre in time for performances to resume in January 1991.

The 1990–91 season will inevitably be limited by the need to adapt productions to the neighbouring Schauspielhaus, where the company is currently performing despite its restricted stage. Some performances are also given in the Alte Oper, particularly during the festival (mid-August to late September).

Frankfurt's first opera was Johann Theile's *Adam und Eva*, presented in 1698 by Johann Velten's touring company. The young Goethe first experienced opera in his native Frankfurt in productions by Theobold Marchand's company, largely German translations of *opéra comique*. Mozart's operas were the staple fare at the Städtisches Comödienhaus, opened in 1782, but the founding of the Museum in 1808 was more significant. Here Weber's *Silvana* was introduced (1810). Spohr was conductor (1817–19), and premiered his *Zemire und Azor*. Wagner directed the 1862 season.

The present Alte Oper, intended exclusively for opera, was opened in 1880. Ludwig Rottenberg's long directorship (1889–1923) witnessed several new works by Franz Schreker, notably *Die Gezeichneten* (1918), and the first German performance of Bartók's *A Kékszakállú herceg vára* (*Duke Bluebeard's Castle*, 1922). Hindemith became leader of the Frankfurt Opera Orchestra in 1915: his *Sancta Susanna* was premiered there in 1922.

The next director, Clemens Krauss (1924–29), often featured his wife, the soprano Viorica Ursuleac. Orff's *Carmina Burana* was unveiled in Frankfurt in 1937. The theatre was bombed in 1943, but was reopened during Georg Solti's directorship (1952–61). The company's 'progressive' reputation under Michael Gielen (1977–87), allied to such producers as Ruth Berghaus, looks set to be continued by Bertini, already off the mark with Cage's *Europeras*.

Schauspielhaus, Theaterpl., 6000 Frankfurt am Main 1   ☎ 069-2562 0   TX 410163   SBUEFO   FX 069-2562 518   ♫ Aug – Jul   Ⓑ As above and Unter-mainanlage 11, 6000 Frankfurt am Main 1   ☎ 069-2360 61.   Mon – Fri 10am–6pm, Sat 10am–2pm.   Discounts for school groups and the disabled   CC None   ⛨ Elevators   ⛐ 839   ⚲ Bars   PT Tram – 11, Theaterpl. Underground – U1, U2, U3, U4 Theaterpl.   Ⓟ Wilhelm Leuschner str.1.

GRAND THEATRE

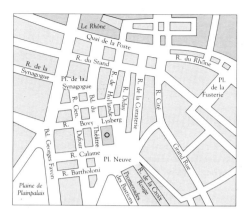

Although Geneva is now a thriving musical centre, it was slow to take up opera. The young Grétry, attracted by the new Parisian vogue for *opéra comique*, and encouraged by Voltaire, wrote a number of ariettas to Favart's *Isabelle et Gertrude*: the one-act result was premiered in Geneva in December 1766. A new theatre, built in 1783, remained the city's chief operatic venue until a replacement – the Grand Théâtre – was opened in 1879 with Rossini's *Guillaume Tell*, the Swiss patriotic opera *par excellence*.

A serious fire closed the Grand Théâtre in May 1951. It reopened in its present guise in December 1962 with a production of the original French version of *Don Carlos* by Marcel Lamy, who remained as director for three years. He was succeeded by the Viennese-born Herbert Graf, whose opening gambit was a production of *Zauberflöte*, with designs by Oscar Kokoschka, conducted by Ernest Ansermet, the founder in 1918 of Geneva's renowned Orchestre de la Suisse Romande. As well as standard repertory, Graf revived works by Swiss composers, including *Macbeth* by Geneva-born Ernest Bloch and Honegger's *Antigone*. In 1966 he premiered Milhaud's last opera, *La Mère Coupable*.

Jean-Claude Riber was appointed director general in 1973, and was succeeded by Hugues Gall in 1980. Under both men, the company's repertory has been an enterprising mixture of old and new allied to a certain penchant for engaging theatrical producers with a limited experience of opera. One of Gall's early gambles was the troika of François Rochaix (producer), Jean-Claude Maret (designer) and Roderick Brydon (conductor), whose string of successes began with Britten's *Turn of the Screw* in 1981, followed in 1983 by his *Death in Venice*. Recent premieres have included Girolamo Arrigo's *Il Ritorno di Casanova* (1985) and Rolf Liebermann's *La Forêt* (1987).

This is an impressive four-tier house, but compact and sympathetic to voices, exuding

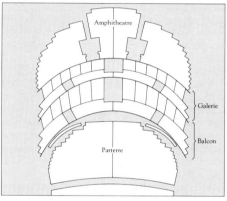

a certain self-assurance. A potential asset, but sometimes proving a liability, is the Suisse Romande Orchestra, which has not always proved amenable to unfamiliar conductors. The company, which includes a ballet troupe, is relatively small, but enjoys substantial government and civic support: large budgets and high attendance figures enable a constant procession of stars to adorn expensive productions. These span works of the last three centuries.

11 Bd du Théâtre, CH-1211 Genève 11
☎ 022-21 23 11 ☐TX☐ 421 132 GTG
♫ Sep – Jun ☐B☐ As above ☐CC☐ None
♿ On request ⸬ 1488 ♟ Buffet
☎ 022-21 56 73 ☐PT☐ Tram – 12, Pl.
Neuve. Bus – 3, Pl. Neuve ℗ Nearby.

OPERA DI GENOVA

The Teatro Carlo Felice was the famous arena used for opera in Genoa from 1828 until it was severely damaged by an air-raid in August 1943. Its replacement – part reconstruction, part addition – is now underway, but delays and scandals within the company have recently conspired to put back completion. In the meantime, an operatic administration, in some disarray, is carrying on in the Teatro Margherita.

The first record of opera in the city is in the early 1640s, when Benedetto Ferrari's *Il Pastor Regio* was staged. The Teatro Falcone, named after its architect, was built in 1650. Throughout the 18th century, the Teatro Sant' Agostino was Genoa's operatic hub. Productions there were haphazard and intermittent; Genoa still lacked a consistent tradition.

The necessary initiative came from King Carlo Felice: he ordered the city council to either enlarge the Sant' Agostino or build a new theatre. The church of San Domenico was demolished forthwith and a new theatre designed by Carlo Barabino built on the site, opening in 1828 with the premiere of Bellini's *Bianca e Fernando*.

In a century of distinction at the theatre, Angelo Mariani was *maestro direttore* from 1852 until his death in 1873, enlarging and improving its orchestra to a position of pre-eminence in Italy.

In his last season at the Carlo Felice (1894), Toscanini conducted 64 performances of seven operas in 58 days (including several matinees), a marathon which no modern conductor would attempt. He also initiated a Wagner – Strauss cult in Genoa. Strauss came to conduct the first Italian performance of his *Arabella*. A shell hole in the roof caused by a British naval ship in November 1941 failed to stop the show; the incendiary bombs of August 1943 did.

Major reconstruction was finally put in hand a few years ago. No-one can guess when it will be ready. The company lacks an artistic director, but Daniel Oren is chief conductor, with 114 players and 77 singers on the payroll of his orchestra and chorus.

Teatro Margherita, Via XX Settembre 33/7, 16121 Genova ☎ 010-53811 [TX] 286354 EATCO [FX] 010-5381233 ♫ Jan – Jun [B] As above ☎ 010-589 329/ 591 697. Daily 10am – 12.30pm. Sun 3.30 – 7pm. On days of performance only. For groups contact box office [CC] None ♿ ☎ 010-53811 ⁙ 1800 and 270 standing 🍷 Bar [PT] Train – Brignole Station (500 m away) Ⓟ Under theatre.

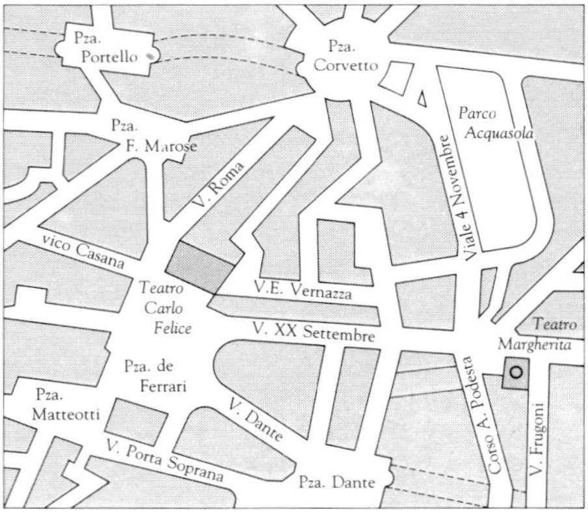

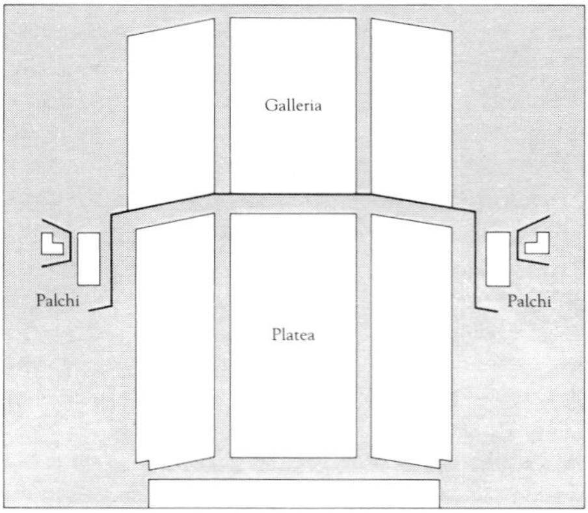

SCOTTISH OPERA

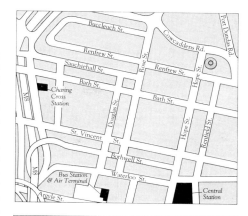

The Theatre Royal, Glasgow, opened its doors in November 1867. Designed by George Bayliss as the Coliseum Theatre and Opera House, it staged the first opera in Glasgow in December that year, when Florence Lancia's Grand English Opera Company performed *Trovatore*.

In 1869 a charter from Queen Victoria conferred the title Theatre Royal. After a fire ten years later, Charles John Phipps designed a replacement which opened in 1880. Meanwhile the Carl Rosa Company had begun the first of many visits. After fire damage in 1895, it was again Phipps who masterminded the reconstruction. The need for a local pool of singers to supplement the Carl Rosa led to the formation in 1905 of the amateur Glasgow Grand Opera Company, which staged the British premieres of *Idomeneo* (1934) and *Les Troyens* (1935).

Scottish Opera, Glasgow's first professional company, established by Alexander Gibson in 1962, was at first only an intermittent operation. Its inaugural season, which opened at the King's Theatre in 1962, alternated *Butterfly* and *Pelléas* for one week with the Scottish National Orchestra in support. The appointment of Peter Hemmings as general manager that autumn provided a forceful foil to Gibson, the artistic director: steady growth culminated in SO's first *Ring* in 1971, and the number of annual performances passed 100 in 1973. The Theatre Royal was acquired in 1974 and extensively converted under Derek Sugden: SO opened there with *Fledermaus* in October 1975.

Hemmings was succeeded by Peter Ebert (1977), John Cox (1981) and Richard Mantle (1986). The American conductor John Mauceri succeeded Gibson in 1987. While maintaining high musical standards, the company enjoyed an uneven relationship with the Scottish Arts Council in the 1980s, falling foul of several experimental producers. Several works by Scottish composers have had successful premieres: Iain Hamilton's *The Catiline Conspiracy* (1974)

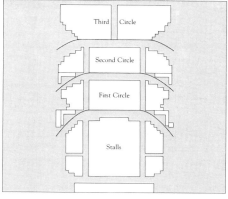

and Thea Musgrave's *Mary Queen of Scots* (1977). SO travels regularly to Aberdeen, Edinburgh, Inverness, Liverpool and Newcastle.

Theatre Royal, Hope St., Glasgow G2 3QA
☎ 041-248 4567 [TX] 776264 SCOTOP
[FX] 041-221 8812 ♫ Varies [B] As above ☎ 041-331 1234/332 9000
[FX] 041-332 3965. Discounts for groups of 20+ [CC] Amex, Diners, MC, Style, Visa ♿ Wheelchair spaces, restrooms, hearing aids ☎ 041-331 1234 ░ 1547 and limited standing ♀ 4 bars
[PT] Train – Glasgow Central/Glasgow Queen St. stations. Bus – Buchanan St. bus station. Underground – Cowcaddens station Ⓟ At Cambridge St., corner of Cowcaddens and Port Dundas Rds.

GLYNDEBOURNE FESTIVAL OPERA

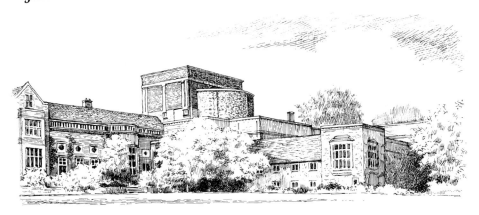

Glyndebourne is a unique institution in British operatic life. An English manor house set in the Sussex downs near Lewes, 50 miles (80 kilometres) south of London, it became a byword for the highest musical standards in 1934 when John Christie, its owner, built an opera house on to the manor. This came in the wake of his marriage to the soprano Audrey Mildmay. She tempered his original desire to present Wagner, and the 311-seat house opened in 1934 with a two-week season of *Figaro* and *Così*. The producer was Carl Ebert, conductor Fritz Busch, with Rudolf Bing as general manager; they gave 12 performances in all. Sceptical critics were unanimously impressed by the meticulous attention to detail in every aspect of the productions: Busch alone had put his orchestra through 24 three-hour rehearsals. Even so, no-one expected Christie would be able to sustain what looked like a rich man's folly.

Yet in 1938 he delivered the British premiere of *Macbeth* and by 1939 there were 38 performances in a theatre now enlarged to 600 seats. Activity ceased during World War II. Glyndebourne's resumption was spectacular, with two Britten world premieres given by the English Opera Group: *The Rape of Lucretia* in 1946, with Kathleen Ferrier in the title role making her

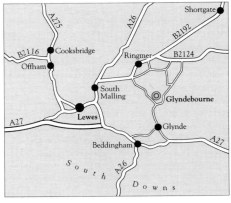

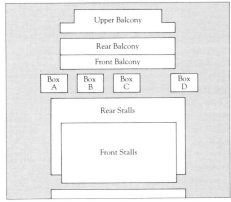

operatic debut, and *Albert Herring* in 1947, conducted by the composer. Bing and Audrey Mildmay founded the Edinburgh Festival in 1947, with Glyndebourne providing its operatic component for the next four years, underwritten by the city. Ebert also produced *Orfeo* that year, with Ferrier in her famous leading role.

Normal seasons were resumed at Glyndebourne in 1950 as industrial sponsorship began: it now provides about one-third of the company's income. The rest comes entirely from ticket sales, most of which are confined to members of the Glyndebourne Festival Society – for which there is a waiting list, despite the necessarily high price of tickets. After a government grant, Busch conducted four Mozart works at the Festival of Britain (1951), including the country's first professional *Idomeneo*. Upon Busch's death that September, Vittorio Gui became music director (1952–64), introducing four Rossini works and the first opera sung in French at Glyndebourne, Gluck's *Alceste* (1953). That year the auditorium was enlarged to seat 700 and the company introduced *The Rake's Progress* to Britain. A year later George Christie, aged 23, succeeded his father as chairman of Glyndebourne Productions Ltd, the controlling company.

Moran Caplat took over as general manager after Bing's departure for the Met in 1950, while Günther Rennert became artistic director (1959–68) in succession to Busch. From 1948 the Royal Philharmonic Orchestra was in the pit and accompanied the first production in the original English of Henze's *Elegy for Young Lovers* (1961). Since 1964 the London Philharmonic has been Glyndebourne's resident orchestra. The exception was the Orchestra of the Age of Enlightenment, which in 1989 played for the first of three 'authentic' productions of Mozart's Da Ponte operas – *Figaro*, *Don Giovanni* and *Così* – conducted by Simon Rattle and due to be completed in 1990/91. Recent music directors have been John Pritchard (1969–77), Bernard Haitink (1977–88), and since late 1988, Andrew Davis.

Brian Dickie, who succeeded Caplat as general administrator in 1981, had been the founding administrator of Glyndebourne Touring Opera from 1967. GTO, which unlike its parent company does receive a government subsidy, visits major English cities in October and November, notably Manchester, Oxford, Plymouth and Southampton, after opening at Glyndebourne. Its casts are generally slightly less experienced than those of the festival company.

Anthony Whitworth-Jones took over from Dickie in 1989. In the previous six years he had orchestrated Glyndebourne's New Opera policy, which produced Oliver Knussen's *Where the Wild Things Are* (1984) and *Higglety, Pigglety, Pop!* (1985), Nigel Osborne's *The Electrification of the Soviet Union* (1987) and the British premiere of Tippett's *New Year* (1990). So there is ample proof that Glyndebourne is moving with the times, although with an ethos all its own.

Special trains are laid on from London (Victoria); evening dress is recommended, though not obligatory; opera goers may dine in the restaurants – there is a 75-minute interval after a 5.30pm start – but are more likely to bring their own picnics to consume in the gardens. What contributes most to Glyndebourne's unique atmosphere is the commitment of its casts, genuinely international and generally on the verge of straddling the world stage. The chorus, too, consists of carefully-chosen young British singers. Billeted locally, all benefit from almost limitless rehearsal. Due to extensive renovation the opera house will be closed for the 1993 season.

Glyndebourne, Lewes, E. Sussex BN8 5UU ☎ 0273-812321 TX 877862 GLYOP FX 0273-812783 ♫ May – Aug B As above ☎ 0273-541111 during season only TX FX As above CC None ♿ Ramps, space for wheelchairs – contact box office ⛲ 830 ♥ Letheby & Christopher restaurant ☎ 0273-812510 FX 0273-813851 Bar PT Train – Lewes station (special transfer, contact box office) Ⓟ In grounds.

STORA TEATERN

Gothenburg (Göteborg) is Sweden's second largest city and its opera company justifiably considered second only to Stockholm's Royal Opera. After a succession of German companies had visited the city in the early 19th century, the taste for opera increased and led to the construction of the Nya Teatern, which was opened in 1859.

Renamed Stora Teatern in 1880, and locally referred to as 'Storan', it has survived several threats to its existence, notably in the 1920s when only a public outcry saved it from becoming a cinema. Recent restorations have maintained its cramped 19th-century theatrical charm and slightly improved is rather dry acoustics, while reducing its capacity to only 617.

Smetana was the first musician of international repute to visit Gothenburg, which was more or less his permanent base for five years from 1856. Flagstad sang her first Agathe (*Der Freischütz*) at the Storan in 1928 and Verdi's *Vêpres Siciliennes* had its Swedish premiere there. Sixten Ehrling was chief conductor during the 1940s before moving to Stockholm. The company has always had an international outlook: The British conductor Nicholas Braithwaite became chief conductor in 1981 and took Lars Johan Werle's *Animalen (The Animals)* to the Wiesbaden Festival that year. The

Scandinavian premiere of Strauss' *Intermezzo* (1982) and the first Swedish performance of Monteverdi's *Il Ritorno d'Ulisse* (1983) were typical of Gothenburg's enterprise.

In 1984 Eskil Hemberg became director (a position previously held by his fellow composer Werle). Before he left for Stockholm in 1987, he was responsible for the European premiere of Argento's *Voyage of Edgar Allan Poe* in 1986, the same year that Gedda starred in a new production of *Ballo in Maschera*.

The tenor Sven-Olof Eliasson, who sang Peter Grimes there during the 1979–80 season, is the present artistic director. He oversees an operation which includes 24 resident soloists, a chorus of 30 and an orchestra of 61. The repertory encompasses everything from Monteverdi to Maxwell Davies and musicals.

Stora Teatern, Kungsparken, Göteborg
☎ 031-17 47 45 FX 031-13 11 35
♫ Aug – Jun B Box 53 116, 400 15 Goteborg ☎ 031-13 13 00. Daily 12 – 6pm. For groups ☎ 031-17 47 45. Mon – Fri 9am – 4pm CC None ♿ Advise when booking for wheelchairs
☎ 031-13 13 00 ⬚ 605 and 12 standing
♣ Bar PT Train – Kungsportsplatsen station. Tram – 1 Ⓟ Nearby at bus terminal.

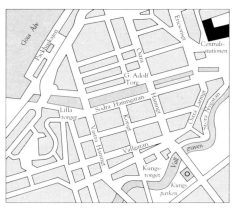

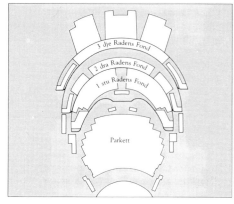

HAMBURGISCHE STAATSOPER

Hamburg has been a leading operatic city ever since 1678, when it opened Germany's first independent public opera house. Standards rose after 1695 under Reinhard Keiser, who wrote over 50 operas for Hamburg and also guided the young Handel. A new playhouse took over in 1765, where Friedrich Schröder directed Mozart and Gluck operas between 1771 and 1812.

The first house on the present site was the Theater am Dammtor, built to designs by Karl Schinkel, which opened with Spohr's *Jessonda* on 3 May 1827. It became the Grosse Oper under Ignaz Lachner (1853–58). With the theatre modernized, there was a golden era under Bernhard Pohl *alias* Pollini (1874–97).

Klemperer was its first important conductor this century (1910–13). Egon Pollak (1917–32) staged the premiere of Korngold's *Die Tote Stadt* (1920) and also oversaw major rebuilding (1925–26), which included modernized stage machinery. The house was officially named Hamburger Staatsoper in 1934 under Böhm's brief tenure (1931–34).

The auditorium was burned out by bombs in 1943. A completely new glass and concrete building, designed by Gerhard Weber, was opened in 1955. Its clean lines have been compared to London's Festival Hall.

The company reached its zenith with the composer Rolf Liebermann as intendant (1959–73). He paid more than lip service to 20th-century opera (especially Schoenberg, Berg and Zemlinsky) and commissioned several new works: Alexander Goehr's *Arden Must Die* (1967), Humphrey Searle's *Hamlet*, Menotti's *Help, Help, the Globolinks!* (1968) and Penderecki's *The Devils of Loudun* (1969) all enjoyed success.

A fire in November 1975 destroyed all the scenery and most of the costumes for 39 operas. This contributed to Christoph von Dohnányi's policy (1977–84) of cutting back on design expenditure. His departure caused some disarray: Liebermann had to be coaxed out of retirement (1985–88). Peter

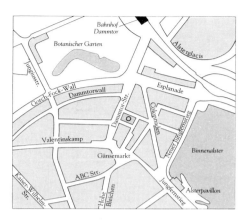

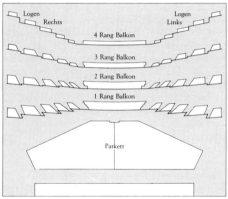

Ruzicka is the new intendant (1988), with Gerd Albrecht replacing Hans Zender as music director from 1989.

Grosse Theaterstr 35,2000 Hamburg 36
☎ 040-35 68 0   ♫ Aug–Jun   B As above   ☎ 040-35 15 55   TX 215020.
Mon–Fri 10am–6pm. Sat, Sun and public holidays 10am–1pm   CC None
& Wheelchair access by elevator to specially designated places in the stalls (*Parkett*)   ⁙ 1674 and 24 standing
♀ Bar   PT Train – Hamburg – Dammtor station. Bus and Underground – Stephanspl.   ℗ At Drehbahn (5 mins).

NIEDERSACHSISCHE STAATSOPER

Hanover celebrated the 300th anniversary of the opening of its first opera house (Schloss-opernhaus) by repeating Steffani's *Enrico Leone*, the work first seen there in 1689. Steffani remained in charge of the company, writing nine more operas for it, until 1698, when Georg Ludwig became Elector of Hanover. Handel was *Kapellmeister* for nine months from June 1710. Opera declined after Georg left for London to become King George I in 1714. The *Singspiel* was introduced to the city by Seyler's travelling company in 1769.

The composer-conductor Heinrich Marschner was appointed *Kapellmeister* in 1831, remaining in Hanover until his death in 1861: five of his operas were premiered there. The theatre was substantially renovated in 1837 and renamed the Hofoper. In 1843 King Ernst August commissioned Georg Laves to design a new theatre. The new Royal Opera House is the present headquarters of opera in Lower Saxony; *Figaro* was its first opera production after it opened in September 1852. The baroque theatre was pulled down in 1854, the year that the Wagnerian tenor Albert Niemann began a 12-year stint in Hanover.

After World War I, control of the opera house passed into municipal hands. Rudolf Krasselt, who took over as music director (1924–43), brought the company back to prominence. In 1943 the theatre was seriously damaged by bombing.

In less than two months the company was back in business, performing in the Galeriegebäude in the suburb of Herrenhausen. Franz Konwitschny was conductor from 1945 to 1949. Reconstructed very much as before, on broadly baroque lines, the old house reopened on 30 November 1950 with *Rosenkavalier* under Johannes Schüler, who gave the first German *Albert Herring* (1950) and the premiere of Henze's *Boulevard Solitude* (1952). Günther Wich (1961–65) earned the credit for presenting Schoenberg's three one-act operas for the

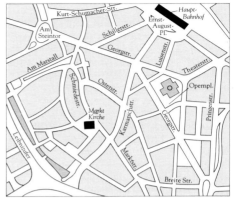

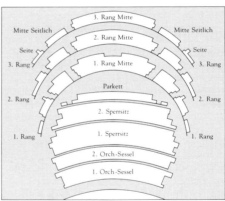

first time as a triple bill, in 1963.

George Albrecht, who succeeded him in 1965, remains as chief conductor, with Hans-Peter Lehmann as intendant.

Opernplatz 1, 3000 Hannover 1
☎ 0511-168 6161   TX 511 85 69 NSH
♫ Sep – Jun   B As above
☎ 0511-168 6140. Mon – Fri 10am – 1pm and 3 – 5.30pm, Sat 10am – 1pm, Sun 11am – 1pm. Discounts for groups
CC None   ♿ Wheelchair space
⬚ 1207   ♟ Restaurant   PT Train – Hannover station nearby. Underground – Marienstrasse   Ⓟ Underneath the theatre.

FINNISH NATIONAL OPERA

Finnish opera is on the crest of a wave: composers are writing successful new works and a magnificent purpose-built opera house is due to open in Helsinki during the 1990–91 season, with Aulis Sallinen's *Kullervo* planned for the inauguration. Finland has not had the depth of operatic tradition enjoyed elsewhere is Europe, having gained independence only in 1917.

In the early 19th century, German opera companies would stop over en route to St Petersburg. Despite publication in 1835 of the Finnish national epic, the *Kalevala,* Swedish-speaking socialites long felt the need for something more cosmopolitan: they eventually mounted *Il Barbiere di Siviglia* with Finnish performers in 1849. The first native opera was *Kung Karls jakt* (*King Charles' Hunt*), written by the German immigrant Fredrik Pacius (who became known as 'the father of Finnish music') and successfully staged in 1852.

Count Nikolai Adlerberg, a culturally sensitive governor-general, established a Russian Theatre company in 1868 whose success led to the building of the Alexander Theatre on Helsinki's Bulevardi in 1880.

A rising tide of musical nationalism, fuelled by Sibelius (whose only opera, however, was in Swedish), encouraged the composition of the first opera in Finnish, Oskar

Merikanto's *Pohjan Neiti* (*Maid of the North*) in 1899. It received an open-air premiere at Viipuri in 1908. Finland's first permanent company, the Domestic Opera, was founded in 1911 by Edward Fazer and the soprano Aïno Ackté (first to sing Salome in Britain), becoming the Finnish Opera (Suomalainen Ooppera) in 1914. After Independence, the company was given the Alexander Theatre as its 'temporary' base.

With Sibelius as patron, the artists' committee of Finnish Opera started an appeal fund for a new building in 1950. Completion is now expected in 1992.

The National Opera has this century staged 38 of the more than 80 operas composed in Finland. Artistic director Jorma Hynninen and principal conductor Ulf Söderblom continue to oversee an adventurous repertory which still attracts large houses.

Alexander Theatre, Bulevardi 23–27, SF-00181 Helsinki ☎ 0-12921
TX 123401 OPERA FX 0-1292 301
♫ Aug – May B Albertinkatu 34 B, SF-00180, Helsinki ☎ 0-129 255.
Mon – Fri 11am–5pm, Sat 10am–1pm. Discounts for groups of 30 + CC None
♿ 1 reserved box ▒ 500 ♟ Bar – advance orders ☎ 0-12921/292 PT Tram– 3,6. Bus – 14 Ⓟ In nearby square.

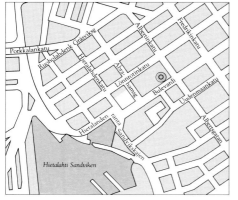

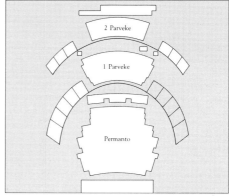

HOUSTON GRAND OPERA

Houston boasts the newest cultural complex in North America, the $72 million Wortham Center for the Performing Arts. Opened in May 1987, it houses both the Houston Grand Opera and the Houston Ballet in a complex which includes two arenas, the Alice and George Brown Theater (capacity 2176), and the Lillie and Roy Cullen Theater (capacity 1066).

The architect, Eugene Aubry, modelled the central arch of the grand entrance foyer upon that of England's Tewkesbury Abbey. The outside is faced with Texas brick trimmed with red granite, a colour which is picked up in the dark red furnishings within. The crescent shape of the larger auditorium ensures that no seat is further than 130 feet (40 metres) from the stage; the spacing between rows and the raking of stalls seats ensures superb vision. It has lively acoustics, and the singers are further helped by the stage, which slightly overhangs the orchestra pit – a style described as 'modified Bayreuth' – although this can muffle the orchestra. The pit, which houses up to 110 players, can be adjusted to provide an extra 70 seats at the front of the stalls or raised to add more 'thrust' to the stage.

None of this has been lightly achieved. The company's history goes back to 1955 with the formation of the Houston Grand

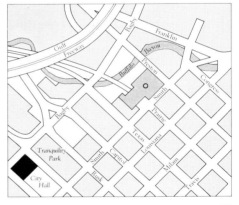

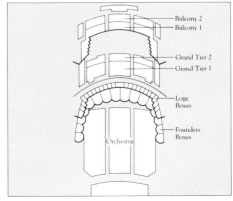

Opera Association by the Viennese-trained conductor Walter Herbert, who had been general director at New Orleans Opera since 1943. Operatic tradition in Houston before that time was shallow indeed. Founded as the capital of the Republic of Texas in 1836, it experienced its first grand opera only in April 1867 – two Verdi productions which were coolly received. So were other touring companies, until the arrival of the Metropolitan Opera in 1901, coincidentally the year when oil – which has since underwritten a huge cultural explosion – was first discovered at nearby Spindletop.

Herbert's company was the first resident opera group. Always with the highest standards, it grew during his tenancy from an opening season of *Salome* and *Butterfly* in the Music Hall on a mere $40,000 to 30 performances with a budget increased tenfold. In 1966 it moved to the new Jesse H. Jones Hall for the Performing Arts. David Gockley took over as general director in 1973 and put HGO even more firmly in the big league. His repertory is relatively conventional, but he has introduced at least one new work each year, either a premiere by an American – Bernstein's *A Quiet Place* (1983) was the most successful – or a 20th- century masterpiece such as *Lulu* or *Grimes*. He has started a light opera series in English, free staged performances in a Spring Opera Festival (which has included Scott Joplin's

Treemonisha and Sondheim's *Sweeney Todd*), a touring offshoot, Texas Opera Theater, and the Houston Opera Studio for young American singers.

There is strong evidence of Gockley's international perspective: productions in 1986 were imported from Drottningholm, Düsseldorf and Toronto; co-productions with the English and Welsh National Operas followed soon after. John Adams' *Nixon in China* was given its premiere during HGO's opening season at the Wortham and subsequently taken to Edinburgh; Philip Glass' *The Making of the Representative for Planet 8*, based on the Doris Lessing novel, was unveiled in 1988. But his greatest coup to date has been the world premiere of Sir Michael Tippett's fifth opera, *New Year*, in October 1989.

Wortham Theater Complex, 550 Prairie St., Houston Tx 77002 ☎ 713-546 0240 TX 910 881 5551 FX 713-247 0906 ♬ Oct – Jun B As above ☎ 713-228 2787. Mon – Fri 9.30am – 5.30pm, Sat 10am – 5pm. Discount for groups of 10 + CC Amex, MC, Visa ♿ Wheelchair space, sight and hearing aids, advance booking preferred ⛲ 2172 ♐ Bars and buffet PT Bus – 16, 17, 84, 39, 40, 75, 85, Texas St. and Smith St. ☎ 713-635 4000 Ⓟ Nearby in Civic Center Garage.

ISTANBUL STATE OPERA

Turkey's interest in Western music has been expanding since the war – there are important opera houses in Ankara and Istanbul – but opera has been known there since 1797, when an Italian company visited what was then Constantinople. Turkey's first Western-style theatre was the city's Naum, opened in 1844 with Donizetti's *Lucrezia Borgia*. It survived a serious fire, and in 1848 was reopened by its Syrian founder, Mihail Naum, with *Macbeth*.

An Italian company of 36 staged six operas by Bellini, Donizetti and Verdi during the 1849–50 season, with Meyerbeer's *Robert le Diable* and Verdi's *Attila* added in the following year. Naum continued to promote opera until 1870, when his theatre burned down irreparably.

Four comic works by the founder of Armenian opera, Tigran Chukhadjian (nicknamed *Il Verdi Armeno*), were first performed in Constantinople (1872–91) by the Benliyan operetta group. This operetta tradition was established and survives today: Istanbul State Opera stages at least two each year, with Leo Fall's *Rose of Stambul* included in the repertory.

While opera enjoyed an intermittent existence, operettas and musicals became popular, notably at the Sehir Tiyatrosu Theatre during the 1930s where the works of Cemal Resit Rey were regularly performed. The true founder of modern-day Turkish opera, however, was Adnan Saygun, who attempted a synthesis of native classical styles with Western influences.

Opera finally received proper state support with the building of the Atatürk Kültür Merkezi (Atatürk Culture Centre) in 1969, designed by one of Turkey's most prominent architects, Hayati Tabanlioğlu. The Centre includes an opera house and a concert hall. It is the home of the Istanbul State Opera and Ballet, which also embraces a resident orchestra of 55 players. The company presents a well-balanced repertory, which includes at least one Turkish opera and one opera in the original language. It also tours regularly to Ankara, Izmir, Bursa and Cyprus. The director is Mesut Iktu, the musical director Alexander Schwinck.

Atatürk Kültür Merkezi, 80090 Taksim, Istanbul ☎ 01-151 5600 TX 24410-IDDB ♬ Oct – May B As above ☎ 01-143 20 14/151 56 00/145 16 36. Daily 9am–8pm. For groups write 1 month in advance to Mr Ridvan Kaya ☎ 01-145 16 36 CC None ♿ Special access and elevator ☎ 01-151 56 00 x279 ☼ 1307 ♟ Bar ☎ 01-143 28 79 PT Bus ℗ 3-storey car park.

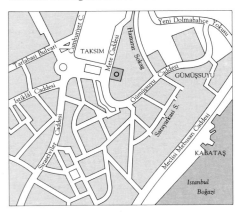

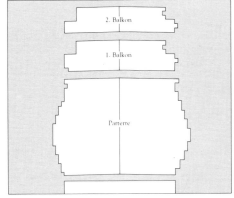

ROYAL THEATRE

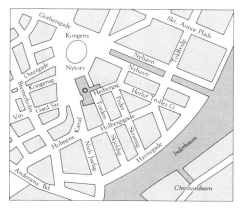

A theatre has stood for well over 200 years on Kongens Nytorv, Copenhagen's central and most attractive square, where the 17th-century Charlottenborg Palace is situated. With renovations and rebuilds, it lasted until 1874, when the present Royal Theatre was opened. From the beginning, opera shared the theatre with ballet and drama: the three continue to cross – fertilize one another.

Foreign companies began to appear in Copenhagen from the 1720s onwards: Gluck came as a conductor with the Pietro Mingotti company from Italy. He celebrated the birth of Crown Prince Christian with his *La Contesa de' Numi* (1749) at the Charlottenborg, conducting it himself.

A distinctive Danish style began to emerge in the late 18th century, pioneered by a group of German-born musicians, notably Johann Schulz, 'father' of Danish national music and director of the Royal Theatre (1787–95), his successor Friedrich Kunzen (1795–1818), and Friedrich Kuhlau, whose incidental music to *Elverhøj* (*The Elf's Hill*, 1828) is the most frequently performed work in the Royal Theatre's repertory. August Bournonville, chiefly remembered as the founding director of the Royal Danish Ballet, produced the first Wagner, *Lohengrin,* in Denmark in 1869.

The new Royal Theatre has enormous atmosphere. Now known as the Old Stage because a new one mainly used for drama and ballet, was added in 1931, it is decorated in red plush, accented with cream and gold. A red lamp lit outside the theatre to signify a full house is a custom later adopted elsewhere.

Carl Nielsen, Denmark's most famous composer, had both his operas produced at the Royal Theatre, *Saul og David* in 1902, *Maskarade* in 1906: both are still in the repertory. Melchior made his stage debut there in the baritone role of Silvio in *Pagliacci* (1913); it was 1918 before he emerged as a tenor. Despite the occupation, *Porgy and*

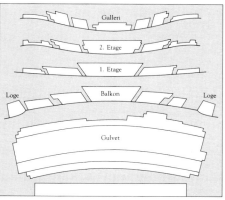

Bess had its first performances outside the USA there in 1943 together with other works banned in Nazi Germany, a typical act of Danish independence The newly (1986) enlarged pit now allows even more scope for this imaginative company, whose director is the conductor Poul Jørgensen.

Det Kongelige Teater, Kongens Nytorv, Tordenskjoldsgade 3, 1055 København ☎ 01-15 22 20 [TX] 15524 DKT [FX] 01-14 46 06 ♫ Sep–Jun [B] Kongens Nytorv, P.O. Box 2185, 1017 København ☎ 01-14 10 02. Mon–Sat 12.15–5pm [CC] None ♿ Wheelchair space ⸬ 1300 ♟ Bars, restaurant ☎ 01-12 42 79 [PT] Bus – 1, 6, 9, 10, 28, 41, 7 ℗ Nearby.

OPER DER STADT

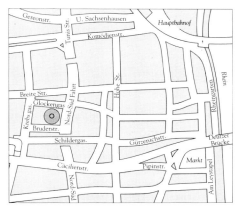

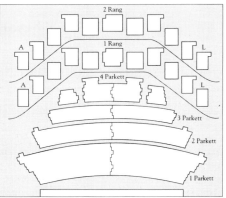

Cologne's first attempts at home-grown opera were in 1661, when the cathedral organist Kaspar Grieffgens wrote *Vanitas Vanitatum*. But it was a full century before French touring companies began to visit the city, playing Pergolesi, Gluck, Dittersdorf and Mozart. The first permanent theatre, built in 1822, specialized in Weber and Rossini. Lortzing was one of its singers.

The conductor – composer Ferdinand Hiller, a close friend of Wagner, was city *Kapellmeister* (1850 – 84) and at once introduced him to Cologne: its first *Tannhäuser* was in 1853 and *Lohengrin* in 1855. Wagner personally conducted a fund – raising concert for Bayreuth at the Gürzenich (City Hall) in 1873. The Theater in der Glockengasse was opened in 1872, with the Theater am Habsburger, specifically for opera, added to it in 1902. Klemperer was its first great director (1917 – 24), conducting the premiere of Korngold's *Die Tote Stadt* (1920), and the first German *Kátya Kabanová* (1922).

Cologne was severely bombed in 1943: both the Gürzenich and the theatre were destroyed. Begun in 1954, designed by Wilhelm Riphahn, the present Grosses Haus was inaugurated in May 1957 with Weber's *Oberon*, conducted by Otto Ackermann. Its functional architecture and trapezoid shape make it a landmark in the city.

Cologne Opera has maintained high standards in recent decades. In its first modern season it premiered Fortner's *Bluthochzeit* (after Lorca). Under Kertész, who was musical director from 1964 to 1973, it staged the first German performance of Prokofiev's *The Fiery Angel* (1960) and unveiled Zimmermann's *Die Soldaten* (1965). Michael Hampe, a talented producer who has been intendant since 1975, appointed Sir John Pritchard as principal conductor in 1978. Since then the company has travelled widely and also made television recordings ranging from Cimarosa to Tchaikovsky. Its broad repertory includes an acclaimed Mozart cycle conceived by Jean-Pierre Ponnelle. It is accom-

panied by the Gürzenich Orchestra. In 1988 it introduced surtitles to Germany for the first time. James Conlon became principal conductor in 1989.

Offenbachpl., D – 5000 Köln 1
☎ 0221-2218204/2218205
TX 8881225 OPER   FX 0221-2212211
♬ Sep – Jun   B As above and
Opernkasse, Postfach 18 0241, D – 5000 Köln 1 ☎ 0221-2125 81. Discounts for children at certain performances   CC None
♿ 4 Wheelchair spaces, elevator, restrooms   ☷ 1330 and 16 standing
♟ 2 bars and restaurant ☎ 0221-233291
PT Train – Köln Hauptbahnhof. Bus – Neumarkt. Underground – Neumarkt   Ⓟ 2 car parks next to theatre.

OPERA NORTH

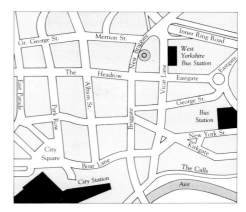

The opening of the Grand Theatre and Opera House in 1878 created an immediate demand for opera: the Carl Rosa and D'Oyly Carte companies soon became regular visitors. Designed by George Corson, the Grand was considered one of the best equipped in Europe. In the 1980s, under Clare Ferraby, extensive refurbishment, with ornate maroon and gold decoration, confirmed its reputation as the most elegant Victorian theatre in the north of England.

The first *Ring* cycle in the English provinces was staged at the Grand by the Ernst Denhof Opera Company in March/April 1911. The British National Opera Company (from 1923) and the Covent Garden Opera (from 1955) began to include Leeds on their tours. The centrepiece of the Leeds Centenary Music Festival in 1958 was Handel's *Samson* under Raymond Leppard, starring Sutherland and Vickers.

A City Council trust took over the Grand in 1971. Plans for a new opera company were announced by Lord Harewood in 1975, but the local authorities withheld essential financial support. Only in late 1977 could a company be founded under the aegis of the Arts Council of Great Britain. Conceived as an offshoot of the English National Opera, with Harewood as managing director of both companies, it was initially known as the English National Opera North. It opened in November 1978 with *Samson et Dalila*, conducted by its music director, David Lloyd-Jones, with a resident orchestra (the English Northern Philharmonia) of 62 players and a chorus of 40.

The company became independent of ENO in 1981, changing its name to Opera North; Nicholas Payne took over as general administrator in 1982. It achieved an early reputation for its vigorous chorus and versatile orchestra. In its first decade, ON staged 70 operas by 40 composers, including the premiere of Wilfred Josephs' *Rebecca* (1983), and the first British stagings of Krenek's *Jonny spielt auf* (1984) and Strauss'

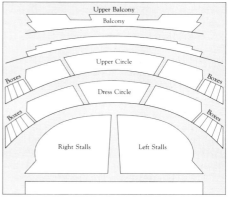

Daphne (1987). The British premiere of Verdi's *Jérusalem* was performed in 1990, when Paul Daniel became musical director. ON tours to Hull, Manchester and Nottingham.

Leeds Grand Theatre and Opera House, 46 New Briggate, Leeds LS1 6NZ
☎ 0532-456014 [FX] 0532-435745
♫ Sep – Oct, Dec – Jan, Apr – May
[B] As above ☎ 0532-459351/440971.
Daily 10am – 7.30pm. Discounts for groups of 10 + [CC] Amex, Diners, MC, Visa
& Wheelchair space, elevator, restroom, hearing aids ⋯ 1550 and 80 standing
🍷 8 bars, private parties catered for
☎ box office [PT] Train – Leeds City station. Bus – Central bus station
Ⓟ At the Headrow, Vicar Lane and nearby.

KIROV OPERA

The Kirov's operatic pedigree reaches back to the 1730s, though its actual name is only 50 years old. The Neapolitan composer Francesco Araia brought a troupe to present his *La Forza dell'Amore e dell'Odio* at the St Petersburg court in 1736; his *Cephalus and Procris*, premiered there in 1755, was the first opera ever to be performed in Russian. Later Italian composers-in-residence included Galuppi (1765–68), Paisiello (1776–83) and Cimarosa (1789–91): all benefited from the building of the Bol'shoy Kammeniy (Grand Stone) Theatre in 1757. After restoration in 1836, it reopened with the premiere of Glinka's *A Life for the Tsar*, which was so successful that it opened every season for several decades thereafter. He capped it with *Ruslan and Lyudmila* there in 1842.

Catterino Cavos conducted at the Bol'shoy from 1798 until 1840. His son, Alberto, designed the important Maryinsky Theatre – now the Kirov – which opened in 1860. Its chief conductor from 1869 to 1911, the Czech composer Eduard Nápravník, presided over an extraordinary run of premieres: Verdi's *La Forza del Destino* (1862), Dargomïzhsky's *The Stone Guest* (1872), *Boris Godunov* (1874), Rimsky-Korsakov's *Snow Maiden* (1882), Tchaikovsky's *Queen of Spades* (1890), and works by other leading Russians. The bass Fyodor Stravinsky, father of Igor, was a leading member of the company (1876–1901).

After the Revolution, it reopened as the State Academic Theatre in 1920; it became the Kirov Theatre in 1935. At first progressive, it became reactionary after the notorious premiere of Shostakovich's *Lady Macbeth of Mtsensk* (1934) at the Maly Theatre (originally the Mikhaylovsky).

Since 1977 its artistic director has been Yuri Temirkanov. A chorus of 120, an orchestral pool of 160 and a ballet company of 240, between them stage an average of seven performances a week, all the year round. Productions at the Kirov tend to be old-fashioned and large-scale, whereas at the smaller Maly (capacity 1212) the company leans towards the experimental. The best time to visit is during the White Nights Festival at midsummer.

1 Teatralnaya Ploshchad, 190000 Leningrad
☎ 7812-216 1211　♫ Sep – Jul　B As above, Intourist Service Bureaux, 'Kassas' (street stalls), 11am – 7pm　CC Amex, Diners, MC　& None　♿ 1780 and standing for students　♟ Buffet
PT Tram – 1, 5, 11, 15 from Basilevsky Ostrov. Bus – 43, 3, 27. Underground – Ploshchad Mira, Metro Nevsky Prospekt.

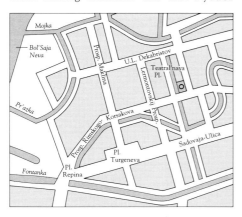

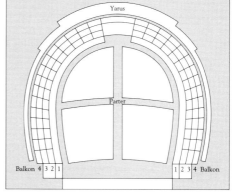

TEATRO NACIONAL DE SAO CARLOS

The Royal Palace Theatre was the venue for the first opera by a Portuguese composer, Francisco Almeida's *La Pazienza di Socrate* (1733), performed in Italian during the carnival season. At the same time, Italian composers, such as Leo and Caldara, were popular at the public Academia da Trindade (1735), later rivalled by the native Carvalho. Lisbon's operatic history might have been very different had the Teatro dos Paços da Ribeira survived. Opened in 1755 with *Alessandro nell'Indie* by David Perez, it was said to be the most splendid anywhere in Europe, but it succumbed to the catastrophic earthquake of November that same year. Opera continued at a variety of theatres, notably the Teatro do Bairro Alto, where the celebrated Portuguese mezzo Luisa Todi made her debut in 1771.

A replica of the famous Neapolitan Teatro San Carlo was opened in Lisbon, in 1793, with Cimarosa's *La Ballerina Amante*, conducted by António Moreira. A year later, the first opera to be sung in Portuguese was staged there, Moreira's *A Vingança da Cigana*. During his term as director of the São Carlos (1800–07), Marcos Portugal premiered 14 of his own Neapolitan-style *opere serie*, but only allowed one Mozart work, *La Clemenza di Tito*. Throughout the 19th century, the São Carlos was on the itinerary of most of Europe's finest singers, but it fell into decline around 1910, just as a number of orchestras were springing to life. Meanwhile, the Coliseu dos Recreios, which holds 7000, had opened in 1894 and staged magnificent productions of operetta and ballet until 1910; it is still used intermittently for opera.

The São Carlos reopened in 1940 with Rui Coelho's *Dom João IV*. But it really became a serious entity in the operatic firmament under João de Freitas Branco, who became its director in 1970. The repertory is still largely Italian, but with a steady trickle of Iberian works: Jerónimo Lima's *Lo Spirito di Contradizione* (1972) was successfully revived in 1985 and Luis de Pablo's *Kiú* was premiered in 1987.

Rua Serpa Pinto 9, 1200 Lisboa
☎ 1-346 84 08 TX 12978
FX 1-37 17 38 ♫ Nov – Jun B As above ☎ 1-346 59 14 FX As above.
Daily 1 – 7pm CC MC, Visa
♿ Elevators ⚎ 1148 ♀ Snackbar
PT Train – Rossio and Cais do Sodré stations. Tram and Bus – Largo do Camões, Largo do Chiado, Rua do Alecrim, Rua da Misericórdia. Underground – Rossio
Ⓟ Nearby.

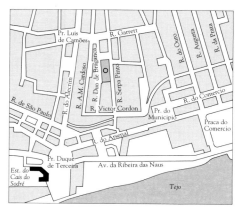

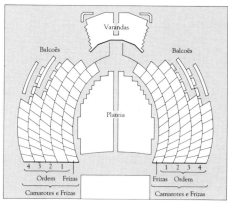

THE ROYAL OPERA

Three theatres have occupied the site in Covent Garden now known as The Royal Opera House, which is home to the leading opera company of Great Britain. Previously it was used as the garden of a Roman Catholic convent. Then Henry VIII gave it to the Russell family, later the Dukes of Bedford, who leased it in turn to John Rich. With letters patent originally granted by Charles II, Rich opened his Theatre Royal at Covent Garden in December 1732. Though not primarily an opera house, it presented the premieres of several Handel operas (1734–37), including *Alcina* and *Ariodante*, and 16 of his oratorios (1736–57). His *Messiah* had its London premiere in 1743. The premiere of Arne's *Artaxerxes* (1762) took place in a climate that was gradually embracing English light opera.

The theatre burned down in 1808, and its replacement was opened a year, less a day, later, on 18 September 1809. The notorious Old Price riots followed in protest against the increased admission prices, the result of high fees paid to foreign singers, notably Angelica Catalani. Weber conducted the premiere of his *Oberon* there in April 1826, less than two months before his death; England's introduction to his *Euryanthe* followed in 1833. Maria Malibran starred in both *Sonnambula* and *Fidelio* on a single night

in 1835. The theatre became the Royal Italian Opera in 1847, after a group of singers under Michael Costa had transferred there from Her Majesty's Theatre. Frederick Gye's enlightened management (1851–77) saw several British firsts, including *Rigoletto*, *Benvenuto Cellini* (both 1853), *Trovatore* (1855), *Aida* with Adelina Patti and *Tannhäuser* with Emma Albani (both 1876). Gye's statue stands in the foyer.

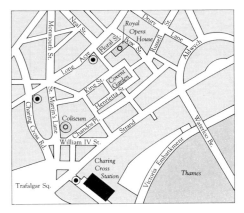

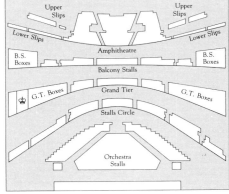

The second theatre burned down in March 1856. Its replacement, the present house, was designed by Edward Barry and opened on 15 May 1858 with *Les Huguenots*. The performance was cut short because public entertainment was forbidden after midnight on a Saturday. After Gye, standards declined until Augustus Harris took over the theatre's lease in 1888. He insisted on original language productions, rather than Italian for everything, a policy which continues today although English surtitles have been adopted. With royal patronage establishing opera as a society pursuit, he ran eight notable seasons, beginning with Nellie Melba's London debut and culminating with Mahler conducting his Hamburg company in Covent Garden's first *Ring* in 1892. That year the company became The Royal Opera.

Thomas Beecham launched his career there in 1910 with the first British productions of *Elektra* (beginning a line of Strauss premieres) and Delius' *A Village Romeo and Juliet*. His own company, formed in 1915, became the British National Opera Company and performed at Covent Garden (1922–24) until 'international' fare was preferred by the 'ruling syndicate'. Bruno Walter then conducted singers such as Lotte Lehmann, Elisabeth Schumann and Lauritz Melchior mainly in German repertory, with Beecham returning as artistic director in 1932. This was the age of the conductor.

The end of World War II (during which the theatre became a dance hall) provided the opportunity for a total reassessment of operatic priorities: a new Covent Garden Opera Trust appointed David Webster general administrator (1946–70), with Karl Rankl as musical director (1946–51), to form a 'permanent national institution' which was to develop its own style in opera and ballet. At first English-language productions returned together with the premieres of Britten's *Billy Budd* (1951) and *Gloriana* (1953), and Walton's *Troilus and Cressida* (1954). With Rafael Kubelik as musical

director (1955–58), an excellent anglophone ensemble was developed, with singers such as Joan Sutherland, Amy Shuard, Jon Vickers and Geraint Evans. Later, under Georg Solti (1961–71), with the Sadler's Wells Opera competing in English-language productions, the trend towards international casts became more pronounced just as English language productions declined. The *stagione* system, concentrating on one work at a time, was adopted. Tippett's first four operas were all premiered by the company, as was Maxwell Davies' *Taverner* (1972) and Henze's *We Come to the River* (1976). Notable achievements included two productions by erstwhile film makers: Luchino Visconti's *Don Carlos* and Zeffirelli's *Tosca*, starring Maria Callas and Tito Gobbi. Webster's successor, John Tooley (1970–88), introduced 'prom' performances and stimulated co-operation with foreign houses. He received powerful assistance from musical director Colin Davis (1971–86), especially over Mozart, but was too often foiled by increasing financial pressures, a situation now reaching crisis point under Jeremy Isaacs, general director since 1988. The company may be in danger of losing its status among Europe's top five. The musical director now is Bernard Haitink.

Royal Opera House, Covent Gdn, London WC2E 9DD ☎ 071-240 1200 TX 27988 COVGAR FX 071-836 1762 ♫ Sep – Jul B 48 Floral St., Covent Gdn, London WC2E 9DD ☎ 071-240 1066/1911. Mon – Sat 10am–8pm. Discounts for groups of 20+ Write to: Marketing Dept., Royal Opera House CC Amex, Diners, MC, Visa ♿ Wheelchair space, hearing aids 2067 and 42 standing ♟ Bars and buffets ☎ 071-836 9453 PT Train – Charing Cross and Waterloo stations. Bus – 1, 4, 5, 6, 9, 11, 13, 15, 68, 77, 77a, 170, 171, 171a, 176, 188, 502, 513, Aldwych. Underground – Covent Gdn, Leicester Sq., Holborn Ⓟ Drury Lane, Museum St and nearby.

ENGLISH NATIONAL OPERA

The genesis of the English National Opera lies in the introduction of opera to the Old Vic (originally Royal Victoria Hall) in 1900 by its manager Lilian Baylis, niece of its leaseholder Emma Cons. Inheriting the theatre, Baylis put on opera twice weekly and alternate Saturday matinees from 1914. Throughout the 1920s, with Charles Corri as chief conductor, the company built a standard repertory of nearly 30 works, all sung in translation and featuring singers such as Edith Coates, Joan Cross and Heddle Nash. In 1931, when Baylis moved to the Sadler's Wells Theatre, the company was known as Vic-Wells Opera. In 1934, it became Sadler's Wells Opera.

The theatre reopened after World War II with the premiere of *Peter Grimes*. There was an adventurous period under Norman Tucker as director (1948–66): he introduced British stage premieres of Janáček's *Káťa Kabanová* (1951), *The Cunning Little Vixen* (1961) and *The Makropulos Affair* (1964), and changed traditional attitudes towards production. The company moved to the Coliseum in August 1968. Built as a music hall by Oswald Stoll in 1904, the Coliseum boasts London's largest stage and the first revolving stage anywhere. After an uneasy start, Colin Graham's production of Prokofiev's *War and Peace*, Britain's first, in

October 1973, proved a turning-point; the following summer the company became the English National Opera.

Since then the 600-strong company under the Earl of Harewood (1972–85), has established a solid reputation for high standards and innovative productions, always in English, with the emphasis on drama. Jonathan Miller's mafia *Rigoletto* is a typical example. Notable premieres included David Blake's *Toussaint* and Harrison Birtwistle's *The Mask of Orpheus*. Peter Jonas is now managing director, with Mark Elder as music director.

London Coliseum, St Martin's Lane, London WC2N 4ES ☎ 071-836 0111
TX 264867 ENO   FX 071-836 8379
♫ Aug–Jun   B As above
☎ 071-836 3161   CC Amex, Diners, MC, Visa ☎ 071-240 5258   ♿ Wheelchair space and restrooms   ☎ 071-836 0111 x318   ⚏ 2356 and approx 75 standing   ♟ The Terrace or The Dutch Bar
☎ 071-836 0111 x324   PT Train – Charing Cross station. Bus – 1, 3, 6, 9, 11, 12, 13, 15, 24, 29, 53, 77, 77a, 88, 159, 170, 172, 176, 500 all stop nearby. Underground – Charing Cross and Leicester Sq. stations   Ⓟ Trafalgar Sq. (Spring Gdns), Bedfordbury and nearby.

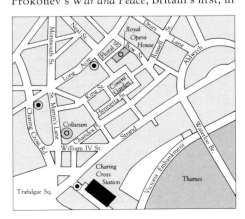

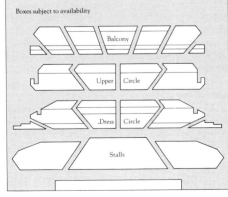

Boxes subject to availability

LOS ANGELES MUSIC CENTER OPERA

Los Angeles has enjoyed a permanent opera company of its own only since October 1986, when Music Center Opera's first season began with Placido Domingo in *Otello* and Maria Ewing in *Salome*.

Touring companies first visited the city in the 1880s, and the US premiere of *La Bohème* was performed there by the Del Conti Opera Company of Mexico in 1897. The Metropolitan Opera appeared there in 1900, while the Chicago Lyric Opera made 11 visits between 1913 and 1930. The San Francisco Opera made annual visits (1936–65), succeeded by the New York City Opera which appeared there annually after 1968.

In 1965 three theatres were opened in a music centre complex. The largest is the Dorothy Chandler Pavilion. It immediately became the home of the Los Angeles Philharmonic Orchestra. The following year saw the foundation of the LA Music Center Opera Association (LAMCO), which began by promoting visiting productions at the Dorothy Chandler. The tempo of operatic activity increased in the 1980s, culminating in visits by Covent Garden in 1984 and West Berlin's Deutsche Oper in 1985.

London-born Peter Hemmings was appointed as LAMCO's general director in 1985. He had been managing director of the London Symphony Orchestra, and before that general manager of both Scottish Opera (1965–77) and The Australian Opera (1977–79). Under his aegis LAMCO has quickly established itself in the front rank.

The company is 'committed to the staging of the traditional repertoire in carefully considered, but innovative, productions that will stir fresh insights'. Not so traditional as to prevent the commissioning of designs from David Hockney for *Tristan und Isolde* (1987–88). Further credibility has been gained by the appointment of Placido Domingo as artistic consultant.

Dorothy Chandler Pavilion, Los Angeles Music Center, lst and Hope Sts., Los Angeles, CA 90012 ☎ 213-972 7219 TX 650290 94 42 MCI UW FX 213-972 7474 ♪ Sep – Apr B Los Angeles Music Center Opera, P.O. Box 2237, Los Angeles, CA 90051 ☎ 213-480 3232. Discount for groups of 20 +, ☎ 213-972 7219 CC Amex, MC, Visa ♿ Wheelchair space, reserved parking, sight and hearing aids, restrooms ⚏ 3098 ♟ Pavilion Restaurant ☎ 213-972 7333, Otto Rothchilds ☎ 213-972 7322 PT Shuttles from several downtown restaurants and airport ☎ 213-626 4455 Ⓟ Garage under Music Center, valet parking on Hope St.

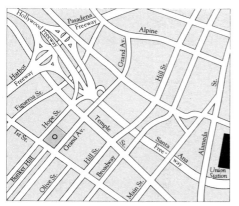

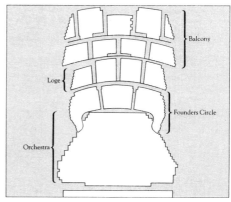

TEATRO LIRICO NACIONAL LA ZARZUELA

The court of Philip IV provided Madrid's first operatic opportunity in 1629, when Lope de Vega's *La Selva Sin Amor* (*The Loveless Forest*) was staged at the Coliseo del Buen Retiro (The Royal Palace Theatre) by Cosimo Lotti, a Florentine designer. After Lope's death in 1635, court theatre was dominated until 1681 by another first-class librettist, Calderón de la Barca. His *La Púrpura de la Rosa* was staged in 1660 to music by Juan Hidalgo, one of the earliest examples of *zarzuela*, a name derived from the brambles (*zarzas*) around the palace. After 1700 Philip V tried to discourage native opera by introducing an Italian company at the Teatro de los Caños del Peral.

In 1737 the noted male soprano Farinelli sang in Madrid with such success that Philip appointed him to sing the same four songs every night as a cure for his melancholia – which he did for 25 years. He also produced several lavish musical spectacles at court in the Italian style. Charles II, who became king in 1759, forced Farinelli into exile, considering Italian opera undignified, thus letting *zarzuela* regain a foothold. Boccherini, a long-time Madrid resident (1769–1805), composed one entitled *Clementina* in 1786. But Italian operas, by Cimarosa and Paisiello, made a come-back a year later.

The Teatro Real, built on the site of the Caños del Peral, opened in 1850 with an Italian company in Donizetti's *La Favorite*. Some 32 operas by Spanish composers were presented there between 1871 and its closure in 1925, all but nine of them premieres. When the Teatro Real reopened in 1966, its (mainly orchestral) season included *Giulio Cesare*. It is now being extensively renovated; present plans call for it to open again in 1992 as the base of the Teatro Lirico Nacional.

The Teatro la Zarzuela, which opened in 1856, always concentrated upon lower-brow entertainment, and was headquarters for a revival of the *zarzuela*. It is currently the opera company's temporary home, where the opening half of the season is liberally spiced with works by composers such as Barbieri, Bretón, Chapí and Caballero. Italian composers, especially Verdi, are regular fare. The artistic co-directors are José Luis Alonso and Benito Lauret.

Jovellanos 4, 28014 Madrid
☎ 1-429 82 25   TX 41493 TZM
FX 1-429 71 57   ♫ Jan – Jul   B As above. Daily 12 – 6pm   CC None
♿ None   ⚱ 1242   ♣ Bars   PT Bus – Puerta del Sol, Pza de Cibeles. Underground – Banco de España, Sevilla, Sol
Ⓟ Pzas de las Cortes, del Rey, de Santa Ana.

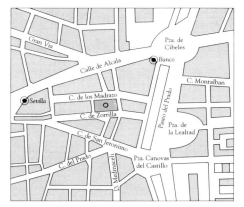

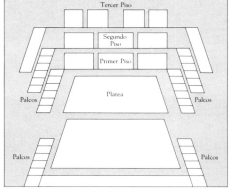

OPERA MUNICIPAL DE MARSEILLE

Marseille has a musical longevity befitting its status as France's second city: the Romans built a Greek-style amphitheatre for plays and concerts in the mid-2nd century BC, when the Phoenician republic became part of the province of Gaul. Pierre Gautier inaugurated the Théâtre de la Rue Pavillon, home of the Marseille Music Academy, in 1685, with *Le Triomphe de la Paix*.

The Grand Théâtre, designed by Benard and constructed by royal permission, was opened in October 1787 in the presence of the Governor of Provence, the Maréchal Prince de Beauveau, whose personal troupe of actors staged Stanislas Champein's *La Mélomanie*. Works by Halévy (still popular there today) and Meyerbeer dominated its repertory in the 19th century.

A disastrous fire in November 1919 reduced the theatre to its outer shell, leaving only the splendid Louis XVI colonnade unaffected. Rebuilding plans submitted by a trio of distinguished architects, led by Gaston Castel, were accepted in 1921 and the new Opéra Municipal de Marseille inaugurated three years later. The company came under municipal control in 1945. A continuous programme of improvements since 1972 has updated its equipment and accentuated the qualities of the interior, one of the rare operatic monuments to early Art Deco, a style underlined by the gold-lacquered decoration of the auditorium. The proscenium arch is a bas-relief by Emile-Antoine Bourdelle depicting the Birth of Beauty surrounded by representatives of all the theatrical arts. The painted ceiling by Carréra recounts the Orpheus legend.

L'Opéra de Marseille is a company of nearly 400, including the 90-member Orchestre Philharmonique de Marseille, whose founder-director – also the musical director of the Opéra – is Janos Fürst. There is a ballet group of 26 and a chorus of 56. The producer Jacques Karpo is the artistic director. The repertory is largely traditional but has included the French stage premiere of

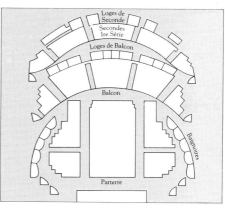

Milhaud's *Christophe Colomb* (1984).

2 rue Molière, 13000 Marseille
☎ 091-55 21 09   ♫ Oct – Feb, Apr – Jun   B As above
☎ 091-55 21 22/55 21 23. Tues - Sat 10am – 12.30pm, 3 – 6pm, Sun 10am – 12.30pm. Discounts for groups of 10 +   CC None   ♿ Contact Service d'Accueil at above address or ☎ 091-55 14 99/55 21 07/55 11 11   ⌨ 1350 and 485 standing   ♟ None   PT Train – Gare St. Charles. Bus and trolleybus – most lines stop nearby   Ⓟ Nearby – P1. Montyon and Cours d'Estienne-d'Orves.

VICTORIA STATE OPERA

Melbourne has produced a greater number of distinguished opera singers than any other Australian city. Perhaps the greatest of them all, Helen (Nellie) Mitchell, displayed her pride in her native city by adopting Melba as her surname when fame had overtaken her. By virtue of the Australian Opera's residence in Sydney, however, Melbourne is not quite the hub of operatic activity it would like to be.

From 1860 onwards there were at least four months of opera each year: the American impresario William S. Lyster managed as many as 100 English-language performances annually between 1861 and 1880. The Melba-Williamson Company toured to Melbourne in 1911 – and again in 1924, by which time (1918) Dame Nellie had become its guiding spirit. Opera became a casualty of the Depression, although the foundation of the National Theatre Movement (NTM) in Melbourne in 1935 brought some musical theatre in its wake.

Melba's modern-day counterpart has been Dame Joan Sutherland. Like Melba, she teamed up with the Williamson organization and toured to Melbourne in 1965. This laid the groundwork for visits promoted by the Elizabethan Theatre Trust, successor to the NTM, and eventually the formation of the professional Victoria

State Opera in 1977 from its predecessor, the Victorian Opera Company. In the meantime, the Australian Opera had been giving an annual two-month season at the Princess Theatre since 1956, a tradition which continues to this day.

A typical season now includes seven productions of Australian Opera (March – May) and a further four by VSO at other times. Most are given at the large State Theatre in the Fitzroy district of Melbourne, which opened in 1985. Under the musical directorship of Robert Divall since 1981, VSO has become a lively, broad-minded company. Ken Mackenzie-Forbes is its general manager.

The State Theatre, Victorian Arts Centre, 100 St Kilda Rd, Melbourne 3004
☎ 03-417 5061 TX AA33705 ELWOL
FX 03-419 5071 ♬ Jul – Dec
B Smorgon Family Plaza + as above
☎ 03-11566, 03-11500 (credit card charge). Mon – Sat 9am–9pm CC Amex, Diners, MC, Visa ♿ Wheelchair space, hearing aids. Contact House Manager
☎ 03-617 8211 ∷ 2000 ♟ 3
Restaurants – The Vic ☎ 03-617 8180. Bar PT Train – Princess Gate, Flinders St. Stations. Tram – St Kilda Rd. Ⓟ Under the Centre.

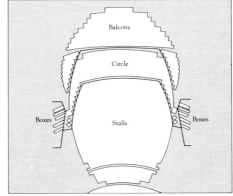

OPERA NACIONAL

Mexico can claim to be the first country in the Americas to develop a viable musical life of its own. The earliest opera to be composed in the New World was Manuel de Zumaya's *La Parténope*, premiered in 1711 in the viceregal palace. But the Italian-born Ignacio Jerusalem, *maestro de capilla* at Mexico City cathedral in the mid-18th century, turned operatic tastes towards Europe. The Coliseo Nuevo, which had opened in 1735, increasingly moved away from Spanish repertory – *zarzuela* and *tonadilla* – towards Italian opera. The 1806 production of Paisiello's *Il Barbiere di Siviglia* was a typical mixture of local and imported elements. It was sung in Spanish with Mexican dances between its four acts.

In 1821, half a century after Independence, opera was invariably performed in Italian, even when written by Mexican composers such as Melesio Morales, whose *Idelgonda* was the first Mexican opera to be staged abroad – in Florence in 1868. Aniceto Ortega broke the language rule with his nine-scene opera *Guatimotzin*, about the defence of Mexico by its last Aztec ruler, Cuauhtémoc: its cast at the premiere in the Gran Teatro Nacional in September 1871 included Mexico's first prima donna, Angela Peralta, with the renowned Enrico Tamberlik as the Aztec king.

The Mexican Revolution of 1910, while it encouraged a new nationalism among composers, discouraged visits by foreign opera companies. Caruso, however, regaled an audience of 25,000 in a bull-ring. The Revolution may also have delayed work on the new Palacio de Bellas Artes. Begun under the Italian architect Boari in 1900, it finally opened in 1934.

A Viennese refugee, Franz Steiner, made the first effort to establish a permanent company there in 1941, importing conductors such as Beecham and Kleiber. Two years later the contralto Fanny Anitua founded the Opera Nacional. In 1950 Callas appeared there in *Aida*. The Mexican contralto Oralia Dominguez made her stage debut there in the same

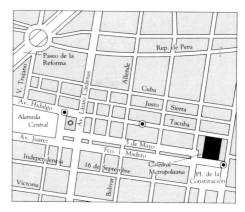

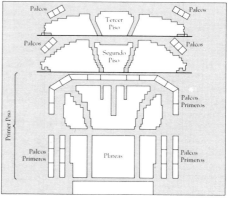

year. Domingo, who was born in Spain but grew up in Mexico, made his debut there – as a baritone – in a *zarzuela* by Caballero called *Gigantes y Cabezudos* in 1957. Today the company may not produce singers of quite such quality, but its mainstream repertory continues to attract the brightest international stars in the operatic firmament.

Palacio de Bellas Artes, Av. Hidalgo No.1, Mexico D.F. 06050 ☎ 905-521 36 68 ♬ Mar – Jul, Sep – Dec B As above ☎ 915-510 13 83. Mon – Sat 11.30am – 3pm, 5 – 9pm, Sun 8.30 – 1pm, 4 – 9pm CC None ♿ None ⚏ 1750 ♙ Bars and buffets PT Bus – many. Underground – 2, Bellas Artes Ⓟ Nearby.

TEATRO ALLA SCALA

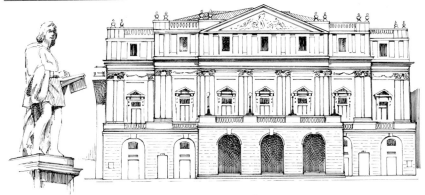

La Scala is one of the world's great operatic shrines. Its unique atmosphere, allied to the highest possible standards, means that La Scala is the supreme test for any singer or producer. Success or failure in Milan invariably makes news in the operatic world.

A pastoral fable (drama with music) called *Armenia* was staged in the Salone Margherita of the ducal palace in 1599. The Margherita burned down in 1708, the year when Austria took over the rule of Lombardy from the Spanish. In 1717, it was replaced by the Teatro Regio Ducale, whose distinguished history included the premieres of four of Gluck's first eight operas (1741–45) and three of the young Mozart's earliest stage works: *Mitridate, Rè di Ponto* (1770), when he

was not yet 15 years old, *Ascanio in Alba* (1771) and *Lucio Silla* (1772).

Fire destroyed the Regio Ducale in 1776. Its 96 box-holders took immediate action to build a replacement. Maria Theresa, Empress of Austria and Duchess of Milan, shared their enthusiasm and gave permission for a new theatre to be built on the site of the demolished Santa Maria alla Scala church.

La Scala opened on 3 August 1778 with Salieri's *Europa Riconosciuta*, specially commissioned for the occasion and accompanied by an orchestra of 70 (large at the time), with no less than 36 horses on stage. At that period it had 2800 seats, including 260 boxes, arranged on six levels above the spacious parterre. Subscribers could buy

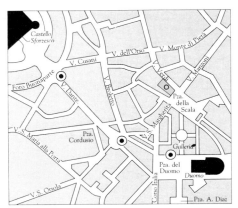

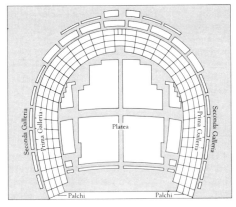

their own box, together with its anteroom where refreshments were served, and decorate it to their personal taste. However, except at the front, the acoustics in a box are poor. Externally, La Scala was (and is) a plain building, with a neoclassical façade of pilaster strips. In 1807 the stage was enlarged, in 1838 the whole theatre was renovated, and in 1857 the buildings opposite were demolished to permit a full view of it from across the piazza.

Milan changed political hands several times during the Napoleonic Wars and La Scala seems to have been the centre of celebration on each occasion. Rossini produced a powerful impression upon the Milanese in 1812 with *La Pietra del Paragone;* another four of his operas were premiered there, including *La Gazza Ladra* (1817). Nearly 250 performances of Rossini operas were presented during a two-year term by the English impresario Joseph Glossop (1824–26). Domenico Barbaia, following his success in Naples, succeeded Glossop in Milan, staying there until 1832. He immediately commissioned Bellini's *Il Pirata* (1827) and subsequently capped it with *Norma* (1831).

Under Bartolomeo Merelli (1836–50 and 1861–63), the theatre 'discovered' Verdi: *Oberto* was staged there first (1839). Verdi's next three operas were also unveiled at La Scala, the best of them *Nabucco* (1842). Thereafter his only significant commissions for Milan were *Otello* (1887) and *Falstaff* (1893).

La Scala reached its peak during Toscanini's three terms as artistic director. He announced his intentions by launching the first of these (1898–1903) with *Die Meistersinger*: Wagner was to become a vital part of the company's repertory from then on. Cleofonte Campanini conducted the disastrous first performance of the two-act version of *Madama Butterfly* (1904). But Toscanini returned in 1906–08 and again from 1921–28, to conduct the first Italian performances of *Pelléas et Mélisande* (1908) and Charpentier's *Louise* (1923), the premiere of Boito's *Nerone* (1924) and of *Turandot* (1926), perhaps the climax of his achievements there. After he had fallen out

with the Fascists and left Milan in 1929, Toscanini was never again to conduct opera in an opera house, except as a guest at the Bayreuth and Salzburg festivals.

Bombs ruined the theatre in August 1943 – along with sets and costumes for more than 100 productions – and it was nearly three years before it was rebuilt in almost the original style. Toscanini, by now in his eightieth year, returned to conduct the gala concert reopening it on 11 May 1946: it was also Tebaldi's debut at La Scala, where she remained until 1955. Callas was a regular visitor throughout the mid-1950s, appearing in several Visconti productions (notably *Sonnambula* and *Traviata*), often with Giulini conducting. In 1955 the Piccola Scala was opened within the main building with Cimarosa's *Il Matrimonio Segreto*: it is regularly used for 17th- and 18th-century works and chamber opera.

For the last two decades the company has particularly benefitted from Claudio Abbado's term as artistic director (1971–80); he remained chief conductor until 1986, when Riccardo Muti took over. With Paolo Grassi as *sovrintendente* (1972–77), there was an attempt to democratize the audience. It was already, and still is, an audience ready to boo and berate anything not to its taste, just as much as it unstintingly cheers excellence. The current repertory is naturally broad: in recent years there has been a preponderance of Verdi and – exceptionally for Italy – slightly more Mozart than Puccini, with Rossini and Donizetti the runners-up. Eastern European works have had short shrift, and there is always a world premiere every year. The *sovrintendente* is Carlo Maria Badini, the artistic director Cesare Mazzonis.

Pza della Scala, 20121 Milano
☎ 02-887 91   TX 335328 SCALAN
FX 02-887 9388   ♬ Dec – Jul   B As above ☎ 02-807041/809126   CC Amex, Diners, Visa   ♿ Wheelchair spaces at orchestra level ☎ Box office   ⸬ 2015 and 150 standing   ♨ Bars   PT Tram – 1. Bus – 61. Underground – 1   Ⓟ Difficult.

OPERA DE MONTE CARLO

Sumptuous entertainments were long a feature of the Grimaldi court, which has ruled Monaco since the 13th century. Gropallo's *Le Vittorie de Minerva*, produced for Prince Honoré II in 1655, may well have been the first opera written there. Musical activity flourished sporadically at court until the French Revolution, when artistic activity ceased. Comic opera was revived during the reign of Prince Florestan, notably the works of Dalayrac, a pupil of the Monaco-born Honoré Langlé. Florestan commissioned Charles Garnier, fresh from his triumph with the Paris Opéra, to design a new opera house: this intimate auditorium, a jewel of the *Belle Epoque*, opened on 25 January 1879 with Celestine Galli-Marié (who created Carmen) in Planquette's *Le Chevalier Gaston*. Almost immediately it became one of Europe's most fashionable houses.

The arrival in 1893 of Romanian composer-impresario Raoul Gunsbourg as director began a stunning era. Before his retirement in 1951, at the age of 91, he had presented an extraordinary number of premieres, including the stage version of Berlioz's *La Damnation de Faust* (1893), Fauré's *Pénélope* (1913), Puccini's *La Rondine* (1917), Ravel's *L'Enfant et les Sortilèges* (1925) and works by Franck, Saint-Saëns and Honegger. Furthermore Massenet, in his latter years, almost became Monte Carlo's resident composer: six of his operas were first staged there, including *Le Jongleur de Notre-Dame* (1902), *Thérèse* (1907) and *Don Quichotte* (1910) with Chaliapin in the title role. Gunsbourg engaged all the leading international singers, including Patti, Melba, Caruso and Garden.

A parallel development was the Monte Carlo Opera Orchestra, founded in 1863 by E. Lucas, its conductor until 1876. Now known as the Orchestre Philharmonique de Monte Carlo, its chief conductor is Lawrence Foster. Diaghilev's Ballet Russe created *Le Spectre de la Rose* there in 1911, to designs by Picasso; exiled after World War I, it used Monte Carlo as its base.

Although today the company is less prestigious, it maintains a respectable standard under its director, John Mordler.

Salle Garnier, Casino de Monte Carlo, Pl. du Casino, MC98007, Monaco
☎ 93-50 69 31   [FX] 93-30 07 57
♫ Jan – Mar   [B] Casino de Monte-Carlo, B.P. 139, MC 98007, Monaco
☎ 93-50 76 54   [FX] As above
[CC] None   ♿ Elevator up to theatre
⸬ 500   ♠ Nearby   [PT] Train – Monte-Carlo station. Bus – check at hotels   ℗ In front of Opera House.

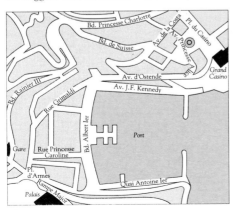

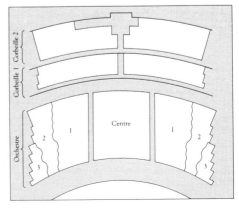

L'OPERA DE MONTREAL

Montreal has had great difficulty in setting up a permanent opera company of its own. Not for want of trying: over the last century, no fewer than seven different companies enjoyed success and then foundered. L'Opéra de Montréal, however, which was started in 1980 with tenor Jean-Paul Jeannotte as artistic director, appointed an American, Bernard Uzan, as its general director in 1988 and looks well set to establish itself. The excellent Montreal Symphony Orchestra provides accompaniment, with bilingual surtitles.

Joseph Quesnel's comic *Colas et Colinette*, premiered at Montreal's Théâtre de Société in 1790, is widely regarded as the first opera to be written in Canada and probably North America. The brewer John Molson erected the Theatre Royal, Canada's first institution devoted to the performing arts, in Montreal in 1825 and it was there that Italian opera was first seen in 1841.

The Société d'Opéra Français (1893–96) was the first attempt at a permanent company, but its early success was short-lived. The Metropolitan Opera presented five works in Her Majesty's Theatre in 1899. Its return in 1901 caused an enormous upsurge in operatic interest. The Montreal Opera Company (1910–13), originally the Montreal Musical Society, gave nearly 300 performances in Eastern Canada.

For the next 30 years operetta took precedence, first through the Société Canadienne d'Opérette (1921–33), founded by Honoré Vaillancourt, and then with its successor, the Variétés Lyriques (1936–52), which provided a springboard for the singers Léopold Simoneau and Joseph Rouleau.

Beginning in 1964 the modern era has its origins in the Montreal Symphony Orchestra's occasional operatic sorties inspired by its dynamic chief conductor Zubin Mehta. These in turn were made possible by the opening in 1963 of the Salle Wilfrid-Pelletier, home of the present company, later to become part of a three-theatre complex, the Place des Arts. La Scala, the English Opera Group, the Vienna

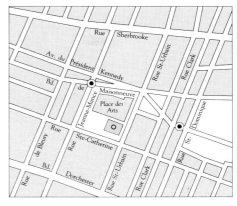

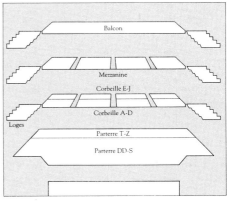

State, the Bolshoi, the Hamburg State and Royal Swedish Operas all made their North American debuts during Expo 67, the Montreal World Fair of 1967.

Place des Arts, 1157 Ste-Catherine Est, Montreal, Quebec H2L 2G8
☎ 514-521 5577   TX 21-55-61201
FX 514-521 8751   ♫ Sep – May
B 1151 rue Jeanne Mance, Montreal, Quebec H2X 1Z9   ☎ 514-842 2112
CC MC, Visa   ⑬ Contact box office for details   ⋯ 2874   ⬤ None
PT Underground – Place des Arts   Ⓟ Garage under theatre.

BOL'SHOY THEATRE

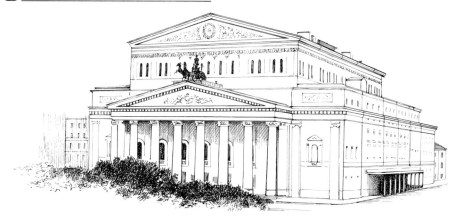

The first opera in Russia was Ristori's *Calandro*, staged in 1731 by an Italian company based at the Polish court. The first opera house was the Operny Dom, opened in 1742 for the Empress Elizabeth's coronation with Hasse's *Tito Vespasiano*. Most of the early Russian comic operas, such as Sokolovsky's *The Miller-Magician*, were given in the Petrovsky Theatre, built in 1780; it burned down in 1805.

The worldwide reputation of Russian opera rests on the shoulders of the Bol'shoy (Grand) Theatre, not merely the building, but the opera (and ballet) company which inhabits it. The first Bol'shoy was built in 1825 on the site of the former Petrovsky Theatre. Inauspiciously, it burned down in 1853 and was rebuilt three years later by Alberto Cavos (who also designed St Petersburg's Maryinsky – later the Kirov – Theatre). A cathedral of an opera house, with an enormous stage, it was always destined for 'great' things: spectacular productions on the grand scale, usually enhanced by an enormous, awe-inspiring chorus. These features survive today.

Its standards were set early by Alexey Verstovsky, overall director of the Moscow theatres (1842–60): his opera *Askold's Tomb* (1835), similar to *Freischütz*, was given over 400 performances in Moscow. His musical

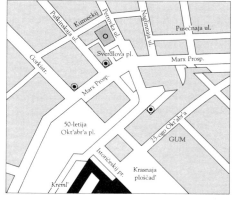

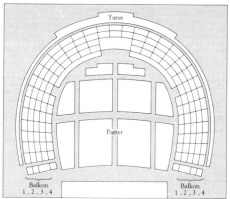

director at the Bol'shoy for 20 years was Ivan Johannes. Inherited, French-inspired attitudes demanded elaborate sets and extravagant gestures. Some reaction set in, and from 1885 Savva Mamontov's Moscow Private Russian Opera introduced a more intimate realism into its production styles. Sergey Zimin kept this tradition afloat from 1904 to 1924 at the Solodovnikov Theatre, where Rimsky-Korsakov's *Golden Cockerel* was premiered in 1909. Chaliapin worked under both directors, creating Salieri in Rimsky-Korsakov's *Mozart and Salieri* (1898).

Meanwhile, the Bol'shoy had entered a new era, with conductors such as Rakhmaninov (1904–06) and Václav Suk (1906–32); its ballet company under Alexander Gorsky had also established a lasting tradition of excellence. It was reorganized after the 1917 Revolution, at first under the tenor Leonid Sobinov. Perhaps the most significant development in the Bol'shoy Theatre's history was the establishment in 1918 of its Opera Studio under the direction of Konstantin Stanislavsky: this marked the birth of the modern concept of 'producer's opera'. He strove to integrate singing, words and movement in an attempt to infuse psychological truth into music theatre, though always emphasizing the pre-eminent importance of the score. Separated from the Bol'shoy, the studio was renamed the Stanislavsky Opera Theatre in 1926. Meanwhile, in 1919, Vladimir Nemirovich-Danchenko had started his Moscow Arts Theatre Music Studio along similar lines. The two groups were to merge in 1941 to form the Stanislavsky/Nemirovich-Danchenko Music Theatre, which to this day remains Moscow's most important venue for opera after the Bol'shoy. Its productions are much more adventurous. Y.P. Privegin is its director.

A useful half-way house between composers and the operatic stage was the Soviet Opera Ensemble of the All-Union Theatrical Society, started in 1934: it organized concert performances of more than 75 operas, including several premieres, notably Shaporin's *The Decembrists* (1937)

and Prokofiev's *War and Peace* (1944).

Today, the Bol'shoy is an enormous organization, numbering some 3000 full-time staff. These include a chorus of 200, an orchestral pool of 250, a further 120 non-singing supernumeraries, and a vast in-house technical and production staff, as well as its own ballet company. In addition, there are in residence some 100 soloists, 15 répétiteurs, five conductors and three producers. Many of these are on something approaching life contracts. The more senior singers appear in the Bol'shoy Theatre itself, which seats 2155 on six levels; something like a 'B' team may be heard, less frequently, in the Kremlin Palace of Congresses, a barn of a building with 6000 seats put up in 1961. Some 30 performances are given each month. All this is financed by huge state subsidies – there is no dependence upon box office receipts – with the result that an ideological orientation, not to mention complacency in some of the leading stars, pervades many productions.

But *glasnost* may be taking hold: recent productions by the mezzo Elena Obraztsova (of *Werther*) and the film director Sergei Bondarchuk (of Tchaikovsky's *Mazeppa*) have departed from tradition. Between 20 and 25 operas are given in a full season. The repertory is not wide, covering the standard Russians such as Glinka, Darghomizhsky, Rimsky-Korsakov and Tchaikovsky – often including works little seen in the West – but very little Verdi or Wagner, and no Strauss. The director is Stanislav Lushin, the chief conductor Yuri Simonov.

Ploshchad Sverdlova 1, Moskva
☎ 095-292 6534   ♫ Sep – Jul   B As above, or book through Intourist Service Bureau at hotels, if none available use 'Hotel Rossiya', 6 Ulitsa Razina
☎ 095-229 4250, 11am–7pm   CC Amex, Diners, Visa   ♿ None   ♒ 2153 and standing for students   ♟ Buffet
PT Trolley bus – 3, 23. Bus – many to Ploshchad Sverdlova or Red Square. Underground – Ploshchad Sverdlova.

BAYERISCHE STAATSOPER

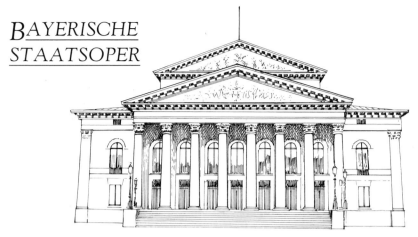

Munich became the capital of Bavaria in 1255. Four centuries later it staked its claim as the operatic headquarters of southern Germany: Giovanni Maccioni's *L'Arpa Festante* (1653), promoted by Maximilian I's daughter-in-law, Henriette Adelheid, was Munich's first opera, given in the Herkules-Saal of the electoral Residenz. Three years later the court opera was able to rival Europe's finest when the so-called Haber-kasten (previously a corn-exchange) on the Salvatorplatz was inaugurated as an opera house – Germany's first – with Johann Kerll's *L'Oronte*. Under Kerll and his successor as *Kapellmeister*, Ercole Bernabei (1674–87), there were a number of magnificent productions.

One of the most perfect rococo opera houses anywhere, the Residenztheater in the electoral palace, was erected in 1753 by the Belgian architect François Cuvilliés. Italian opera thereafter enjoyed its heyday in Munich, with the premiere of Mozart's *La Finta Giardiniera* in 1775, commissioned by the court intendant, Count von Seeau, for performance in the Redoutensaal on Pran-nerstrasse. A pinnacle was reached in 1781 with the premiere of *Idomeneo* at the Residenztheater. Six years later opera in Italian was banned by Elector Karl Theodor, who favoured *Singspiels* by Mannheim composers: none have stood the test of time.

But German opera eventually regained lost ground. There was a notable Residenz-

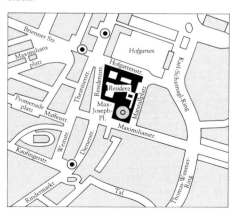

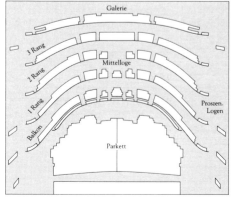

theater premiere in Weber's *Abu Hassan* (1811), and Meyerbeer's first opera was introduced there in the following year. To replace the old Haberkasten, demolished in 1802, a new Hof-und Nationaltheater, designed by Karl von Fischer, was opened in 1818. It took an immediate hold on the public: when it burned down in 1823 funds for rebuilding were raised quickly through a *Bierpfennig* (beer tax). It reopened two years later. Modelled on the Paris Odéon, in severe classical style, the Nationaltheater has been Munich's operatic flagship almost continuously since then.

From 1836, high orchestral standards were reinstated under Franz Lachner's musical direction and the repertory hugely expanded. At first with a blind spot for Wagner, he later relented sufficiently to introduce the final version of *Tannhäuser* (1855) and Munich's first *Lohengrin* (1858).

King Ludwig II's patronage of Wagner led to the appointment in 1864 of Hans von Bülow (whose first wife Cosima, Liszt's daughter, later left him for Wagner) as Lachner's successor. He directed the resoundingly successful premieres of *Tristan* (1865) and *Meistersinger* (1868); Franz Wüllner followed him with the first *Rheingold* (1869) and *Walküre* (1870): a remarkable sequence that established Munich's international credibility once and for all. This owed a good deal to the initiative of intendant Karl von Perfall (1867–93) who, in 1875, inaugurated what has now become an annual July festival: at first dedicated to Mozart and Wagner, it now also favours Richard Strauss among a broad range of composers. Intendant Ernst von Possart (1894–1905) instigated the erection of the Prinzregententheater specifically as the main festival venue. Modelled on Bayreuth, it opened in 1901 with *Meistersinger*. It thrived during and immediately after World War II, when the Nationaltheater was bombed, but is now used mainly for the Akademie's orchestral concerts.

Richard Strauss, born in Munich in 1864, became a favourite son of its opera company. He was conductor there while still in his mid-twenties. After World War I his works became a feature of the repertory: *Friedenstag* was premiered in 1938 and *Capriccio* in 1942. Munich's love-affair with Strauss reached an extraordinary peak in 1988, when all 15 of his operas were performed in the July festival, several as new productions.

Bruno Walter, musical director (1912–22), brought the company into the modern era, with the premiere of Pfitzner's *Palestrina* (1917) and new works by Schreker and Korngold. His successor, Hans Knappertsbusch, established the Strauss tradition, which was taken up by Clemens Krauss in 1937. The Nationaltheater was destroyed in 1943; it eventually reopened in 1963 as the permanent home of the Bavarian State Opera with its supporting 150-member Bavarian State Orchestra. It is now among Germany's most elegant opera houses, superbly equipped. The company, whose standards are consistently high, still favours a sprinkling of international stars in productions which can be alluringly lavish. Its Strauss tradition is without equal. Wolfgang Sawallisch has been musical and artistic director since September 1982. Meanwhile, inside the next-door Residenz is the Cuvilliés-Theater (capacity 436), whose sparkling interior had been stored away during the war and was reassembled in 1958 to provide a jewel-box setting for small-scale works.

Max-Joseph-Pl. 2, 8000 München 22 ☎ 089-2185 1   FX 089-2185 304 ♬ Sep – Jul   B Maximilianstr. 11, 8000 München 22   ☎ 089-221316 Mon – Fri 10am–1pm, 3.30–5.30pm, Sat 10am–12.30pm Discounts for the disabled CC None   ♿ Wheelchair spaces, hearing aids   ⠿ 1773 and 328 standing ♨ Restaurant Kaefer   ☎ 089-2185 303 PT Train – S-Bahn S1 to S6. Bus – 50, 55, Odeonspl. Underground – U3, U5, U6 Ⓟ Underground carpark attached to the opera house.

TEATRO SAN CARLO

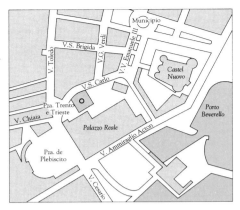

The date usually given for the first public performance of opera in Naples, at the Teatro di San Bartolomeo, is 1654. The work was *Orontea Regina d'Egitto* by Francesco Cirillo, but it is now thought that Francesco Provenzale's *Il Ciro* was presented a year earlier.

Provenzale is recognized as the 'father' of the enormously influential 'Neapolitan School', which dominated opera throughout Europe until Gluck's 18th-century reforms. Neapolitan-style operas were often based on a libretto by Pietro Metastasio. The composers, all of whom were connected with Naples, include Alessandro Scarlatti, Pergolesi, Paisiello, Cimarosa and Hasse.

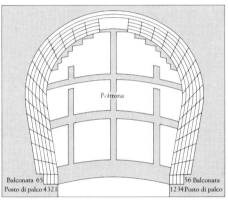

The heyday of the San Bartolomeo was during the viceroyalty of the Duke of Medinaceli (1695–1702), when it was enlarged and improved. It was then that Scarlatti consolidated his own and Naples' position at the peak of the operatic firmament. In 1737, Charles III of Bourbon built a new theatre, the Teatro di San Carlo, which opened in 1737 with Domenico Sarro's *Achille in Scirro*.

The shrewd Domenico Barbaia, director at the San Carlo and the most famous impresario of his day, lured Rossini to Naples, where he stayed from 1815 to 1822.

Despite losing his mistress, the Spanish soprano Isabella Colbran, to Rossini, Barbaia remained the composer's staunchest ally. The best-known of the eight Rossini operas he premiered at the San Carlo are *Mosè in Egitto* (1818) and *La Donna del Lago* (1819). Colbran starred in both. Premieres of no less than 17 of Donizetti's operas were presented at the San Carlo, of which *Lucia* (1835) and *Roberto Devereux* (1837) were the most successful.

The San Carlo went into a decline during the later part of the 19th century, but began to recapture some of its former glory, after World War II, under the directorship of Pasquale di Costanzo. Two Prokofiev works had their Italian premieres there, *The Gamb-*

ler (1953) and *Betrothal in a Monastery* (1959). Bartók, Berg, Hindemith, Schoenberg and Shostakovich shared billing with the old Neapolitan favourites, Bellini, Donizetti, Rossini and Verdi. Renzo Giacchieri became director in 1988.

Via San Carlo 981, 80132 Napoli
☎ 81-7972111   TX 721606 TESCAR
FX 81-7972306   ♬ Dec – Jun   B As above   CC None   & None   ⛲ 1450
♀ Bar   ☎ 81-7972370/7972412
PT Train – Napoli Centrale. Bus – 150, Pza Trieste e Trento   Ⓟ Pza Trieste e Trento, Pza del Plebiscito.

NEW ORLEANS OPERA

New Orleans has the distinction of being the first North American city to have its own permanent opera company. French-Creole influence is strong and has been a determining factor in its cultural development.

A French troupe under Louis Tabary arrived in 1791 and set up shop the following year in Le Spectacle de la Rue St Pierre. Here the city's first full-length opera, Grétry's *Silvain,* was performed in 1796. Closed for some time, the theatre was restored and reopened by Jean-Baptiste Fournier in 1804. When he was ousted by Tabary's comeback two years later, he set up the rival Théâtre de la Rue St Philippe.

In 1819 another French immigrant, John Davis, opened the (second) Théâtre d'Orléans, and staged 52 US premieres in his first five years. He was succeeded in 1837 by his son, Pierre, who oversaw several outstanding American 'firsts', particularly *Lucia* (1841), Halévy's *La Juive* (1844) and Meyerbeer's *Le Prophète* (1850). But New Orleans opera was to see a yet more golden era. Charles Boudousquié, who had taken over the Orléans in 1853, left it six years later to build an even more splendid edifice. His new building, the French Opera House, designed by James Gallier Jr., was constructed in a mere eight months, opening with *Guillaume Tell* on 1 December 1859, three days after completion. Among a host of fine singers, Patti made one of her very earliest appearances there, at the age of 17, in Flotow's *Martha* (1860) and returned for the title role of Meyerbeer's *Dinorah* the following year. Seventeen American premieres were given there, among them Massenet's *Le Cid* (1890) and Saint-Saëns *Samson et Dalila* (1893). The French Opera House was totally destroyed by fire in 1919.

To some extent opera in New Orleans has never been the same since. There were only occasional productions until 1943, when Walter Loubart founded the New Orleans Opera Association. It presented mainstream repertory in the unsatisfactory Municipal

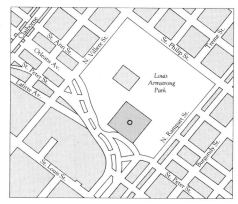

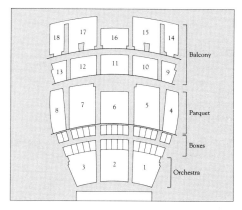

Auditorium until 1973, when the modern Theatre of the Performing Arts was opened. Four operas are now presented each season, one of them normally a new production and one taken from the French repertory. Visitors may also find operatic activity at any one of the four colleges in the city.

New Orleans Theatre of the Performing Arts, 801 N. Rampart Street., New Orleans, LA 70116 ☎ 504-529 2278
♬ Oct – Mar Ⓑ New Orleans Opera Assn, 333 St Charles Av., Suite 907, New Orleans, LA 70130 ☎ As above
CC MC, Mr. Bol, Visa ♿ Elevators, ramps, wheelchair spaces, hearing aids
⸬ 2317 ♟ Bar PT Taxi only Ⓟ In grounds.

THE METROPOLITAN OPERA

One of the world's great companies, the Metropolitan Opera – universally known as the Met – has a relatively short history, stretching back just over a century. Before that, after the usual run of visiting companies from the mid-18th century, Italian opera only started there in earnest when Manuel Garcia and his daughter, the mezzo Maria Malibran, founded a company at the Park Theater in 1825: it gave the first American *Don Giovanni* (1826). The Italian Opera House was opened in 1833, but burned down in 1839. Other houses were similarly short-lived until the Academy of Music, an opera house despite its name, was built at Irving Place and 14th Street. It opened in 1854 with *Norma*, and enjoyed annual seasons until 1886 under such impresarios as 'Colonel' Mapleson.

The Academy's popularity indirectly gave birth to the Met: a group of businessmen unable to get boxes decided to build their own opera house. Setting up the Metropolitan Opera as an institution in 1880, they subscribed $800,000 and inaugurated their new building with *Faust*, starring Christine Nilsson in 1883; Henry Abbey was the leaseholder. American premieres of *Tristan*, *Meistersinger* and most of *The Ring* were staged in the 1880s. With nearly 70 boxes in two tiers, the house had an initial capacity of

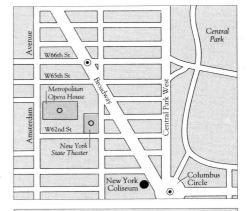

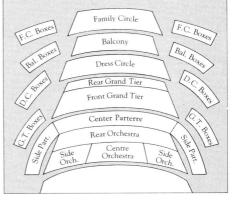

3045; rebuilding after a serious fire in 1892 increased this to 3849. The theatre enjoyed its first golden age under impresario Maurice Grau (1891–1903), who owned the lease of both the Met and Covent Garden. His casts regularly included the De Reszke brothers and Lilli Lehmann. His successor Heinrich Conried (1903–8) introduced Caruso to the USA and scandalized his reactionary patrons with America's first *Salome* (1907).

A new production company was established under Giulio Gatti-Casazza, who began his long tenure (1908–35) with Toscanini as principal conductor; Mahler also conducted eight productions. The first operatic specialist to run the Met, Gatti-Casazza achieved consistently profitable seasons. In December 1910 he presented the world premieres of Puccini's *Fanciulla* and Humperdinck's *Königskinder*, and in the 1920s commissioned a series of new American works. He also engineered Rosa Ponselle's operatic debut, as Amneris in 1925. His successor, the Canadian tenor Edward Johnson (1935–50), instituted vital economies in the wake of the Depression and organized a buy out of the theatre by the company from its boxholders in 1940. He encouraged specifically home-grown talents such as Risë Stevens, Eleanor Steber and Leonard Warren. Broadcasts from the Met began with *Hänsel und Gretel* on Christmas Day 1931; the weekly Texaco-Met live radio broadcasts, now reaching some 10 million listeners, started in December 1939. A formative influence on operatic taste throughout the continent, they have also raised millions of dollars by public contributions to the Met.

Purse strings were loosened again under the Viennese-born, British-naturalized Rudolf Bing (1950–72). With the postwar dollar reigning supreme, he was able to lure back international casts to productions enhanced by the latest developments in stage design, largely learned from Broadway. He ended the Met's tacit colour bar with Marian Anderson as Ulrica in *Ballo* (1955) and premiered Samuel Barber's Pulitzer prize-winning *Vanessa* in 1958, though his choice of repertory was generally conservative.

The climax of Bing's regime was the company's move to the Lincoln Center for the Performing Arts, whose largest arena became the Metropolitan Opera House. Designed by Wallace Harrison and built for $46 million, mostly privately subscribed, it opened in 1966 with a Zeffirelli production of Barber's new *Antony and Cleopatra*. Its auditorium is visually austere but offers superb backstage and production facilities. It also enjoys unrivalled acoustics and a more egalitarian audience than in the old Met, without the use of surtitles.

Although Göran Gentele died within seven weeks of succeeding Bing in 1972, he had by then appointed James Levine principal conductor. His foresight was confirmed when Anthony Bliss, who had taken over management of the Met in 1975, announced Levine's promotion to artistic director from 1986/7, a position he still holds. Bruce Crawford succeeded Bliss in 1985, but resigned in 1989. Despite a certain inconsistency in its guest singers during the 1980s, the Met boasts America's finest opera orchestra and a chorus renowned for its disciplined power. The company gives seven performances a week for 32 consecutive weeks. Apart from the New York City Opera, productions of better than average competence may also be seen at the Amato Opera Theater, the Juilliard School's American Opera Center and the Manhattan School of Music.

Lincoln Center, New York, N.Y. 10023
☎ 212-362 6000   FX 212-874 2659
♫ Sep – May   B As above   CC Amex, Diners, MC, Visa   ♿ Wheelchair space
☎ 212-799 3100 X2204, libretti in braille and large print ☎ 212-582 3512
⦂⦂⦂ 3800 and 265 standing   ♟ Grand Tier Restaurant ☎ 212-799 3400   PT Bus – M5, M7, M11, M66, M104.
Underground – No. 1, 66th St. station
Ⓟ Lincoln Center Park ☎ 212-874 9021.

NEW YORK CITY OPERA

New York City Opera is the city's 'other' company, a more adventurous counterpart to the Met and easier on the opera goer's pocket. It has always preferred up-and-coming American talent to international stars, and has been the proving ground for any number of young Americans who have later achieved fame abroad.

It was founded in 1943 as the City Center Opera Company by New York's progressive mayor Fiorello LaGuardia. Its declared aim was 'to present opera with the highest artistic standards, while maintaining the civic and democratic ideas of moderate prices, practical business planning and modern methods'. The energetic, but spiky, László Halász was its first musical director. He was dismissed in 1951 as a 'threat to the City Center's prosperity and advancement'. He was succeeded by the Polish-born Joseph Rosenstock, who conducted the American stage premiere of Bartók's *Duke Bluebeard's Castle* (1952) and oversaw the world premiere of Copland's *The Tender Land* (1954).

Julius Rudel, who had emigrated from Vienna and joined the company right at the start as a repetiteur, became director in 1957 at the age of 36. His was a vintage era. A breath of fresh air was felt as world premieres such as Hugo Weisgall's *Six Characters in Search of an Author*, after Pirandello

(1959), and Rorem's *Miss Julie* (1965), jostled with Monteverdi, Gilbert & Sullivan, Prokofiev and Gershwin. He supervised the move to the New York State Theater in Lincoln Center, where it opened with Ginastera's *Don Rodrigo* in February 1966.

One of Rudel's greatest successes was Handel's *Giulio Cesare in Egitto* (1971), in which Beverly Sills sang Cleopatra, the highlight of her quarter century as the company's unofficial prima donna. When Rudel resigned in 1979, she was a popular choice as his successor, the first non-conductor to be appointed. Under her inspiration, NYCO's policy became even more eclectic as musicals rubbed shoulders with grand opera, operetta and new commissions. Miss Sills resigned as general director in 1988 to be succeeded by Christopher Keene in 1989.

New York State Theater, Lincoln Center, New York, NY 10023 ☎ 212-870 5600 FX 212-724 1120 ♬ Jul – Nov Ⓑ As above. Discount for groups CC Amex, MC, Visa ♿ Contact theatre ☷ 2779 and limited standing ♙ Cafe and bar ☎ 212-870 5600 PT Train – Columbus Station. Bus – M5, M7, M11, M66, M104. Underground – Columbus Circle Ⓟ Lincoln Center Garage.

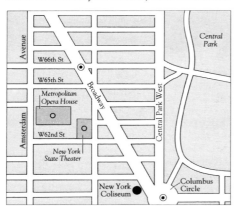

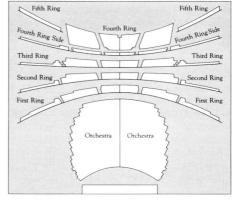

DEN NORSKE OPERA

Opera has enjoyed an unbroken existence in Norway only for the past 30 years, but is now thriving, at least in the capital. The Norwegian National Opera (Den Norske Opera) averages 150 performances a year, divided about 60/40 between opera and ballet. It is an ensemble company, with 26 resident principals. Under Bjørn E. Simensen, its artistic director since 1984, it is beginning to come to terms with the current internationalization of opera.

From 1380 until 1814, Norway was twinned with Denmark, with Copenhagen the capital. While based there as conductor of the renowned Mingotti company in 1749, Gluck is reputed to have travelled with it to Christiania, known after 1924 as Oslo. Those performances are generally regarded as Norway's introduction to opera. The first Norwegian opera (1825) was Waldemar Thrane's *Fjeldeventyret* (*The Mountain Adventure*).

A surge of theatrical nationalism, centred on Ibsen, led in 1899 to the building of the National Theatre, which included opera in its repertory. Opera flourished for three years from 1918 in the purpose-built Opéra Comique, which foundered when its benefactor Christoffer Hannevig went bankrupt. The Norwegian soprano Kirsten Flagstad's flourishing international career after 1933 rekindled local operatic interest. In 1950 the Norsk Operaselskap (Norwegian Opera Society) was started by the brothers Gunnar and Jonas Brunvoll. In turn this led to the foundation of Den Norske Opera in November 1957. Flagstad was appointed its first artistic director; the company opened in 1959 with d'Albert's *Tiefland*, in which she had made her own 1913 debut.

A critical appointment was that of the Czech conductor Martin Turnovsky, who became musical director (1975–80): he raised standards considerably and broadened the repertory beyond Mozart, Verdi and Puccini. The present musical director, Heinz Fricke, appointed in 1984, is

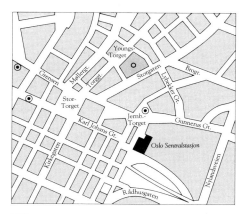

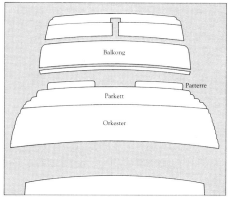

continuing in similar vein.

Operas were commissioned from five Norwegian composers in 1985: the first to be produced was Oddvar S. Kvam's *I 13 Time* (At the 13th Hour) in 1987. The company has declared its intention to erect a purpose-built opera house by New Year's Eve 1999.

Folketeatret, Storgaten 23, 0184 Oslo 1 ☎ 02-42 94 75 FX 02-42 78 77 ♫ Aug – Jun B P.O. Box 8800 Youngstorget, 0028 Oslo 1 ☎ 02-42 77 24. Discounts for groups of 10+ CC MC, Visa & Elevators 1050 and 40 standing ♟ 3 bars, meals on request to: Marketing Dept at box office address PT Train – Sentralstasjon. Bus/tram – Operaen. Underground – Jernbanetorget Ⓟ For 150 cars.

TEATRO MASSIMO

Although the Sicilian Vespers rebellion, later immortalized by Verdi's opera, began in Palermo in 1282, opera took a long time to filter down to the toe of Italy. Cavalli's *Giasone,* imported from Venice via Naples, was staged there in 1655 in the Teatro della Misericordia. It was followed by several more from Cavalli's generous output. The birth of Alessandro Scarlatti in Palermo in 1660 undoubtedly encouraged the frequent performance of his works there, beginning with *Il Pompeo* in 1690.

Throughout the 18th century the Unione dei Musici, a semicharitable organization, promoted Neapolitan opera at the Teatro di Santa Cecilia, which it had opened in 1693. Competition came from the 500-seat wooden Teatro di Santa Lucia, built in 1726 for comic opera. It was owned by the noble Valguarnera family. In 1809 it was enlarged to 700 capacity, substantially rebuilt in brick, and renamed Real Teatro Carolino. Because it operated all the year round, it attracted several great names as conductors, including Donizetti who wrote his *Alahor in Granata* for it in 1826. Michael Balfe was its principal baritone in 1829–30, producing his first opera there, *I Rivali di se Stessi.* Renamed the Real Teatro Bellini, it eventually became a cinema and burned down in 1964.

The Bellini's decline owed much to its inadequate facilities and the inauguration in 1874 of the Politeama Municipale, which was renamed Politeama Garibaldi on the death of the statesman in 1882. Toscanini made his Sicilian debut here in 1892.

The Politeama's quarter-century of operatic success came to a halt with the opening of an altogether more grandiose theatre. The architect Filippo Basile emerged victorious from a municipal competition organized in 1864, and after endless wrangling the Teatro Massimo was finally completed in 1897, opening with *Falstaff.*

The Massimo, true to its name, is one of the largest opera houses anywhere, covering

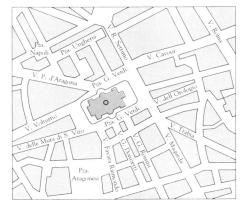

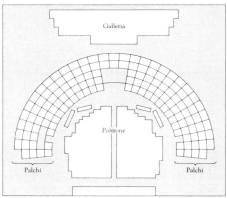

a total of 9245 square yards (7730 square metres). Although its auditorium is Italy's fifth largest, its stage is smaller only than those of Paris and Vienna. It has 142 boxes arranged in five tiers. Caruso, barely 24, appeared in *La Gioconda* during its opening season: to this day, the company has preferred to engage young prospects rather than established greats.

Pza G. Verdi, 90138 Palermo
☎ 091-583600   ♫ Oct – Jun   B As above ☎ 091-581512. Tue – Sun 10am – 1pm, 4 – 7pm   CC None
♿ None   ⬚ 1316   ♟ Bar   PT Bus – 1, 2, 3, 4, 10, 12, 14, 15, 16, 19, 21, 24, 27, 31. Transport info
☎ 091-222398   Ⓟ Nearby.

OPERA BASTILLE

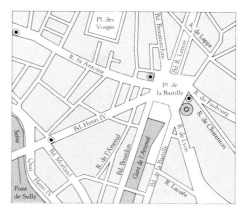

Opéra Bastille was originally destined to become the new home of the Paris Opera in 1989, to commemorate the bicentenary of the French Revolution. Although the building opened on the eve of Bastille Day, 13 July 1989, with a gala featuring Teresa Berganza and Placido Domingo, political shenanigans delayed the operatic opening until March 1990.

The project was the brainchild of President Mitterand, combining a monument to his 'reign' and an opera house for the 21st century. Ideas for a new opera house were first mooted in 1968; various reports were commissioned from Maurice Béjart and Pierre Boulez, among others. The decision to build in the Place de la Bastille was made in March 1982. An international competition was held for a suitable design and, in November 1983, Carlos Ott was declared the winner from 787 entrants. Born in Uruguay in 1946, Ott trained there as an architect and in the USA. He emigrated to Canada in 1974 and is now based in Toronto.

Preparation of the site began the following November and the foundations were laid in February 1985. While building proceeded smoothly enough, there were serious disagreements behind the scenes. These reached crisis point in the spring of 1989 when the Bastille's artistic director, Daniel Barenboim, announced his plans for the 1989/90 season. The administration considered these too unambitious for such a prestigious project, and he resigned shortly afterwards. Several other prominent musicians then renounced their Bastille contracts, in sympathy with Barenboim. His place was taken by Myung-Whun Chung. By now all hope of preparing a production for July 1989 had vanished; a less pretentious opening ceremony had to be devised.

Seating 2716, the Grande Salle is the largest auditorium ever built for opera in France. Its two balconies are designed like a series of giant sledges descending into the

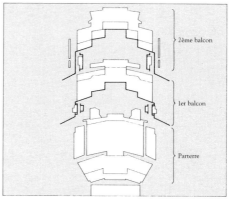

enormous stalls area. The walls are blue-tinted granite, while the seats combine pearwood and black velvet. Rounded surfaces are intended to give excellent acoustics in any part of the house. Stage facilities are extremely flexible: scenery can be prepositioned on five adjacent secondary platforms identical in size to the main stage, to facilitate quick scene-changes.

120 rue de Lyon, 75012 Paris
☎ 01-40 01 17 89   FX 01-43 44 94 01
♫ Oct – Jul   B As above
☎ 01-40 01 16 16   TX 215 356
FX As above   CC Visa   ♿ Special seats
⁙ 2716   ♥ Cafe, Restaurant Fouquet's
PT Bus – 91, 87, 86, 76, 69, 65, 29, 20.
Underground – 1, 8   Ⓟ 34 rue de Lyon.

OPERA DE PARIS

The very word 'Opéra' has traditionally meant the Paris Opéra, such has been its prestige since it began.

Sacrati's *La Finta Pazza* (1645) was the first opera seen in Paris, but Robert Cambert and Pierre Perrin's *Pomone* was the first French opera performed at their new Académie d'Opéra in 1671. Lully took over their royal warrant and, after Molière's death (1673), was given the Grande Salle of the Palais Royal, where his Académie Royale de Musique (known as the Opéra) staged 17 operas (including ballets) in a grand style, which was influential for more than two centuries. The Opéra orchestra was also much the most important in Paris.

The mid-18th century was dominated by Rameau with 13 premieres (1733–60), notably *Les Indes Galantes* (1735) and *Castor et Pollux* (1737). Controversy raged between the conservative Lullistes and the progressive Ramistes, reflected in the famous Querelle des Bouffons (1752–54) – heated exchanges over opposing French and Italian styles – and still later embodied in the operas of Gluck (beginning with *Iphigénie en Aulide* in 1774) and his rival Piccinni. The theatre burned down in 1763, was renovated and destroyed by fire again in 1781.

In 1821, after 40 years involving frequent changes of name and base, the Opéra finally

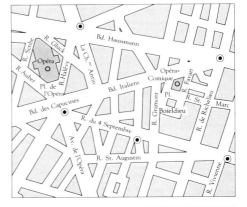

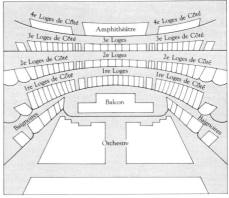

settled in the Théâtre de l'Académie Royale de Musique, built by Debret in the rue Le Peletier, where gas lighting vastly improved stage effects. The era of French grand opera, which dominated Europe for more than half a century, had been ushered in by Spontini's *La Vestale* (1807) and reached a climax with Meyerbeer's *Les Huguenots* (1836) and Rossini's *Guillaume Tell* (1828). Spurred on by sumptuous productions by Cicéri and Daguerre (the photographer), new works by Meyerbeer and Halévy were later joined by Verdi's first French opera, *Les Vêpres Siciliennes* (1855), and by *Tannhäuser* (1861, with ballet), which was a disaster.

In 1858, Napoleon III decided on the construction of a new opera house that was to become the keystone in the plans for Parisian re-urbanization under Baron Haussmann. After a competition for its design was won by Charles Garnier, construction began in 1861, but was delayed by the Franco-Prussian War. When fire destroyed the building in rue Le Peletier in 1873, work was speeded up and the new Palais Garnier finally opened on 5 January 1875.

One of the most magnificent opera houses anywhere, it is let down by its indifferent sightlines. Four tiers of balconies rise above the stalls, themselves on two levels. Garnier not only drew the designs, but personally directed the various sculptors, painters and mosaicists, channelling them into what he called 'Art Officiel'. The stage is nearly 598 square yards (500 square metres), generally regarded as the largest in the world. Superbly equipped, the building even included stabling for 20 horses to be used in Meyerbeer spectaculars. For all its original gold and velvet, the auditorium is now dominated by Marc Chagall's *Bouquet de Rêves* ceiling, painted in 1964. The great sweep of the white marble grand staircase is the building's most breathtaking feature. In a sense, the very lavishness of decoration in the Palais Garnier, designed to provide a backdrop for splendid audiences, has proved an embarrassment to anti-élitist sentiment in today's France. Hence the company's move to the more populist Bastille, which took place in 1990.

At first, only *Aida* and Rossini were allowed to join the solidly French repertory based on Gounod and Massenet. Wagner was only allowed in under the directorship (1884–1908) of Pierre Gailhard whose production of *Lohengrin* (1891) was greeted angrily. Messager finally completed the Wagner cycle in 1911 with *Parsifal*. He also succeeded in disbanding the notorious *claque* of professional applauders.

After World War I Paris saw a steady reaction against the more pretentious aspects of Opéra life in favour of operetta and cabaret, although there were premieres of Roussel, Honegger and Milhaud. Nationalized after World War II, the Opéra was hamstrung by bureaucracy until Rolf Liebermann emerged as director (1973–80) with Georg Solti as musical adviser. Together they transformed its parochialism into an international showcase again. They also commissioned Messiaen's *Saint-François d'Assise*, premiered there in 1983. There was some attempt to keep up morale under its last regime, with Jean-Louis Martinoty as administrator and Lothar Zagrosek as musical director: they gave the first French performance of Busoni's *Doktor Faust* in 1989. The unsettled start at the Opéra Bastille may well extend the Palais Garnier's lease of life beyond being a mere purveyor of Bastille revivals, as has been threatened.

Pl. de L'Opéra, 75009 Paris
☎ 01-47 42 57 50   TX 230366 T'OPERA
FX 01-42 66 50 10   ♫ Sep – Jun   B 8
rue Scribe, 75009 Paris   ☎ 01-47 42 53 71
TX 240508 LOCOPER. Mon – Sat 11am – 8pm. Discounts for groups, write to: Responsable du Service Location par Correspondance at box office address
CC MC, Visa   ⅍ None   ⁘ 1991
♟ Bars   PT Train – Gare St Lazare. Bus – 21, 27, 29, 68 (and many more). Underground – Opéra, Chausseé d'Antin
℗ Bd. Haussmann.

OPERA-COMIQUE (SALLE FAVART)

The origins of the Opéra-Comique lie in the two great Théâtres de la Foire, the Paris fairs which started in the 16th century: the Foire St Germain (3 February to Easter) and the Foire St Laurent (17 June to late September), where vaudeville originated. The *comédiens* of the St Germain and the Académie Royale de Musique merged as the Opéra-Comique in 1715. The Comédie-Italienne, which had arrived in Paris during Henri III's reign (1551–89), took over the St Laurent company in 1721; it eventually amalgamated with the Opéra-Comique in 1762. Together they moved to the Salle Favart in 1783, playing *opéras comiques* by Grétry and Dalayrac. A rival Opéra-Comique, which premiered Cherubini's *Médée* in 1797, inevitably bankrupted both and they merged to form a new Théâtre National de l'Opéra-Comique in 1801.

It gave a string of brilliant first performances in a variety of theatres, ranging from Méhul's *Joseph* (1807) to Donizetti's *La Fille du Régiment* (1840), when it settled back into the second, redesigned, Salle Favart. There it stayed until the building burned down in 1887. Further moves ended with the inauguration of the present Salle Favart in 1898. At this period, especially under Léon Carvalho (1876–87, 1891–97) and Albert Carré (1898–1914), the Opéra-Comique rivalled the Opéra with several prestigious premieres: *Carmen* (1875), *Les Contes d'Hoffmann* (1881), *Manon* (1884) and *Pelléas et Mélisande* (1902).

From 1936 onwards, the fortunes of the Opéra-Comique became more closely linked to those of the Opéra: they shared administrations from 1959. The appointment of Louis Erlo as director in 1971 saw the company reconstituted as the Opéra-Studio, a training-school for all aspects of opera. When this moved to Lyons in 1976, the company reverted to the old name, Salle Favart, under Liebermann of the Opéra.

Opera is also found in the Théâtre du Châtelet, opened in 1862, which was home to Diaghilev's Ballet Russe (1909–13), and in the Théâtre des Champs-Elysées, scene in its opening season (1913) of the notorious premiere of Stravinsky's *The Rite of Spring*.

Pl. Boieldieu, 75002 Paris ☎ 1-42 60 0499/ 1-42 96 1220 ⊤ⅹ 213886 OP COM Fⅹ 1-42 86 8578 ♫ Sep–Jul Ⓑ 5 rue Favart, 75002 Paris ☎ ⊤ⅹ Fⅹ As above. Discount for groups Ⓒ Ⓒ None ♿ None ⚏ 1300 and some standing ♟ Bars ☎ 1-42 60 0499 ⓟⓣ Train – Gare du Nord, Gare de L'Est. Bus – 39, 48, 67. Underground – Richelieu Drouot.

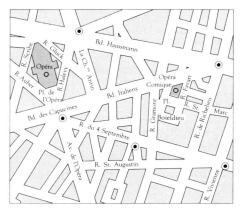

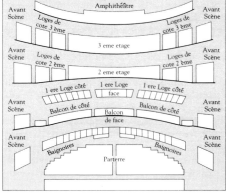

TEATRO REGIO

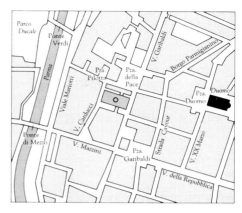

Parma has a distinguished operatic history, reaching back to the Farnese dukes in the early 17th century. Duke Ranuccio I commissioned a theatre from the architect Gian Battista Aleotti in 1618: the huge Teatro Farnese, seating 4500, was built entirely of wood on the first floor of the Palazzo della Pilotta. It opened in 1628 with *Mercurio e Marte*, a *torneo regale* (royal tournament), to music by Monteverdi, celebrating the marriage of Odoardo Farnese to Margherita de' Medici. Its last performance honoured the arrival of Carlo I of Bourbon in 1732.

The arrival of the Duchess Marie-Louise, Napoleon's second wife, in 1815, gave a considerable fillip to music in Parma. A year later she founded the court orchestra and a school of choral singing, which eventually became the city's present conservatory. She authorized the demolition of the convent of Sant'Alessandro, to accommodate the Nuovo Teatro Ducale. It was modelled by Nicola Bettòli on Milan's La Scala, and similarly decorated in gold and white with red velvet. It opened, after eight years of construction, in 1829 with the disastrous premiere of Bellini's *Zaira*. After the first war of independence in 1849, it became known by its present name, Il Teatro Regio.

Parma is particularly associated with Verdi, who was born some 30 miles (48 kilometres) away in Le Roncole. Parma has managed to stage only one Verdi premiere, the first performance in Italy of *Les Vêpres Siciliennes* (1855), then entitled *Giovanna di Guzman* for fear of Austrian censorship. Toscanini was born in Parma in 1867. Although as a student he played his cello in the Regio orchestra, he never conducted opera there. Renata Tebaldi grew up in Parma, where she began her studies.

The amusingly baroque arena is gloriously lit by a central chandelier. It contains 113 boxes, each with its own individually furnished anteroom ranged on four levels, with a *loggione* (gallery) above. The gorgeous nymphs on the ceiling as well as the drop-curtain,

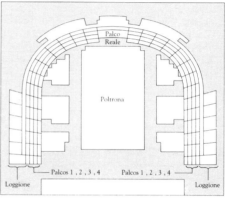

depicting The Triumph of Knowledge, were painted by Gian Battista Borghese. Opera is accompanied by the Orchestra Sinfonica dell' Emilia Romagna 'Arturo Toscanini'. Despite recent financial cutbacks, there has been no apparent loss of quality in its shortened season and a willingness to stage premieres as well as exploring lesser-known Verdi. Angela Spocci is its director.

Via Garibaldi 16, 43100 Parma
☎ 0521-79 5687   TX 532233 T REGIO
FX 0521-284283   ♫ Dec – May   B As above   ☎ 0521-795678   TX   FX As above   CC None   ᕃ None   ☷ 1392 and 48 standing   ♀ Two bars
PT Train – Stazione Parma. Bus – 1, 2, 8
Ⓟ Piazza della Pace.

OPERA COMPANY OF PHILADELPHIA

Philadelphia's early operatic history is British, dating from the ballad opera *Flora, or Hob in the Well*, performed by an English company in Plumsted's Warehouse in 1754. The Southwark Theatre opened in 1766 with Arne's *Thomas and Sally*. It relied upon importing London productions of English comic opera. In recent years, however, the company has tended to obtain its principals from Italy. The city's Italian bias is crystallized in the person of Gian Carlo Menotti, who studied at its Curtis Institute of Music.

The Italian connection traces its origin to Mozart's librettist, Lorenzo da Ponte, who brought the first Italian companies to the city. Starting in 1829 they performed in the Chestnut Street Theatre, once known as 'Old Drury' but aptly renamed the Italian Opera House.

An important cornerstone in American operatic history was the opening in January 1857 of the Academy of Music: the oldest opera house in continuous use in the USA, it doubles as the home of the present company and the renowned Philadelphia Orchestra. Patti sang in Flotow's *Martha* there at the age of 16 in 1859.

The Met first appeared at the Academy in 1885, where it performed the city's first *Ring* cycle in 1889. It moved in 1908 to the new 4000-seat Philadelphia Opera built by Oscar Hammerstein, acquiring it from him in 1910, when it was renamed the Metropolitan Opera House. Until 1968 the Met gave between six and 25 performances annually, returning to the Academy after the cavernous Metropolitan was ruined by fire in 1948.

Meanwhile, two local companies had been started. The Philadelphia Civic Opera (renamed the Philadelphia Lyric Opera in 1958) opened in 1924, and the Pennsylvania Grand Opera in 1927. In 1975 they merged under Carl Suppa's direction to form the present Opera Company of Philadelphia.

The Academy of Music, Broad and Locust Sts, Philadelphia, PA 19102 ☎ 215-732 5814 TX 379 1595 PHILOP FX 215-790 1104 specify Opera Co. of Philadelphia ♫ Oct – May B 1500 Walnut St., Suite 504, Philadelphia, PA 19102 ☎ 215-732 5813. Discounts for special groups CC Credit cards taken by telephone only – Academy Charge, Amex, MC, Visa ☎ 215-893 1999 3 weeks before performance ♿ Wheelchair ramp and seating ☎ 215-893 1935 ⸬ 2818 ♀ Bar PT Train – Amtrak 30th St., SEPTA Suburban and Market East, PATCO regional line Bus – various SEPTA routes ☎ 215-547 7800 Underground – Broad St. ℗ Nearby.

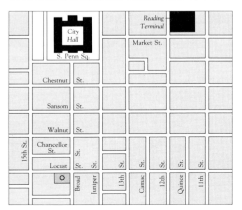

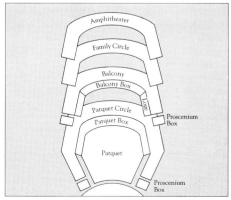

PITTSBURGH OPERA

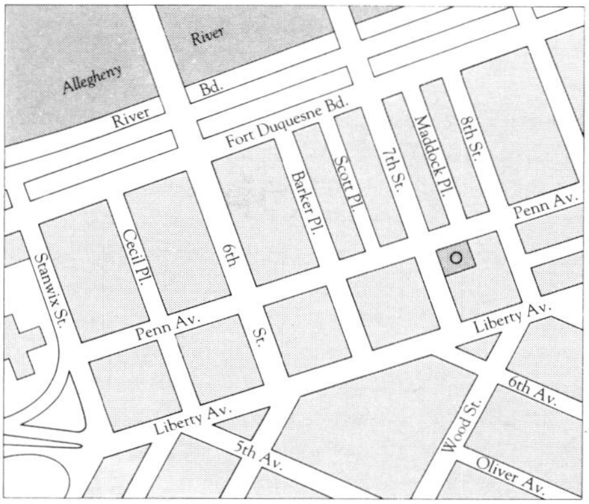

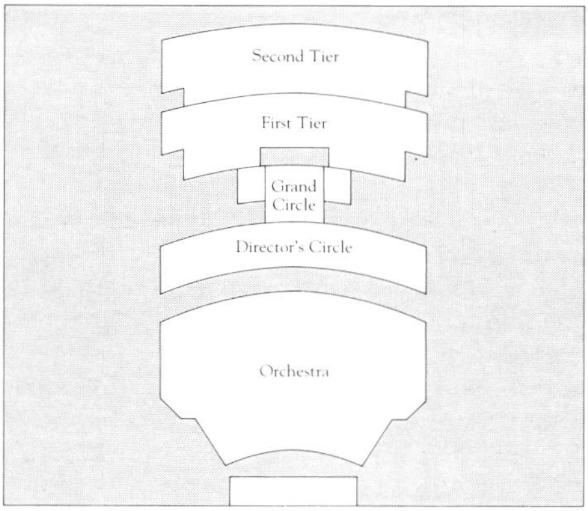

Pittsburgh Opera, the fifth oldest opera company in the USA, celebrated its fiftieth anniversary during the 1988/89 season. Founded as the Pittsburgh Opera Society in the autumn of 1939, it promoted sporadic productions in a variety of venues until Viennese-born Richard Karp, a violist with the Pittsburgh Symphony, was appointed music and artistic director in 1942. Karp masterminded the Society's move to the Syria Mosque in 1945, which marked its first steps towards wider recognition. International stars such as Regina Resnik, Licia Albanese, Robert Merrill, Eleanor Steber and Richard Tucker performed there.

A lavish production of *Aida* heralded the company's transfer to the newly renovated Heinz Hall in the autumn of 1971. A year after Karp's death in 1977 Vincent Artz became general manager, with James de Blasis as his artistic advisor. Pittsburgh Opera's current policies, however, may be said to have originated with the Argentine-born Tito Capobianco, who has been involved with the company intermittently as a producer since 1971, becoming general director in 1983.

Capobianco signalled a new era with the American professional stage premiere of Verdi's *La Battaglia di Legnano* in 1984, and the introduction the following year of Op-Trans, with English translations projected above the stage. He also expanded the number of performances per production from two to four. Since October 1987, Pittsburgh Opera has been housed in the ornately decorated Benedum Center for the Performing Arts.

The company's repertoire ploughs a fairly conservative furrow, hardly surprising considering Capobianco's reputation as a Verdi producer. Healthy financial underpinning has enabled a return to its earlier policy of engaging international talent: Agnes Baltsa, José Carreras, Joan Sutherland and Sherrill Milnes have all appeared in recent years. The highlight of the Golden Jubilee celebrations was a new production in May 1989 of *Werther*, with Luciano Pavarotti making his debut in the title role.

Benedum Center, 719 Liberty Ave., Pittsburgh, PA 15222 ☎ 412-281 0912 TX 265451 MONREF ♫ Oct – May B 711 Penn Ave., Pittsburgh, PA 15222 ☎ 412-456 6666. Mon – Fri 10am – 6pm, Sat – Sun 12 – 4pm. Discounts for groups of 20 +, and the disabled ☎ 412-281 9189 CC Amex, Horne, Kaufmann, MC, Visa ♿ Seats, ramps, headsets, usher assistance, restrooms ⁙ 2800 🍷 For large receptions and meals ☎ 412-456 2600 PT Transport info. ☎ 800-821 1888. Underground – Wood St. Ⓟ Nearby.

NATIONAL THEATRE

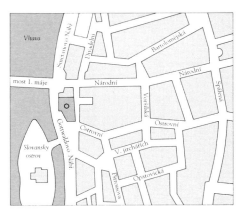

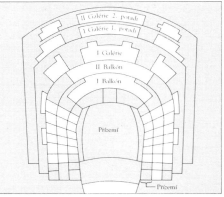

Opera is important to Prague: it can be seen at three venues, since the Tyl and Smetana Theatres are also under the control of the National Theatre. The city's early tradition was entirely Italian. Even works on Czech subjects, such as Bartolomeo Bernardi's *La Libussa* (1703), were performed by visiting companies. The first theatre was built on the citadel in 1681. Here Gluck conducted Locatelli's company in his own *Ezio* (1750) and *Issipile* (1752). However, a purpose-built opera house was provided by Count Nostitz in 1783. Known first as Nostitz's National Theatre, it became the Estates Theatre (1798) and finally the present Tyl Theatre (1945).

The National won almost instant fame. Mozart was invited to Prague after the success there of *Seraglio* (1783) and *Figaro* (1786), and conducted his new 'Prague' Symphony. He was asked to compose a new opera for the royal wedding celebrations: the result was *Don Giovanni*, which he conducted on 29 October 1787. He returned to conduct the first performance of *La Clemenza di Tito* on 6 September 1791, just three months before his death. The resultant Mozart cult was fostered by Weber, who was intendant at the Estates Theatre (1813–16).

The premiere of František Škroup's *Dráteník* (*The Tinker*, 1826), the first opera in Czech, touched off a widespread urge for a separate Czech theatre. This eventually led to the building of the Provisional Theatre in 1862. The most important Czech opera, *Prodaná Nevěsta* (*The Bartered Bride*), was first presented there in May 1866. Smetana was appointed principal conductor, remaining until 1874. Public subscription paid for the new National Theatre (Národní Divadlo), designed by Josef Zítek, which opened in June 1881 with the first performance of Smetana's *Libuše*. The theatre burned down in July, but public donations again paid for rebuilding. It reopened in 1883. Most of Dvořák's operas were first seen there, notably *Rusalka* (1901), as well as the

premiere of Schoenberg's *Erwartung* (1924).

Massive reconstruction (1977–83) has given the National a deeper stage, splendid backstage and technical facilities, an ultra-modern Chamber Theatre seating 500, and a golden, glittering auditorium. František Vojna is head of opera, Zdeněk Košler the principal conductor.

Národní Divadlo, Ostrovní St., Praha 1
☎ 02-21 44 111   [TX] 122 556 ND
♬ Sep – Jun   [B] Dept. of Commerce, Národní Divadlo, P.O. Box 865, Praha 1
☎ 02-20 31 28   [TX] as above   [CC] None
♿ Special box   ⬚ 986   ♀ Theatre restaurant ☎ 02-20 63 81. Bars
[PT] Underground – line B. Tram – 6, 9, 21, 22, 17, 18   ℗ At theatre.

ICELAND OPERA

Iceland Opera is an example of what a nation of not much more than 200,000 people can achieve. Regular professional opera in Iceland dates from the foundation of the 661-seat National Theatre at Reykjavík in 1950: it is legally required to stage at least one opera a year. Its major shortcoming is a pit limited to 40 players.

Iceland Opera was formed in 1979, with the tenor Gardar Cortes as its director. It opened that autumn with *Pagliacci*. A sizeable bequest a year later from Sigurlidi Kristjánsson, a partner in a grocery chain, enabled the company to purchase the Gamla Bíó, a cinema built in the 1920s. It is a short distance from the National Theatre, in the centre of the city. Modifications were carried out and new lighting installed, providing a capacity of 505 seats.

The new house opened with Strauss' *Zigeunerbaron* on 9 January 1982 – eight days late, because the Austrian producer imported for the occasion had to be asked to leave prematurely. Despite this apparent setback, the production then ran for 49 sold-out performances.

Encouraged by the new company's triumphant start, the National Theatre replied the same June with perhaps the greatest operatic success by a native composer, Atli Heimir Sveinsson's *Silkitromman* (*The Silken Drum*). Based on a 14th-century Japanese Noh play, it was performed as part of the seventh Biennial Reykjavík Arts Festival, conducted by the American Gilbert Levine and produced by Sveinn Einarsson, the opera-keen director of the National Theatre.

Iceland Opera, meanwhile, has maintained a schedule of three productions a year and regularly plays to full houses. Apart from Cortes, who remains as director but who makes occasional sorties abroad – for example, to sing Macduff in Opera North's *Macbeth* and *Otello* for Jutland Opera – the tenor Kristján Jóhansson is another Icelander who has recently carved out a career abroad, notably in the United States. He

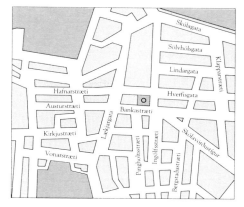

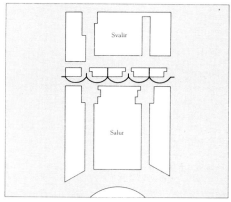

returned to Reykjavík in 1988 to sing the Duke in *Rigoletto*. A considerable proportion of Icelanders sing in choirs, and the opera chorus is known for its high standards. Members of the Iceland Symphony Orchestra, many of whom are imported, provide the accompaniment and all operas are now sung in the original language with Icelandic surtitles.

Gamla Bíó, Ingólfsstraeti, 121 Reykjavik
☎ 91-27033/621077   FX Nearest post office R – 1 91-29323   ♬ Oct – May
B As above   ☎ 91-11475. Discounts for groups of 20 +   CC MC, Visa
♿ Wheelchair space   ☷ 505
♀ Non-alcoholic refreshments
PT Bus – Hafnarstraeti   ℗ Nearby.

TEATRO MUNICIPAL

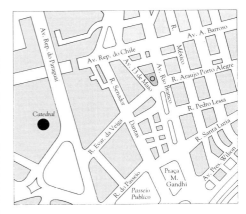

As Brazil's former capital, Rio still holds a prominent place in the country's musical life. Music, opera and ballet are all performed in its Teatro Municipal; the city is frequently included in South American tours by foreign opera companies, orchestras and ensembles.

Opera was first seen in Brazil at the city's Opera Velha, which flourished under Father Ventura in the late 1770s. Before Brazil achieved independence in 1822 the first major stimulus to music in Rio was the transfer there of the Portuguese royal court in 1808.

It was Manuel da Silva, composer of the Brazilian national anthem, who first encouraged the use of the vernacular in opera. The Imperial Academy of Music and National Opera was founded in 1847 to further the cause. Its most successful graduate was Carlos Gomes, who achieved extraordinary fame in Europe with his opera *Il Guarany*, first performed at La Scala in 1870. Rio secured a certain retrospective glory when a talented, but obscure, cellist touring in 1886 with an Italian company, became stand-in conductor for *Aida* at the Teatro Lirico – which he did from memory. This was the operatic debut of Toscanini.

The remodelling of the city, begun under President Rodrigues Alves, inspired a start to be made on a new opera house in 1905: the Teatro Municipal was eventually inaugurated in 1909. Since then it has attracted a steady stream of international stars.

The theatre was extensively redesigned in 1934, and further modifications were carried out between 1976 and 1978. The theatre is again being renovated in celebration of its eightieth anniversary.

In recent years the company's operatic enterprises have been somewhat erratic, partly due to unpredictable funding. There have been occasional glimpses of native opera: Villa-Lobos' tragedy based upon Lorca's play *Yerma*, first performed in Santa Fe in 1971, had its Brazilian premiere in 1983; *Il Guarany* was revived in 1986.

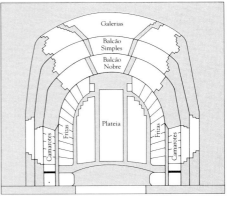

The 100-member Orquestra Sinfônica do Teatro Municipal was founded in 1934: its chief conductor is Mario Tavares. The theatre also has a 120-voice chorus and a full-size ballet company. A new regime under Luis Paolo Sampaio, appointed opera co-ordinator in 1988, promises a return to high standards.

Av Rio Branco, 20040 Rio de Janeiro ☎ 021-210 2463 ♫ Mar – Dec Ⓑ As above. Daily 9am – 5pm. Discounts for groups of 30+ CC None & None ⠿ 2357 ☻ Café do Teatro ☎ 021-262 3935 PT Bus – various (check at hotels for details). Underground – Cinelandia Station Ⓟ In street next to theatre.

TEATRO DELL'OPERA

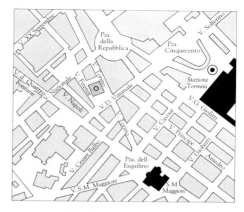

For all its importance as Italy's capital, Rome has never had an opera house to rival Milan or Venice. But it certainly has a proud operatic history. Its first public theatre, the Teatro Tordinona, opened in 1670 with Cavalli's *Scipione Affricano* and, after a turbulent history it was demolished in 1889.

Rome's other major operatic site was the Teatro Argentina. Built by the Duke Giuseppe Sforza-Cesarini in 1732, it mainly deserves to be remembered for staging the premiere of Rossini's *Almaviva*, later to become known as *Il Barbiere di Siviglia*, in 1816. The work received a rude reception. The theatre is still used occasionally for concerts.

With two of the city's three main theatres out of operatic action by the late 1870s, a wealthy builder, Domenico Costanzi, opened the Teatro Costanzi, still incomplete, in 1880 with Rossini's *Semiramide*. The management of the Costanzi was taken over in 1888 by the Milanese music publisher Edoardo Sonzogno. He organized two competitions for composers which produced a winner in Mascagni's *Cavalleria Rusticana*, premiered in 1890. The theatre's greatest occasion was undoubtedly 14 January 1900, the world premiere of *Tosca*: it consolidated the Costanzi's reputation as the unofficial headquarters of the *verismo* movement in opera, already moving away from 'slice of life' realism.

The theatre was taken over by the city authorities in 1926. Renovated and modernized it was reopened in 1928 as the Teatro Reale dell'Opera with Boito's *Nerone*. In 1946 it became known as the Teatro dell'Opera. Its positive attitude to contemporary opera continued, with the Italian premieres of Britten's *The Rape of Lucretia* (1949) and Hindemith's *Mathis der Maler* (1951).

The 1988/89 season, with Alberto Antignani as *sovrintendente* and Bruno Cagli as artistic director, revealed continuing enterprise: new productions of Donizetti's *Poliuto*, Cimarosa's *Gli Orazi ed i Curiazi* and

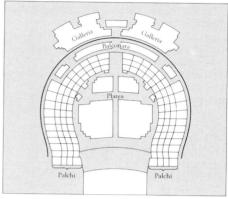

Rossini's *Zelmira* – hardly mainstream repertory – together with the world premiere of Lorenzo Ferrero's *Charlotte Corday*, written to commemorate the bicentenary of the French Revolution. The summer season at the Baths of Caracalla is organized by the Teatro dell'Opera.

Piazza Beniamino Gigli 1, 00184 Roma
☎ 06-46 36 41   TX 626402 EATO
FX 06-46 12 53   ♫ Nov – Jun   B As above   ☎ 06-46 17 55 Tues – Sat 10am – 1pm, 5 – 7pm and until beginning of perf., Sun. 10am – 1pm. Groups ☎ 06-46 17 55   CC None   & None
⫴ 1600   ♟ 3 Bars   PT Bus – 64, 70, 65, 62, 492. Underground – Repubblica
Ⓟ Opposite entrance.

OPERA THEATER OF ST LOUIS

In a country where opera has always tended towards the grand, the Opera Theater of St Louis has carved a distinctive niche for itself. Smaller scale productions employing younger, mainly American, singers have characterized a company which emphasizes the theatrical in its relatively confined arena. In its wooded setting eight miles (13 kilometres) out of town, the Loretto-Hilton Theater of Webster College encourages rapport between cast and audience, both during the performance as well as on the lawns outside. Furthermore, the unusual and the contemporary in the company's programming are a natural concomitant of the enterprising attitudes of the St Louis Symphony Orchestra, America's second oldest orchestra.

St Louis' early operatic history is fairly typical of American cities of its size (population about a half million). A local company gave its first grand opera, Auber's *La Muette de Portici*, in 1830. A huge variety of touring companies appeared throughout the 19th century, culminating in 1884 with the Metropolitan Opera, whose visits continued until 1966.

A significant landmark was the huge Pageant and Masque of St Louis, staged in 1914 to mark the city's 150th anniversary. A cast of 7000 performed in Forest Park before an audience of 500,000. The enthusiasm it generated led to the formation of the St Louis Municipal Opera Association, which has presented summer seasons of musicals, operettas and, occasionally, operas since 1919, when the huge (capacity 11,475) Municipal Opera Theater was opened.

The current era began in 1976 with the foundation of the Opera Theater of St Louis by the English-born Richard Gaddes. He put St Louis on the world map with a production of *Albert Herring* for the WNET and BBC television networks in 1978, and later invited Jonathan Miller to direct a six-year Mozart cycle. Colin Graham, the artistic director from 1986, produced the American premiere of Rossini's *Il Viaggio a Reims*, and

followed up equally successfully with Stephen Oliver's *Beauty and the Beast* in 1987, also an American first.

Loretto-Hilton Center, 130 Edgar Rd., St Louis, MO 63119 ☎ 314-961 0170 [FX] 314-961 7463 ♫ May – Jun [B] P.O. Box 13148, St Louis, MO 63119 ☎ 314-961 0644. 10am–4pm. Special group arrangements [CC] Amex, MC, Visa ♿ Reserved parking, seating, hearing aids, restrooms ⚏ 954 ♟ Picnics – Mon – Sat 6 – 7.15pm, Sun 5 – 6.15pm ☎ 314-961 0644, bar [PT] Taxi only Ⓟ Nearby.

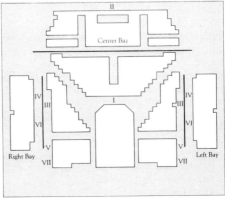

GROSSES FESTSPIELHAUS

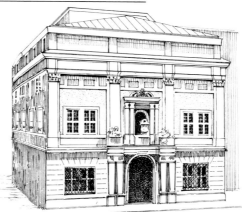

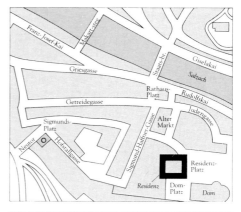

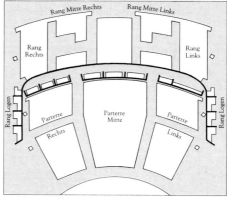

As the birthplace of Mozart, Salzburg is an obvious candidate for a musical pantheon. Since 1922 it has been the scene of one of the world's great festivals, while also providing the summer home of the Vienna State Opera.

An Italian 'Hoftragicomedia', staged in the archbishop's residence on 10 February 1614 by Francesco Rasi, one of the Florentine *camerate*, was probably the first opera performance anywhere outside Italy. A year later the Archbishop, Marcus Sitticus, created the outdoor Steintheater at nearby Hellbrunn, the oldest surviving garden theatre in the German-speaking world. Georg Muffat's *Le Fatali Felicità di Plutone* (1687) and Heinrich Biber's *Alessandro in Pietra* (1689) were typical of the two composers central to musical developments in Salzburg in the late 17th century.

Antonio Caldara staged a good 20 of his operas in Salzburg (1716–27), including *Dafne* which opened the Heckentheater in the gardens of the Schloss Mirabell in 1719. It was here that the 13-year-old Mozart's *La Finta Semplice* was produced in 1767, followed by *Il Sogno di Scipione* (1772) and *Il Rè Pastore* (1775). Mozart was appointed honorary *Konzertmeister* to the archbishop's court (1769–77). After a stagnant start to the 19th century, Franz von Hilleprandt founded the Dommusikverein und Mozarteum in 1841, to promote all branches of music. As the Mozarteum, it later became a renowned public music school with an 807-seat Grosses Saal.

Under the auspices of the International Mozart Foundation, begun in 1870 by Karl von Sterneck, Salzburg's first music festival was held in 1877, with the Vienna Philharmonic Orchestra playing outside the capital for the first time. After a further seven festivals – Mahler conducted *Figaro* in 1910 – the Salzburger Festspielhaus-Gemeinde was founded in 1917 to establish an annual festival devoted to drama and Mozart. It began in 1920, with the first operas – *Giovanni, Così, Figaro* and *Seraglio* – performed in 1922 at the Stadttheater (built in 1893, now the 724-seat Landestheater) conducted by Richard Strauss and Franz Schalk.

The first Festspielhaus, originally designed by Eduard Hütter, but remodelled by Clemens Holzmeister with Anton Faistauer's famous foyer frescoes, was officially opened in 1926: its first opera was *Fidelio* with Lotte Lehmann, conducted by Schalk in August 1927. Its auditorium was turned 180 degrees in 1937 and a new fly-tower built, while in 1962–63 it was completely redesigned by Erich Engels and Hans Hofmann to improve acoustics and sightlines. Now wood panelled, it is known as the Kleines Festspielhaus, seating 1323 (plus standing-room for 60) on two levels divided by 16 open boxes. It is used for drama and small-scale opera.

The old open-air Felsenreitschule (Summer Riding School) which had been hewn out of the Mönchsberg rock in accordance with plans drawn up by Johann von Erlach in 1693, was used as a drama venue from 1926 onwards. When Herbert von Karajan realized that its excellent acoustics made it appropriate for opera, he conducted Gluck's *Orfeo* there in 1948. Since then, and with the

addition of an extendible waterproof awning, a lighting bridge and a lower stage area in 1969, it has proved a popular operatic auditorium. Indeed, it more nearly captures the Salzburg spirit than any other arena. It seats 1549.

The appointment of Salzburg-born Karajan, who had first conducted at the festival in 1933, as artistic director (1957–60) coincided with a period of astounding growth in popularity. Work was begun in 1956 to remove a great quantity of rock from the Mönchsberg to accommodate the high fly-tower of a new Grosses Festspielhaus designed by Holzmeister. It opened on 26 July 1960 with Karajan conducting *Rosenkavalier*.

The stage is one of the largest in the world. The proscenium width can be adjusted up to 34 yards (32 metres). The orchestra pit, which holds 120, can be raised to form an apron stage in front of the so-called 'iron curtain', which weighs 37 tons (38 tonnes). The auditorium has superb acoustics. This is the festival's main operatic arena, also used by orchestras and *Lieder* recitalists.

Karajan initiated the Salzburg Easter Festival in 1967, which runs from Palm Sunday to Easter Monday and which includes an opera, often by Wagner. He had resumed his position (1964) as artistic director of the summer festival, but his death in 1989 left a question mark over Salzburg's future direction. At the moment Mozart is pre-eminent, followed by Richard Strauss, whose *Liebe der Danae* (1952) was a notable Salzburg premiere. Other European opera and drama, together with baroque opera and contemporary works, complete the Salzburg menu.

A–5020 Hofstallgasse 1, Salzburg
☎ 0662-842 5 41   TX 633880   FX 0662-842 541 401   ♫ Jul – Aug   B As above
CC None   ♿ Wheelchair space. Apply to box office for tickets   ⚱ 2177   ♥ Bar
PT Bus – 1, 2, 15, 29   ℗ Nearby.

SAN DIEGO OPERA

San Diego had to subsist on a diet of touring companies until after World War I. The city's Civic Grand Opera mounted some 40 productions of French and Italian repertory between 1919 and 1932. When this enterprise foundered there was a long hiatus until the foundation in 1950 of the San Diego Opera Guild, a group of volunteers dedicated to presenting visiting companies. San Francisco Opera accepted this challenge with three productions each year until 1962. In May 1965, with the completion of the New Civic Theatre, SDO became a company in its own right, opening with a production of *La Bohème* under Walter Herbert's direction. Operas were invariably sung in English during his regime, mainly standard repertory. He also presented the first American performance of Henze's *The Young Lord* (1967) and the world premiere of Alva Henderson's *Medea* (1972).

Upon Herbert's death in 1975 the mantle passed to Tito Capobianco, who became general director in 1977, retaining that position until 1983. His reign was notably adventurous. He ran six Verdi summer festivals between 1978 and 1984, emphasizing lesser-known early works such as *Un Giorno di Regno* and *Giovanna d'Arco*.

Capobianco resigned at the end of the 1983 season. He was succeeded by an Australian, Ian D. Campbell, who had previously been assistant artistic administrator at the Met. Campbell has overseen a return to more popular programming as an antidote to his predecessor, who had lost the support of too many subscribers. Apart from the US professional premiere of Verdi's *Oberto* in 1985, his has been a cautious administration. Financial consolidation has become the name of the game: the season is concentrated into the first four months of the year, and the annual budget now approaches $4 million, which puts the company in the American 'top ten'.

Superstars are rarely seen, their places taken by up-and-coming American talent.

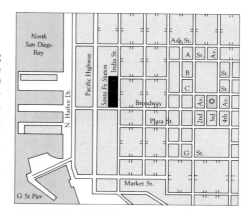

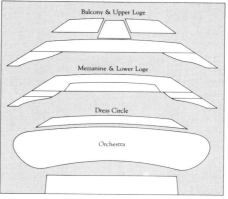

The Peking Opera appeared there in January 1989. Subscribers now account for more than 70 per cent of all tickets sold. The signs look good for a complete recovery of the company's former fortunes.

Civic Theatre, 202 'C' St., San Diego, CA 92101 ☎ 619-232 7636
FX 619-231 6915 ♫ Jan – Apr
B Center Box Office, 202 'C' St. MS–57, San Diego, CA 92101 ☎ 619-236 6510.
Mon – Fri 9am–5pm. Discounts for groups of 15+ ☎ 619-232 7636 CC MC, Visa ♿ Wheelchair space, hearing aids
⠿ 2992 and 84 standing ♨ Bar
PT Train – Kettner Bd station. Bus – 2nd Av. and Broadway ☎ 619-233 3004
Ⓟ At theatre.

SAN FRANCISCO OPERA

The Gold Rush of 1848 lured German and Italian refugees from European revolutions to the promised land of America's West Coast. Yearning for their native music, these adventurers idolized singers such as soprano Elisa Biscaccianti and the Irish mezzo Catherine Hayes, who duly amassed fortunes.

San Francisco heard its first full-length opera in 1851, when the Pellegrini troupe performed *La Sonnambula* at the Adelphi Theater. This sparked a craze for opera which burgeoned further upon the completion of the transcontinental railway in 1869. Between 1851 and the earthquake of 1906, touring companies flocked to the city. The largest theatre was Wade's Opera

House, built in 1876. It was later expanded, as the Grand Opera House, from 2500 to 4000 seats, to become the second largest in the USA. The Metropolitan Opera appeared there from 1890, and gave San Francisco its first *Ring* cycle in 1900. A mere two days into its 1906 season – only a few hours after Caruso had appeared in *Carmen* on 17 April 1906 – the catastrophic earthquake struck. The golden era had come to an abrupt end.

Opera was slow to re-establish itself after such widespread destruction. A handful of touring companies continued to appear, led in 1909 by W.A. Edwards' International Grand Opera Company, whose conductor was Gaetano Merola. He, encouraged by the

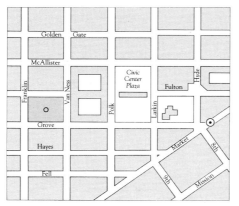

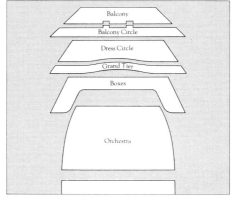

fund-raising efforts of the Italian community, staged three operas in Stanford University's football stadium in 1922.

Merola's success led to his founding the San Francisco Opera in the following year. His aim was a short autumn season of established Italian, French and German repertory, with singers from the Met, before the New York season opened. The International Exposition of 1915 had seen the construction of a 12,000-seat auditorium on the site of the present Civic Center. Renamed the Civic Auditorium, it was used for all SFO's productions until 1932. Merola was reasonably adventurous in those early years, introducing a few rarities such as the American premiere of Ravel's *L'Enfant et les Sortilèges* (1930). Thereafter, it was for its high musical standards in mainstream works that the company established its expanding reputation. He masterminded the move to The War Memorial Opera House, where it opened with *Tosca* in October 1932.

Merola confined his season to the autumn, partly for fear of losing his audience if New York stars could not be found for principal roles, and partly in order not to clash with the San Francisco Symphony Orchestra whose players he invariably used. To this day, no symphony concerts are performed during the opera season. In 1943, Merola appointed Viennese-born Kurt Herbert Adler as his chorus master, later to be his right-hand man. Upon Merola's death in 1953, Adler duly succeeded him as general manager and promptly ushered in a more expansive, adventurous era. As a result, the season now begins on the Friday after Labor Day (the first Monday in September), involving ten productions over a 12-week period. There is also a free 'Opera in the Park' concert two nights later in the Music Concourse of Golden Gate Park, a popular annual event.

Adler's choice of repertoire was wide-ranging and he was responsible for the American premieres of several major works. He lessened the company's dependence upon stars from the Met by engaging international singers before they appeared in New York, cut down its travel commitments, introduced new staging techniques (notably through the producer Jean-Pierre Ponnelle), widened the repertoire, and set up new organizations to train young singers. Schwarzkopf, Geraint Evans, Te Kanawa, Nilsson and Rysanek all made their US debuts in San Francisco, where also Sutherland sang her first Mary Stuart and Jess Thomas his first Tristan. The company became known as 'Covent Garden West'. Adler was succeeded in 1982 by the Canadian Terence McEwen, who trimmed some of Adler's more expensive projects, concentrating them in the new San Francisco Opera Center. He turned the sizeable deficit, which he had inherited, into a surplus by dropping the summer season, despite the success of a new *Ring* cycle introduced in 1985 and announced for revival in the summer of 1990. Ill-health forced his early retirement in 1988, when he was succeeded by Iranian-born Lotfi Mansouri, who previously had been general director of the Canadian Opera Company.

Western Opera Theater takes full-length productions in English to communities not normally exposed to opera. In March 1987 it became the first American opera company to tour mainland China. Brown Bag Opera provides live operatic entertainment in everyday locations. Festivals devoted to Mozart and Rossini are planned by SFO for the summers of 1991 and 1992, respectively.

War Memorial Opera House, 301 Van Ness Av, San Francisco, CA 94102
☎ 415-861 4008　[TX] 34459 SF OPERA SFO　[FX] 415-621 7508　♬ Sep – Dec
[B] As above ☎ 415-864 3330. Mon – Sat 10am–6pm. Discounts for groups of 20 +
☎ 415-861 4008 x440　[CC] Emporium/ Capwell, MC, Visa　& Wheelchair space, hearing aids　☎ 415-861 4008 x125
⁙ 3176 and 300 standing　♟ Restaurant, bars ☎ 415-864 1958　[PT] Train – BART to Civic Center. Bus – stop outside. Underground – MUNI to Van Ness Station　Ⓟ Nearby at Civic Center Garage and at Performing Arts Garage.

SANTA FE OPERA

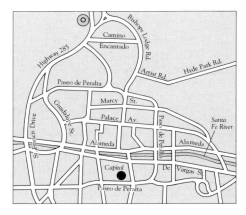

Santa Fe, state capital of New Mexico, has a population of only 50,000, but its opera company's reputation far exceeds what might be expected from a city of that size – and deservedly so. The Opera Association of New Mexico, which later became the Santa Fe Opera, was founded as recently as 1956 by John O. Crosby, who continues to be its general director. From his first season, which opened in July 1957, Crosby underlined his commitment to the 20th century by including Stravinsky's *The Rake's Progress*, in a production personally supervised by the composer, and the world premiere of Marvin David Levy's *The Tower*. Such imaginative programming has continued to this day, helped by a budget of $6 million, which puts Santa Fe among the top ten American opera companies.

For a decade the company operated at an open-air theatre which burned down during the night of 26 July 1967, a few hours after the American premiere of Hindemith's *Cardillac*. A year later a new 1773-seat theatre opened on the original site. This open-air amphitheatre sits on a hillside seven miles (11 kilometres) north of the city centre. Situated some 9000 feet (2700 metres) above sea level, it commands a panoramic view of the foothills of the Sangre de Cristo Mountains. Stage and pit are covered, but the bowl is partly open to the skies, sometimes falling prey to the weather. Equally it is magical under a starlit sky.

Crosby's enterprise has embraced six world and 30 American premieres, among them five works by Richard Strauss, for whom Santa Fe is renowned, a further five by Henze, *Lulu* in both the two-act and three-act versions (1963 and 1979), Schoenberg's *Die Jakobsleiter* (1968) and Britten's *Owen Wingrave* (1973). The first American performance of Penderecki's *The Black Mask* was given there in 1988 and that of Judith Weir's *A Night at the Chinese Opera* in 1989. From an initial company of 67, SFO numbered nearly 500 by the 1989

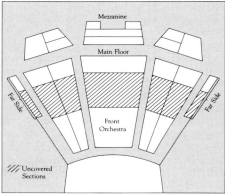

season. Its orchestra comprises 90 players drawn from major American orchestras, and a number of its singers have been nurtured through its own Apprentice Artist Program. John Crosby continues to fulfil a unique triple role as conductor, impresario and administrator.

Santa Fe Opera Theater, Highway 84-285 (7 miles nth of S.F), NM ☎ 505-982 3851 FX 505-989 7012 ♫ Jun – Aug B P.O. Box 2408, Santa Fe, NM 7504 ☎ 505-982 3855. Mon – Sat 10am – 4pm. For groups contact box office CC Amex, MC, Visa ♿ Access available ⚏ 1773 and 200 standing ♨ Pre-opera buffets ☎ 505-982 3855 PT Shuttle service ☎ 1-800-452 2665 Ⓟ In grounds.

TEATRO MUNICIPAL

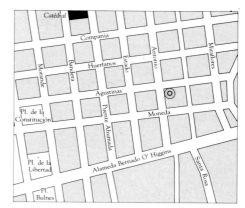

Santiago is the fulcrum of Chilean musical life and the Teatro Municipal its unofficial headquarters. Even before an independent constitution was framed in Chile in 1830, opera had been extremely popular. That year the first full-length production was presented, Rossini's *L'Inganno Felice*.

In 1853 opera moved to the Teatro de la Républica. In 1857 the new Teatro Municipal was inaugurated with a performance by an Italian company of Verdi's *Ernani*.

Tragedy struck on the night of 8 December 1870 when, immediately after a recital by Patti, the theatre was destroyed by fire. Reconstruction began almost immediately. Built to the same plans, the new Teatro Municipal was opened in July 1873 with a performance of *La Forza del Destino*. The repertory now began to broaden out from its Italian origins, and embraced Gounod, Halévy, Massenet and Bizet, together with the Spanish *zarzuela*. The first Mozart, *Don Giovanni*, was heard there in 1870; Wagner for the first time in 1889, with *Lohengrin*. It was not until 1895 that the first opera by a native composer was staged in Chile, *La Florista de Lugano* by Eleodoro Ortiz de Zárate, although his *Juana la Loca* had received its premiere at La Scala three years earlier.

The house continued to rely upon touring companies until well into the 20th century. The breakthrough came in 1955 when two resident ensembles were established at the Municipal: the Orquesta Filarmónica (Santiago Philharmonic) founded with a playing staff of 100 by Juan Matteucci, who remained its permanent conductor until 1963; and the Ballet Municipal, now the resident Ballet de Santiago, which undertakes regular tours.

Over the past decade the number of annual productions has been reduced from six to five, which has not allowed much room for manoeuvre outside the standard repertory. A sprinkling of international stars is invited each year: Carlo Cossutta sang

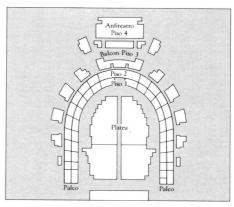

Otello in 1982, Renata Scotto played Butterfly in 1985 and Mimi a year later, while Rosalind Plowright sang Norma in 1987. Young Chilean singers often take over for the final night of a run. The posts of artistic and general director are combined in Andres Rodriguez; the musical director is Roberto Abbado.

San Antonio 149, Santiago Centro
☎ 02-712 900/335 689   TX 440407
TEMUN   FX 02-332 160   ♬ May – Nov
Ⓑ San Antonio 191, Santiago
☎ 02-330 752. For group discounts contact the Sales Manager at the theatre   CC Diners, MC, Visa   ♿ Ramp access   ∷ 1200
♀ Non-alcoholic bar   PT Underground – Santa Lucia Ⓟ Nearby.

SEATTLE OPERA

The Century 21 World's Fair of 1962 may fairly be said to have thrust Seattle on to the world map. It also provided a new artistic impetus: the Civic Auditorium was refurbished and inevitably became the home of the Seattle Opera Association. This was founded in 1963 and the following spring opened to the public with two performances each of *Tosca* and *Carmen*. The Civic Auditorium is now known as the Opera House.

The presiding genius of Seattle Opera's first two decades was general director Glynn Ross, whose career began in 1945 with two years as stage director at the Teatro San Carlo, Naples: he became the first American to direct in a major Italian opera house. A mere three years after the start of the Seattle Opera, Ross guided it into a season of five productions which earned the highest per capita opera attendance of any city in the USA. A star system was the main attraction: Sutherland sang the title role in Delibes' *Lakmé* for the first time there in 1967. There were notable world premieres, too: Carlisle Floyd's *Of Mice and Men*, after Steinbeck's novel, was staged in 1970 and Thomas Pasatieri's *Black Widow* in 1972.

The decisive initiative came in the summer of 1975 with SO's production of the *Ring* cycle, directed by the Montreal-born bass-baritone George London. Under the banner of the Pacific Northwest Wagner Festival, this became an annual celebration with the cycles performed in both German and English.

Glynn Ross was succeeded in 1983 by Speight Jenkins, who was responsible for a controversial new production of the *Ring* in 1986, sung in German with surtitles. In 1988 this was displaced by *Satyagraha*, an opera about Mahatma Gandhi by Philip Glass, although there was a return to Wagner in 1989 with a new François Rochaix production of *Meistersinger*. An exchange production of *War and Peace* with the Soviet Union in 1990 makes the summer of 1991 the target for the next *Ring*. The Jenkins regime is

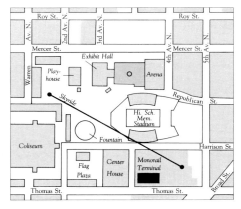

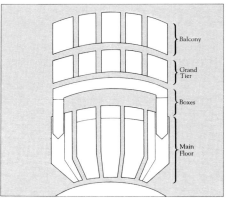

slightly more conservative than its predecessor, but superstars and premieres have given way to productions – 15 new ones in his first four years alone – which are more theatrically unified and, ultimately, more satisfying.

Opera House, 225 Mercer St., Seattle, WA 98109 ☎ 206-443 4700 TX 160595 SEOPRA FX 206-443 2533 ♫ Sep – May B P.O. Box 9248, Seattle, WA 98109 ☎ 206-443 4711. Mon – Fri 9am – 5pm CC MC, Visa & Hearing aids ⋯ 3017 ⚲ In Seattle Center, special dinners, ☎ 206-345 4081 PT Seattle Center Monorail Ⓟ In Center and opposite on Mercer St.

OPERA NATIONAL DE SOFIA

In 1890, the pianist and composer Angel Bukureshtliev founded the Stolichnata Dramatichna Opera Trupa (Capital Dramatic Opera Company), which gave several performances of excerpts from *Trovatore* and *The Merry Wives of Windsor* a year later. The opening of the country's first music school (later the State Music Academy) in 1904 helped to provide singers to form the new Operna Druzhba (Opera Association) in 1908. Its guiding spirit was the Russian-trained tenor Konstantin Mikhaylov-Stoyan, who had been a soloist at the Bolshoi through the 1890s. He staged the first opera performed in Bulgarian, *Pagliacci*, at the Naroden Teatar (National Theatre) in 1909.

The first Bulgarian opera was Emanuil Manolov's unfinished *Siromakhkinya* (*The Poor Woman*). Completed by others, it was produced in Sofia in 1910. The company's chief composer was Georgi Athanassov, a pupil of Mascagni who is considered to be the founder of Bulgarian opera; his works, notably *Borislav*, are still highly regarded.

The Opera Association became the present Sofiyska Narodna Opera (Sofia National Opera) in 1921 and received its first state subsidy a year later. Under Moysey Zlatin, it now became a fully fledged professional ensemble. The National Theatre was destroyed during the war and a monumental replacement erected. Since then a succession of eminent singers has emerged, notably basses: Boris Christoff, in many ways Chaliapin's successor, Nikolai Ghiaurov, who made his debut in Sofia as Basilio in *Barbiere* (1955), and Nikola Gyuzelev, whose debut was as Timur in *Turandot* (1960). The sopranos Raina Kabaivanska (debut 1957) and Anna Tomowa-Sintow (1965) also have international reputations.

Sofia National Opera is the most important of five national companies in Bulgaria. Its total staff of 850 includes two orchestras, the 96-member National Opera Choir, 80 soloists, and a ballet company of more than 100 dancers. The choir, which since 1966 has given more than 60 tours throughout Europe, has been directed for the last three decades by Lyubomir Karoleev: it is undoubtedly the jewel in Sofia's operatic crown. The company's general director is Svetozar Donev.

National Theatre, Bd. Dondukov 58, Sofia–1000 ☎ 02-87 70 11/87 70 12/ 87 70 13 TX 23198SNO ♬ Sep - Jul
B As above. For groups ☎ 02-88 16 58
CC None ♿ None ⛲ 1200
♀ None PT Tram – 3, 4. Trolley bus – 9
Ⓟ Difficult.

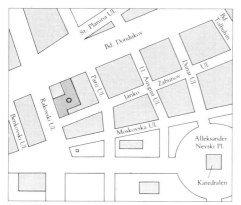

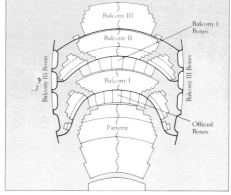

ROYAL OPERA

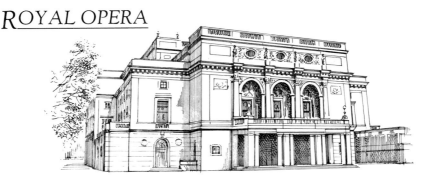

The autocratic reign of King Gustaf III (1771–92) was one of enormous revival for Swedish opera. He dismissed the French company resident in Stockholm and created the Royal Opera, by converting the old Bollhuset (the 'ball house', where real tennis had been played) on the hill by the Royal Castle. It opened in January 1773 with the first opera written in Swedish, *Thetis och Pelée* (*Thetis and Pelée*) by the Italian born Francesco Uttini (who continued as chief conductor until 1788). Such was the confidence of the times that the work was parodied in *Petis och Thelée* (*Petis and Thelée*) (1779) by the tenor Carl Stenborg, who had sung Peleus in Uttini's original production.

In 1782 the company moved to a theatre designed by Carl Fredrik Adelcrantz. The New Opera House opened in September of that year with J.G. Naumann's *Cora och Alonzo* (*Cora and Alonzo*), whose melodies are still popular. One of its greatest successes was Naumann's *Gustaf Wasa* (1786), a lyric tragedy based upon a play by the King. The theatre was also used for concerts and masked balls, one of which in March 1792 was the scene of the King's assassination, later to be immortalized in Verdi's *Un Ballo in Maschera*. Göran Gentele's controversial 1958 Stockholm production of the work, which has since been revived, was thought a particularly accurate re-enactment of the original tragedy.

Opera continued at a variety of venues in Stockholm throughout the 19th century. It produced several eminent singers, among them the 'Swedish nightingale', Jenny Lind, who trained at the Royal Opera School in Sweden before making her formal debut as Agathe in *Der Freischütz* (1838). She had,

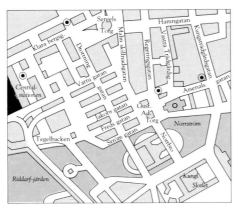

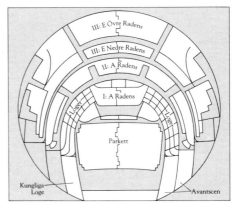

however, made her true singing debut three years earlier in Adolf Lindblad's *Frondörerna* (*The Rebels*) – the only Swedish opera to be successfully staged in the first half of the century. Sweden's most distinguished composer, Franz Berwald, had several of his operas premiered at the Royal Opera, notably *Estrella de Soria* (1862) and *Drottningen av Golconda* (*The Queen of Golconda*, 1864). His cousin, Johan Fredrik Berwald, was chief conductor at the Opera from 1823 until 1849. The most popular Swedish 19th-century opera was Ivar Hallström's *Den Bergtagna* (*The Bride of the Mountain King*, 1874).

The opera house was eventually demolished in 1891, and replaced by the present building on the same site. Designed in neoclassical style by Axel Anderberg, it was inaugurated in 1898 with extracts from *Estrella*— –which was revived there in full in 1946 to celebrate the 150th anniversary of Berwald's birth. The first opera written for the new building was Andreas Hallén's *Waldemarsskatten* (1899), which perfectly fitted the growing Swedish penchant for all things Wagnerian. After Stockholm's first *Ring* cycle in 1907, there were no holds barred. Many Wagnerian singers have graduated from the Royal Opera during the 20th century. Among the most notable have been the sopranos Nanny Larsén-Todsen, Birgit Nilsson and Berit Lindholm, mezzo Kerstin Thorborg, tenors Set Svanholm and Helge Brilioth, and bass- baritone Joel Berglund.

There has been a strong tradition of appointing former singers to the post of director, beginning with baritone John Forsell (1924–39). Berglund (1949–56) and Svanholm (1956–63) were to follow. Perhaps the Royal Opera's most successful producer was Göran Gentele. Between 1952 and 1962 he was responsible for 16 productions, including the famous *Ballo* and Karl-Birger Blomdahl's 'space opera' *Aniara* (1959), which travelled widely including to the Edinburgh Festival (1959) and Montreal's Expo 67. In 1963 Gentele succeeded Svanholm as director, leaving for the Met in 1971.

The same house which had nurtured Björling in the thirties – he had made his debut as the Lamplighter in *Manon Lescaut* there in 1930 – has, since the war, produced others of similar calibre in Söderström (debut 1947), Gedda (1952), mezzo Kerstin Meyer (1952), who now directs the Royal Opera School, and baritones Ingvar Wixell (1955) and Håkan Hagegård (1968). A simultaneous drop-off in company morale and box-office receipts during the mid-1980s seems to have been stemmed by the appointment of Eskil Hemberg as director in 1987. Repertoire is fairly mainstream apart from a consistently supportive policy towards native composers: Hans Gefors scored a notable success in 1986 with an opera based on Sweden's redoubtable Queen Christina.

Officially known as the Royal Theatre (Kungliga Teatern), the opera house contains both a main stage (Stora Scenen) and an annexe, the Rotunda, which was opened in 1964 with Werle's *Drömmen om Thérèse* (*Dream about Thérèse*). It is still used mainly for contemporary chamber opera staged in the round. The Royal Theatre is headquarters for the Royal Orchestra, the country's largest and oldest (founded in the 16th century), which numbers 120 players, though a maximum of 90 can be accommodated in the pit. Sweden's largest full-time choir, the 70-voice Royal Opera Chorus, as well as the Royal Opera Ballet, also the country's largest, are both based there. The Royal Opera is an ensemble company and maintains about 50 resident soloists. The American conductor Gary Berkson is its musical director.

Kungliga Teatern, Gustaf Adolfs Torg, 111 52 Stockholm ☎ 08-22 17 40
♫ Aug – Jun   Ⓑ Jakobs Torg 2, 111 52 Stockholm ☎ 08-24 82 40. Daily 11am – 7.30pm. For groups ☎ 08-23 05 30
Ⓒ None   ♿ Wheelchair space, elevator
⋮⋮⋮ 1090 and 10 restricted view   ♀ Non-alcoholic bar   Ⓟ𝕋 Bus – 62, 55 Gustav Adolfs Torg; 46, 76 Karl XII Torg; 59, 43 Jakobsgatan or Riksdaghuset. Underground – Kungstradgarden
Ⓟ Galleria Garage.

OPERA DU RHIN

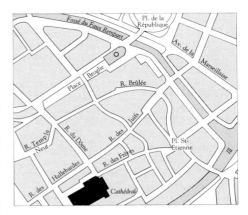

Opéra du Rhin is really three companies in one, covering Colmar and Mulhouse as well as Strasbourg. The first Strasbourg opera house was built in the Place Broglie in 1701. When it burned down in 1799, the church of St-Etienne was converted into a temporary theatre. It was May 1821 before a new opera house was inaugurated on the site of the previous one, with Grétry's *La Fausse Magie*. The theatre was wrecked during the Franco-Prussian War of 1870.

The present Théâtre Municipal was opened in 1873, a graceful auditorium in muted neo-baroque style, its four narrow balconies steeply raked. With Strasbourg now in Prussian hands, the repertory was exclusively German. Otto Lohse was musical director (1897–1904), combining the post with Covent Garden for the last three years. His successor was Hans Pfitzner, who became general director (1910–20) and appointed Klemperer as his deputy (1914–17); he wrote his *Palestrina* there, although it was premiered in Munich (1917).

The city reverted to French control in 1919 and under Paul Bastide the company quickly reinstated the staples of French repertory. Hans Rosbaud took over during World War II (1941–44), but Bastide returned in 1945. With government subsidies falling short of provincial needs, the three cities joined operatic forces in 1972.

The company maintains a chorus of 42 and Le Ballet du Rhin with 36 dancers. It also has first call on two orchestras: the 108-member Orchestre Philharmonique de Strasbourg under Theodor Guschlbauer (who is also musical director of the Opéra), and the 56-member Orchestre Symphonique du Rhin-Mulhouse under Luca Pfaff. The producer René Terrasson has been general director since 1980. Repertory is largely French, but quite adventurous: there was a rare production of Massenet's *Grisélidis* in 1986, while the 1988/89 season included two world premieres, René Koering's *La Marche de Radetsky* and Renaud Gagneux's *Orphée*.

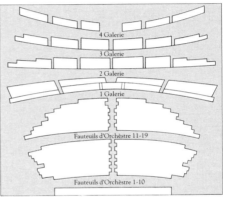

Colmar's Théâtre Municipal opened in 1849; Mulhouse's identically named theatre, where Pons (1928) and Crespin (1950) made their debuts, opened in 1868.

Théâtre Municipal, 10 Pl. Broglie, 67008 Strasbourg ☎ 88-36 71 12 TX 890261 OPERHINO, Théâtre Municipal, 39 rue de la Sinne, 68100 Mulhouse ☎ 89-45 20 24, Théâtre Municipal, rue des Unterlinden, 68000 Colmar ☎ 89-41 29 82 ♩ Oct – Jun B As above CC Amex, MC, Visa, all French CC & ☎ Box office ⌗ Stras-1143,Mul-867,Col-707 ♠ Bar PT Train – Gare Centrale for all theatres. Bus – Stras-Pl. Broglie, Mul-rue de la Sinne, Col-rue des Unterlinden Ⓟ Nearby.

WURTTEMBERGISCHES STAATSTHEATER

A permanent opera company was first established in Stuttgart at the Komödienhaus in 1696. From 1744, the regime of Giuseppe Brescianello (1716–55) was much enhanced by the patronage of Duke Carl Eugen, who opened Stuttgart's new Hoftheater in 1750. Keen to put the city on the musical map, the Duke appointed the prolific Nicolò Jommelli as director of opera and concerts (1753–69). German opera eventually flourished under Johann Zumsteeg (1793–1802), when the city enjoyed its first taste of *Die Zauberflöte* (1795) and *Don Giovanni* (1796). Only a year later Goethe described the operatic poverty which followed the Duke's death.

A revival began under Franz Danzi (1807–12), who encouraged Weber's early operas, notably *Abu Hassan*; Hummel introduced *Fidelio* to the Hoftheater in 1817. Peter Lindpaintner – 'the best conductor in Germany' according to Mendelssohn – injected a new professionalism into the company and wrote several Weberian operas (1819–56). His death brought a long-term decline in Stuttgart's operatic fortunes.

In 1908 the appointment of Max von Schillings rejuvenated opera and led to the opening of the present Grosses und Kleines Haus in September 1912. It had scored an immediate coup: the premiere of *Ariadne auf Naxos* with Maria Jeritza in the title role and Strauss personally conducting. Fritz Busch (1918–22) continued his ambitious approach to repertory with works by Hindemith (two one-act premieres), Pfitzner and Stravinsky; Carl Leonhardt (1922–37) masterminded complete Weber and Wagner cycles.

The theatre reopened after World War II with Germany's first performance of Hindemith's *Mathis der Maler* (1946). Ferdinand Leitner's considerable tenure as music director (1950–69) established Stuttgart's (continuing) reputation for works by Strauss and Wagner: Wieland Wagner produced for him regularly and casts included Anja Silja, Wolfgang Windgassen and Fritz Wunderlich. He also took the company to Edinburgh, Paris and Vienna. The Opera Ballet acquired similar status under John Cranko's direction (1961–73). Now under intendant Wolfram Schwinger (since 1989) and musical director Garcia Navarro (since 1987).

Oberer Schlossgarten 6, 7000 Stuttgart 1
☎ 0711-20320   TX 723 777 STAST
FX 0711-2032 389   ♬ Sep – Jul
B Postfach 104345, 7000 Stuttgart 10
CC None   ⬚ 1400   ♟ Bars
PT Train, bus, underground stations – 3 mins away   Ⓟ Underground parking at the theatre.

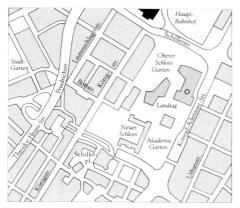

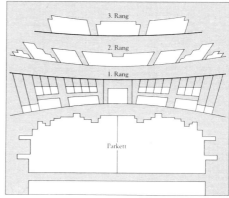

AUSTRALIAN OPERA

In terms of sheer publicity, Sydney Opera House has a worldwide reputation. In fact, its name is misleading. It is a performing arts complex consisting of five arenas, of which the opera theatre is only the second largest. It is spectacularly sited on the Bennelong Point peninsula, close to Sydney Harbour Bridge.

Whatever one's reaction to the building itself, there is no denying that Australia has long been a breeding ground for top-rank singers, from Melba to Sutherland. Australia's early cultural history was powerfully influenced by immigrants from the mother country. The earliest to make a distinctive contribution was the multitalented Isaac Nathan, who wrote two operas, *The Merry Freaks in Troublous Times* (1843) and *Don*

John of Austria, produced at Sydney's Victoria Theatre in 1847. In 1845 an Italian political refugee, Count Carandini, founded a company in which his wife was prima donna, and presented successful performances of several Italian works. An American impresario, William Saurin Lyster, toured a company for two decades until 1880, regularly using local singers. Martin Simonson's company which toured in 1886–87 included several Italian singers whose *bel canto* was to set high standards for budding native talents. Touring companies with international casts regularly gave polyglot performances, with each singer using his or her own language.

Nellie Melba (born Helen Mitchell) made the first of three tours of her homeland in

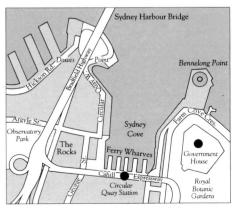

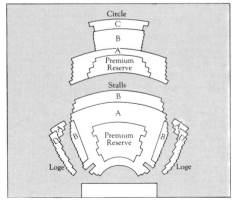

1911, returning in 1924 and again for her farewell appearances in 1928. She died in Sydney in 1931 when nearly 70. Beecham came as conductor of the Quinlan Opera Company in 1912, returning a year later to give the Australian premiere of *Die Meistersinger*. By now a burgeoning musical nationalism encouraged the writing of more native operas, typified by Alfred Hill, who worked mainly in Sydney, and who grafted aboriginal material on to his essentially Romantic style. His *Lady Dolly* (1900), *Teora* (1928) and *The Ship of Heaven* (1933) were all premiered in the city.

It took until after World War II for a resident opera company to emerge in Sydney. In 1952 the New South Wales Opera Company attempted to join forces with Melbourne's National Theatre Opera Company. Developing rivalries were quelled by the Elizabethan Theatre Trust under Hugh Hunt in 1954, who turned the new company into the Australian Opera a year later. It was intended to be a national touring company and opened with a Mozart season in 1956.

1955 was also the year when the Sydney Opera House saga began. At the instigation of Sir Eugene Goossens, the NSW State Government announced an international competition to design the new building, and in January 1957 awarded the prize – on the basis of imaginative but flimsy sketches – to a Dane, Jørn Utzon. Construction began two years later, but the original designs proved impossible to realize.

Utzon redesigned the roof faults with a distinctive spherical geometry which enabled them to be precast. Amid continuing controversy, he resigned in 1966, when Peter Hall took over as architect. The large hall, originally intended for opera, now became the Concert Hall (capacity 2690), while the smaller hall became the Opera Theatre (capacity 1547). Meanwhile, costs soared: the original estimate was A$7 million, the eventual cost A$120 million.

The complex was officially opened by Queen Elizabeth II on 20 October 1973, although the first performance in the Opera Theatre, Prokofiev's *War and Peace* in a production by Sam Wanamaker conducted by Edward Downes, had taken place on 28 September. Downes was the Australian Opera's music director from 1972–76. He was succeeded by Richard Bonynge, whose reign was a mixed blessing. A succession of operas were staged as star vehicles for his wife, Dame Joan Sutherland. It was his shortcomings as a conductor which finally led to disagreements with the administration. This in turn depressed morale, caused desperate financial straits, and an official Australia Council enquiry.

Peter Hemmings survived three years as general manager until 1980, succeeded by Patrick Veitch (formerly of the Met) who lasted until the end of 1986. A planned *Ring* cycle had to be abandoned in midstream and only a government injection of A$2.5 million rescued the company from terminal illness. In 1987 Donald McDonald became general manager, the first native Australian to hold that position, while Bonynge was effectively moved aside into the new post of chief guest conductor. There are now positive signs of recovery and even talk of a new purpose-built theatre more suited to the company's needs. The artistic director is Moffatt Oxenbould.

Sydney Opera House, Bennelong Point, Sydney 2001, NSW ☎ 02-250 7111 TX 25525 AA FX 02-221 8072 ♫ Jan – Mar, Jun – Oct B P.O. Box R239, Royal Exchange, 2000 Sydney, NSW
☎ 02-250 7777. Mon – Sat 9am – 8.30pm, Sun 9am – 4pm. For groups ☎ 02-250 7250 CC Amex, Bankcard, Diners, MC, Visa ﾠ Parking, elevators, wheelchair space, hearing aids, access to Bennelong and Harbour restaurants, telephone, restrooms, guide dogs allowed ☎ 02-250 7185 ⋮⋮⋮ 1547 and 22 standing ♟ Harbour Restaurant ☎ 02-250 7581/7191, Bennelong Restaurant ☎ 02-250 7578/ 7548 PT Train, bus and ferry – Circular Quay terminal. Transport info. ☎ 02-29 2622 Ⓟ Park and Ride service from Domain parking station.

NEW ISRAELI OPERA

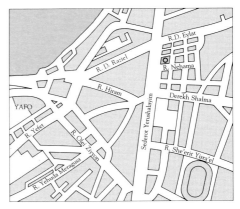

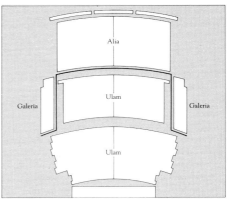

The New Israeli Opera has its roots in pre-Israeli history. The foundation of the Palestine Opera Company in 1923 owed its financial backing to a benefit concert given in Petrograd, now Leningrad, three years earlier by Chaliapin. When its promoter, the conductor Mordecai Golinkin, emigrated to Palestine, he was able to devote the proceeds to a performance of *La Traviata* in a Tel Aviv cinema. He went on to present more than 20 productions in Hebrew until the company was forced to disband in 1927. Undaunted, Golinkin continued to promote opera, founding the Palestine Folk Opera in 1941.

Shortly after her arrival in Palestine in 1945, the soprano Edis de Philippe launched a new initiative. On the very day that the United Nations voted to partition Palestine and create Israel (29 November 1947) she promoted a gala evening of operatic excerpts by her new Hebrew National Opera, whose success prompted a full production of Massenet's *Thaïs* the following year, in which she took the title role. In 1958 the Israel National Opera moved into the former Knesset (parliament) building.

In 1959 a further boost to the operatic scene were the staged performances by the Israel Philharmonic Orchestra under Giulini which began with *Falstaff*. The INO achieved some 43 productions in its first 25 years.

The death of Miss de Philippe in July 1978 ended an era. Alexandru Szinberger, appointed her successor, was unable to maintain standards and the company fell on hard times financially. During a three-year hiatus, the Cologne Opera under Sir John Pritchard began the first of several visits in 1984. Zubin Mehta continued the Giulini/ Israel PO tradition with nine performances of *Butterfly*, introducing Hebrew surtitles. In June 1985 a combination of national and municipal subsidies enabled the formation of the New Israeli Opera.

By 1989 the company was able to schedule four productions, divided between the Noga Hall and the Duhl Auditorium. Visits are also made to Jerusalem and Haifa. Plans have been drawn up for a new Performing Arts Center on the seashore near Tel Aviv, but its completion looks unlikely before the mid-1990s. The company's managing director is Uri Ofer, its musical director Yoav Talmi, and Gary Bertini acts as artistic advisor. The future for opera in Israel looks bright once again.

Noga Hall, 7–9 Jerusalem Bd, Jaffa, Tel Aviv
☎ 03-2622 56 9   TX 371 795 OPA
FX 03-265701   ♫ Feb – Jun
B 1 King David Bd, 64953 Tel Aviv
CC None   占 None   ☲ 830
♟ Restaurant   ☎ 03-812121   PT Bus –
18, 26, 44, Shdepoth Jerusalem
Ⓟ Nearby.

NISSEI THEATRE

There is a great deal of operatic activity in Tokyo, but – strangely for a city of its size and wealth – there is no permanent or dominant company. Performances take place in a variety of theatres, of which the Nissei is the best appointed.

Although Hispanic missionaries introduced European music into Japan in the 16th century, Christianity was banned later and it was only after the Meiji Restoration of 1868 (when Tokyo became the capital) that Western influences began to take hold upon the Japanese imagination. The first opera – extracts from *Faust* – was staged in 1894. Western-style composers were not long in appearing. The Berlin-educated Kosaku Yamada wrote his *Ochitaru Tennyo (The Depraved Heavenly Maiden)* in 1912, although it had to wait until 1929 for its premiere; his *Ayame (The Sweet Flag)* was first staged at the Theatre Pigalle, Paris, two years later.

The first breakthrough occurred in 1933 with the formation of the Fujiwara Opera Company by the tenor Yoshie Fujiwara. The company was responsible for the premiere of Ikuma Dan's *Yuzuru (The Twilight Heron)* in 1952, which has since become the most popular opera by a Japanese composer. The Fujiwara has no permanent base, but frequently performs at the Tokyo Bunka Kaikan (the city's most important concert hall).

The Fujiwara's chief rival is the Niki-Kai Opera Group, a singers' cooperative founded in 1952. It is renowned for its productions of Wagner and has also encompassed Japanese works in recent years.

The Niki-Kai mainly performs in the Nissei Theatre, which opened in 1963 with the Berlin Deutsche Oper production of *Fidelio* under Böhm, which featured Fischer-Dieskau, Christa Ludwig and James King. Designed by Togo Murano, the auditorium has undulating walls faced with glass mosaic and a curved plaster ceiling studded with pearl oyster shells, all in light cobalt blue.

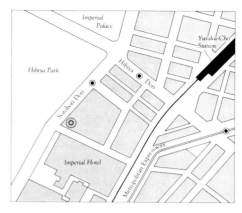

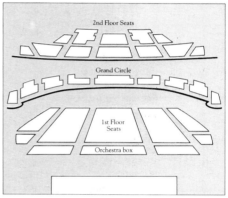

The most important of the remaining ensembles promoting opera has been the Tokyo Chamber Opera Group, founded in 1970, with Hiroshi Wakasugi as one of its guiding lights.

Opera is also staged from time to time in the 4000-seat NHK Broadcasting Corporation Hall, the Shinjuku Bunka Centre and in the new Globe Theatre, opened in 1988.

1–1–1 Yuraku-Cho, Chiyoda-ku, Tokyo
☎ 03-503 3111   [FX] 03-501 6816
♫ Nov [B] As above   [CC] None
♿ None   ⚱ 1238   ♟ Bars, Actress Restaurant ☎ 03-503 3111   [PT] Train– JR Yuraku-Cho Station. Underground – Hibya, Ginzai   ⓟ Nearby.

TEATRO REGIO

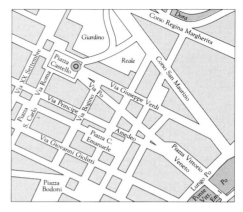

Although Turin has the newest opera house among the front-line companies in Italy, the name Teatro Regio has a distinguished history. Turin was the seat of the dukes of Savoy, when the marriage of Carlo Emanuele I to the Spanish Infanta in 1585 was marked by Giovanni Battista Guarini's famous pastoral *Il Pastor Fido*, which was a forerunner of true opera. A more important determinant of future trends was the marriage of Louis XIII's sister, Marie Christine, to Vittorio Amedeo I in 1619: thereafter French influence was paramount.

In 1727 the 40 members of the Nobile Società dei Cavalieri invited the noted Sicilian architect Filippo Juvarra to draw up plans for an opera house. After his death, these were realized by Benedetto Alfieri: work began in 1738, and on 26 December 1740 the new Teatro Regio was inaugurated with a performance of Francesco Feo's *Arsace*. The theatre's 2500 capacity made it Italy's finest opera house, at least until the opening of La Scala (1778).

The theatre was modified and enlarged in 1838 by Pelagio Palagi. It still, however, took itself very seriously: no *opera buffa* was staged there until *Barbiere* and that only in 1855, nearly 40 years after its premiere.

Puccini's *Manon Lescaut* had its world premiere at the Regio on 1 February 1893, *La Bohème* three years later to the day, this time with Toscanini conducting: he had already consolidated Turin's Wagnerian reputation with the Italian premiere of *Götterdämmerung* in 1895.

After its closure (1901–5) for modernization by Ferdinando Cocito, the Regio became a temple to Wagner and Strauss. An era ended with a *Ring* under Fritz Busch in January 1936: a short circuit caused a fire which destroyed all but the theatre's façade in February.

It was 30 years before architects were appointed to design a replacement. The phoenix duly rose from the ashes and on 10 April 1973 the present theatre was

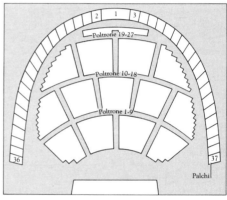

inaugurated with Verdi's *I Vespri Siciliani*, in a collaborative production between Callas (her first) and Di Stefano, with choreography by Serge Lifar. Its sleek modern auditorium consists of one enormous swathe of red seating with a single row of boxes above. The *sovrintendente* is Ezio Zefferi, the artistic director Piero Rattalino.

Pza Castello 215, 10124, Torino
☎ 011-88151 [TX] 220277 REGTOR
[FX] 011-8815214 ♬ Nov–May [B] As above ☎ 011-548 000 Groups contact box office at least 20 days before performance [CC] None ⑁ Limited seating avail. Contact box office
⠿ 1754 ♀ Bar [PT] Transport info. ☎ 011-500 900/591 297 ⑫ Nearby.

CANADIAN OPERA COMPANY

The Canadian Opera Company, based at Toronto's O'Keefe Centre for the Performing Arts, has been the flagship of opera in Canada for nearly 40 years.

A company from Rochester, New York, gave Toronto its first taste of opera in 1825. Jenny Lind appeared there in 1851, but the first grand opera was *Norma*, given at the Royal Lyceum Theatre by the touring Artists' Italian Opera in 1853. The Holman English Opera Troupe, Canada's earliest attempt at a permanent opera company, resided at the Lyceum between 1867 and 1873.

The present company's roots go back to 1946, when the Royal Conservatory of Music set up its own Opera School under Arnold Walter, with Nicholas Goldschmidt as music director. Herman Geiger-Torel joined as stage director two years later. Together they mounted the School's first Opera Festival in February 1950 with *Don Giovanni*, *Rigoletto* and *La Bohème*: such was its success that an Opera Festival Association was formed to sponsor annual presentations and underwrite future festivals. This is generally regarded as the genesis of the Canadian Opera Company.

After 1954 the Opera Festival began to use professional singers in all but minor roles, mounting its own productions under the name Opera Festival Company of Toronto.

Geiger-Torel was promoted to artistic director in 1956 and was the company's inevitable choice as general director in 1959 when it assumed the name Canadian Opera Company.

The COC's first base of operations was the Royal Alexandra Theatre, but since 1960 it has shared the new O'Keefe Centre with the National Ballet of Canada. The O'Keefe has attracted considerable criticism over the years for its unflattering acoustics. Singers are normally discreetly amplified. Plans have recently been announced for a new home for the COC to be completed in the mid-1990s.

Lotfi Mansouri, who became general director in 1977, left at the end of 1988 and was succeeded by Brian Dickie, former general administrator at Glyndebourne.

The O'Keefe Centre, 1 Front St. East, Toronto, Ontario M5E 1B2
☎ 416-363 6671   FX 416-363 5584
♫ Oct–Jun   B 227 Front St. East, Toronto, Ontario M5A 1E8
☎ 416-393 74 69. Discount for groups of 25 +   ☎ 416-363 66 71   CC Amex, MC, Visa   ♿ Special parking and seating
☎ 416-393 7469   ⚏ 3167   ⚲ 2 bars, restaurant ☎ 416-393 7478   PT Train – Union Station 5 mins. Bus – Gardiner and Don Valley Expressways 5 mins   ℗ Front of The O'Keefe Centre.

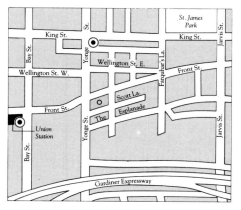

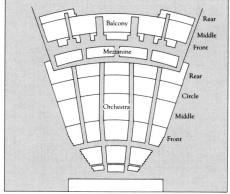

THEATRE DU CAPITOLE

Toulouse has had a theatre as part of its town hall since its 16th-century Logis de l'Ecu. In 1737 a new Salle du Jeu du Spectacle, designed by Guillaume Cammas, was inaugurated for the Capitouls – the 12 town councillors – after whom it was nicknamed, like its predecessor, Théâtre du Capitole. After the Revolution, renamed the Théâtre de la République, it deteriorated irreparably and a replacement was opened on the same site in 1818. Always in financial difficulties, it finally closed its doors in 1878.

Completely redesigned by Dieulafoy and Thillet in neo-baroque style, it reopened in 1880 – the fourth Capitole. This was reduced to a skeleton by fire in August 1917. The fifth Capitole, in Edwardian style by Paul Pujol, opened its doors with Meyerbeer's *Huguenots* in November 1923. Here the company developed a reputation for operetta which remains to this day. But the building was soon considered to be in bad taste and, in 1950, when it came under municipal control, it was again completely remodelled, this time by Roger Brunerie: this sixth Capitole, almost stripped of decoration, opened in November with *Faust*.

All the city's theatrical enterprises were now concentrated under the direction of tenor Louis Izar (1948–67). Inevitably, the restless Toulousains would not endure these spartan surroundings for long. In 1973 the conductor Michel Plasson took over as general director and immediately set about devising a thorough modernization.

Opened in 1975, the present, seventh Capitole offers improved comfort and sight-lines, and has better working conditions backstage. It maintains the same layout as its predecessor of 1818. Its main feature is a spectacular assortment of blown-glass tubes arranged into a crescent-shaped chandelier on the ceiling.

The company's own Orchestre National du Capitole also gives a separate concert series in La Halle aux Grains (Cornmarket). The Opéra includes a ballet group of 40 and a chorus of 45. The season now normally includes six operas and five operettas, mostly French and Italian, as well as four full-length ballets. Most of its productions are shared with other provincial companies, particularly Bordeaux and Marseilles.

Pl. du Capitole, 3100 Toulouse
☎ 061-23 21 35   TX 530891   ♫ Oct –
Jun   B As above   ☎ 061-22 80 22,
Tue – Sat 9am – 12.30pm, 2.30 – 5.45pm.
Discounts for organized groups
CC None   ♿ ☎ 061-23 21 35 × 431
⬝⬝⬝ 1200   ♟ Buffet   PT Special coaches
Ⓟ Next to theatre.

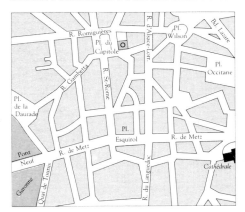

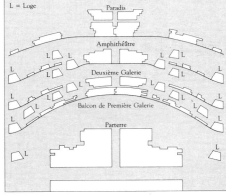

TEATRO COMUNALE GIUSEPPE VERDI

Originally Italian, Trieste, the capital of the Friuli-Venezia Giulia region, was for long ruled by the dukes of Austria. Only in 1954 did it become fully part of Italy, after a United Nations settlement. Trieste's nearest equivalent to an operatic debut was in February 1684, when *La Fidutia in Dio*, by the native-born Pietro Rossetti, was performed with choruses and dances at the end of each act. Hasse's comic intermezzo *La Contadina* was staged in 1721 and Giuseppe Orlandini's *Serpilla e Bacocco* in 1730 on the movable stage of the Palazzo del Comune. In 1751 it became a permanent theatre with 800 seats and in 1760 was officially named the Cesareo Regio Teatro di San Pietro. It closed in 1800.

Trieste was by now ready for something on a grander scale. Antonio Selva, architect of Venice's La Fenice, was commissioned to build what began life as the Teatro Nuovo. It opened in 1801 with Simon Mayr's *Ginevra di Scozia*, specially written for the occasion. It changed its name to Teatro Grande in 1821. The theatre became known as the Comunale in 1861, to which was added Verdi's name in 1901, two days after his death.

The Teatro Verdi became an autonomous company in 1936. With Giuseppe Antonicelli as *sovrintendente*, it opened its account with *Otello* in January 1937. Apart from a six-year break (1945–51) when he conducted at the Met, Antonicelli remained in charge until 1966. The Teatro Verdi has apparently enjoyed more success with out-of-the-way and modern repertory than potboilers, possibly the fruit of composer Raffaelo de Banfield's long sojourn (since 1972) as artistic director. Eastern European works have done especially well: Mussorgsky's *Khovanshchina* (1984), Janáček's *Jenůfa* (1985), Dvořák's *Rusalka* (1986) and Shostakovich's *Ledi Makbet Mtsenskovo uyezda* (*Lady Macbeth of Mtsensk*, 1987) have maintained a consistent standard. The Italian premiere of Kodály's *Háry János* was

staged in 1987 and that of Girolamo Arrigo's *Il Ritorno di Casanova* in 1988. There is also a summer season of operetta (late June – early August). The present musical director is Spiros Argiris.

Pza Verdi 1, 34121 Trieste ☎ 040-62 931 ♫ Dec – May, Jun – Aug Ⓑ As above ☎ 040-36 26 54. Tues – Sun 9am – 1pm, 4 – 7pm. For groups ☎ 040-3626 54 CC None ♿ None ▦ 1235 and 353 standing ⚑ 3 bars PT Train – Stazione Centrale. Bus – 5, 9, 10, 11 Ⓟ Nearby on quaysides or Pza Unita d'Italia.

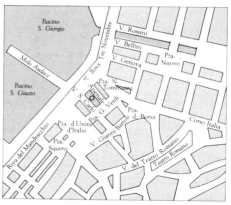

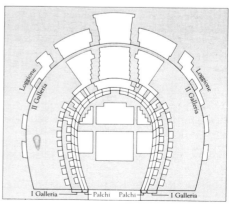

VANCOUVER OPERA

Vancouver Opera Association celebrated its thirtieth anniversary in 1989, but its origins go back a century. The opening of the Canadian Pacific Railway's Vancouver Opera House in 1891, nearly four years after the completion of the transcontinental railway, was the city's splendid initiation into opera. For the then princely sum of $10,000, Emma Juch's Grand Opera Company staged *Lohengrin*. Its sequel took a long time to materialize. Operetta was the staple fare at the Theatre Under the Stars (1940–63), which operated from Stanley Park's Malkin Bowl, a small replica of the Hollywood Bowl.

The real impetus for a resident opera company came from the Vancouver International Festival (1958–68), an annual event which included at least one opera. Among these was the North American premiere of Britten's *A Midsummer Night's Dream* (1961). The Vancouver Opera Association was founded just as its base, the Queen Elizabeth Theatre, was opened by Her Majesty on 15 July 1959. Its first artistic director, Irving Guttman, produced *Carmen* for its debut in April 1960 with Nan Merriman and Richard Cassilly. He was succeeded in 1974 by Richard Bonynge who had made his conducting debut there in 1963. Joan Sutherland, his wife, sang her first Norma there in 1963 and her first Lucrezia Borgia in 1972.

Hamilton McClymont became general manager in 1978, while Anton Guadagno succeeded Bonynge as principal conductor in 1980. A period of financial difficulty was finally overcome in 1984 by the apppointment of Brian McMaster as artistic director. He held the same position simultaneously with the Welsh National Opera until, in 1989, the strain of long-distance commuting became too much. His tenure brought several benefits, notably the sharing of several productions with WNO: Kupfer's *Fidelio*, Giles Havergal's *Barbiere* (which originated in Vancouver) and Pintilie's *Carmen* were outstanding examples. Guus Mostart took over from him in 1989.

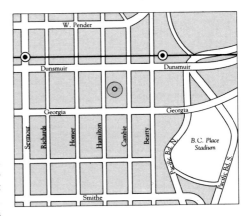

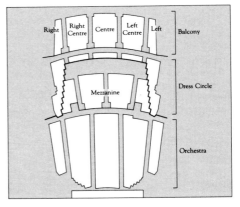

Queen Elizabeth Theatre, 1132 Hamilton St. Vancouver, B.C., V6B 2S2
☎ 604-682 2871   TX 04-352848
FX 604-682 3981   ♬ Oct, Jan, Mar – Apr
B 1304 Horny St., Vancouver, B.C. V6Z 1W6   ☎ 604-280 4444
FX 604-684 0905. Discounts for groups of 10 +   ☎ 604-682 2871   CC Amex, MC, Visa   ⬥ Wheelchair spaces
☎ 604-683 0222 for wheelchair booking
☎ 604-665 3050   ⠿ 2821   ♀ Queen Elizabeth Theatre Restaurant
☎ 604-684 6595   PT Transport info
☎ 604-261 5100, Skytrain – Stadium, Bus – Granville and Georgia or from out of town – Cambie and Dunsmuir
Ⓟ Theatre Parkade 649 Cambie St.

TEATRO LA FENICE

Venice has as glittering an operatic history as any city in the world. Because its constitution under the doges precluded the celebration of royal weddings, that avenue to operatic activity was barred. So it was not until 1630 that the first true opera, Monteverdi's *Proserpina Rapita*, was given in the Palazzo Mocenigo Dandolo. The world's first public opera house was the Teatro San Cassiano, which opened in 1637 with Francesco Manelli's *L'Andromeda*. It had been a private theatre built around 1600 by the Tron family. After it burned down in 1629, the Trons made a deliberate decision to open its successor to the public. It staged the premieres of Monteverdi's *Il Ritorno d'Ulisse* (1641) and, between 1639 and 1650, ten of the first 12 operas by Venice's most popular 17th-century composer for the medium, Francesco Cavalli. The Cassiano lasted until about 1800.

The Teatro La Fenice's immediate forerunner was the Teatro San Benedetto, one of many opera houses founded in the wake of the Cassiano's success. It opened in 1755 but was severely fire damaged in 1774, after which it unexpectedly went back into private ownership. A competition was organized for the design of a phoenix (*fenice*) to rise from its ashes (although the Benedetto was eventually rebuilt and sur-

vives today as the Rossini cinema). The award went to Gianantonio Selva and building began in May 1790.

Selva was unpopular, and when he inscribed the word Societas (referring to the Nobile Società which funded the enterprise) on the theatre's façade, the Venetians turned it into a Latin acronym: *Sine Ordine Cum Irregularitate Erexit Theatrum Antonius Selva* ('In disorderly fashion and irregularly Antonius Selva put up the theatre'). The work was completed quickly and the theatre opened on 16 May 1792 with Paisiello's *I Giuochi d'Agrigento*, specially written for the occasion. La Fenice's immediate popularity survived the decline in opera houses caused

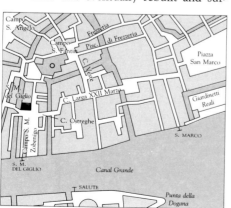

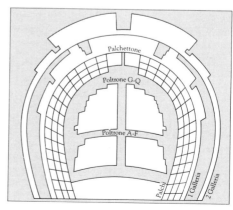

by the high salaries demanded by the leading singers. The earliest significant premiere given at La Fenice was Rossini's first great *opera seria*, *Tancredi* (1813), to be followed by his *Sigismondo* (1814) and *Semiramide* (1823).

By now La Fenice had a national name and Bellini was next on its roll of prominent composers with his Romeo and Juliet opera *I Capuleti ed i Montecchi* (1830); less successful was his *Beatrice di Tenda* (1833), though it was revived in 1987. Having scored one success at La Fenice with his *Belisario* (1836), Donizetti wrote *Lucia* for the start of the Carnival season (26 December) that year. But fire – a recurrent theme in Venetian theatre history – destroyed all but the walls, the foyer and the Sale Apollinee (suite of public rooms above it) on 12 December, and *Lucia*, delayed by only a day, had to open at the Teatro Apollo (now Goldoni).

La Fenice was immediately rebuilt and reopened on 26 December 1837. Donizetti's new *Pia dei Tolomei* was part of the first season. When asked for a new work for the 1844 Carnival season, Donizetti demanded an exorbitant fee. The commission went instead to the young Verdi and *Ernani* was the result. It gave the composer an international reputation, and led to several other Fenice commissions.

Rigoletto (1851) was an instant hit. *Traviata* (1853) was a near disaster; although Fanny Salvini Donatelli sang well elsewhere in the title role. The news in Act III that she was shortly to die of consumption – coming from one with a *troppo prosperosa* figure – caused a roar of mirth. Revived a year later, in a production moved back by a century, it was unanimously acclaimed.

The unification of Italy turned the spotlight away from Venice towards larger centres such as Milan and Rome, so that La Fenice's star waned during the second half of the century. There was a major restoration in 1854, in which the proscenium arch was altered and the present ceiling painted. In 1938, when the company became an autonomous corporation, the orchestra pit was enlarged.

La Fenice's modern reputation stems partly from the several world premieres it gave during the early years of the Venice Festival (discontinued in 1973): *The Rake's Progress* in 1951, *The Turn of the Screw*, with Britten himself conducting, in 1953 and Prokofiev's *The Fiery Angel* in 1955, as well as works by several Italians notably the Venetian, Gian Francesco Malipiero. The company's present diet is catholic, leaning towards its favourite sons, Rossini and Verdi (including the first complete performance of the former's *Zelmira* in 1988) but with more than a nod towards Mozart and the revival of baroque opera.

The company is no longer quite in the very top rank in Italy. But the theatre itself is a *sine qua non* for the visitor to Venice. Its neoclassical entrance façade is relatively plain, without much decoration, hardly a preparation for what lies within. The auditorium is breathtaking. It has been described as gentle and feminine. Decorated in a florid, late-Empire style in duck-egg blue, cream and gold, it has 95 boxes arranged on five levels, with a royal box at the centre. The pink velvet armchairs in the stalls are arranged in widely spaced rows, which give easy access and plenty of leg room. Venetian glass was used for the foyer chandeliers. When La Fenice was built, a canal was dug alongside at the same time – it is still possible to arrive by gondola. The artistic director is Gianni Tangucci.

Campo San Fantin, 30124 Venezia
☎ 041-786511/786500   TX 215647
FX 041-786562 Mon – Sat
9.30am – 12.30pm, 4 – 6pm (closed Mon when there is a Sun perf.) For groups contact box office CC None & Written requests to box office ⸬ 800
♠ Bar PT Motoscafo (Motor-boat). ACTV No 2 S. Zaccaria. Ⓟ Piazzale Roma.

TEATR WIELKI

A version of *Acis and Galatea* by Santi Orlandi is reputedly the first opera to be staged in Warsaw, promoted by the Prince Regent in 1628. As Wladyslaw IV, he sponsored an Italian opera company (1634–48). A court theatre (Operalnia) flourished between 1725 and 1772, and the first public theatre opened in 1765. It staged the first Polish opera, Maciej Kamieński's *Misery Made Happy*, in 1778. One of its singers, Wojciech Boguslawski, organized the Warsaw Opera within the Polish National Theatre (opened in 1779), with Józef Elsner as chief conductor (1799–1824), but opera still lacked an exclusive theatre.

Opera in Warsaw had long been a focal point of Polish nationalism. So the opening of the Teatr Wielki (Grand Theatre) in 1833, with *Barbiere* in Polish, was an event of unusual significance: under the Russian occupation, the Polish language could only be heard publicly in opera, not in straight theatre. The Wielki was designed for opera by the Italian architect Antonio Corazzi.

Karol Kurpiński succeeded Elsner until 1840: as operatic composers and teachers, both men were instrumental in tapping the emergent nationalism in Polish music. The stage premiere of Moniuszko's *Halka* (1858) – the most popular Polish opera ever written – led to the composer's appointment as director (1859–72). He wrote several more operas, notably *Straszny Dwór*, (*The Haunted Manor*, 1865). A prominent later director was Emil Mlynarski (1898–1903 and 1919–29), who consolidated the native tradition with premieres such as Szymanowski's important *King Roger* (1926).

Financial stringencies caused interruptions during the 1930s. The theatre was completely destroyed, apart from its handsome façade, by bombs in 1944. Opera resumed in the Roma Hall after the war, and the company was named the Warsaw State Opera in 1948. But it was not until 1965 that the Wielki was able to reopen, with *The*

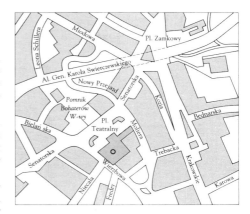

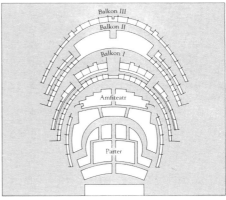

Haunted Manor. Robert Satanowski was appointed general director in 1981. His repertory is based around a large selection of Polish works, with Mozart and Verdi running distant seconds. With the exception of Salzburg and Bayreuth, the Wielki's stage is the largest in the world. Some 300 performances are given each year, by a company that includes 70 resident principals, a chorus of 140 and a ballet company of over 100. Chamber opera is also given in the theatre's Mlynarski Room.

Pl. Teatralny 1, 00-950 Warszawa
☎ 22-263 001/267 001 TX 817473
B As above ☎ 22-265 019 TX As above CC None & Elevator ░ 1800 and 100 standing PT Bus P Nearby.

THE WASHINGTON OPERA

Washington is typical of the post-war resurgence in American opera. Until 1956 it had no regular opera season. Only with the opening of the John F. Kennedy Center for the Performing Arts in 1971 did it acquire a permanent company. Before that it relied on touring companies for 150 years.

The New Company of Philadelphia gave summer seasons of ballad opera (1800–14). The first European opera was *Barbiere*, sung in English by Philadelphia's Walton Opera Company (1836). Operetta and musical comedy predominated in the second half of the century, centred on the works of Sullivan, Lecocq and Johann Strauss; grand opera was, however, given at Albaugh's Opera House after 1884. A black company

had been organized in 1872, playing in Washington and Philadelphia, and 20 years later Sissieretta Jones (the 'Black Patti') sang at the White House. The Washington National Opera Association performed during the 1920s, and was the first to present opera in the newly built Auditorium when it opened in 1924. The National Negro Opera Company, formed by Mary Cardwell Dawson, first appeared in Washington in 1943, and was based there from the late 1940s until her death in 1962, giving traditional repertory with all-black casts as well as homegrown rarities such as Clarence Cameron White's *Ouanga*.

The present era began in 1956, when the Opera Society of Washington was founded

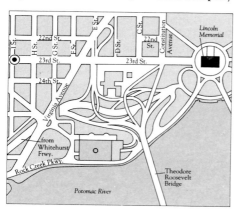

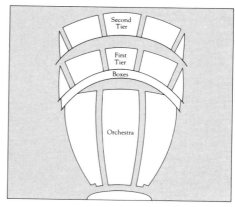

to present unusual operas on a low budget. Its original venue, the Lisner Auditorium of George Washington University, proved unsatisfactory, but the society survived to establish a reputation for enterprise and excellence. Its first music director (1957–65) was Paul Callaway, who had been organist at the Episcopal Cathedral since 1939; he conducted the American stage premiere of Berlioz's *Béatrice et Bénédict* in 1964. Productions in the original of Tchaikovsky's *Queen of Spades* and Strauss' *Ariadne auf Naxos*, together with the US premiere of Schoenberg's *Erwartung* (1960), typified the company's early adventurousness. Hindemith conducted his own one-act fantasy, to a Thornton Wilder libretto, *The Long Christmas Dinner*, in 1961; Stravinsky conducted his own *Oedipus Rex*.

The Kennedy Center opened in 1971, and two days later the Opera Society staged the world premiere of Ginastera's *Beatrix Cenci*, specially commissioned for the occasion and sung in Spanish. With its red and gold decor, the Center's Opera House has become the company's permanent home, although smaller-scale productions are staged in the more intimate atmosphere of the wood-panelled Eisenhower Theater (capacity 1142). Music theatre is also given in the 512-seat Terrace Theater, a gift from the Japanese people, which was opened in 1979. The Kennedy Center, which was designed by Edward Durell Stone, is an impressive complex on the banks of the Potomac River: its halls are lined with Carrara marble and its huge Grand Foyer, more than 188,000 square feet (17,500 square metres), stretches up some 98 feet (30 metres) above a bust of President Kennedy. The Center also contains a 2759-seat concert hall, a cinema, a theatre laboratory and a performing arts library.

The company became known as The Washington Opera in 1977. Ian Strasfogel was appointed its first general director in 1972, introducing Delius' *A Village Romeo and Juliet* (1972) and Monteverdi's *Il Ritorno d'Ulisse* (1974) to America. He was succeeded in 1975 by Canadian-born bass-baritone George London. Martin Feinstein has been general director since 1980. The company underwent considerable expansion during the 1980s, tripling its output to 48 performances of seven productions by the end of the decade. Casts are predominantly American, but guest conductors of international standing are regularly brought in: Daniel Barenboim made his American conducting debut there in *Così Fan Tutte*.

Productions are generally given in the original, but with English surtitles. In keeping with the Kennedy Center's role as a national showcase for the arts, the company imports the best productions from major American companies, as well as originating its own. Repertory continues to favour the offbeat, with at least one work by a contemporary American each year. Stephen Paulus' *The Postman Always Rings Twice* (1989) and Dominick Argento's *The Aspern Papers* (1990) are typical examples. Another recent coup was the premiere of Menotti's *Goya* (1986), with Placido Domingo in the title role. The Kennedy Center is also a popular venue for visiting foreign companies: Deutsche Oper, Berlin, gave two *Ring* cycles during the summer of 1989. Despite its relative youth, The Washington Opera looks set to join the front rank of American companies before long.

The John F. Kennedy Center for the Performing Arts, Washington DC 20566
☎ 202-822 4700   [FX] 202-653 5749
♬ Oct – Mar   [B] Hall of States then as above   ☎ 202-254 3770 Instant charge
☎ 202-857 0900 Discount for groups
☎ 202-634 7201   [CC] Amex, Diners, MC, Visa ♿ Wheelchair reservation
☎ 202-254 3774 hearing aids
☎ 202-254 3906, restrooms, special performances   ⫶⫶ 2318 and 40 standing
♟ Roof Terrace Restaurant
☎ 202-833 8870, Hors d'Oeuvrerie, Curtain Call Cafe   [PT] Bus – 46, 81, M-5, M-12. Underground – Foggy Bottom
℗ Kennedy Center Garage, Rock Creek Parkway. Columbia Plaza Garage, 2400 Virginia Ave N.W.

STAATSOPER

The Vienna State Opera is not only one of the world's great companies, it is a symbol of Austria's devotion to music and theatre. What began as court entertainment in the 1620s had become a source of pride and joy for all citizens by the time the present building was erected in 1869.

Italian musicians were first attracted to Vienna by the marriage of Ferdinand II to Eleonora Gonzaga in 1622. The 'Fedeli' probably gave Vienna its first opera, *Arcas* (1627), although Ludovico Bartolaia's *Il Sidonio* (1633) was the first documented production. The Habsburgs spent huge sums on opera, notably when Cavalli was working under Ferdinand III, himself a composer. Leopold I's long reign (1657–1705) saw some 400 new operas: for his marriage to the Infanta Margherita of Spain in 1668 he commissioned Antonio Cesti's celebrated *Il Pomo d'Oro*, which was given in a specially built theatre (where the Austrian National Library now stands). Later this became the Burgtheater, which opened in 1748 with Gluck's *Semiramide Riconosciuta*. While music director there, Gluck incorporated his operatic reforms into ten new works, beginning with *Orfeo* in 1762.

There were parallel developments in German opera. Emperor Joseph II sanctioned the arrival of the *Singspiel* with the formation

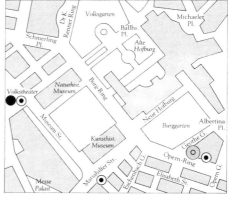

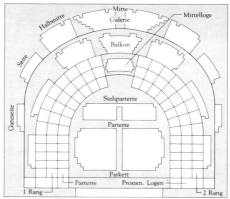

of the National Theatre Company at the Burgtheater, where in 1782 Mozart's *Entführung* received its first performance. *Figaro* was unveiled there in 1786, *Così* in 1790, while *Zauberflöte* had its premiere in 1791 at its librettist Emanuel Schikaneder's own Theater auf der Wieden in the suburbs. Schikaneder replaced this with the Theater an der Wien in 1801 and staged the first version of *Fidelio* there in 1805; it later became a major house for operetta, including the premiere of *Fledermaus* (1874), and is now the official base of the annual (May/June) festival.

The Theater an der Wien's main rival was the Kärntnertortheater (where the Hotel Sacher now stands), which opened for straight drama in 1708, but became home of the Imperial Court Opera from the 1780s. The final version of *Fidelio* was given here in 1804. Weber's *Euryanthe* was specially commissioned for it in 1823, and there were several outstanding Rossini seasons under Domenico Barbaia. Donizetti's *Linda di Chamounix* (1842) and Flotow's *Martha* (1847) were its only other notable premieres.

The reconstruction of central Vienna, begun in 1857, meant the Kärntnertortheater's demolition and its replacement by an opera house on the new Ringstrasse. After a competition, August von Siccardsburg's ground plan and Eduard van der Nüll's interior decor were chosen for the new opera house, which opened in 1869 with *Don Giovanni*. Moritz von Schwind's 14 frescoes in the foyer, and his *Zauberflöte* cycle of paintings in the loggia, were major features of this neo-Renaissance masterpiece. After a decade of financial uncertainty, it became the musical fulcrum of central Europe. Wilhelm Jahn, its intendant (1881–97), established an atmosphere of sumptuousness which was enhanced by Hans Richter as musical director.

Into a Vienna steeped in the hedonistic malaise of the Habsburgs' latter years came Mahler as director (1897–1907). He virtually gave his lifeblood to raising the Opera to standards unequalled anywhere else: Vienna, led by the Opera, burst into bloom

once again. Despite considerable opposition, he ruthlessly eliminated false traditions (restoring cuts to Wagner and the harpsichord to Mozart), banned the claque, built up a first-class ensemble and wiped out the deficit he had inherited. Alfred Moller was his invaluable chief designer.

Renamed the Vienna State Opera after World War I, the company regained some of its former glory: soloists such as Elizabeth Schumann, Jan Kiepura and Richard Tauber made Vienna their base, under conductors who included Richard Strauss (1919–24), Clemens Krauss (1929–34) and Bruno Walter (1936–38). During the war, Karl Böhm's Mozart productions with Seefried, Schwarzkopf and Dermota became legendary. After being bombed in March 1945, only the façade, the central staircase, the loggia and the 'tea salon' behind the central box remained intact.

For a decade the company played in the Volksoper and the Theater an der Wien. Restored by Erich Boltenstern, with three levels of boxes and two balconies, but with its capacity reduced by 670, the Oper am Ring reopened in 1955 with Böhm conducting *Fidelio*. Karajan's stormy directorate (1956–64) introduced numerous 20th-century works and restored productions to their original language. Standards declined thereafter, to be rescued by Lorin Maazel (1982–84). Since 1986, Claus Helmut Drese has been intendant, Claudio Abbado music director. A vast budget and the Vienna Philharmonic Orchestra are their vital allies in sustaining a repertory of nearly 50 works.

Opern-Ring 2, A-1015 Wien
☎ 01-51444 2960/2959 TX 113775
FX 01-51444 2969 ♬ Sep – Jun
B Osterreichischer Bundestheaterverband/Bundestheaterkassen, A-1010 Wien,
Hanuschgasse 3 ☎ TX FX As above
CC Air Plus, Amex, Diners, MC, Visa
♿ 2 wheelchair spaces and 2 attendants
🎭 1709 and 567 standing 🍸 Several bars
PT Train – Badnerbahn, Strabenbahn, D, J, 1, 2. Underground – U1, U2, U4
Ⓟ Garage nearby.

VOLKSOPER

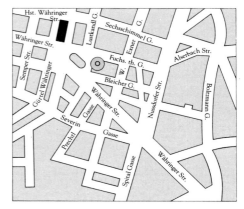

The Volksoper is Vienna's second opera house. Plainer than the Opera, it is nevertheless comfortable and intimate. It was founded by Adam Müller-Guttenbrunn as a home for German drama. Originally known as the Kaiser Jubiläums Stadttheater, it opened on 14 December 1898 to celebrate Franz Joseph's golden jubilee. Initially unprofitable, it was leased by the Cologne impresario Rainer Simons, who announced a programme of popular opera at popular prices under the name Volksoper. This began in September 1904 with a production of *Freischütz* conducted by Alexander von Zemlinsky.

After building up his audiences with operettas, Simons confronted the Opera head on in 1907 with the sensational Viennese premiere of *Tosca* in which Maria Jeritza initiated the tradition of singing '*Vissi d'arte*' from a prostrate position. She also starred in the city's first *Salome* (1910), which had similarly been rejected by the Opera's censor. Repertory, under the enterprising Simons, was broad enough to include Dukas' Bluebeard opera and Humperdinck's *Königskinder*.

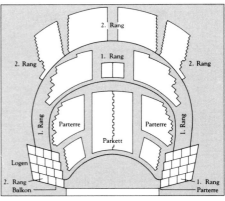

During Felix Weingartner's term as director (1919–24), Vienna saw its first *Boris Godunov*; *Parsifal* and even the *Ring* entered the Volksoper's repertory. Schoenberg's fiftieth birthday celebrations produced the premiere of *Glückliche Hand* (1924). Singers such as Viorica Ursuleac and Richard Tauber made regular appearances during the 1920s.

From 1938 to 1944 the theatre came under municipal control as the Opernhaus der Stadt Wien. Less than two months after the bombing of the Opera in March 1945, the company had restarted at the Volksoper – which it continued to use for a decade until the Opera had been rebuilt. But the Volksoper staged its own revival, ranging from Lortzing to Britten and Orff. After the Opera's departure, Franz Salmhofer became director (1955–63), adding a ballet company to the chorus and orchestra already resident at the Volksoper. Karl Dönch (1973–87) deliberately introduced new works by Austrian composers. The baritone Eberhard Wächter, his successor, now directs a balanced programme of opera, operetta, musicals and ballet, in company with a Mozart cycle begun in 1988.

Währinger Str. 78, 1090 Wien
☎ 514 44 3188/3319 TX 115097
♫ Sep – Jun B Osterreichischer Bundestheaterverband, Bundestheaterkassen, Hanuschgasse 3, 1010 Wien ☎ 514-44 2960/2959 and above CC Amex, Diners, MC, Visa ♿ Wheelchair space ♨ 1473 and 102 standing ♟ Buffet PT Tram – 40, 41, 42, 8. Underground – DG, G ℗ Difficult.

OPERNHAUS

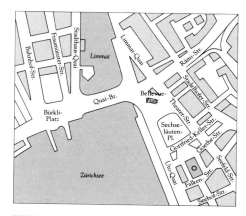

Full-time opera began in Zurich in 1834 in the Aktientheater, which was the headquarters for Wagner's activities during his Zurich exile (1849–50): there he conducted his own edition of *Don Giovanni* and wrote the entire poem for *The Ring*. Productions were accompanied by the renowned Tonhalle Orchestra, which is still the nucleus of the city's musical life. The theatre burned down in 1890, but its library was rediscovered in 1974 and is now preserved in the Zentralbibliothek.

In 1891 a new theatre, designed by the Viennese architects Pellner and Helmer, was opened. At first called the Stadttheater, it became known as the Opernhaus in 1964. Furtwängler began his operatic career in Zurich as repetiteur during the 1906–7 season. Zurich held its first international festival of opera in May 1909, and in 1913 staged the first authorized production of *Parsifal* outside Bayreuth – a 1905 performance in Amsterdam had been against copyright – under Ernst Reucker's direction.

Zurich has inevitably been a magnet for Swiss composers with aspirations: Othmar Schoeck's *Venus* was premiered at the Opernhaus in 1922; Arthur Honegger and Frank Martin both worked there. Its greatest years stem from the directorate of Hans Zimmermann (1937–56), who scored an immediate success with the world premiere of *Lulu* in his first season, followed by Hindemith's *Mathis der Maler* (1938) and Honegger's *Jeanne d'Arc au Bûcher* (1942).

The influential Hans Rosbaud celebrated his appointment as chief conductor of the Tonhalle in 1957 with the stage premiere of Schoenberg's *Moses und Aron*. More recently, the theatre enjoyed a vintage era under Claus Helmut Drese's direction (1975–86). He masterminded the renowned Monteverdi cycle, conducted by Nikolaus Harnoncourt and produced by Jean-Pierre Ponnelle.

Ferdinand Leitner's term as chief conduc-

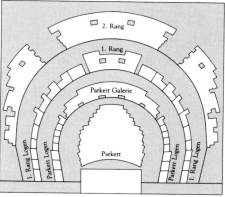

tor (1969–83) largely coincided with Drese's, who remained long enough to supervise a major two year renovation and extension to the opera house. The present chief conductor is Ralf Weikert; Christoph Groszer has succeeded Drese as artistic director. The facilities also house the Zurich Opera Ballet under Uwe Scholz.

Falkenstrasse 1, CH-8008 Zurich
☎ 01-251 69 20   TX 815 988 OHZ
♬ Sep – Jun   B As above
☎ 01-251 69 22/251 69 23   CC Amex, Diners, MC, Visa   ⅃ Elevator   ⸬ 1100
♀ Restaurant – Belcanto. Several coffee bars   PT Transport info. – 01-221 22 83
Ⓟ In front of opera house and multistoreys nearby.

ADDITIONAL OPERA HOUSES AND COMPANIES

AUSTRALIA

Lyric Opera of Queensland, Lyric Theatre of the Queensland Performing Complex, **S. Brisbane** ☎ 7-846 1177 TX 140472 FX 7-844 5352 ♫ May – Aug B PO Box 677, South Brisbane 4101, Queensland ☎ TX FX As above CC Amex, Diners, MC, Visa ♿ Parking bays under complex, elevators, wheelchair area, hearing-aids ☷ 2100 ♀ Lyrebird restaurant ☎ 7-846 4646 Coffee shop, bars PT Train – from Southside – Ferny Grove, Shorncliffe; from Northside – Beenleigh, Cleveland. Bus – Cityxpress 501, 502, 503, 504, 505, 506, 511, 518–28, 522, 529, 583, 584; Citybus – 121, 131, 141, 151, 160, 170, 180; for details phone Bus Hotline 7-225 4444 ℗ Art Gallery Carpark opposite and Performing Arts Complex, World Expo.

Formed in 1982, a relatively new company, whose orchestra and chorus already provide a solid foundation for its conservative repertory.

AUSTRIA

Vereinigte Bühnen Graz Steiermark, Kaiser Josef Platz 10, A-8010 **Graz** ☎ 0316-82 6451 FX 0316-82 6451 204 ♫ Sep – Jun B As above ☎ 0316-82 7422 Discounts for groups CC None ♿ Wheelchair access, elevator and restroom ☷ 1271 and 200 standing ♀ Several buffets PT Bus – 31, 89 Kaiser Josef Platz. Tram – 1, 7 Kaiser Josef Platz ℗ 3 carparks nearby.

Traditionally a breeding-ground for German-speaking musicians, this enterprising company (also heard at the Styrian Autumn Festival) acquired soprano Gundula Janowitz as opera director in 1990.

Tiroler Landestheater, Rennweg 2, A-6020 **Innsbruck** ☎ 0512-52074 FX 0512-52074333 ♫ Sep – Jun B As above. Discounts for groups of 18 + CC None ♿ Hearing-aids ☷ 793 and 30 standing in large theatre, 364 in small theatre, 99 in workshop theatre ♀ Buffets in large and small theatres PT Train – Innsbruck Station. Bus – A, C, D, E, K, OA, and from station ℗ Nearby.

This compact 1846 theatre, reopened in 1967 after a complete rebuild, makes a happy arena for such a vigorous company, which has a first-class chorus.

BELGIUM

Opera Royal de Wallonie, Lyric Centre of the French Community, 1 rue des Dominicains, B 4000 **Liège** ☎ 041-235910 TX 42131 ORW LGB ♫ Sep – Jun B As above ☎ 041-236765 TX As above. Mon – Sat 11am – 1pm, 2 – 6pm. Discounts for groups of 30 + CC Amex, Diners, MC ♿ Elevator and restrooms ☷ 1048 ♀ Restaurant ☎ 041-235910 Ext 19 PT Bus – Théâtre Royal ℗ Nearby.

Established in 1967, this enterprising company with a natural bias towards French repertory has an excellent orchestra and tours to Charleroi, Mons and Verviers.

DENMARK

Den Jyske Opera, Musikhuset Arhus, 8000 **Arhus** C ☎ 06-4586137266 TX 06-4586194386 ♫ Aug – May B As above 🆑 None ♿ elevator, restroom and special seats ⚏ 1477 ♟ restaurant and cafe ☎ 06-4586134344 PT Train – Arhus station. Bus – all city-lines stop at concert hall Ⓟ Nearby.

Den Jyske Opera, Denmark's second largest company, founded in 1947, gives up to six productions, all of which it tours round the country.

FRANCE

Opéra de Lyon, Auditorium Maurice Ravel, 141, rue Garibaldi, 69003 **Lyon**
☎ 78-71 05 73 ♫ Sep – Jun B 9 Quai Jean Moulin, 69001 Lyon
☎ 78-28 09 07/78-28 09 60 TX 305286
FX 78-27 88 05 Discounts for groups
🆑 Amex, Diners, MC ♿ Contact box office for details ⚏ Large theatre – 1350, small theatre – 200 ♟ Restaurants nearby PT Bus – 3 Ⓟ Nearby.

An old-established but particularly enterprising company that devotes considerable attention to 20th-century works. The opera house is closed for renovation until 1993 but is performing at alternative venues until then.

Théâtre de Metz, 4 – 5 Place de la Comédie, **Metz** ☎ 87-55 51 71 ♫ All year
B As above 🆑 None ♿ Contact box office for details ⚏ 700
♟ Restaurants nearby PT Bus – stop for Metz Theatre Ⓟ In front of theatre.

The company has surmounted recent administrative difficulties with the city to give refreshing productions on its relatively unsophisticated stage.

Opéra de Nancy et de Lorraine, 1 rue Sainte-Catherine, 54000 **Nancy**
☎ 83-37 65 01 TX 850740
FX 83-32 90 96 ♫ Oct – Jun B As above ☎ 83-32 08 54. 10.30am – 12.30pm, 7 days before performance. Discounts for groups, over 60s and under

25s 🆑 None ⚏ 920 ♟ Buffet
☎ 83-32 08 54 Ⓟ Nearby.

An up-and-coming company alive to the benefits of international co-productions in its beautiful, compact theatre.

Opéra de Nice, 6 rue Saint François de Paule, 06300 **Nice** ☎ 93-80 59 83
TX 470593 OPERANI FX 93-80 34 83
Sep – Jun B As above. Discounts for groups 🆑 None ♿ None ⚏ 800 and 200 standing ♟ Bar ☎ 93-85 67 31
PT Train – Gare de Nice, Bus – Gare des Autobus Ⓟ Nearby at Corvesy.

Almost a second home to American singers in Europe, this charming theatre is beginning to show its age.

GERMANY

Oper der Stadt Bonn, Am Boeselagerhof 1 D-5300 **Bonn** 1, Postfach 2440
☎ 0228-72 8 1 TX 885 295
FX 0228-63 03 73 ♫ Sep – Jun
B Mülheimer Platz 1, 5300 Bonn 1
☎ 0228-77 36 66-7/728 350 🆑 None
♿ Register one day in advance, access by elevator from underground car park, restrooms ⚏ Grobes Haus – 896, Werkstättbuhne – approx 176
♟ Restaurants in both theatres
PT Train – 62, 64, 66. Bus – 620, 622, 624, 625, 628, 630, 631, 634, 635.
Underground – Schnellbahn 635, 640, 550 Ⓟ Underground car park.

This recent (1965) theatre beside the Rhine maintains an admirably sound operatic tradition in mainstream repertory accompanied by the Beethovenhalle Orchestra.

Staatstheater Braunschweig, Am Theater, 3300 **Braunschweig** ☎ 0531-484 2700
♫ Sep – Aug B Advance booking 14 days before performance
☎ 0531-484 2800 🆑 None
♿ Elevators, 4 wheelchair spaces in large

theatre ⛶ Large theatre – 900 and 60
standing, small theatre – 210
♨ Snackbars ☎ 0531-484 2795
[PT] Bus – 12, 13, 16, 18 to large theatre,
18 to small theatre ⓟ Nearby.

With one of Germany's most reliable
middlebrow companies, Brunswick has a
history of exploring operatic byways.

Bremer Theater, Am Goetheplatz,
Postfach 10 10 46, 2800 **Bremen**
☎ 0421-3653333 ♫ Daily [B] As
above ☎ 0421-35 36 37, 10am–7pm
[CC] Amex ♿ Wheelchair spaces
⛶ 900 ♨ 2 restaurants [PT] Train –
Lines 2, 3. ⓟ Theatre garage.

International casts and Romantic works not
commonly staged in Germany mark out the
repertory in this 1950 theatre.

Staatstheater Darmstadt, Marienplatz,
6100 **Darmstadt** ☎ 06151-2811 211
[FX] 06151-2811 226 ♫ All year, Tues –
Sun [B] As above, Tue – Fri 9.30am–
1pm, 5–6.30pm. Sat 10am–12pm. Sun
11am–12pm. Discounts for children
[CC] None ♿ Ramps, elevators and special
box available on request ⛶ 956
♨ Snackbar [PT] Bus – stops 5 mins
away ⓟ Underground.

This modern theatre houses a company
renowned for innovation in a city strongly
committed to 20th-century music.

Theater Dortmund-Opernhaus, Kuhstr.
12, 4600 **Dortmund** ☎ 0231-542 25547
[TX] 82-22 87 [FX] 0231-542 22877
♫ Sep – Jun [B] Advance booking Tue –
Fri 10am–1pm, 4.30–6.30pm, Sat 10am–
1pm ☎ 0231-542 22412. 1 hour before
performance ☎ 0231-542 22444
[CC] None ♿ Two disabled parking
places, ramp, restroom ⛶ 1160
♨ Snackbar and 2 buffets [PT] Train –
Dortmund Central. S-Bahn-Stadttheater
ⓟ Underground opposite theatre.

Industrial prosperity in Westphalia has
helped to broaden the perspectives of this
opera house, opened in 1966.

Musiktheater im Revier, Kennedyplatz,
Postfach 101854, 4650 **Gelsenkirchen**
☎ 0209-40970 [FX] 0209-4097 250
♫ Sep – Jun [B] As above ☎ Evenings
0209-4097 200. Discounts for groups
of 25+ [CC] None ♿ 4 wheelchair
spaces, restroom ⛶ 1034 in large theatre,
374 in small theatre ♨ Snackbar
☎ 0209-495565 [PT] Train –
Gelsenkirchen Station. Tram –
Musiktheater. Bus – Musiktheater
ⓟ Nearby, 300 places.

In alliance with Bochum, the Musiktheater
im Revier's consistent enterprise embraces
unusual works given to high standards, in
spite of financial constraints.

Badiches Staatstheater Karlsruhe,
Baumeisterstr. 11, D-7500 **Karlsruhe** 1
☎ 0721-1521 [FX] 0721-373223
♫ Sep – Jul [B] As above
☎ 0721-60202, Mon – Thur, 2–3pm, 8pm
Fri – Sat 2–3pm, 7.30pm. Discounts for
groups of 20+ [CC] None ♿ Special
access, restroom ⛶ 1002 in large theatre
and 100 standing, 330 in small theatre
♨ Snackbar ☎ 0721-152330 [PT] Train –
Karlsruhe Station. Tram – Baumeisterstr.
ⓟ Underground nearby.

A well-balanced if conservative company
with a better reputation in mainstream
repertory than in 20th-century works.

Staatstheater Kassel, Friedrichsplatz 15,
3500 **Kassel** ☎ 05611-10940
[FX] 0561-11094 204 ♫ All year [B] As
above [CC] None ♿ None ⛶ 953
♨ Snackbar ☎ 05611-15859 [PT] Tram –
6, 3, 1 Friedrichspl. Bus – 18, 19 Altmarkt
ⓟ Nearby.

An enterprising, industrious company,
inclined to over-produce but still delivering
solid fare with musical integrity in a theatre
opened in 1959.

Bühnen der Landeshauptstadt Kiel,
Rathausplatz 4, D-2300 **Kiel** 1
☎ 0431-9012880 ♫ Sep – Jun
[B] Vorverkaufskasse im Opernhaus, 6 days

before performance ☎ 0431-92100.
Mon – Fri 4.30 – 7pm, Sat 11am – 1pm.
Discounts for school groups of 15 +. Adult
groups 20 + CC None ⚅ Wheelchair
spaces ⛭ 866 ♟ Snackbars PT Train –
Kiel main station. Bus – Rauthsplatz
℗ Nearby.

Performing in the rebuilt Stadttheater
(1953), the company spans a broadly
Germanic repertory including operetta and
modern works.

Bühnen der Hausestadt, Grosses Haus,
Beckergrube 10 – 14, D-2400 **Lübeck**
☎ 0451-1224200 ♫ Daily B As above
☎ 0451-74552/1224238. Discounts for
groups CC None ⚅ None ⛭ 913
♟ Snackbars ☎ 0451-1224267
PT Train – Lübeck Hauptbahnhof.
Bus – Beckergrube, Koberg and Markt.
℗ Multistorey and nearby.

Despite moderate resources, the company
maintains an enterprising repertory in its
1908 theatre.

Nationaltheater, Am Geotheplatz, 6800
Mannheim ☎ 0621-1680 220 ♫ No
fixed programme B Day-Collinstr 26,
6800 Mannheim ☎ 0621-24844.
Evenings – theatre ☎ 0621-252, Mon
and Sat 11am–1pm. Tue – Fri 11am–1pm
and 2 – 6pm CC None ⚅ Elevators and
special box ⛭ 1154 ♟ Buffet
PT Bus and Tram – 32, 33, 34, 36, 71, 75
℗ At theatre and multistoreys nearby.

A versatile company now consolidating its
huge repertory with three or four new
productions each year.

Staatstheater Am Gärtnerplatz,
Gärtnerplatz 3, Postfach 140569, 8000
München 5 ☎ 089-20241-4 TX 5213 318
STAG ♫ Oct – Jul B As above
☎ 089-2016767 Mon – Fri 10am – 1pm and
3.30 – 5.30pm. Sat 10am – 12.30pm
CC None ⚅ Elevator to stalls at
Reichenbachstrasse entrance ⛭ 823 and
85 standing ♟ Snackbars PT Bus – 52,

56 Gartnerplatz. Underground 1, 2,
Fraunhoferstr ℗ Jakobsplatz and
Mariahilfplatz nearby.

Munich's second opera house, home to a
large and lively company with an eclectic
repertory, covering modern opera, musical
comedy and Mozart with equal facility.

Stadttheater Bühnen Nürnberg, Richard
Wagner Platz 1 – 3, 8500 **Nürnberg** 70
☎ 0911-22990 TX 626929 BRNBY
♫ Oct – Jun B Frânkischer
Beosucherring, Opernhaus Nürnberg
Lessingstr 1, Nürnberg CC None
⚅ Wheelchair spaces and hearing-aids
⛭ 1061 ♟ Snackbars PT Train –
Nürnberg Hauptbahnhof (5 mins walk).
Underground – Line 2, Opernhaus ℗ At
theatre.

This self-reliant company, which includes
its own substantial orchestra and chorus,
covers a refreshing range of repertory and
has staged several premieres in recent years.

Hessisches Staatstheater Wiesbaden, Am
Warmen Damm, 6200 **Weisbaden**
☎ 06121-1321 FX 06121-132 337
♫ All year B As above
☎ 06121-132 325, 11am – 1.30pm,
4.30 – 6pm. Sat, Sun and Bank Holidays
11 – 12.30pm CC None ⚅ Ramps,
restroom, 2 wheelchair spaces in large
theatre, 1 wheelchair space in small theatre,
hearing-aids, doctor present at each
performance ⛭ 1041 in large theatre, 328
in small theatre, 89 in studio
♟ Restaurant PT Train – S-Bahn from
Frankfurt airport to Wiesbaden. Bus –
several services from main railway station
℗ Multistorey carpark opposite theatre.

An attractive repertory supplemented by at
least one new work each year and foreign
companies at the annual May festival.

Wuppertaler Bühnen, Spinnstrasse 4, 5600
Wuppertal 2 TX 8591871 SKW
FX 0202-554765 ♫ Daily
B Opernhaus ☎ 0202-550050/556607
Schauspielhaus ☎ 0202-444462/453880.
Ticket sales 10 days before performance, or

20 days if guest performance, reduced tickets available by advance booking. Discounts for groups of 10 + [CC] None & Elevator and restrooms ⸬ OH-845, SH-792 ♞ Bar [PT] Train – Wuppertal-Elberfield Station. S-Bahn-Adlerbrücke. Bus – Adlerbrücke. Cable car ℗ At theatre.

Fourteen productions, half of them new, are presented annually by this often innovative company, the first in Germany to reopen after World War II.

ITALY

Teatro Petruzzelli, Via Cognetti 26, **Bari** ☎ 080-5241741 [TX] 812270 [FX] 080-5210527 ♫ Oct – Jan [B] As above. Discounts for groups [CC] None & Ticket reductions ⸬ 2000 ♞ Cafe 'Il Ridotto' ☎ 080-5241761 [PT] Train – Bari Station (5 mins walk). Bus – Teatro ℗ Public car park nearby.

The Politeama Petruzzelli, an enormous theatre opened in 1903, annually hosts a handful of large-scale productions, with guest principals.

Teatro Sociale, Piazza Folengo 4, 46100 **Mantua** ☎ 0376-362739 [FX] 0376-362739 ♫ Oct – Jun [B] As above. Discounts for groups [CC] Contact box office for details & Contact box office for details ⸬ 1100 ♞ Bars ☎ 0376-323860 [PT] Train – Mantua Station (5 mins walk). Bus – Local service ℗ 5 – 10 mins walk.

The first Italian city after Florence to stage opera, which is now given in traditional productions at both the Teatro Sociale (1822) and the Teatro Andreani (1862).

Teatro Comunale Città di Modena, Via Fonteraso 8, 41100 **Modena** ☎ 059-225443 [TX] 583322 MUNIMO [FX] 059-214775 ♫ Oct – May

[B] Corso Canalgrande 85 ☎ 059-225183 10am – 12.30pm, 4 – 8pm [CC] None & None ⸬ 1000 and 150 standing ♞ Bar [PT] Train – Modena Station ℗ Nearby.

Opera on the spacious stage of the Teatro Comunale (Nuovo), which was completed in 1841, tends to be given in 'safe', imported productions.

Teatro Municipale, Via Giuseppe Verdi 41, 29100 **Piacenza** ☎ 0523-492253/545556 [FX] 0523-29273 ♫ Dec – Mar [B] As above ☎ 0523-492251 [CC] None & None ⸬ 1055 ♞ Bars [PT] Train – Piacenza Station. Bus – 1, 2, 3, 6 ℗ Nearby.

Sound productions of Italian works, cleanly sung, are found in the imposing Teatro Municipale of 1804, which boasts five rows of boxes.

Teatro Municipale Valli, Piazza Mantiri, 7 Luglio, **Reggio Emilia** ☎ 0522-434244 [TX] 531835 [FX] 0522-46605 ♫ Jan – Apr [B] As above. Discounts for groups [CC] None & Contact box office for details ⸬ 1070 ♞ Bars [PT] Train – Reggio Emilia Station (5 – 10 mins walk) ℗ Nearby.

The beautiful Teatro Municipale Romolo Valli (1857), with 106 boxes, regularly exchanges productions with major companies in the region.

Teatro Comunale, Corso del Popolo 31, 31100 **Treviso** ☎ 0422-53336/546355/56467 [FX] 0422-52285 ♫ Oct – Dec [B] As above [CC] None & None ⸬ 700 and 50 standing ♞ Bar ☎ 0422-546355 [PT] Train – Treviso station. Bus – local service ℗ None.

The season at the Teatro Comunale (1869), which was restored in 1961, is confined to the Autunno Trevigiano, which concentrates on intelligent explorations of Italian repertory.

SOUTH AFRICA

State Theatre Pretoria, Church Street, **Pretoria** ☎ 012-322 1665 ⊤X 3-20753 FX 012-322 3913 ♬ Feb – Nov B c/o Performing Arts Council of Transvaal, 320 Pretoria Street, Pretoria 0002. Discounts for groups of 10+ ☎ ⊤X FX As above CC None ♿ Elevators, ramps and wheelchair spaces ⛶ 1322 ♜ Buffet de L'Opéra, Goldfields and Allegro Restaurants ☎ 012-322 1665 PT Bus – Main route into city P Underground garage.

PACT (Performing Arts Council Transvaal) Opera's production standards (also seen in Johannesburg) have not always kept pace with casts which are often enlivened by foreign principals.

SWEDEN

Folkoperan, Hornsgatan 72, 117 21 **Stockholm** ☎ 08-669 0095 FX 08-84 41 46 ♬ Sep – Dec, Jan – May B As above. Discounts for groups 15+ CC None ♿ Ramp and restroom facilities ⛶ 585 and some standing ♜ Snackbars ☎ 08-585300/25 PT Trains – Grand Central Station, Bus – 45, 69. Underground – Red line 'Norsborg' or 'Fruängen' to 'Mariatorget' P Nearby.

A lively company that provides a focal point for young Swedish talent in stimulating productions that border on the experimental.

SWITZERLAND

Stadttheater Berne, Nageligasse 20, 3011 **Berne** ☎ 31-211711 ♬ All year B As above. Group bookings 2 months in advance, single bookings 1 month in advance ☎ 31-220777 CC None

♿ None ⛶ Large theatre – 690, small theatre – 770 ♜ Snackbar PT Bus – 15. Tram – 9 P Nearby.

Intelligent stagings by some of Switzerland's leading producers characterize the company's reliable performances in the 1903 Stadttheater.

USA

Central City Opera House, Eureka Street, **Central City**, Denver, Colorado ☎ 303-292 6500 FX 303-292 4958 ♬ Jul – Aug B 621 17th Street, Suite 1625, Denver, Colorado 80293 ☎ 303-292 6700. Discounts for students and groups of 20+ CC Amex, MC, Visa ♿ Limited seating and wheelchair access ⛶ 756 ♜ Teller House Restaurant adjacent to Opera House PT Bus – tour buses for Opera House P Limited parking adjacent to Opera House.

A charming Victorian theatre in this Rocky Mountain mining town has been home since 1932 to the company's (summer) season, which includes two operas and an operetta.

Michigan Opera Theatre, Fisher Theatre, 3011 W. Grand Boulevard, **Detroit**, MI 48202. Masonic Temple Theatre, 500 Temple Avenue, **Detroit**, MI48201 ☎ 313-874 7850 FX 313-871 7213 ♬ Nov – Dec (Fisher), Apr – May (Temple) B Fisher: as above; Temple: 6519 Second Avenue, Detroit, Michigan 48202 ☎ Fisher: 313-872 1000; Temple: 313-874 SING CC Amex, MC, Visa ♿ Wheelchair access ⛶ Fisher - 2100; Temple – 4300 ♜ Fisher – restaurant, bars; Temple – bars PT Fisher: Bus – City of Detroit buses and SMART; Masonic: Train – Amtrack to city. Bus – Detroit City Buses and SMART ☎ 313-962 5515. Overground – People Mover within city P Adjacent to both theatres.

A fast-growing company, gives three of its wide-ranging productions at the Fisher Theatre, three at the Masonic Temple Auditorium (also used by the Met).

Lyric Opera of Kansas City, Lyric Theatre, 1029 Central, **Kansas City**, Missouri 64105
☎ 816-471 4933   FX 816-471 0602
♬ Sep – Oct and Apr   B As above   CC Amex, MC, Visa
&   ☎ 816-471 4933 wheelchair access, restroom and seating   ⸬ 1659
♟ Bars   PT Trains – limited, Amtrack stops once a day. Bus – from mid-town, through downtown   Ⓟ 3 car parks adjacent to theatre.

The company performs at the Lyric Theater, a Masonic building of the 1920s, using up-and-coming American talent singing in English.

Greater Miami Opera, Dade County Auditorium, 2901 West Flagler Street, **Miami**, Florida 33135   ☎ 305-854 1643
FX 305-856 1042   ♬ Nov – May
B 1200 Coral Way, Miami, Florida.

Discounts for groups of 20 +
☎ 305-854 7890   CC Amex, MC, Visa
& Wheelchair access and special seating
⸬ 2400   ♟ Stands and Bar   PT Train – Amtrak, Tri-Rail. Bus – Metro-Dade Buses and Metro-Rail   Ⓟ Behind Auditorium.

International stars lend glamour to the company's five annual productions at Dade County Auditorium, which usually include one rarity among otherwise mainline repertory.

The Virginia Opera, Center Theater, 160 Virginia Beach Bd, **Norfolk**, Virginia 23510
☎ 804-627 9545   FX 804-622-0058
♬ Oct – Mar   B P.O. Box 625, Norfolk, Virginia 23501. Discounts for groups of 15 +   CC Amex, MC, Visa   & Seating, restrooms and access   ⸬ 1729   ♟ Bars
PT Bus – city buses to Virginia Beach Bd   Ⓟ At theatre.

Founded in 1974, Virginia Opera stages four works a year (with surtitles), regularly including a premiere or offbeat production.

FESTIVALS

AUSTRIA

Bregenz Festival, Platz der Wiener Symphoniker, A-6900 **Bregenz**
TX 05574-57539   FX 05574-22811 242
♬ Jul – Aug   B As above
☎ 5574-22811-227   CC None
& Wheelchair space in Festival Hall and open air theatre, Theater am Kornmarkt has seats for wheelchairs users   ⸬ Festival Hall – 1800, Theater am Kornmarkt – 633, Open air theatre – 4400   ♟ Restaurant
PT Train – Bregenz Station   Ⓟ Nearby.

A splendidly spectacular production on the floating stage and another in the nearby Festspielhaus plus top-quality orchestras.

EIRE

Wexford Festival Opera, Theatre Royal, High Street, **Wexford**   ☎ 053-22240
FX 053-24289   ♬ Oct – Nov   B As above   ☎ 053-22144   CC MC, Visa
& None   ⸬ 550   ♟ Wine bars and reception areas   PT Train and Bus – Wexford station   Ⓟ Adjacent to theatre.

The compact 1832 Theatre Royal, charmingly restored in 1987, is centre for productions that take over the whole town and introduce new talents.

ENGLAND

Buxton International Arts Festival,
Buxton Opera House, Water St, **Buxton**,
SK17 6XN ☎ 0298-70395
[FX] 0298-72289   ♫ Jul – Aug
[B] Festival office, 1 Crescent View, Hall
Bank, Buxton SK17 6EN ☎ 0298 72190.
Discounts for groups of 10 + [CC] Amex,
MC, Visa ⅌ Special seating and access
⸬ 980 and 50 standing ⚲ Bars,
restaurant nearby [PT] Train – Buxton
station ℗ Car park behind Opera House.

Lovely Edwardian opera house with warm
acoustics, totally refurbished in 1979, as
centre of multi-faceted indoor/outdoor
entertainment amid stunning landscape.

FINLAND

Savonlinna Opera Festival, Olavinlinna
Castle, 57150 **Olavinlinna**
☎ 358-57 514 700 [TX] 81057007
[FX] 358-57 21866 ♫ Jul [B] Olavinkatu,
35, SF-57130 Savonlinna, ☎
[TX] [FX] As above [CC] MC,
Visa ⅌ 2 wheelchair spaces ⸬ 2262
⚲ Cafes and restaurants in
castle [PT] Train – good connections from
Helsinki. Walking distance from
centre ℗ Nearby.

Half-covered inner courtyard of
Olavinlinna Castle, set on its own tiny
island, is a striking setting for productions
imbued with Finnish national pride.

FRANCE

**International Festival d'Art Lyrique et de
Musique d'Aix-en-Provence**, Palais de
L'Ancien Archevêché, 13100,
Aix-en-Provence ☎ 16-42233781
[TX] 410065F FESTAIX [FX] 16-42961261
[B] As above [CC] Visa ⅌ Contact box
office for details ⸬ Variety of venues
⚲ Nearby [PT] Train – Avignon station
℗ Nearby.

Up to five productions run in repertory,
interspersed with oratorios, with
international casts and a penchant for
Mozart.

GERMANY

Ludwigsburger Schlossfestspiele,
Hohenzollernstrasse 45, Postfach 1022,
7140 **Ludwigsburg** ☎ 07141-25035
[TX] 726 4451 LUSF [FX] 07141-901011
♫ May – Oct [B] Kartenbüro der
Ludwigsburger Festspiele, Postfach 1022,
7140 Ludwigsburg ☎ 07141-28000
[CC] None ⅌ Elevator, seating,
wheelchair spaces, restroom. Access
problems in some areas ⸬ 250 – 1200
⚲ Snackbar ☎ 07141-941719
[PT] Bus – S-Bahn ℗ Nearby.

Handsome former early 18th-century royal
palace used for Mozart, now complemented
by splendidly equipped new Forum am
Schlosspark (1988), for a variety of concerts
and opera.

Munich Opera Festival, Nationaltheater,
Max Joseph Platz 2, 8000 **München** 22
☎ 089-21 85 1 [FX] 089-21 85 304
♫ Dates vary, contact box office
[B] Tageskasse der Bayerischen Staatsoper,
Maximilianstr 11, 8000 München 22
☎ 089-22 13 16 [CC] None ⅌ Contact
box office for details ⸬ 1677 and 321
standing ⚲ Snackbars ℗ Underground
opposite theatre.

Bavarian State Opera's annual adventure
into summer festivity is tight-knit,
action-packed and musically unrivalled, a
sure magnet for the opera buff.

ITALY

Stagione Lirica, Arena Sferisterio, 1-62100
Macerata ☎ 0733-40735/49508
[TX] 560413 ARSFER ♫ Jul – Aug
[B] As above, book 12 months in advance
[CC] Amex, MC, Visa ⅌ None

:::: Approx 2000   ♀ Snackbars
[PT] Bus – local to Arena   ℗ Nearby.

Open-air Arena Sferisterio, set in the Apennine foothills and built for a unique 19th-century ball-game, provides an acoustically superb back-drop – an enormous wall – for ambitious productions.

Rossini Opera Festival, Teatro Rossini, Via Rossini 37, 61100 **Pesaro**
☎ 0721-697360   [TX] 560215 PP PSI
[FX] 0721-30979   ♫ Aug – Sep   [B] As above, tickets should be requested by 1st March   [CC] None
& None   :::: Theatre – 350, Auditorium – 250   ♀ Nearby
[PT] Train – Pesaro Central. Bus – Pesaro Central   ℗ Nearby.

The old town, in a beautiful valley open to the sea, is a museum to its most famous son, Rossini, whose every note is lovingly cherished.

Festival dei Due Mondi (Festival of the Two Worlds), Teatro Nuovo and Caio Melisso, **Spoleto**   ☎ 0743-28100/40700   ♫ Jun – Jul   [B] As above   ☎ 0743-40265 and Teatro Giulio Cesare, Viale Giulio Cesare 229, 00196 Roma   [CC] None
& Contact box office   :::: Teatro Nuovo – 800, Caio Melisso –300   ♀ Bars
[PT] Train – Spoleto station. Bus – special and regular services   ℗ Nearby.

Festival dei Due Monde (Two Worlds), started by Menotti in 1958 in parallel with Spoleto USA (near Charleston), achieves high standards without stars.

Festival Pucciniano, Piazzale Belvedere Puccini 4, 55048 **Torre del Lago**
☎ 0584-350567/340235
[FX] 0584-6350562   ♫ Jul – Aug   [B] As above   ☎ 0584-359322/350897
[CC] None   & Free entry, elevator
:::: 4000   ♀ Restaurant, bars
[PT] Train – to Via Pisa. Bus – from Viareggio   ℗ Nearby.

Set beside the lake, Puccini's villa, where he wrote most of his operas, provides inspiration for a festival mainly devoted to him.

Ente Lirico Arena di Verona, Piazza Bra' 28, 37121 **Verona**
☎ 045-590966/590726/590109
[TX] 480 869 OPERVR   [FX] 045-590201
♫ Festival Anfiteatro Arena – Jul – Aug, Teatro Filarmonico – Spring, Autumn and Winter   [B] As above   [CC] None
& Discounts   :::: Arena – 16,663, Filarmonico – 1137   ♀ Arena – bars
☎ 045-596517/8005151, Filarmonico – 1 bar   ☎ 045-8002880   [PT] Train – Verona Station at Porta Nuova. Bus – AMT 1, 8, 10, 51 Piazza Bra' and San Luca   ℗ Porta Nuova Station, Via Pallone, Via Bentegodi.

Perhaps the most famous of the outdoor festivals, making spectacular use of the Roman arena, notably in its staple *Aida*.

SCOTLAND

Edinburgh International Arts Festival, 21 Market Street, **Edinburgh**, EH1 1BW
☎ 031-226 4001   [TX] 728 115
[FX] 031-225 1173   ♫ Aug – Sep   [B] As above   ☎ 031-225 5756   [CC] Amex, Diners, MC, Visa   & Variety of venues   ♀ Bars in King's Theatre, Playhouse and Leith Theatre   [PT] Train – Waverley Station   ℗ Nearby.

Opera is always a strong, if haphazard, component of this huge festival, largely involving foreign companies dotted around this historic city (which still lacks a proper opera house).

SWEDEN

Drottningholms Slottsteater, Drottningholm, Nr Stockholm
☎ 08-665 1400 [FX] 08-661 01 94
♫ May – Sep   [B] Drottningholms Teatermuseum, 'Fôrestàllningar', Box

27050, S-10251, Stockholm
☎ 08-660 8281 CC Amex ♿ Two
wheelchairs per performance ⚄ 450
♟ Restaurant nearby ☎ 08-759 04 25
PT Boat – from Klara Målarstrand. Bus –
direct from Grand Hotel and Central
Station. Underground – to Brommaplan
and Màlaröbus to Drottningholm
Ⓟ Next to theatre.

The Court Theatre, a unique time-capsule
preserving all its original 1766 decor and
stage machinery, is the elegant backdrop to
Classical opera, accompanied on authentic
instruments (plus ballet and concerts).

USA

Baltimore Opera Company Inc., Lyric
Opera House, Mount Royal Ave.,
Baltimore, Maryland 21201
☎ 301-727 0592 FX 301-727 7854
♫ Oct – Apr B 527 North Charles
Street, Baltimore, Maryland 21201
☎ 301-685 0692 CC Amex, Diners,
MC, Visa ♿ Ramp, wheelchair spaces,
hearing-aids, restroom ⚄ 2600
♟ Nearby PT Train – Metrobus. Bus –
Amtrack Ⓟ Theatre.

With only rare excursions into native
works, Baltimore Opera takes a traditional

line in production and repertory, but has
made some works with its annual
International Vocal Competition.

Glimmerglass Opera, Alice Busch Opera
Theater, P.O. Box 191, **Cooperstown,** New
York 13326 ☎ 607-547 5704
FX 607-547 6030 ♫ Jul – Aug B As
above ☎ 607-547 2255. Discounts for
groups of 20 + CC Amex, MC, Visa
♿ Wheelchair access and seating
⚄ 900 ♟ Bars, light snacks available in
grounds ☎ 607-547 2255 PT Own
transport only Ⓟ At theatre site.

Two operas and an operetta, spread over
the summer with concerts and recitals, in
the sylvan setting of the Alice Busch Opera
Theater close to Lake Otsego.

Lake George Opera Festival, Adirondack
Performing Arts Center, P.O. Box 2172,
Glens Falls, New York 12801
☎ 518-793 3858 FX 518-793 6719
♫ Jul – Aug B As above. Discounts for
groups CC MC, Visa ♿ Special
seating ⚄ 450 ♟ Limited
refreshments ☎ 518-793 3866 PT Taxis
only Ⓟ Next to Arts Center.

Self-assured productions in the local high
school of this small summer resort by the
lake, set in the unspoilt Adirondack
mountains.

COMPLETE LIST OF COMPOSERS AND OPERAS

The operas in this guide fit into one of two categories: *either* they are so popular that they form part of the regular repertoire *or* they hold a sufficiently important place in the history of opera to justify their occasional revival.

The major operas and the shorter summaries are in chronological order headed by a biography of their composer. The format of the entry for each major opera presents the general details beside a list of the principal characters, followed by a synopsis of the story. In the left-hand margins are highlights to watch out for (whether arias or significant lines). This is intended to give a quick picture of what to expect. The translations given are not necessarily exact, but capture the spirit of what is being sung. Equally, some directors give highly individual interpretations to the original stage directions, particularly in operas where the plots are susceptible to political preaching (for example *Fidelio*).

Most can be enjoyed at first sight: Mozart's *Don Giovanni*, for example, or Puccini's *Tosca*. But with some, preliminary study (listening to a recording, reading the libretto) is essential: to ensure enjoyment of Wagner's *Ring*, for example.

In the shorter summaries, the following abbreviations have been used: **(b-bar)** bass baritone; **(bar)** baritone; **(c)** contralto; **(c-t)** counter-tenor; **(col-s)** colloratura soprano; **(ms)** mezzo-soprano; **(s)** soprano; **(sp)** speaking part; **(t)** tenor; **(tr)** treble.

LUDWIG VAN BEETHOVEN

Born Bonn 1770, died Vienna 1827. Beethoven had early
success as a pianist and played the viola in the Bonn
Opera orchestra before moving to Vienna in 1792. He
was taught at different times by Haydn and Salieri. His
first two piano concertos were written between 1792 and
1795, and the first of his symphonies appeared in 1800.
Fidelio, commissioned by the Theater an der Wien, is his
only complete opera. Like another of his choral works,
the *Missa Solemnis*, it demands great rigour of the singers.
Beethoven worked on *Fidelio* over a period of ten years,
composing three 'Leonore' overtures (frequently performed as symphonic pieces) before the final 'Fidelio'
overture, first heard in 1814. The brilliance and energy of
the orchestral writing announced a new era in German
and in dramatic opera.

FIDELIO

Florestan, a political prisoner	tenor	
Leonore (Leonora), his wife, disguised as Fidelio	soprano	
Rocco, chief jailer	bass	
Marzelline (Marcellina), his daughter	soprano	
Don Pizarro, the prison governor	baritone	

Seville, 18th century: the story of unjust
political imprisonment and conjugal devotion. Leonore, disguised as the young
Fidelio, discovers her husband Florestan in
the cells and bravely stands between him and
his persecutor, the prison governor Don
Pizarro.

The libretto is by Joseph von Sonnleith-
ner after the play *Léonore, ou l'Amour Conjugal* by Jean Nicolas Bouilly. *Fidelio* was first
performed in three acts, at the Theater an
der Wien, Vienna, in 1805; the final two-act
version was not completed for a further nine
years.

ACT I

The state prison

Oh wär ich schon mit dir vereint
('Oh if only you and I
together'): Marzelline's
expression of longing to marry
Fidelio

Mir ist so wunderbar ('I see such
wonder'): the stylized quartet
in which each comments on the
situation as it would appear

In the prison Rocco's daughter Marzelline is being wooed
by one of the jailer's colleagues but she has fallen in love
with her father's new assistant Fidelio, not realizing that
the young man is actually Leonore, wife of the prisoner
Florestan, in disguise. Rocco is by no means averse to the
idea of Fidelio becoming a member of the family and the
four of them join together in a formal canon, each in turn
hoping for joy to come. Rocco follows this with a song in
praise of money in a marriage.

Although worried about deceiving Marzelline,
Leonore drives herself on, as Fidelio, to persuade Rocco

Hat man nicht auch Gold beineben ('Money is a necessity'): Rocco's aria idolizing gold

Ich habe Muth ('I am brave enough'): Leonore's insistence that she can bear the sight of the starving prisoner

Ha! welch' ein Augenblick! ('Ah! What a moment!'): Don Pizarro's violent aria determining on the murder of Florestan

Abscheulicher! ('Oh loathsome villain'): Leonore's splendid and moving outburst of anger, determination and hope

O welche Lust ('What happiness'): the Prisoners' Chorus

The prison dungeon
Gott! welch' Dunkel hier!: ('God, how dark it is down here'): Florestan's notoriously difficult aria, evoking the depths of human despair

Euch werde Lohn ('May heaven reward you'): Florestan's simple gratitude, Leonore's love and Rocco's pity combined in a beautiful trio

O namen-, namenlose Freude! ('What indescribable joy'): Florestan and Leonore's joyful reunion

The castle parade ground
Wer ein solches Weib errungen ('Whoever wins such a wife'): the chorus' acclaim for a heroic wife

to trust her to help in the dungeons. The old jailer welcomes this idea but pronounces that there is one prisoner whom no-one must see and who in any case is unlikely to survive much longer as on the governor's orders he is being deliberately starved. This seems to bear out Leonore's intuition that her missing husband is indeed below. Her determination that she can face any hardship leads Rocco to agree to ask the governor's permission.

The governor is on his tour of inspection. He receives a warning that the minister may be about to pay a visit and he decides that Florestan, his political opponent, must be eliminated. Detailing a trumpeter to watch out for the minister, Don Pizarro orders Rocco to kill Florestan. Rocco, realizing that this is something that even the reward of gold cannot justify, refuses; but he agrees to dig the grave. Leonore, having overheard, places her faith in Heaven to guide her either in rescuing her husband or in dying with him.

On Leonore's initiative the prisoners are let out into the sunlight to enjoy the fresh air. Pizarro orders that they return immediately. Rocco defuses his anger by reminding him of the more important task ahead.

ACT II

Florestan, in chains, gives way to despair. He seems to see a vision of his wife, perhaps an angel, bringing him peace. He sinks down exhausted as Rocco and Leonore approach. They begin the grim task of preparing a grave while Leonore tries to see the prisoner's face. He stirs, and at last she is able to recognize him. He asks Rocco about the governor of the prison. When he learns that it is Pizarro, whose crimes he had denounced, he gives up all hope. Rocco, urged on by Leonore, offers him some wine and she then is able to give her husband some bread. He does not recognize his wife in Fidelio.

Pizarro descends to taunt and despatch his victim. But the supposed Fidelio flings herself in front of her husband, warning the governor that he must first kill her, Florestan's wife. As Pizarro prepares to do so, she draws a pistol, and at that moment a trumpet call announces the arrival of the minister. The defeated Pizarro is led upstairs as Florestan and Leonore fall into each others' arms.

With the prisoners all assembled, the minister is overjoyed to recognize his old friend Florestan. Pizarro's attempt to incriminate Rocco is dismissed and he is led away as a prisoner. Leonore is permitted to unchain her husband, applauded by all.

VINCENZO BELLINI

Born Catania 1801, died Puteaux 1835. The operas of Bellini epitomize the Italian *bel canto* style, which is characterized by long, highly ornamented vocal lines. Born into a family of musicians, Bellini completed his education at the Naples Conservatory and was given his first commission by the San Carlo Opera, Naples. The manner in which *Bianca e Gernando* (1826) was received led to a commission from La Scala, Milan, and the success of *Il Pirata* in 1827 established Bellini's reputation internationally. With Felice Romani, the most famous librettist of the day, he wrote a series of operas, including *I Capuleti e i Montecchi* (1830), *La Sonnambula* (1831) and *Norma* (1831), in which *bel canto* singers can exhibit the full range and quality of their voices. Bellini's last opera was *I Puritani* (1835).

LA SONNAMBULA

(THE SLEEPWALKER)

Teresa, a mill-owner	mezzo-soprano
Amina, her foster daughter	soprano
Lisa, an innkeeper	soprano
Elvino, a young farmer	tenor
Count Rodolfo	bass

Switzerland, early 19th century: Elvino's wedding to Amina is delayed when she is found in another man's bedroom. The explanation – that she was walking in her sleep – is only accepted after she is seen sleepwalking again.

The libretto is by Felice Romani; the first performance was at the Teatro Carcano, Milan, in 1831.

A village square

Tutto è gioia ('Everyone else is rejoicing'): Lisa's expression of misery amidst the general rejoicing

Come per me sereno ('How peacefully for me'): Amina's aria on her contentment

Prendi, l'anel ti dono ('Take this ring'): Elvino's duet with Amina as he presents her with a ring

ACT I

Lisa the innkeeper has the only sad face in the village because the man she loves, Elvino, is to be married to Amina and it upsets her to hear the villagers serenading the future bride and groom. Nor is she made any happier by having, herself, a suitor whom she despises. Amina by contrast has never been happier and is especially grateful to her foster mother Teresa, who owns the local mill. However, her attempts to congratulate Lisa on her own future wedding are not well received. The notary prepares the marriage contract and Elvino gives Amina a ring. All is now ready for the wedding.

The celebrations are interrupted by the arrival of a stranger's carriage. Rodolfo, wearied by travelling, is offered accommodation at Lisa's inn. He seems to recognize the village. The villagers tell him that the old

Son geloso del zefiro errante ('I am jealous of the wandering breeze'): Elvino tells Amina that he is jealous of anything that touches her

At the inn that night

D'un pensiero e d'un accento ('Never, even in my thoughts'): Amina's passionate protestation of her innocence

A wood near Teresa's mill

Ah! perchè non posso odiarti ('Even now I cannot hate you'): Elvino's anguished aria admitting that he loves Amina still

The square

Ah! non credea mirarti ('Who could have believed'): Amina's wistful song of the flowers that have withered with her happiness
Ah! non giunge ('No-one could believe'): Amina's last aria as the couple are reunited

count has been dead for some years and that the son is missing. Rodolfo says he knows the son is alive (it is of course himself) and laughs at their superstitious fear of the ghost at the castle. Told about the wedding, he admires the bride. Elvino's jealousy is aroused but Amina reassures him, and they part for the last time before the wedding.

Lisa has guessed that Rodolfo is the young count. She is not pleased when, visiting him to see that all is in order, they are disturbed. The door creaks open and as Lisa hides next door – in her haste leaving her scarf – Amina enters, walking in her sleep. She is dressed in white and for a moment he thinks she is the ghost. Amina believes Rodolfo is Elvino and that they are already married. Dreaming, she encourages him to embrace her but he restrains himself and leaves her sleeping on the bed, though not before Lisa has seen them together. She fetches Elvino and the villagers, who burst into Rodolfo's bedroom and find Amina sleeping on his bed. Her confusion on being woken by the noise only makes her guilt seem more certain. She is cast aside by all except Teresa, who picks up the scarf and ties it round Amina's neck. Amina falls into her arms.

ACT II
The villagers are on their way to ask the Count to defend Amina if she is indeed innocent. Amina, supported by Teresa, meets Elvino and they reproach each other: she for his lack of trust, he for her infidelity. The villagers call out that the Count confirms her innocence, but this only increases Elvino's rage. He snatches back the ring, bitterly regretting that he still loves her.

Elvino seeks consolation with Lisa, who is delighted by the turn of events. As he prepares to take her into the church, where all is ready for a wedding, Rodolfo stops them and explains that Amina is a somnambulist: that she walks in her sleep. Elvino is not persuaded; and indeed the entire village voices its disbelief, bringing Teresa out to ask them to be quiet as Amina is sleeping. Lisa tells Teresa that it is she who is to marry Elvino. She deserves him for she does not spend her evenings alone in a gentleman's room. *Menzognera!* ('Lying woman!') Teresa produces the scarf she found in Rodolfo's bedroom. Elvino is aghast. Suddenly Amina can be seen sleepwalking across the bridge of the mill. They are all terrified in case she wakes and falls. At last she is on firm ground and, still asleep, sings of her lost happiness.

Convinced at last, and guided by Rodolfo, Elvino slips the ring back on Amina's finger, and she awakes and forgives Elvino's incredulity.

NORMA

Norma, High Priestess of the Druid temple	soprano	
Adalgisa, a virgin of the temple	soprano	
Pollione, Roman proconsul in Gaul	tenor	
Flavio, a centurion	tenor	
Oroveso, Norma's father	bass	

Gaul, 1st century BC: the tragedy caused by a Roman proconsul's love for two women – Norma, who has borne him two sons, and the young Adalgisa, her acolyte.

The libretto is by Felice Romani after Alexandre Soumet's play *Norma, ou L'Infanticide*. The first performance was given at La Scala, Milan, in 1831 and established him as Italy's leading composer of opera. Maria Callas and Joan Sutherland have been especially associated with the title role.

In the sacred forest of the Druids

ACT I

Oroveso leads the Druids in prayer against their Roman masters. Pollione, the Roman proconsul, is watching with Flavio; he tells the centurion that he has fallen in love with a young priestess in place of Oroveso's daughter Norma, by whom he already has two children. He tells Flavio of his dream that, having taken Adalgisa back to Rome with him, they were parted by the supernatural presence of Norma. Flavio persuades him to leave as Norma enters. The Druids are begging for her blessing on an uprising, but she tells them that Rome's power will fade by reason of its own vices and that they must remain at peace. She calls upon the Moon to calm the unhappy Gauls. Her followers are still crying for the death of the Romans and in particular of Pollione, but Norma confesses to herself that what she most desires is that Pollione should love her again.

Casta Diva ('Chaste Goddess'): Norma and the priestesses address the Moon as she cuts the sacred mistletoe

Adalgisa, now alone, blames herself for falling in love with the man who has made her a traitor to her vows. Pollione returns. She begs him to leave her, but he pleads with her to yield to love and find eternal happiness with him. At last she promises to go with him to Rome and to renounce her religion.

O Dio! Perduta io son! ('My soul is lost'): Adalgisa appeals for God's pity and protection

Va, crudele ('Oh cruel woman'): Pollione would rather die than be parted from Adalgisa

Norma's dwelling

Norma, at home, is worried about the future of her children. While she and her companion discuss the news that Pollione has been recalled to Rome, and whether he will take Norma with him, Adalgisa comes to confide in the High Priestess. She tells Norma that she has fallen in love. When she repeats the words used by her lover, Norma is reminded of her own experiences. She absolves Adalgisa from her vows. As she asks which man it is that

Io fui così ('It was just the same for me'): Norma reflects that she felt enchantment like Adalgisa's without knowing it was for the same man

No, non tremare, o perfido
('Tremble not for her but for
yourself'): Norma accuses
Pollione of treachery

**Beside the cradle of the
children**
Mira, O Norma ('See these
lovely children'): as Norma
determines to die, Adalgisa
calls for her to have pity on her
children: the greatest of all
Italian duets for two sopranos

The forest

Guerra! guerra! ('War! War!'):
Norma unleashes the Gauls
against their Roman
oppressors

Adalgisa loves, Pollione arrives, and Adalgisa points to
the father of Norma's children. This leads to an impassioned trio in which Adalgisa rejects Pollione utterly.
Both women unite in cursing and renouncing Pollione.

ACT II

Norma contemplates killing her children in preference to
abandoning them to a stepmother in a foreign country,
but before making up her mind she calls for Adalgisa.
Having made Adalgisa swear to obey her instructions, she
tells her to take the children and leave with Pollione.
Adalgisa refuses and in a duet undertakes to restore
Pollione to Norma and the children.

The Gauls are still eager to fight, and anxious to attack
Pollione before he leaves. They are restrained by
Oroveso, who orders them to follow his daughter's
inspired orders. Norma is waiting at the temple and her
maid brings the news that Adalgisa has failed to change
Pollione's mind. At first Norma believes Adalgisa has
betrayed her; then she learns that Adalgisa is renewing
her vows and that Pollione intends to drag her away by
force. She summons the Gauls and orders immediate
battle.

Their rites demand the sacrifice of a victim. Norma
reassures them that a victim will be found. At that
moment Pollione is brought in a prisoner. He asks to be
sacrificed without delay, and it is Norma's duty as high
priestess to strike with the sacred dagger. As she approaches him, she stops and orders the others away so that
she may question him first.

Alone with Pollione, she offers him freedom if he will
renounce Adalgisa. When he refuses, she threatens first
to kill his children, then to slaughter all the Romans and
to burn Adalgisa. The more he begs her to kill him and
spare Adalgisa, the more enraged she becomes. At last she
calls the Druids back and orders them to build a pyre,
announcing that it is she herself who will be the victim
and confessing her past guilt. As the people express
disbelief, Pollione at last recognizes her as the woman he
truly loves. Exacting from her father the promise to
protect her children as the crowd turns to curse her,
Norma and Pollione throw themselves on to the
sacrificial fire.

I CAPULETI E I MONTECCHI

(THE CAPULETS AND THE MONTAGUES)

In four parts (two acts), text by Felice Romani after Luigi Scevola's *Giulietta e Romeo*, loosely based on Shakespeare's *Romeo and Juliet*. Premiere: La Fenice, Venice, 1830. Typically Bellinian tunefulness is given momentum by dramatic accent and rhythm.

Verona, 13th century: Tebaldo (**t**, Tybalt), betrothed to Giulietta (**s**), warns of Romeo's hostile intentions towards the Capulets. Romeo (**ms**), incognito, pleads for his own marriage to Giulietta to seal peace between the warring clans, but her father Capellio (**b**, Capulet) rejects the idea. In love with Romeo, Giulietta takes a sleeping draught to feign death and avoid marriage to Tebaldo. Believing her dead, Romeo takes poison. She awakes too late and dies of grief.

I PURITANI

(THE PURITANS)

In three acts, text by Carlo Pepoli after Jacques-Arsène Ancelot and Saintine's *Têtes Rondes et Cavaliers*, in turn taken from Walter Scott's *Old Mortality*. Premiere: Théâtre Italien, Paris, 1835. Bellini's last opera, requiring a powerful quartet of soloists.

A fortress near Plymouth, during the English Civil War (1640s): Charles I's widow Enrichetta (**s**, Queen Henrietta) is imprisoned under the Puritan governor Gualtiero (**b**, Lord Walton), who reluctantly agrees to his daughter Elvira (**s**) marrying Arturo (**t**, Lord Talbot), a cavalier. Disguised in Elvira's bridal veil, the Queen escapes with Arturo's help, but they are spotted by Elvira, who imagines Arturo unfaithful and loses her sanity: *'Qui la voce sua soave'* ('It was here in sweetest accents'). She regains her senses when Arturo, at great risk, returns and is pardoned after the Puritans are victorious.

ALBAN BERG

Born Vienna 1885, died Vienna 1935. Berg wrote two of the most powerful and original music dramas of the 20th century: *Wozzeck* and *Lulu*. He was 19 when he began his formal musical training with the composer Schoenberg. In 1914 he started to write the libretto and music for *Wozzeck*. His experiences in the Austrian Army in World War I intensified his understanding of the central character in Büchner's play *Woyzeck*, on which he based the opera. *Wozzeck* was immediately recognized as a work of genius and produced in other European houses. In 1926 he began work on *Lulu*, but the intricate score, employing 12-tone techniques, was uncompleted at the time of Berg's death. The third act was edited and orchestrated by Friedrich Cerha.

WOZZECK

Franz Wozzeck	baritone
Marie, his mistress	soprano
Margret, a neighbour	contralto
Drum Major	tenor
Andres, a friend of Wozzeck	tenor
Captain	tenor
Doctor	bass

Leipzig, 1824: the painful story, with a tragic outcome, of a poor man's humiliating struggle to support a woman and their child as his mind becomes contorted by her infidelity and the experiments of an ambitious doctor.

Based on a play by Georg Büchner, found after the writer's death, *Wozzeck* is a psychological drama set to continuous music but with *Sprechstimme*, the words produced half way between speaking and singing. It was first staged at the Berlin Staatsoper in 1925 after 100 rehearsals.

The Captain's room

Wir arme Leut! ('We poor people'): Wozzeck surprises the Captain with a well-argued retort

A field near the town

ACT I
The Captain muses on Time and Eternity. Wozzeck is shaving him and the Captain reprimands him for immorality because he has an illegitimate child. Wozzeck retorts that God does not blame children for their parents' oversights and suggests that morality is the preserve of those who can afford it. The Captain, tired of the conversation, sends him off with plenty of good advice.

Cutting wood with his friend Andres, Wozzeck is convinced that the wood is haunted. Wozzeck becomes so unbalanced and confused that his friend insists on leading him back to the town.

Marie's room
Soldaten, Soldaten ('Soldiers, Soldiers'): Marie sings along with the band

Mädel, was fängst Du jetzt an? ('Where are you going my pretty?'): Marie's lullaby

Marie, the mother of Wozzeck's son, is watching the soldiers with Margret. They both admire the Drum Major. When rebuked by her neighbour for encouraging him, Marie goes indoors to sing to her child. Wozzeck returns, still very disturbed. She tries to interest him in his son, but without even looking at him Wozzeck rushes out, leaving Marie to reflect on their grim existence: they are unmarried and so very poor.

The Doctor's study next day
Oh! meine Theorie! ('My very own theory'): the Doctor has ambitions to make his name over Wozzeck's case

The Doctor has many theories, which he tries out on Wozzeck. He is particularly interested in his patient's growing obsessions and visions. He sees here an opportunity to establish himself as an expert on this form of paranoia.

The street in front of Marie's house

Marie is flirting with the Drum Major and he takes her in his arms. She breaks free, but when he persists she leads him into the house.

Marie's room

Mädel, mach's Lädel zu! ('Shut the window tight'): Marie's grim lullaby sung to her child

ACT II
Marie, admiring her new earrings in the mirror, tries to persuade her child to go to sleep. Wozzeck returns with some money for her and realizes what has happened. He runs out, leaving Marie full of remorse.

The street
Ein langer Bart unter dem Kinn ('The longer the beard'): the Doctor and the Captain tease Wozzeck about Marie

The Doctor is in a rush. When the Captain detains him, he offers a highly discouraging diagnosis of the Captain's health. Meeting Wozzeck, they cannot resist teasing him about Marie and the Drum Major until he becomes desperate.

The street in front of Marie's house

When Wozzeck returns to Marie he is raving. She pushes him away saying she would rather be dead than have him touch her. His head is full of thoughts about his knife.

A beer-garden
Ein Jäger aus der Pfalz ('A huntsman from the Rheinland'): a local hunting song
Blut? Blut! ('Blood? blood!'): the Idiot's mention of blood increases Wozzeck's dementia

Marie and the Drum Major are together at a party. Wozzeck, watching them, is beside himself with jealousy. His friend Andres joins him and tries to calm him until an Idiot comes up and tells Wozzeck that he stinks of blood.

The barracks
Einer nach dem Andern! ('It's just one after another'): Wozzeck's anguished obsession with Marie's infidelity

Wozzeck's mind is divided between prayer and the image of a large knife. The Drum Major staggers in drunk to give them the details of the woman he has been with. He taunts Wozzeck. They fight and he throws Wozzeck to the ground before releasing him. The others go to sleep while Wozzeck is left staring into space.

Marie's room

Heiland, Du hast Dich ihrer erbarmt ('Oh my Redeemer, Thou hadst pity on her'): Marie finds a parallel in the Bible to her own predicament

ACT III

Marie is reading from the Bible to her child. She reads about the woman taken in adultery, about an orphan and about Mary Magdalene. She prays for mercy.

Later, in a wood by a pond

Marie and Wozzeck are walking near a pond in the wood. He insists on sitting down. He kisses her before drawing his knife and cutting her throat, crying out that no-one else shall have her.

An inn at night

Es ritten drei Reiter ('Three horsemen rode by'): Wozzeck's ballad as he tries to simulate gaiety

Wozzeck watches the happy couples dancing. When Marie's neighbour joins him, he tries to entertain her. But she sees that his arm is red and smells of blood. As the others crowd around, Wozzeck leaves in a hurry.

By the pond

Wozzeck is searching for the knife when he hears someone calling 'Murderer'. Then he realizes that it is his own voice. He finds Marie's body and compares the red necklace of blood to the earrings as the rewards for sin. He grabs the knife and throws it into the water. Even the moon seems bloodstained. He wades into the pond to try to wash off the stains. The Doctor and the Captain pass. They hear Wozzeck's dying groans and hurry away.

The street outside Marie's house

Hopp, hopp! ('Hop, hop'): the awful irony of the child playing happily, unable to comprehend what has happened

Marie's child is playing with a hobbyhorse. Some children come skipping past and tell him that his mother is dead. He goes on playing with his toy after they leave; then hops off to join them.

LULU

Lulu	soprano
Dr Schön	baritone
Alwa, his son	tenor
Schigolch	bass
Countess Geschwitz	mezzo-soprano
Athlete	baritone
Artist	tenor
Schoolboy	contralto

A city in Germany, Paris and London, late 19th century: a series of bizarre episodes illustrates Lulu's rise from artist's model to châtelaine, destroying throughout whatever she touches. The reversal in Lulu's fortunes concludes with her murder.

Berg wrote the libretto, adapted from Frank Wedekind's plays *Erdgeist* and *Die Büchse der Pandora*. The first two acts were ready in 1934 but were not performed until after his death: at the Stadttheater, Zurich, in 1937. Not until Berg's widow died did a substantially realizable third act become available. The three-act version was first performed at the Paris Opéra in 1979.

PROLOGUE

A circus animal tamer introduces the characters in words and music, with Lulu characterized as a snake.

An artist's studio

ACT I

Lulu is being painted as Pierrot, watched by Dr Schön. His son Alwa drops in and the two of them admire Lulu before they leave. Alone with her, the Artist chases her round the studio and then locks the door as she yields to him. There is a hammering on the door and soon her husband breaks it open. Agitation at what he finds causes him to suffer a stroke, from which at first Lulu believes he will recover. On realizing that he is dead, it dawns on her that she is now rich.

Ich möchte tauschen ('I'd rather exchange'): the Artist's prophetic fears about Lulu's influence

The Artist is shocked at Lulu's amorality and while she dresses reflects that he is frightened almost to the point of preferring to change places with the corpse.

A grand drawing-room, Lulu's portrait in a brocade frame over the fireplace

Lulu and the Artist are now married and he is excited by the money he is getting for his pictures. When the doorbell rings, Lulu begs him not to let anyone interrupt them, but he is eager for more work and leaves her alone with a lame beggar – or so he believes. It is in fact Schigolch, an old and sinister figure from her past. He is immensely impressed by the Pierrot portrait. The doorbell rings again and Schigolch leaves as Dr Schön enters. He recognizes Schigolch as the man he has always believed to be Lulu's father. Schön has been her lover for some years. He has arranged both her marriages to try to free himself of her, and now he tells her that he himself is to be married.

The Artist returns and during a bitter argument with Schön discovers much about Lulu's past. He rushes from the room and kills himself in the kitchen. Schön's son Alwa arrives.

He and Lulu encourage Schön to invent a revolution in Paris for his newspaper so as to hush up the scandal which would threaten his engagement.

A theatre dressing-room, a poster of Lulu's portrait as Pierrot on the wall

Lulu is changing behind a screen while Alwa pours her some champagne. She tells him that a prince intends to marry her and carry her off to Africa. After she has left for her dance act, the Prince arrives. A bell rings and Lulu rushes in, apparently having fainted on stage when she saw Dr Schön with his fiancée. Coming back-stage to remonstrate with her, Dr Schön manages to get rid of everyone, including, reluctantly, the Prince. Tortured by the prospect of her going to Africa, he weakens, and within minutes she is dictating his farewell letter to his fiancée.

A grand room in German renaissance style hung with tapestries, Lulu's portrait, now in a massive gold frame, on an easel

ACT II

Countess Geschwitz has come to visit Lulu, who is now married to Dr Schön. A bowl of white flowers stands on a table. Lulu accompanies the Countess outside while Dr Schön gives way to jealousy.

Drawing a revolver, he pulls one of the curtains aside to see if anyone is hiding from him. Lulu returns, embarrassed by the Countess' flowers and attentions, and reproaches her husband for neglecting her. He says he has to go the Stock Exchange but she manages to draw him into the bedroom just as Schigolch, the Athlete and the Schoolboy appear, expecting to find her husband out. Lulu returns and jokes with them until the butler announces Dr Schön's return. The men hide, and then Alwa enters. While she flirts with him even the butler has difficulty in concealing his passion for her. Alwa throws himself at her feet and, though she admits to having poisoned his mother, he declares his love for her. Dr Schön has silently reappeared at the top of the stairs and, having witnessed the scene as well as observed the Athlete hiding behind the curtains, he screams at her and hands Lulu his revolver, insisting that she shoot herself. She fires a shot into the ceiling. The Athlete bursts from cover and dashes away up the stairs. Dr Schön crosses the room to look behind a screen and comes out holding Countess Geschwitz. Again he demands that Lulu kill herself. When she suggests divorce, he angrily refuses to contemplate another man succeeding him. Everyone involved with her has always had what they wanted, she claims, and she has never pretended to be other than she is. When he shouts at her, the Schoolboy jumps out from under the table. As Dr Schön turns round, Lulu empties the revolver into his back, continuing to press the trigger even when the gun is empty. *'Der Einzige, den ich geliebt!'* ('The only man I ever loved') she says as she pours herself a glass of champagne. The dying Doctor warns his son that he will be the next. Then the police arrive.

Du kreatur ('You animal'): Dr Schön's savage denunciation of his wife's amorality

Wenn sich die Menschen ('If men must kill themselves'): Lulu defends herself, saying that men bring upon themselves their own doom

The music of the *entre-acte* (which Berg had intended to accompany a film sequence) describes in cyclical form Lulu's trial and imprisonment, and her deliberate infection with cholera by the Countess Geschwitz, who infects herself by wearing the underclothes of a victim of the plague. She exchanges them with Lulu's while visiting her in prison. Both end up in the isolation ward of the hospital, where the Countess does all she can to make her face resemble Lulu's.

Part of the plan for Lulu's escape involves the Athlete posing as her husband, but he is worried about the cholera. With the Athlete's doubts, Lulu's influence

The same room, dusty and with an air of desertion, the portrait propped up with its face to the wall

Durch dieses Kleid ('Beneath
this dress'): Alwa's declaration
of desire

Paris. A huge *salon*
dominated by the Pierrot
portrait

London. A miserable attic
enlivened only by the sound of
a barrel-organ in the street

shows the first sign of waning.

Schigolch appears with the passports, and he and the
Countess, recently discharged, set off to the hospital.
Lulu and the Countess once again will exchange clothes.
The Athlete tries to extract money from Alwa without
success and is further angered by the return of the
Schoolboy. At last Lulu, very weak and wearing the
Countess' dress, enters, supported by Schigolch. The
Athlete is further unnerved by her appearance and leaves,
threatening to betray them. Alwa is overcome at seeing
Lulu again. She tells him how she managed to escape,
leaving the Countess lying in prison as Dr Schön's
murderess, and he puts her portrait back on the easel. She
kisses him and draws him on to the *chaise longue*.
Entranced by her, he never falters, even when she
murmurs that this was the sofa on which his father bled to
death.

ACT III
Lulu and Alwa, living grandly among a dissolute group of
friends on the prospects of their railway shares, entertain
lavishly. The Athlete has reappeared to blackmail her
(she is still an escaped murderess) and a procurer is eager
to recruit her for a brothel in Cairo. The whole set-up
collapses with the Stock Exchange, and Alwa and Lulu (in
disguise) only just manage to evade the police.

Living as a prostitute in London, Lulu now supports
Alwa and Schigolch with her earnings. Countess Ges-
chwitz manages to find them. She has succeeded in
acquiring Lulu's Pierrot portrait in Paris. First Alwa is
killed trying to protect Lulu and then Lulu herself is
murdered by a visiting client (Jack the Ripper). He stabs
the Countess as she kneels adoringly before the portrait.
The stricken Countess crawls towards the bedroom:
Lulu Mein Engel!
Lass dich noch einmal sehen!
Ich bin dir nah! Bleibe dir nah!
In Ewigkeit!
('Lulu my Angel
I must see you just once more
I am here
I will stay here with you for ever')
As the Countess dies, the cycle is complete.

HECTOR BERLIOZ

Born La Côte-St-André 1803, died Paris 1869. The son of a doctor, Berlioz was sent in 1821 to study medicine in Paris, where his passion for music soon led him to enrol at the Conservatoire. He won the Prix de Rome in 1830, the year his *Symphonie Fantastique* was first performed. Gluck, Weber and Beethoven were important influences on him at this time. In 1834 he was commissioned by the violinist Paganini to write a piece for the viola, and he composed *Harold in Italy*. In 1838 his first opera, *Benvenuto Cellini*, failed. From 1840 he toured Europe as a conductor, writing *La Damnation de Faust* (1846) and the oratorio *L'Enfance du Christ* (1854). Between 1855 and 1858 he wrote the music and libretto for *Les Troyens*. This was followed by the *opéra comique Béatrice et Bénédict*, based on Shakespeare's *Much Ado About Nothing*, in 1862.

BENVENUTO CELLINI

Pope Clement VII (Cardinal Salviati in performances when the Pope may not be portrayed on stage)	bass
Balducci, papal treasurer	bass
Teresa, his daughter	soprano
Benvenuto Cellini, a goldsmith	tenor
Fieramosca, sculptor to the Pope	baritone

Rome, 16th century: Benvenuto Cellini, to win Teresa from Fieramosca, his rival in love and art, must mollify the Pope and cast his statue of Perseus in bronze.

The libretto, by Léon de Wailly and August Barbier, is based on the renaissance craftsman's autobiography. *Benvenuto Cellini* was first performed at the Paris Opéra in 1838. The complicated score was subsequently revised by Liszt and Berlioz. Today's productions usually contain elements from both versions.

Balducci's apartments

Entre l'amour et le devoir ('Between love and duty'): Teresa's cavatina, torn between love and duty

O Teresa, vous que j'aime plus que ma vie ('O Teresa, I love you more than life itself'): the

ACT I

Cellini is courting Teresa, daughter of the Pope's treasurer. The old man is summoned to the Vatican and Cellini, hidden among the maskers, throws Teresa a note promising to visit her. She is delighted, though when he arrives she pretends to be alarmed.

Fieramosca has brought flowers. He is Cellini's rival both as a sculptor and for Teresa. Seeing Cellini, he hides and overhears Teresa saying she would rather die than marry Fieramosca and planning to run away with Cellini. He and his friend will be disguised as monks: Cellini in white and his apprentice in brown. They are to meet in

beautiful trio between the two lovers and the jealous Fieramosca

Piazza Colonna, Shrove Tuesday

La gloire était ma seule idole ('Fame was my only goal'): Cellini recognizes that his love for Teresa is more important that his search for glory as a sculptor

Cette somme t'est due par le Pape Clément ('This is Pope Clement's debt to you'): the apprentice's aria delivering money on account for the statue of Perseus in return for the promise of its completion

Le moine blanc ('The white friar'): the second time that Balducci has seized the innocent Fieramosca in compromising circumstances

Cellini's studio with the plaster model of the statue of Perseus

the Piazza Colonna, where a new opera is to be given, and they will escape to Florence during the performance. Suddenly Balducci returns. As Cellini slips out, Teresa pretends that she heard an intruder. She is astonished when her father discovers Fieramosca, whom he favours as Teresa's husband, hiding in her bedroom. Fieramosca's attempts at an explanation are indignantly ignored and he only just escapes being thrown naked into the fountain by their outraged neighbours.

ACT II

Cellini, singing of his love for Teresa, is waiting in the tavern with his friends. Their chorus praises the beautiful materials with which they work – gold, rubies, marble – matching the beauties of nature. When they order some more bottles of wine, the innkeeper refuses further credit until they have paid for the previous 130.

Cellini's apprentice brings some money from the Pope in return for the promise that the statue of Perseus will be cast the following day. Cellini accepts the bargain. Finding that Balducci, the treasurer, has sent only a small sum, they plan to take revenge by making fun of him. Meanwhile, Fieramosca and a friend plan to abduct Teresa, disguised as monks like Cellini.

The opera, *King Midas*, begins. Balducci has come, reluctantly, with his daughter. Cellini and his apprentice are there disguised. The crowd is tremendously excited, particularly when they see a character looking like Balducci on stage. Balducci is enraged. A second pair of monks have appeared in white and brown robes, and Teresa is confused. In the fight that ensues Cellini kills Fieramosca's friend. Cellini is seized by the crowd; but as a cannon shot rings out, the Piazza is plunged into darkness and Cellini escapes. Balducci grabs hold of the unfortunate Fieramosca (dressed, like Cellini, as a monk in white), who is taken to be the murderer.

ACT III

Teresa and the apprentice wait anxiously for news of Cellini. A band of white friars passes and she prays for his safety. At last he appears and explains that he was able to escape capture by hiding among the friars. Cursing the Pope and the statue, he plans immediate escape with Teresa, but they are interrupted by Balducci and Fieramosca. Balducci commands Teresa to marry Fieramosca immediately. Fieramosca, however, is too cowardly to stand up to Cellini. Then the Pope enters. While Balducci and Fieramosca point to Cellini as a murderer and abductor, the Pope is concerned only with his statue and decides that someone else should complete the casting in bronze. He orders the arrest of Cellini, and the sculptor seizes a hammer and threatens to smash the model. He demands of the Pope absolution and the hand of Teresa as well; and time to cast the statue. The Pope chooses to overlook Cellini's presumption and consents, with the condition that if the statue is not cast immediately Cellini will be hanged that night. While the Pope congratulates himself on saving the model and disposing of Cellini, Teresa mourns what seems the inevitable death of her lover. Cellini, however, welcomes the challenge.

The work begins. Then Fieramosca arrives to challenge Cellini to a duel. They leave and the workers decide to down tools. Fieramosca reappears and tries to bribe them to leave, and Teresa in despair believes Cellini is dead. However, the irrepressible Cellini reappears in time to urge on the work.

More and more metal is needed and the fire threatens to go out. Cellini throws all his other work into the crucible. An explosion, clouds of smoke, and the completed work is revealed as a masterpiece. The Pope, content with his statue, forgives Cellini. The lovers are reunited and the opera ends with a chorus in praise of art.

The bronze foundry

Du métal! du métal! ('More metal, more metal'): Fieramosca, fired with enthusiasm by his love of art, is converted to assisting Cellini.

LES TROYENS

(THE TROJANS)

Cassandre (Cassandra), Trojan prophetess	soprano	
Chorèbe (Choroebus), her betrothed	baritone	
Enée (Aeneas), a Trojan hero	tenor	
Ascagne (Ascanius), his son	soprano	
Didon (Dido), Queen of Carthage	mezzo-soprano	
Anna, her sister	contralto	
Narbal, her chief minister	bass	

Troy, 1183 BC: the story of Enée (Aeneas) from the fall of Troy to his final departure for Italy. Seeking refuge in Carthage on the way, he wins the love of Didon (Dido).

The libretto of *Les Troyens* was written by the composer, after Vergil's *Aeneid*. It is a colossal work and only the second part, The Trojans at Carthage, was performed during his lifetime. This was given for the first time at the Paris Théâtre Lyrique in 1863. The complete opera – including the first part, The Capture of Troy – was first performed at Karlsruhe in 1890. It is rarely seen as conceived by Berlioz.

The plains of Troy

Malheureux Roi! ('Unhappy King'): Cassandre's aria prophesying the destruction of King Priam and his city

Dieux protecteurs de la ville éternelle ('You gods who guard our eternal city'): hymn to the Trojans' gods

A room in Enée's palace

Complices de sa gloire ('Sharing her glory'): the Trojan women agree to follow Cassandre in death rather than face dishonour at the hands of the Greeks

Didon's palace at Carthage

Gloire à Didon ('Glorious Dido'): the Carthaginian royal anthem

Reine d'un jeune empire ('Queen of a young empire'): Anna and Didon's duet concerning the Queen's duty to re-marry and at the same time to remain faithful to the memory of her husband

ACT I

After ten years the Greeks besieging Troy have apparently left for home. The joyful Trojans emerge to look over the deserted camp and the one strange relic: a gigantic wooden horse. But Cassandre foretells the immediate destruction of their city. It was her fate to prophesy truly but never to be believed.

The leaders of Troy, including King Priam and Enée, and his son Ascagne, enter to a splendid march and chorus. Rejoicing, they watch a series of games and matches. The appearance of Hector's widow and son brings a moment of sadness, however, and Cassandre continues with her gloomy forebodings. Suddenly Enée rushes back to tell the King of the terrible death of the priest Laocoön, devoured by sea monsters in retribution for urging the crowds to burn the wooden horse. Believing the gods to be displeased by the lack of respect for the horse, Enée leads the procession to drag the horse ceremoniously into the city.

ACT II

That night the ghost of Hector comes to warn Enée that Troy is doomed and that he, Enée, must found a new city in Italy. A soldier rushes in: the whole city is in flames, ignited by Greek soldiers who were hiding in the horse and have opened the gates for their comrades to return. While Enée rallies the remaining Trojans, Cassandre and the women have taken refuge by the altar of Vesta. Warning them what to expect if they are enslaved, Cassandre encourages them to stab and strangle themselves to avoid capture as the Greek soldiers burst in upon them.

ACT III

Since the murder of her husband, Didon has spent seven years founding the city of Carthage, and her people sing in chorus of their devotion to the Queen. She replies with a splendid aria expressing pride in her subjects. There follows a march past of all the people – workmen, sailors, builders and farm workers – who have contributed to the establishment of their city. Alone with Didon, her sister Anna tells Didon that it is time she married again.

A messenger brings news of strange ships seeking shelter from the storm in their harbour. Didon orders that they be made welcome. The sailors reveal themselves to be Trojans. Enée is disguised as one of them; it is his son Ascagne who speaks for them all. Didon acknowledges Enée's renown.

Her chief minister Narbal arrives in agitation to announce a Numidian invasion, warning her that they are

C'est le dieu Mars qui nous rassemble ('The God of War unites us'): the great ensemble led by Didon and Enée as Trojans and Carthaginians join forces

An African forest

Didon's garden
De quels revers ('What disasters'): Narbal's well-founded unease is put aside by Anna

O blonde Cérès ('Oh golden Ceres'): the harpist's hymn to the Goddess of the Harvest

Tout conspire à vaincre mes remords ('Everything conspires to overcome my remorse'): a quintet during which Didon reflects on her love for Enée

Nuit d'ivresse ('In such a night as this'): the great love duet between Didon and Enée

The sea shore

Inutile regrets! ('Useless regrets'): Enée's anguish at having to leave Didon and determining on a last farewell

likely to be overwhelmed. At this Enée flings off his disguise and asks the Queen to allow his soldiers to fight alongside hers. She is impressed both by his courage and by his dazzling appearance. Willingly she accepts the duty of looking after his son while Enée leaves to lead the combined armies against the invaders.

ACT IV
Either at the beginning or at the end of this act is generally performed the famous symphonic pantomine, Royal Hunt and Storm. Water nymphs and satyrs play by a pool in the forest. The court is attending a hunt but a storm drives Didon and Enée alone together into a cave. As the landscape is animated by the celebrating creatures of mythology and the storm turns the stream into a torrent, offstage can occasionally be heard the prophetic cry 'Italie'.

The Numidians have been defeated. Narbal confides in Anna that he is made anxious by Didon. Her love for Enée means she is neglecting her royal duties, and there is the constant threat that Enée must soon sail on to Italy.

A march marks the entrance of Didon and her guest. They watch a series of ballets before Didon, exhausted by all the dancing, orders her harpist to sing something gentle and simple. Afterwards, Didon encourages Enée to continue telling her the story of Troy. Relating how Hector's widow eventually remarried, she sees a parallel with her own situation. Ascagne symbolically takes her wedding ring from her finger. Didon takes it back but does not put it on again.

Didon and Enée are alone together and in a beautiful duet of Shakespearean inspiration they give expression to their love. As they leave, the figure of Mercury appears. He strikes Enée's shield where it has been left hanging on a pillar, and a sombre cry can be heard: 'Italie, Italie, Italie'.

ACT V
A young Trojan sings sadly of Troy, lost to him forever. The Trojan leaders, fearful of the portents, hurry down to the harbour determined to leave soon for Italy. The sentries are less keen to depart, preferring their life in Carthage to an unknown Italy. Then Enée enters. He has told Didon that he must continue his journey and is distressed by her silent grief.

A chorus of Trojan ghosts appear to Enée, urging him not to delay in fulfilling his duty to found a new city in place of Troy. Fortified, Enée rouses his soldiers and prepares to sail at dawn. As a storm breaks, Didon comes down to reproach him. She is overcome with grief and

Errante sur tes pas ('Following you'): the last duet between Didon and the departing Enée

Didon's palace

Didon's garden

Mon souvenir vivra parmi les âges ('My fame will live on'): Didon prophesies that a future Carthaginian, Hannibal, will avenge her

Haine éternelle à la race d'Enée! ('Perpetual hatred for Enée's race'): the Carthaginians swear eternal vengeance for the loss of their Queen

humiliated by his soldiers' sneers. Again and again he tells her that he loves her but that he must obey his gods. Leaving him with a last curse, she hastens away as the Trojans board their ships to the cry of '*Italie*'.

Didon demands that her sister go and entreat Enée not to leave, while Anna bitterly regrets encouraging this fatal passion. Soon they hear that the Trojan ships have already put to sea. Didon's first reaction is to send her fleet to burn the ships: then she orders that a pyre be built and all Enée's relics destroyed. This done, she gives way to terrible and violent grief. Then comes the realization that she cannot continue to live without him.

Calmly bidding farewell to her magnificent city, she goes to the pyre on which are piled Enée's toga, armour and bed. While Anna and Narbal intone a curse against Italy and her priests pray that Didon may be cured of her wounded heart, she flings herself sobbing on to Enée's bed. She seizes his sword and stabs herself. Her horrified subjects pour curses upon Enée's descendants. Didon, expiring, has a last terrible vision of Rome's ultimate triumph over Carthage.

GEORGES BIZET

Born Paris 1838, died Bougival 1875. The son of musicians, Bizet studied at the Conservatoire (under Gounod among others) and in 1857 won the Prix de Rome. In that year his one-act opera *Le Docteur Miracle* won a competition sponsored by Offenbach and had its premiere in Paris. In 1863 *Les Pêcheurs de Perles* had a moderate success at the Théâtre Lyrique, its oriental setting much *à la mode*. *Carmen* (1875) was acclaimed not in Paris, where the bourgeois audience found the realism distasteful and contrary to the conventions of *opéra comique*, but later in Vienna. The dialogue spills over into melody appropriate to the opera's themes of love and jealousy. Dying at the early age of 36, Bizet did not witness its rise to universal popularity.

CARMEN

Carmen, a gypsy	soprano
Micaela, a peasant	soprano
Don José, a corporal	tenor
Escamillo, a toreador	baritone
Lieutenant Zuniga	bass

Seville, c.1820: Don José, infatuated with Carmen, deserts Micaela, the girl from his own village; but Carmen tires of him. She takes up with the glamorous toreador Escamillo and is murdered by her jealous admirer.

Bizet died only three months after *Carmen's* premiere at the Opéra-Comique in Paris in March 1875. Its later success is due to his dazzling score and the powerful novel by Prosper Merimée on which the opera is based. The librettists were Henri Meilhac and Ludovic Halévy.

A square in Seville

ACT I

While the soldiers on guard stand around watching the life of the square, Micaela comes to look for Don José, a corporal. He is due to return soon. Resisting their invitations, she leaves again just before Don José arrives with the relief guard. He admits to his officer, Lieutenant Zuniga, that he is in love with Micaela. The girls come tumbling out of the cigarette factory. The soldiers' favourite is Carmen and as they flirt with her she sings of the unpredictability of love. Intrigued by Don José's lack of interest, Carmen approaches him and gives him her flower. Micaela returns to tell him that his mother sends some money and a kiss, and is longing for his return. They sing together of the pleasures of their village home

L'amour est un oiseau rebelle ('Love flies free'): Carmen sings that love cannot be caged

Ma mère, je la vois ('I see my

mother now'): Don José thinks nostalgically of his mother at home

Près des remparts de Séville ('Near the ramparts of Seville'): Carmen's seductive aria, sung when Don José tells her not to talk

Lillas Pastia's inn
Les tringles des sistres ('At the sound of a guitar'): the Gypsy Song

Toréador, en garde! ('Toreador, on guard'): the refrain to the Toreador's Song

Je vais danser en votre honneur ('I will dance in honour of you'): Carmen's tribute to Don José, released after serving a prison sentence for allowing her to escape

La fleur que tu m'avais jetée ('The flower you gave me'): Don José's love was sustained in prison by the flower that she had given him

The smugglers' camp near Don José's village

Je dis que rien ne m'épouvante ('Nothing should scare me'): Micaela's aria expressing her determination to recover Don José's love

before Micaela leaves, promising to return. His mother's letter urges him to marry Micaela, which he fully intends to do. Don José is about to throw away Carmen's flower when suddenly there is uproar among the cigarette girls. Zuniga sends him over: it seems that Carmen attacked another girl. Zuniga places her under arrest in the custody of Don José, whom she immediately sets out to seduce.

She promises to meet him at Lillas Pastia's inn and, pretending that she knocks him over, he lets her escape just as Zuniga returns.

ACT II
Carmen and her friends sing and perform a gypsy dance. Among the audience is Zuniga, who tells her that Don José, imprisoned for letting her escape, will shortly be free. Escamillo the toreador arrives, a romantic figure full of his own importance. When Carmen rejects his advances, he says that he is happy to wait his turn. Zuniga, too, is rebuffed. Two of the gypsies are recruited by some smugglers but Carmen refuses to go as she is waiting for Don José. At last she hears him arriving and, reunited with him, she begins to dance. He stops her when he hears the regimental bugles sounding the retreat. She taunts him for being ready to obey the call so quickly and for loving her so little, begging him to take her away into the mountains. They are about to part when Zuniga returns to continue his pointless pursuit of her. Seeing his corporal with Carmen, he orders him out. Don José draws his sword and Zuniga is overpowered with the help of the returning smugglers. Don José now has no option but to join Carmen and the others.

ACT III
While the smugglers sing of the dangers and excitement of life on the run, Don José's remorse about his mother is counteracted by his jealous rage when Carmen encourages him to return home. Two girls are telling fortunes with cards and Carmen joins in. She finds herself with the cards of death for herself and 'him'. Cutting the cards again, it is the same.

The smugglers set off on a mission, leaving Don José on guard. Micaela, who has been tracking them down, appears. She, with God's help, intends to rescue the man she loves from her beautiful rival who has bewitched him. As she approaches, she sees him fire a shot at a shadow. It is Escamillo, who has come for Carmen. He is told she has grown tired of her lover – some soldier or other. Don José is outraged and challenges the toreador, who is greatly amused by his own mistake. He nearly dies for it, but Carmen restrains Don José as he is about to strike.

Escamillo goes off, inviting them all to the bullfight just as Micaela is discovered. She begs Don José to return with her to his mother. Carmen encourages him but he refuses. The news that his mother is dying finally persuades him, and as he leaves he hears the toreador's triumphant song.

Outside the bullring
Si tu m'aimes, Carmen ('If you love me, Carmen'): Escamillo enters proudly with Carmen on his arm and they sing in duet

ACT IV
Escamillo is preparing to fight in the bullring and excited crowds are gathering. Carmen is with him and they shout compliments to each other. She has been warned that Don José is looking for her but she refuses to be afraid and goes to meet him. He cannot understand that she no longer feels anything for him, while she cannot understand why he continues to pursue her. As the crowds shout for Escamillo, she turns to join her new lover demanding her right to be free. He grabs her but she breaks free, disdainfully turning her back. With a last cry of despair, he plunges his knife into her. As he watches her die, he proclaims his guilt and falls across her body.

LES PECHEURS DE PERLES
(THE PEARL FISHERS)

In three acts, text by Michel Carré and Eugène Cormon. Premiere: Théâtre Lyrique, Paris, 1863. A weak libretto bolstered by melodies on a par with *Carmen*.

Ceylon, in tribal antiquity: Zurga (**bar**) is chosen fisher-king and is reunited with his former friend Nadir (**t**): 'Au fond du temple saint' ('In the depths of the temple'). A veiled priestess, who must remain a virgin, arrives to preside over the fishing season. Nadir recognizes her as Leïla (**s**), the cause of his earlier break-up with Zurga. They resume their relationship and are caught by the high priest Nourabad (**b**), who denounces them publicly. But Zurga discovers that Leïla had long ago saved his life: he helps the lovers to escape by setting the village on fire, himself dying in the flames.

ARRIGO BOITO

Born Padua 1842, died Milan 1918. He composed only two operas, the other being *Nerone*, left incomplete in 1915 but sometimes performed in a version finished by Toscanini and Vincenzo Tommasini. A skilled librettist, he wrote the texts of Verdi's *Simon Boccanegra*, *Otello* and *Falstaff*, and Ponchielli's *La Gioconda*.

MEFISTOFELE
(MEPHISTOPHELES)

In a prologue, four acts and an epilogue, to the composer's own text, after Goethe's *Faust*, Premiere: original (unsuccessful) edition La Scala, Milan, 1868; revised (successful) edition Bologna, 1875.

Germany, Middle Ages: Mefistofele (b) wagers in heaven that he can win the soul of the philosopher Faust (t), who duly agrees to accept damnation in exchange for one moment of perfect bliss. Restored to youth, Faust attracts Margherita (s) and seduces her; he is shown the Witches' Sabbath. Abandoned, Margherita drowns her child by Faust, and dies in prison after they attempt a reconciliation. Transported to Ancient Greece, Faust meets Helen of Troy (s). Finally, returned to old age, Faust repents, repudiates the Devil and is saved.

NERONE
(NERO)

In four acts, with text by the composer and score completed by Tommasini and Toscanini. Premiere: La Scala, Milan, 1924. A work of consistent craftsmanship and occasional charm, contrasting oriental and Christian influences on Rome in decline.

Rome, c. 60 AD: Nerone (t, Nero), burying the ashes of the mother he has murdered, is met by the sorcerer Simon Mago (bar). Confronted by Asteria (s), who loves him, Nerone flees; Simon tries to enlist her services by promising access to Nerone, Fanuél (bar), a Christian leader admired by Rubria (ms), is not persuaded by Simon's materialism. Simon pretends to work miracles; Nerone is not duped but has him arrested. After several intrigues, Nerone holds games for the people while Rome burns: Christians are martyred, among them Rubria.

BENJAMIN BRITTEN

Born Lowestoft 1913, died Aldeburgh 1976. Britten began studying musical composition aged 12 with Frank Bridge. After leaving the Royal College of Music, London, he composed scores for film documentaries and the theatre. His first opera, *Paul Bunyan*, with libretto by W.H. Auden, had its premiere in New York. An award from the Koussevitzky Foundation enabled him to write *Peter Grimes* (1945). Commissions later produced *Billy Budd* (1951), for the Festival of Britain, *The Turn of the Screw* (1954), for the Venice Biennale, *Gloriana* (1952), for the Coronation, and *Owen Wingrave* (1971), for BBC television. The English Opera Group was formed for the performance of *The Rape of Lucretia* (1946) and *Albert Herring* (1947) at Glyndebourne, and it went to Aldeburgh for the first season of the Festival in 1948.

PETER GRIMES

Peter Grimes, a fisherman	tenor
Captain Balstrode, his friend	baritone
Ellen Orford, a widowed schoolmistress	soprano
Mrs Sedley, a neighbour	mezzo-soprano

A Suffolk fishing town, c.1830: scandal surrounds the death of Peter Grimes' apprentice. The widowed Ellen Orford supports him until a second boy disappears.

The opera was inspired by an article by E.M.Forster on George Crabbe, whose poem *The Borough* was partly concerned with a sinister fisherman working from Aldeburgh. The first performance of *Peter Grimes* was at Sadler's Wells, London, in 1945. Aldeburgh subsequently became central to Britten's life and music

The Moot Hall

Here is a friend: Ellen and Peter plan together to restore his good name

A street by the sea

Let her among you without fault cast the first stone: Ellen again supports Peter

PROLOGUE
Peter is called to explain the death of an apprentice at sea. The coroner, returning a verdict of accidental death, advises him to employ no more children. Despite general suspicion that he was responsible for the boy's death, Peter is supported by the widowed schoolmistress Ellen.

ACT I
After an orchestral interlude, expressive of the sea, the general life of the Borough is portrayed. Peter needs help with his work. Another boy is available from the workhouse and Ellen at last agrees to help look after him in the face of rising protest. Balstrode sees that a storm

has been signalled and the people chorus their fear.

Balstrode tries to persuade Peter to join him in the inn. Peter states his preference for a solitary existence, and his old friend suggests that he might be better off away from the Borough, at sea. But Peter admits that he is rooted in his native soil. He thinks back to his awful ordeal, afloat with the dead boy. He believes that his problems will be resolved if only he can make himself rich and marry Ellen.

A second interlude mirrors the storm. The scene changes to the inn where everyone has taken refuge from the rain. When Peter enters he is like a storm himself. He feels himself completely alienated from his neighbours, even when they all join in a sea song. At last Ellen arrives with the new apprentice, soaked from their journey. Peter immediately drags him off to his home on the cliff.

ACT II

The third interlude shows that the storm is over. It is Sunday morning and Ellen is resting with the new apprentice while others hurry to church. As the service can be heard proceeding off stage, Ellen chatters to the silent apprentice. She is appalled to find his coat torn and his neck bruised. Peter's behaviour may be repeating itself.

When Peter arrives to summon the boy to work, Ellen protests that they have already worked all week. She begs him to let the boy rest, but he persists and finally knocks her down in inarticulate frustrated anger.

The church-goers emerge, some of them having overheard the quarrel. In spite of Ellen's pleas, it is decided that the men must go and inspect what is happening in Peter's hut. The women are left debating the faults of their men.

The interlude which follows, as desolate as the apprentice's miserable existence, prepares for the scene of Peter's home: an upturned boat perched above the cliff. Peter enters, thrusting the boy in front of him. As the boy crouches sobbing in the corner, Peter urges him to prepare for work, for catching fish while there are some. Again he dreams of how life would be with Ellen. Gradually the sound of the approaching townspeople alerts him to their unwanted interruption. As he orders the exhausted boy to climb down the cliff, a scream suggests that he has fallen. Peter clambers after him and when the rector and the men arrive they find the hut empty with no cause for complaint. Balstrode however notices the boy's clothes and climbs down alone after his friend.

Outside the Moot Hall

In the sea the prentice lies: Mrs Sedley has her suspicions of 'murder most foul'
Embroidery in childhood was a luxury of idleness: Ellen's aria mourning the fact that her childhood pastime should now provide evidence against the man she loves
Who holds himself apart: Peter can expect little sympathy from the people he has always despised

By the sea

In ceaseless motion comes and goes the tide: the final chorus mirrors the sea's dispassionate continuity

ACT III

An interlude represents the quiet surge of the sea under the moonlight. There is a barn dance and plenty for the neighbours to talk about. Mrs Sedley, the town gossip, is convinced that the boy's disappearance means that he has been murdered by Peter. Even Ellen, having found the boy's embroidered jersey on the beach, and Balstrode are deeply concerned about Peter. Mrs Sedley calls repeatedly for the coroner (who is also the mayor), and eventually he summons the constable and a posse of men to be sent out to discover the truth.

The sixth interlude paints a bizarre picture of Peter's confused mental state. As the foghorn sounds across the water, Peter appears by his boat, talking deliriously and singing to himself. When Ellen and Balstrode find him, it is clear that he is beyond help. Ellen wants to lead him to safety but his friend quietly advises Peter to sail his boat back out to sea and sink it. As Peter's boat leaves the shore, Balstrode leads Ellen away.

To the echo of the first prelude, life in the Borough quietly returns to normal. As the different characters get on with their lives, news suddenly spreads that there is a boat sinking out at sea. No-one take much notice.

ALBERT HERRING

Albert Herring	tenor
Mrs Herring, his mother	mezzo-soprano
Sid, a butcher's boy	baritone
Nancy, his girlfriend	mezzo-soprano
Lady Billows	soprano

Loxford, 1900: the virtuous Albert Herring is elected King of the May by Lady Billows and her committee. His lemonade laced with rum by mocking friends, Albert goes out on his first spree.

The opera is a comic vignette of English village life, the libretto by Eric Crozier inspired by Maupassant's short story *Le Rosier de Madame Husson*. Written for the English Opera Group, *Albert Herring* received its first performance at Glyndebourne in 1947.

Lady Billows' house

Are Loxford girls all whores?: Lady Billows' outburst against what she hears about local life

ACT I

Lady Billows, magnate and self-appointed guardian of local morality, is joined by her committee to choose the Queen of the May. This title, with a £25 prize, must be held by someone of unimpeachable moral standing and

*Albert Herring's clean as
new-mown hay*: the
superintendent's aria
commending Albert for his
sober life

Mrs Herring's shop

Bounce me high, bounce me low:
the schoolchildren's song
*Girls mean Spring six days a
week*: Sid tries to lead Albert
astray
Meet me at quarter past eight:
trio of Sid and Nancy, planning
to meet, while Albert cannot
help overhearing

**A marquee in the vicarage
garden**

I'm full of happiness: Lady
Billows' considerable oration

Er, er, thank you very much: the
full extent of Albert's speech of
reply

Mrs Herring's shop
Albert the good: Albert's song of
praise for himself as the new
King of the May

every girl they mention proves to have something known against her. Eventually the police superintendent suggests a 'King' of the May. He nominates Albert Herring, who works in his mother's greengrocer's shop. Lady Billows is unenthusiastic, but the vicar suggests that the straightforward test of virtue is surely all that is important and so they all agree to send Albert the news, thankful that a decision has been reached.

The orchestra introduces children playing in the widow Herring's shop. They pocket some apples and are chased off by Sid, who has come to buy herbs from Albert. All Sid's attempts to get Albert to join him in some fun are met with stolid resistance. Nancy comes in and Sid buys her two peaches, using his employer's petty cash. They plan to meet again that evening.

Albert thinks about all the fun he is missing tied to his mother's apron strings. He carries on serving until the shop is invaded by Lady Billows and her committee. They tell Albert and his mother the good news that he is to be crowned as Loxford's King of the May. They try to counter Albert's extreme unwillingness to be dressed up in white by telling him about the £25. After they have gone, he tells his mother that he will definitely refuse. She shouts and bullies him, sending him up to his room.

ACT II

Everything is ready for the great celebration. The girls are waiting for Sid to bring the meat and, when at last he arrives, he has a plan for a practical joke. He is going to fill Albert's glass with rum. The schoolchildren practise the May anthem and eventually Albert, all in white and crowned with orange blossom, is led in to be subjected to lengthy speeches from Lady Billows and the mayor.

Albert finds his lemonade unusually delicious. After many refills he can hardly stand. When he appears overcome by the event, his supporters only make matters worse by pouring him some more 'lemonade' before all settling down to the magnificent feast.

Later that evening Albert stumbles back to the shop, completely drunk. He sings a song while he bangs on the door and rings the bell. When he hears Sid's whistle summoning Nancy to their encounter, he is struck by the dreariness of his existence. After all, he has £25 in his pocket. He spins a coin, heads for 'Yes', and sets off, whistling like Sid, in search of adventure. When his mother returns to find the shop silent, she assumes he has gone to bed.

Mrs Herring's shop the following afternoon	**ACT III** The shop is more than usually subdued, Albert's mother is resting. There has been no sign of Albert, and suicide is suspected. Nancy is worried and remorseful about the trick they played. Sid comes in wringing wet from searching the river. Everyone in the village is out and about, helping or hindering the search and gossiping
In the midst of life is death: Albert's supposed death is greeted with a dirge	about the tragedy. Albert's wreath was found on one of the roads, crushed by a cart. As they form an impromptu congregation to mourn Albert, he suddenly walks in. Angrily reproached for causing so much trouble, he says he is sorry. 'Sorry!' Lady Billows explodes with indigna-
I can't remember everything: Albert's 'off the cuff' description of life on the tiles	tion. Albert is cross-questioned as to how he spent his time and suddenly he bursts into a full account of an extended pub-crawl taking in The Dog and Duck, The Horse and Groom . . . 'Stop!' they all cry, unwilling to hear more of this catalogue of sin from their newly crowned King of the May. Complaining that his mother has driven him to these excesses, Albert politely but firmly sends them all out of the shop so that he can get on with his work. Nancy gives him a big kiss, and he invites
I didn't lay it on too thick, did I?: Albert's tongue-in-cheek question to Nancy and Sid	the schoolchildren in and gives them each a peach. They all agree that Albert is much the better for the last 24 hours as he throws away the orange-blossom wreath.

THE RAPE OF LUCRETIA

In two acts, libretto by Ronald Duncan, based on André Obey's play *Le Viol de Lucrèce*, in turn derived from Shakespeare's poem *The Rape of Lucrece*. Premiere: Glyndebourne, 1946. A Pioneering chamber opera, it exudes an austere nobility from limited resources.

In or near Rome, 500 BC: Male (**t**) and Female (**s**) Chorus set the scene and commentate, drawing a Christian moral. The Roman officers take a bet on the fidelity of their wives in their absence, and return unexpectedly to find only Lucretia (**s**) faithful. Goaded into jealous anger by Junius (**bar**), the arrogant Tarquinius (**bar**) rides to Lucretia's home and rapes her. Devastated by shame, she commits suicide the next day in front of her husband Collatinus (**b**).

THE TURN OF THE SCREW

In a prologue and two acts, libretto by Myfanwy Piper, based on Henry James' story. Premiere: La Fenice, Venice, 1954. A 'screw' theme (all twelve notes of the scale) after the prologue 'turns' through fifteen variations, in a gripping evocation of supernatural oppression.

Bly, an English country house, mid-19th century: two children, Miles (**tr**) and Flora (**s**), come under the care of a new Governess (**s**), who eventually realizes that they are in thrall to the ghosts of her predecessor Miss Jessel (**s**) and the former manservant Peter Quint (**t**). She tries to save the childrens' souls with the help of the housekeeper Mrs Grose (**s**), who takes Flora away. But in revealing the name of his tormentor, Quint, Miles dies in the Governess' arms.

A MIDSUMMER NIGHT'S DREAM

In three acts, text by composer and singer Peter Pears, adapted from Shakespeare. Premiere: Aldeburgh Festival, 1960. The chamber orchestra accompaniment subtly differentiates fairies, lovers and rustics.

Athens and a wood nearby: the fairy monarch Oberon (**c-t**) quarrels with his queen, Tytania (**col s**), and through the agency of Puck (**speaking role**) entangles the love-affairs between Hermia (**ms**) and Lysander (**t**), and Helena (**s**) and Demetrius (**bar**). The rustics' play is a parody of Romantic opera, with Flute (**t**) as Thisby in a full-blown mad scene.

BILLY BUDD

In four (revised in two) acts and an epilogue, with text by E.M. Forster and Eric Crozier, after Herman Melville's novella *Billy Budd, Foretopman*. Premiere: Covent Garden, London, 1951. A head-on confrontation of good and evil, given atmosphere by its nautical setting.

On board *HMS Indomitable*, summer 1797 (year of two naval mutinies): the action is seen in flashback by the ship's captain, Edward Vere (**t**), now retired. Newly press-ganged into naval service, the handsome Billy Budd (**bar**) has only one enemy, the cynical and sadistic master-at-arms John Claggart (**b**), who tries to incite him to mutiny. Under pressure to defend himself against Claggart's false accusations, Billy lapses into a stammer – his one fatal flaw – and strikes Claggart, who dies. A quick court-martial condemns him to death. In old age, Vere consoles himself with Billy's final word, that the captain had no alternative.

LUIGI CHERUBINI

Born Florence 1760, died Paris 1842. He wrote 13 operas in the Italian style, but after moving to Paris (1786) adopted Gluck's style and became the father of French grand opera, beginning with *Lodoïska* (1791), the influential 'rescue' opera (the plot turning on a dramatic rescue). *Médée* is the only one of his 34 operas now performed.

MEDEE
(MEDEA)

In three acts, text by François Benoit Hoffman, after Corneille's tragedy, itself derived from Euripides. Premiere: Théâtre Feydeau, Paris, 1797. A splendid title role (a Callas speciality) which combines classicism, tragic grandeur and psychological passion, usually given with Franz Lachner's recitatives (1854).

The court of Creon in ancient Corinth: through the magical powers of Medée (**s**), his former wife, Jason (**t**) has won the Golden Fleece, but he now spurns her in favour of Glauké (**s**), daughter of Créon (**b**). Allowed to remain in the city one night more, Medée sends a poisoned crown and cloak to Glauké, who dies horribly, and she kills her two sons by Jason. To complete her revenge, she sets fire to the temple.

FRANCESCO CILEA

Born Palmi, Calabria, 1866, died Varazze 1950. He wrote the first of his six operas, Gina (1889), while still at the Naples Conservatory and adopted *verismo* fashion with *La Tilda* (1892). He had limited success with *L'Arlesiana* (1897), still occasionally performed, but made his name with *Adriana Lecouvreur*, which leading sopranos have enjoyed for the lyric drama of its title role.

ADRIANA LECOUVREUR

In four acts, text by Arturo Colautti after the play *Adrienne Lecouvreur* by Eugène Scribe and Ernest Legouvé. Premiere: Teatro Lirico, Milan, 1902.

Paris, 1730: Adriana (**s**), actress at the Comédie-Française, has won the love of Maurizio (**t**), Count of Saxony, replacing his former mistress, the Princesse de Bouillon (**ms**). Learning of her rival, the Princess poisons a bouquet of violets and returns them to Adriana, who had previously sent them to Maurizio. Believing herself rejected, Adriana inhales their scent and dies in his arms attended by her other suitor, Michonnet (**bar**). Adriana's motto theme ('*Io son l'umile ancella*': 'I am the humble handmaid') is heard throughout.

DOMENICO CIMAROSA

Born Aversa 1749, died Venice 1801. An international figure in comic opera, unsurpassed in his day except by Mozart, he wrote at least 65 works for the stage. He studied in Naples, was director at the Ospedaletto in Venice from *c*.1782, and worked in St Petersburg and Vienna before returning to Naples in 1793.

IL MATRIMONIO SEGRETO
(THE SECRET MARRIAGE)

In two acts, text by Giovanni Bertati, after George Colman and David Garrick's comedy *The Clandestine Marriage*. Premiere: Burgtheater, Vienna, 1792. Cimarosa's masterpiece. This is Italian rococo music at its most light-hearted.

Bologna, 18th century: a wealthy merchant Geronimo (**b**) wants his daughters Elisetta (**s**) and Carolina (**s**) to marry into the aristocracy, but the latter has secretly already wed Paolino (**t**). The couple try to arrange for the English Count Robinson (**b**) to propose to Elisetta, but he prefers Carolina and secures the consent of Geronimo, whose sister Fidalma (**ms**) has designs on Paolino. The couple's planned elopement goes awry, all is revealed and the Count agrees to marry Elisetta.

CLAUDE DEBUSSY

Born St-Germain-en-Laye 1862, died Paris 1918. Aged ten, Debussy entered the Paris Conservatoire and won the Prix de Rome in 1884 with his cantata *L'Enfant Prodigue*. His early years were marked by material struggle, and he briefly taught the piano to the chidren of Madame von Meck, patron of Tchaikovsky. Among his early symphonic pieces was *Prélude à l'Après-midi d'un Faune* (1894), evoking an impression in a manner comparable to that of the Impressionist painters. *Pelléas et Mélisande* (1902) is Debussy's only completed opera. It was at once recognized as a landmark in the development of opera, the music closely in sympathy with the inflections of the language of Maeterlinck's text.

PELLEAS ET MELISANDE

Arkel, King of Allemonde	bass
Pelléas, his grandson	tenor
Golaud, Pelléas' half-brother	baritone
Mélisande, Golaud's wife	soprano
Geneviève, mother of Golaud and Pelléas	

The imaginary kingdom of Allemonde, Middle Ages: married to Golaud, who finds her lost in a forest, Mélisande is drawn to his half-brother Pelléas and he to her. Golaud kills Pelléas, and his suspicions are still unsolved at Mélisande's death.

The libretto is a version of Maurice Maeterlinck's play. The opera, which Debussy took ten years to write, was first performed at the Opéra-Comique, Paris, in 1902.

In a forest

ACT I

Golaud, who has lost his way in the forest, finds Mélisande weeping by the side of a pool. She too is lost – and terrified – and she reveals that she has dropped her crown into the water but would rather die than have it returned to her. Unwillingly, she departs with him.

Arkel's castle
Voici ce qu'il écrit ('This is what he wrote'): Geneviève reads out to her father, King Arkel, Golaud's account of his marriage to Mélisande

In Arkel's castle Geneviève, mother of Golaud and Pelléas, reads out Golaud's letter saying that he has married Mélisande. He asks for a lamp to be lit as a signal if the King will receive her. Golaud's first wife has died and it was intended, the King remembers, that Golaud should marry Princess Ursula. Nevertheless the old man is willing to forgive his grandson. Pelléas wishes to leave to visit a dying friend, but he is told to wait for his brother's return and is sent up to light the lamp.

Outside the castle
Hoé, Hisse hoé!: through the mist can be heard the sailors' voices as the ship that brought Golaud and Mélisande sails away

Geneviève has gone down to the harbour to meet Mélisande. Pelléas joins them and together they watch the ship that brought her disappearing into the mist. When he offers his new sister-in-law his hand, she replies that hers are full of flowers. He takes her arm to guide her up the path. He tells her that he is leaving and she seems disappointed.

At a well in the park

Prenez garde de glisser ('Be careful not to slip'): Pelléas becomes anxious when Mélisande seems drawn into the pool

ACT II
There is a well in the park which is said to open the eyes of the blind. Pelléas and Mélisande visit it together and she lets her hair down into the water. While telling Pelléas how she tried to fend off his brother, she throws her wedding ring into the air and it falls into the water just as the clock strikes twelve.

A room in the castle

Dis-moi toute la vérité, Mélisande ('Tell me the truth, Mélisande'): the first occasion on which Golaud suspects his wife of hiding something from him

Golaud has been thrown from his horse and he tells Mélisande that it was on the stroke of midday. Mélisande is crying and wants Golaud to take her away. Golaud assumes that Pelléas has been unkind to her. When she gives him her hand, he notices that her ring is missing. She says she dropped it in a cave and Golaud at once orders her out into the night to find it, telling her to take Pelléas with her.

A cave by the sea

Pelléas takes her to a cave so that she is able to describe it to her husband. In the cave they find three old beggars asleep. She walks back alone.

A room in the castle
Mes longs cheveux descendent ('My hair hangs down'): Mélisande sings to herself as she prepares for sleep
Et ils sont doux ('It is so soft'): Pelléas is entranced by the beauty of Mélisande's golden hair

ACT III
As Mélisande lets her hair fall down out of the window to comb it, Pelléas hears her singing and comes out of the twilight to tell her he is leaving. He begs her to let him kiss her hand. She leans out but he cannot reach. Instead he buries his face in her long hair. Telling her how much he loves her, he ties her hair to the tree. Golaud finds them thus and reproaches them for playing like children.

The castle vaults
On the castle terrace
A propos de Mélisande ('On the subject of Mélisande'): Golaud grimly warns his brother to avoid Mélisande.

Later, Golaud takes Pelléas down to a sinister pool in the dungeons beneath the castle. When they climb back into the light – a transformation brilliantly illustrated by the orchestra – he warns Pelléas to keep away from Mélisande.

Outside the castle

Je suis ici comme un aveugle ('I might as well be blind'): Golaud's anger that his son can

Golaud's suspicions are now troubling him. He meets his son (by his first marriage) outside Mélisande's window. Led on by his father, the little boy says that his stepmother and uncle often quarrel about some door which cannot be opened. Golaud presses the child to tell him more and hears that once they kissed. He lifts his son

tell him nothing incriminating about Pelléas' behaviour with Mélisande

Within the castle

Une grande innocence ('Such a great innocence'): Golaud harshly derides the innocence that his grandfather claims to see in Mélisande's eyes

At the well

Qu'elles s'embrassent ('See how they kiss'): locked out of the castle, Pelléas and Mélisande watch their shadows as they embrace

A room in the castle

Ne mens plus ainsi ('Don't deceive me like this'): Golaud cannot believe in his dying wife's innocence

up to spy on Mélisande through the window and the boy reports that they are sitting together silently, staring at the lamp. He becomes frightened and his father lets him go.

ACT IV

Mélisande agrees to meet Pelléas by the well in the park. But first King Arkel joins her, greatly admiring her beauty. Suddenly Golaud bursts in, demanding his sword and ranting at his wife. When his grandfather protests, he grabs her by the hair and forces her to the ground, mocking her supposed innocence.

By the well, Golaud's son is trying to retrieve a lost toy while a flock of sheep is driven past to be slaughtered. As he goes back to the castle, Pelléas enters. He is soon joined by Mélisande, who has torn her dress. They admit that they have loved each other from the beginning. While they stand gazing at each other they hear the castle gates being closed. They have no choice but to stay outside together. As she kisses him, they hear and then see Golaud in the shadows. Frantically they embrace. Golaud rushes forward and cuts his brother down with his sword.

ACT V

Mélisande lies dying. With her are Golaud and the King. She is delirious and asks for the window to be opened. Golaud begs to be alone with her. He asks for her forgiveness at the same time demanding to be told the truth. She tells him that she loved Pelléas but that they were innocent of any guilt. Golaud cannot believe this and persistently demands the real truth.

The King and the doctor return. She has given birth to a tiny daughter but is too weak even to touch the child. The King holds the baby up for her as all the maidservants come in to be with her. Golaud protests and again insists on being alone with his wife. But suddenly the servants fall to their knees. Mélisande is dead.

GAETANO DONIZETTI

Born Bergamo 1797, died Bergamo 1848. Donizetti's early musical training was as a chorister, and he later studied in Bologna. His first opera, *Enrico di Borgogna*, was produced in Venice in 1818, and he wrote more than 30 before achieving international fame with *Anna Bolena*, produced in Milan in 1830 and within a short time in London, Paris, Madrid and Vienna. Writing with legendary rapidity, he composed more than 70 operas altogether. He worked frequently with the librettists Felice Romani and Salvatore Cammarano (who also wrote librettos for Verdi): with Romani he wrote the comedy *L'Elisir d'Amore* (1832) and with Cammarano *Lucia di Lammermoor* (1835). The intensity of Lucia's Mad Scene deeply affected the audience at its first performance. With *La Fille du Régiment* (1840), he again excelled as a writer of *opera buffa*, surpassing even this with *Don Pasquale* (1843).

L'ELISIR D'AMORE

(THE ELIXIR OF LOVE)

Adina	soprano
Nemorino, her admirer	tenor
Dulcamara, a quack doctor	bass
Belcore, a sergeant	baritone

Italy, early 19th century: village life and a rich girl's indifference to her rustic suitor are changed by the arrival of a conceited soldier and an itinerant quack selling a magic potion.

The libretto is by Felice Romani; the music composed in 14 days. The opera was first produced in 1832 at the Teatro della Canobbiana, Milan, where it ran for 33 performances to packed houses.

Adina's farm
Quanto è bella, quanto è cara ('How lovely she is'): Nemorino's aria, interspersed with the villagers' chorus, exclaiming about his distant passion for Adina

Una parola, Adina ('Just one word, Adina'): Nemorino's pleading with Adina is countered by her refusal as an echo of his music

ACT I
The villagers are resting from the harvest and while one of the girls, Gianetta, leads them in a song, Nemorino watches Adina and sings of his love for her. In turn she tells them the story of Tristan and Isolde which she is reading and of how a magic elixir helped Tristan to win Isolde's love.

Belcore arrives. He immediately attaches himself to Adina and tells her of his irresistible qualities. Nemorino at last attracts her attention. She advises him to spend his time looking after his rich uncle, who is ill, rather than mooning around after her. His response is that she can no more ask him to ignore her than ask a river why it plunges headlong towards the sea. She replies that he might as well love the wind.

A village square
Udite, udite, o rustici! ('Pay attention, country people'): Dulcamara advertises his wares

A trumpet announces the arrival of Dulcamara, purveyor of quack medicines. He tells the astounded bystanders that his medicines can cure everything from toothache to the wrinkles of old age, and all for the trifling sum of one scudo. He does good business, Nemorino asking him for the elixir of love that won Isolde. The doctor quickly understands and sells him a bottle of wine. Nemorino downs the liquid and becomes wildly over-confident. Suddenly new orders direct the sergeant to be on his way the next morning. The act ends with Nemorino in despair and Adina finding herself committed to marrying the impetuous soldier.

Caro elisir ('Blessed elixir'): Nemorino's first taste of the elixir

Inside the farmhouse
Io son ricco e tu sei bella ('I am rich and you are pretty'): an impromptu duet by the doctor and Adina to amuse the guests
Sul momento! ('Enlist, and you can have the money in your hand this instant!'): the sergeant insidiously encourages Nemorino's plan to enlist for cash

ACT II
The marriage of Adina and Belcore approaches. The bride and Dulcamara perform a popular duet about a senator and a gondolier girl. Nemorino begs the doctor for some more of his elixir. The doctor is happy to sell him some more wine but the unhappy youth has no money left. Belcore offers to enlist Nemorino in the army for the money he needs: the papers are signed, the money paid and the potion changes hands.

A courtyard

News reaches the village that Nemorino's uncle has died. Without knowing it, Nemorino is now rich. When he appears, the girls treat him with new interest, which he of course ascribes to the elixir. Even the doctor is rather startled by the potion's success. Adina is astounded to find him so at ease and so much admired. When the doctor boasts to her about his magic potion, she suddenly understands his trick. She realizes at last that she does love Nemorino after all. Dulcamara offers to sell her some of his elixir, but she tells him she has a useful elixir of her own: the power of a woman's eyes.

Quanto amore! ('How much he loved me!'): Adina realizes the depth of Nemorino's love

Una furtiva lagrima ('A secret tear'): Nemorino's beautiful aria on realizing that Adina does indeed love him

Nemorino is waiting for Adina. He sings that he now believes that she does love him. She arrives with his enlistment papers, which she has bought back from Belcore, and then modestly makes to leave. He tells her that he would rather stay in the army and die a soldier's death than live without her. After a moment's misunderstanding they fall into each other's arms and Belcore, coming upon the collapse of his own hopes, takes his defeat with good grace. There are, after all, thousands of other women thirsting for his embrace.

Dulcamara is also leaving, and the opera ends with everyone (except Belcore) singing the doctor's praise.

LUCIA DI LAMMERMOOR

Lucia (Lucy Ravenswood)	soprano	
Edgardo (Edgar Ashton), her lover	tenor	
Raimondo (Raymond), the chaplain	bass	
Arturo (Arthur Bucklaw), her intended husband	tenor	
Enrico (Henry Ravens-wood), her brother	baritone	
Normanno (Norman), his servant	tenor	

Scotland, 1695: Lucia's love for Edgardo, the enemy of her family, drives her to murder Arturo, the man she is forced to marry, and leads to her madness.

The libretto is by Salvatore Cammarano and the first performance was at the Teatro San Carlo, Naples, in 1835. The plot is taken from Walter Scott's novel *The Bride of Lammermoor*, published in 1819; this in turn was based on a true story of the Dalrymple family.

The grounds of Ravenswood Castle

ACT I

The Ashton family now occupy Ravenswood Castle, once the home of the disgraced Ravenswoods. Enrico, chief of the Ashtons, continues to scheme against Edgardo, last of the Ravenswoods. While the guards investigate signs of a possible intruder, Enrico tells Normanno and Riamondo, the chaplain, how difficult it is to interest his sister in a plan to ally his family to the influential Arturo.

La pietade in suo favore ('No mercy!'): Enrico's ringing pledge to destroy Edgardo

Normanno's gossip of Lucia's attachment to an un-known figure in the forest is followed by the guards' report of someone seeing Edgardo. This enrages Enrico, who swears to drown their love in blood.

By the fountain
Regnava nel silenzio ('All was silent'): Lucia's aria describing her vision of the Lammermoor ghost

Waiting to meet Edgardo secretly, Lucia tells Alisa, her confidante, of a vision of a previous Ravenswood who in a jealous rage murdered the woman he loved. Alisa sees this as a fatal omen, but Lucia can think only of Edgardo's pledge of eternal love.

Verranno a te sull' aure (My love will reach you'): the love duet between Lucia and Edgardo as he prepares to leave for France

Edgardo arrives, announcing that he has to leave for France. When she advises him against asking Enrico to accept their betrothal, he rages about the blood feud that has separated their families. Lucia begs him to let love take the place of hatred. He will agree if she promises to be faithful to him. Before parting they exchange rings.

Enrico's chamber, several months later

ACT II

Despite Lucia's protests, her brother has arranged that her marriage to Arturo should proceed. All her letters from Edgardo have been intercepted and Normanno has forged a letter proving Edgardo to be unfaithful. Lucia is summoned. Her firm refusal persuades him to show her the forgery and he now builds on the shock of this by

Ad altr'uom guirai mia fè ('I have pledged myself to another'): Lucia's pitiful insistence that she cannot do what her brother asks

Ah! Cedi, cedi ('You must give way'): Raimondo's insistence that Lucia obey

The hall at Ravenswood Castle

Chi mi frena in tal momento? ('What holds me back?'): the famous sextet as Edgardo returns to find Lucia married to Arturo

The same evening

Spargi d'amaro pianto ('Bitter tears'): the Mad Scene, Lucia veering from misery to wild ecstacy

The castle grounds

Tu che a Dio spiegasti l'ali ('You who are already in Heaven'): Edgardo's beautiful lament for his lost love

telling her how he himself is threatened with the scaffold.

To convince Lucia, Raimondo is brought in. He cites her duty to her brother and the imaginary groans of her dead mother urging her to be loyal to the family. Her sacrifice will be rewarded when she dies, he tells her. She seizes on this as the only source of comfort.

The wedding party begins. The bridegroom has heard something about Edgardo but his uneasy questions are put aside. Lucia signs the contract just as Edgardo returns. At first he plans to rescue her. Faced with her signature – she is clearly married to another – he gives way to jealousy and rage. He demands to be killed there, in front of Lucia. The chaplain steps in to prevent this, and the act end with threats of a bloody revenge.

ACT III
(A preliminary confrontation between Enrico and Edgardo is customarily omitted.) Lucia and Arturo have retired and the remaining guests are celebrating. Suddenly Raimondo bursts in. Lucia has murdered her husband. The girl herself appears, dishevelled and blood-stained, imagining that she has married Edgardo. Her prolonged ravings range through a series of delusions before she collapses.

Edgardo is victim to the desperate pain of one who imagines his love in another's arms. Soaked in self-pity, he imagines her ecstasy while preparing himself for suicide. He is interrupted by the approach of the party of mourners. He learns that Lucia is dying and calling for him. As the bell tolls for her passing, his own death no longer seems a senseless act. Stabbing himself, he prays that God will unite them in Heaven as never on Earth.

DON PASQUALE

Don Pasquale, an elderly bachelor	bass	
Ernesto, his nephew	tenor	
Norina, a local girl	soprano	
Dottore Malatesta, a family friend	baritone	

Rome, early 19th century: the ageing Don Pasquale's determination to disinherit his nephew Ernesto and produce an heir by marrying a young wife is frustrated by his friend, the ingenious Malatesta.

Donizetti wrote the libretto with Giovanni Ruffini, basing it on an earlier libretto by Angelo Anelli. Premiered at the Théâtre Italien, Paris, in 1843, it is undoubtedly his comic masterpiece, though written under the shadow of the madness caused by his syphilis.

A room in Don Pasquale's house

ACT I

Don Pasquale is in a dilemma: he needs an heir and would like his nephew Ernesto to marry, but he considers Ernesto's choice (Norina, a young widow of doubtful reputation) to be unsuitable. Ernesto will not give her up.

Reluctantly, he decides to get married himself and consults an old family friend, Malatesta, who pretends to seek a suitable bride while actually plotting to help the young couple.

Bella siccome un angelo ('As beautiful as an angel'): Dr Malatesta's enthusiastic description of his sister

Malatesta arrives to announce that he has found the very person. She is enchanting and, in fact, his own sister Sofronia. Don Pasquale demands to meet her at once; Malatesta goes to fetch this mythical beauty while his friend gloats on the size of his future family.

Sogno soave e casto ('All alone'): Ernesto's sustained aria contemplating his ruined hopes

Ernesto arrives, and his uncle gives him one last chance to marry a suitable girl. Don Pasquale then tells his astounded nephew that he is to get married himself. Ernesto sings of the dreams that have vanished with his uncle's fortune. Rallying, he asks one last favour: that he talk it over first with his old friend Malatesta. The news that it is Malatesta's idea (and the intended Malatesta's own sister) is greeted with incredulity.

Quel guardo il cavaliere ('The gallant's glance'): Norina's extravagant aria ridiculing the novel that she is reading and extolling her own accomplishments

Norina is reading a romantic novel. She laughs at its extravagant tone and declares that she herself knows all there is to be known about love. She finds a despairing farewell letter from Ernesto as Malatesta arrives to explain his plan. She is to be Sofronia, all sweet simplicity before the ceremony and a perfect shrew afterwards.

Ernesto's lodgings
Povero Ernesto! ('Poor, poor Ernesto!'): a further aria of self-pity

ACT II

Alone, Ernesto bewails his inability now to support Norina.

Don Pasquale's house

Don Pasquale, meanwhile, is giving strict instructions that no-one but Malatesta and his sister are to be admitted to the house. They arrive, the bride so shy that she can scarcely speak. Don Pasquale conceals himself to spare her too much excitement and, when he does appear, the sight of a man overwhelms her.

Un uomo! ('A man!'): Sofronia's horror at finding herself in a room with a 'man'

Don Pasquale is enchanted to hear that her idea of an evening's entertainment consists of cooking and sewing. So far so good. When her veil is lifted, he is overcome by her beauty, and Malatesta has to propose for him. She accepts and Don Pasquale calls for a notary (fortunately one is at hand). At that moment Ernesto (still unaware of the plot being worked on his behalf) arrives and is thunderstruck to find that his uncle's bride is in fact Norina. Malatesta has difficulty in making Ernesto understand that he must keep quiet.

Immediately the contract is signed, the bride's manner changes. Rejecting her husband's embrace, she insists that his nephew remains to act as her escort. Don Pasquale is dumbfounded and Malatesta pretends equal surprise. Ringing for a servant, the new mistress of the house doubles all the wages, sends for the jewellers and plans the complete redecoration of the house. When Don Pasquale objects, she abuses him and the act ends with a noisy family row.

Son tradito ('I have been betrayed!'): Don Pasquale's horror at the change in the woman he has married develops into a spectacular quartet

Don Pasquale's house

ACT III

The servants are enjoying the new regime while Don Pasquale examines the bills that are already pouring in. Worse is to come: his new bride is off alone to the theatre – on her wedding night. Enraged, he shouts that she is no better than a whore. At that, she slaps his face and his dreams are over. His life apparently in ruins, he contemplates an early grave.

E finita, Don Pasquale ('It's all over for me'): as Don Pasquale gloomily faces the future, Norina sings of the end justifying the means

Norina leaves, dropping a piece of paper. It is an assignation from an unknown suitor. Don Pasquale hurries to find Malatesta just as the latter is making his final arrangements with Ernesto to impersonate the imaginary rival. Together the two older men plan to surprise the guilty pair: Don Pasquale anticipates his revenge while Malatesta watches gleefully as his friend sinks deeper into the trap.

Aspetta, aspetta, cara sposina ('Just you wait, my precious wife'): Don Pasquale's pleasure at trapping his wife develops into the brilliant patter duet between him and Malatesta

The suitor is heard singing a serenade to entice Sofronia to join him. Don Pasquale and Malatesta creep up and surprise Sofronia, who insists that she is alone as Ernesto slips away.

Don Pasquale's garden

Com'è gentil ('How lovely it is'): Ernesto's serenade pretending to lure Sofronia away from her husband

Malatesta asks Don Pasquale to give him *carte blanche* to solve the problem. Thus armed, he threatens Sofronia with the imminent arrival of Ernesto's fiancée, a girl named Norina, with whom she will have to share the house. She refuses indignantly and announces she would rather leave. Don Pasquale begs her to do so, and Ernesto arrives to be granted Norina's hand and a handsome income by his desperate uncle. Sofronia is promptly revealed to be Norina. 'Ah! *bricconissimi!*' ('You villains') cries the poor old man, distraught. But his relief conquers his anger, and the opera ends with general agreement on at least one point: that old men marry at their peril.

ANNA BOLENA
(ANNE BOLEYN)

In two acts, text by Felice Romani after Ippolito Pindemonte's *Enrico VIII ossia Anna Bolena*, an inaccurate account of Henry VIII's second wife. Premiere: Teatro Carcano, Milan, 1830. Donizetti's first real success, it returned to the repertory after the Callas revival of 1957.

Windsor Castle and London, 1536: Enrico (**b**, Henry VIII) has lost interest in Anna (**s**, Anne Boleyn) and wants to dispose of her in favour of Giovanna (**ms**, Jane Seymour), her lady-in-waiting. He recalls Riccardo (**t**, Lord Richard Percy) from exile to provide evidence of her adultery. Riccardo rediscovers his love for Anna; his attempt at suicide is prevented by the queen's page Smeaton (**c**). All three are imprisoned. Refusing to admit guilt, Anna is sentenced to death, as the new queen is proclaimed.

LA FILLE DU REGIMENT
(THE DAUGHTER OF THE REGIMENT)

In two acts, text by Jules-Henri Vernoy de Saint-Georges and Jean-François-Alfred Bayard. Premiere: Opéra-Comique, Paris, 1840. This was Donizetti's first French opera, full of Gallic wit and charm that prefigures Offenbach.

Swiss Tyrolean mountains, 1815: the orphan Marie (**s**), who has been brought up by Sulpice (**b**) as the 'daughter' of the 21st Grenadiers, falls in love with the peasant Tonio (**t**). He joins the regiment in order to marry her, but she has to leave when claimed by the Marquise de Birkenfeld (**ms**) as her niece and told to marry an aristocrat. The soldiers, including Tonio, storm the Marquise's castle to prevent this. The Marquise confesses that Marie is her illegitimate daughter and allows her marriage to Tonio.

ANTONIN DVORAK

Born Nelahozeves 1841, died Prague 1904. Czech nationalist composer of nine symphonies and 11 operas, along with much delightful orchestral, chamber, keyboard and choral music. Brahms sponsored him. Of his operas, only *Jakobín*, *Čert a Káča* (*The Jacobin*) and *Rusalka* are much performed outside Czechoslovakia.

RUSALKA
(THE WATER NYMPH)

In three acts, text by Jaroslav Kvapil, based on Friedrich de la Motte Fouqué's *Undine* and influenced by Hans Andersen's *The Little Mermaid* and Gerhardt Hauptmann's *The Sunken Bell*. Premiere: National Theatre, Prague, 1901. The colourful, symphonically styled score is dominated by its natural elements.

Beside a lake and in the palace grounds: Rusalka (**s**), daughter of the Spirit of the Lake (**b**), falls in love with a Prince (**t**); helped by the witch Jezibaba (**ms**), she assumes human form so as to marry him. The Prince soon tires of his silent partner (she must remain dumb with him) and takes up with a foreign Princess (**s**). Encountering Rusalka again, the Prince is remorseful and despite warnings to the contrary embraces her. The spell violated, they die in each other's arms.

GEORGE GERSHWIN

Born Brooklyn 1898, died Hollywood 1937. Gershwin began his career as a pianist for a Tin Pan Alley firm in New York, accompanying song pluggers. Songs, often with lyrics by his brother Ira, for revues and musicals such as *Lady Be Good* (1924), and the more serious *Rhapsody in Blue* (1924) and *An American in Paris* (1928), made him famous. All were imbued with an infectious sense of rhythm derived from the vocabulary of jazz. Inspired by DuBose Heyward's *Porgy*, Gershwin spent the summer of 1934 on an island off the coast of South Carolina absorbing the speech patterns and music of the local black population. Though intended for the Met, the first New York production of *Porgy and Bess* was on Broadway. (The Met premiere was not until 1985, with Grace Bumbry as Bess.) He was working on a film score in Hollywood when he died.

PORGY AND BESS

Porgy, a cripple	bass baritone
Bess	soprano
Crown, a stevedore	baritone
Robbins, a gambler	tenor
Clara, a fisherman's wife	soprano
Sporting Life, a dope peddler	tenor

Charleston, South Carolina, 1930s: in the poor, violent waterfront community, Porgy's life is transformed by the love of the loose-living Bess. His new-found self-respect and his trust in the Lord are unassailable.

Edwin DuBose Heyward's *Porgy* was adapted first as a play and then as an opera, with libretto by DuBose Heyward and Ira Gershwin. The first performance of *Porgy and Bess* was in Boston in 1935, and it was 50 years before the work was put on at the Met, having toured Europe successfully in between. Using the dialect and music of the South, *Porgy and Bess* bridges the gap between popular song and opera.

A black tenement in Catfish Row, Charleston
Summertime: the famous lullaby set to the background noise of the rumbustuous life on Catfish Row
When Gawd make cripple, He mean him to be lonely: Porgy's mournful acceptance that women pass him by

ACT I
Clara, wife of an absent fisherman, sings a lullaby to her baby. Though his wife objects, Robbins is determined to gamble. Porgy, a cripple, drives up in his goatcart. He cannot hide his affection for Bess, the disreputable girlfriend of Crown, a local thug. Porgy's protests are brushed aside when Crown and Bess arrive. The game of crap starts and Sporting Life, a dope peddler, sells his 'happy dust' to Crown. Robbins wins and Crown, who is drunk, loses his temper. In the ensuing fight Crown pulls

out a cotton hook and stabs Robbins to death. As his wife flings herself across Robbins' body, Bess urges Crown to run away, promising to wait for him. Getting some 'happy dust' from Sporting Life, she too looks for somewhere to hide. Refused by everyone else, she asks Porgy, who gladly takes her in.

Robbins' house

My man's gone now: Robbins' widow mourns his death

Oh, the train is at the station: Bess' song about the train to the Promised Land

Robbins' body is laid out with a saucer on his chest for contributions to the funeral expenses. When Bess comes in with Porgy, the widow indignantly refuses her money until Bess explains that she is now Porgy's woman. Two white policemen enter. When they threaten to arrest a harmless old man, their victim thinks to escape by telling them the truth about Crown. They decide to lock him up anyway as a material witness.

The undertaker arrives and finds that there is not enough money for the funeral. Robbins' widow is distraught at the prospect of his being handed over for students to dissect. In the end the undertaker agrees to go through with the funeral with her promise that the rest of the money will be raised later. Bess, jumping up, leads them all in a song of farewell to their dead friend.

Catfish Row
I got plenty o' nuttin': Porgy's song of joy at sharing his life with Bess

Buzzard, keep on flyin' over: Porgy tells the bird to take its shadow elsewhere, away from his new-found happiness

Bess, you is my woman now: Porgy and Bess' duet

ACT II
The fisherman are repairing their nets. Porgy's life has been transformed by his happiness with Bess. Sporting Life saunters around trying to sell his drugs. Porgy is swindled by a lawyer offering to get Bess a divorce (the deal costs more when he learns she was never married). Suddenly a buzzard, an ill omen, flies overhead and scares them all.

Sporting Life has always been interested in Bess. He tries to lure her to New York, or at least into buying some more 'happy dust'. Porgy, who has overhead, intervenes and frightens Sporting Life away. He and Bess commit themselves to each other.

The whole of Catfish Row is going on a picnic. Bess wants to stay with Porgy but is encouraged by him to go and enjoy herself with the others.

Kittiwah Island
It ain't necessarily so: Sporting Life's encouragement to look outside the Bible

Oh, what you want wid Bess?: Bess pleads with Crown to be left in peace

On the picnic there is much drinking and dancing. Sporting Life is the star of the show. His shameless song about easy living is interrupted by Robbins' widow warning them of God's wrath. Just as Bess is about to return to the boat, Crown appears from the undergrowth. Bess tells him that she has settled down with Porgy. Crown refuses to let her go. She tells Crown that she is happy with Porgy, who needs her more than he does; but when he kisses her and orders her to join him in the woods, she quietly does as he asks.

Catfish Row

Bess is back with Porgy after two days in the woods. She is delirious and Robbins' widow comes to pray over her. When Bess recovers, Porgy tells her that he knows she has been with Crown but he wants her to stay with him.

I loves you, Porgy: Porgy, given new confidence by Bess' love, promises to protect her from Crown

Bess admits that she told Crown she would go back to him and Porgy says that he certainly would not wish to keep her against her will. Bess in turn tells Porgy that it is he whom she loves.

Robbins' house

Oh, Doctor Jesus: a spiritual that everyone joins in, singing against the storm outside

Huddled together in fear of a storm outside, the whole community joins in a spiritual, praying for salvation. Crown bursts in, grabbing Bess and knocking Porgy to the ground. He mocks their singing. Clara, who has been looking out of the window for her husband's boat, falls back and Bess sees that the fishing boat is upside down. Clara dashes out into the storm and Crown, taunting Porgy, goes off to help her.

A redheaded woman: Crown's song of defiance

Catfish Row

ACT III

After the storm, Bess and the others try to comfort Clara for the loss of her husband. Sporting Life now bases his hopes for Bess on a fight between Porgy and Crown. And he is not disappointed, for when Crown creeps in, Porgy stabs him in the neck and then strangles him.

The police suspect Robbins' widow. Porgy is interrogated, and he is appalled to be asked to identify the body. Sporting Life warns him that Crown's wound will begin to bleed in the presence of his killer. The police drag Porgy off. Sporting Life's plan is now taking shape. Persuading Bess to take some 'happy dust', he warns her that Porgy may be locked up for two years or more and describes the good time to be had with him in New York. Furiously, she refuses, but he is sure her need for drugs will bring her to him.

There's a boat dat's leavin' soon: Sporting Life's picture of the good life to be had in New York

A week later Porgy returns, delighted that he was able to keep his eyes shut when confronted with Crown's corpse. He has brought with him presents, including a red dress for Bess. Jailed for contempt of court, he had made plenty of money gambling. Gradually his neighbours slip away in embarrassment and at last he realizes that Bess has gone. Two of his neighbours, who always disapproved of her, explain that Sporting Life has lured her away because she believed that Porgy would be imprisoned for a long time. Porgy is relieved to find that she is alive. He immediately calls for someone to bring his goat so that he can follow her to New York. He is helped into his cart and sets off on the thousand-mile journey, confident that the Lord will help him on his way.

My Bess! I want her now: the trio between Porgy and his neighbours as he tries to find out what has happened to Bess

UMBERTO GIORDANO

Born Foggia 1867, died Milan 1948. After making an impression in a competition with his one-act *Marina*, he won a commission from the publisher Sonzogno. The result was *Mala Vita* (1892), whose crude realism caused a scandal. The success of *Andrea* *Chénier* and, in Italy at least, *Fedora* was not repeated in his eight other operas. Mostly in *verismo* style, they are more notable for their theatrical power than their musical imagination.

ANDREA CHENIER

In four acts, text by Luigi Illica, a partly fictional account of the life of the poet André Chénier. Premiere: La Scala, Milan, 1896. Giordano's most successful work, it is a passionate treatment of a patriotic subject.

Paris, just before and during the French Revolution: Chénier (**t**) is in love with Maddalena (**s**, Madeleine de Coigny). Carlo Gérard (**bar**), a servant on the Coigny staff, also secretly admires her but despises the nobility. During the Revolution, they renew their affair. Gérard is now a revolutionary leader, whose jealous indictment leads to Chénier's conviction. Maddalena offers herself to Gérard in exchange for Chénier's release; but too late. Bribing her way into Chénier's cell, she goes with him to the guillotine.

FEDORA

In three acts, with text by Arturo Colautti after Victorien Sardou's drama. Premiere: Teatro Lirico, Milan, 1898. Strong dramatic situations characterize Giordano's most successful opera after *Andrea Chénier*.

St Petersburg, Paris and Switzerland, late 19th century. The fiancé of Princess Fedora Romanov (**s**) is murdered by Count Loris Ipanov (**t**), whose wife has had an affair with him. Helped by diplomat De Sirlex (**bar**), Fedora tracks down Loris but falls for him on learning the reason for the crime. But her earlier (annonymous) accusations have resulted in deaths in his family; he vows revenge on the informer. About to be unmasked, she takes poison; Loris forgives her, but too late.

CHRISTOPH GLUCK

Born Erasbach 1714, died Vienna 1787. After composing 20 or more operas in the Italian manner, the music having little relation to the characters or the plot, Gluck contrived to 're-form' opera. In his preface to the score of *Alceste* (1767), he wrote that the music should be secondary to the poetry and drama, that there should be less disparity between arias and recitatives and no interruptions to the action for the purpose of displaying virtuosity. Ranieri da Calzabigi exerted a strong influence on him and wrote the libretto for *Orfeo ed Euridice*, presented to the Viennese in 1762. Gluck made alterations to this for the Paris production of 1774. In Paris there was some hostility between his supporters and those who favoured the conservative composer Nicola Piccini, *Iphigénie en Aulide* was presented in 1774 and the highly successful *Iphigénie en Tauride* in 1779.

ORFEO ED EURIDICE

(ORPHEUS AND EURYDICE)

Orfeo (Orpheus)	contralto
Euridice (Eurydice), his wife	soprano
Amore (Amor), God of Love	soprano

Greece, in legendary times: Orfeo's music conquers the Furies on his way to reclaiming his beloved wife Euridice from Hades, but he is unable to restrain himself from looking back at her.

Set to Ranieri da Calzabigi's text, the opera was first performed at the Burgtheater, Vienna, in 1762. Gluck rewrote it for Paris in 1774, substituting a tenor for a contralto castrato for the role of Orfeo. It is the first opera to incorporate elements of his reforms.

Grotto with the tomb of Euridice
Chiamo il mio ben così ('Calling always for my love'): Orfeo's impassioned lament for the loss of his wife
Gli sguardi trattieni ('Avert your glances'): Amore's aria conveying Jupiter's command that Orfeo must not look upon his wife if he is to reclaim her from the Underworld

ACT I

Orfeo, accompanied by the chorus, scatters flowers on the tomb of his beloved wife. His grief at losing Euridice, echoing through the woods, turns to anger against the gods who took her from him. He determines to follow her to Hades. At this Amore, God of Love, tells Orfeo that Jupiter has had pity on him and will allow him to cross the River Lethe and that, if he plays his lyre well, she will be restored to him. As Orfeo rejoices, Amore tells him that Jupiter imposes one condition: Orfeo must lead his wife from below without looking upon her. As the god departs, Orfeo anticipates that Euridice will not understand his refusal to look at her. He sets out with confidence, however.

ACT II

In the approach to the Underworld, the sinister music reflects the dreadful scene. The Furies dance and sing of their hostility to anyone rash enough to trespass on their territory. Orfeo's first pleas are met with a savage refusal. Suddenly the music softens and the mood of the Furies changes as they listen to Orfeo's song. They allow him to pass.

Entrance to Hades
No! No! No!: the conclusion to the dramatic scene in which Orfeo tries to placate the Furies

Euridice and a chorus of blessed spirits sing of their serene happiness. As they move on, Orfeo arrives and is enchanted by the scene. Orfeo sings of his love for Euridice and the blessed spirits return, bringing her with them. Orfeo, without looking at her, takes Euridice by the hand.

The Elysian Fields
Che puro ciel! ('What wonderful light'): Orfeo admires the blessed refuge
Io dunque, in braccio all'idol mio ('Back in my lover's arms'): Euridice's joy at rejoining Orfeo

The path from Hades

ACT III

Orfeo urges his wife to follow while she wonders whether she is awake or dreaming. She longs to be taken into his arms and cannot comprehend why his back is turned to her. She cannot understand his coldness. Overcome with misery, Euridice feels herself once more to be dying: as she sinks down on to a rock, she pleads in a last tender moment never to be forgotten by Orfeo. Unable to resist, he turns towards her, ignoring the warning. Euridice immediately dies. Orfeo prepares to kill himself so that he may follow her. But Amore judges Orfeo to have suffered enough for his love, and Euridice revives amidst general rejoicing.

Che farò senza Euridice? ('What can I do without Euridice?'): Orfeo's despair as Euridice returns to the land of the dead

ALCESTE
(ALCESTIS)

In three acts, text by Ranieri da Calzabigi, after Euripides. Premiere: Burgtheater, Vienna, 1767; extensively revised version in French (F.L.G. Lebland du Roullet), Opéra, Paris, 1776. A tragedy that with *Orfeo ed Euridice* spearheaded Gluck's operatic reforms, enumerated in the work's historic preface.

Ancient Thessaly: the oracle of Apollon (**bar**, Apollo) confirms for Alceste (**s**, Alcestis) that the illness of her husband Admète (**t**, Admetus) will be fatal unless a friend dies in his stead. She resolves to sacrifice herself: '*Divinités du Styx*' ('Gods of the Styx'). Evander (**t**) reveals to Admète, now recovered, the oracle's message. Refusing to accept it, Admète follows Alceste into Hades and confronts the God of Death, Thanatos (**bar**). With help from Hercule (**bar**), the pair is reunited on earth after Apollon's intervention.

IPHIGENIE EN TAURIDE
(IPHIGENIA IN TAURIS)

In four acts, text by Nicolas-François Guillard and F.L.G. Lebland du Roullet, after Euripides. Premiere: Opéra, Paris, 1779. This is Gluck's most sustained achievement in dramatic and lyrical intensity, the sequel to *Iphigénie en Aulide* (1774).

The temple of Diana on the isle of Tauris, after the Trojan War: Iphigénie (**s**, Iphigenia), unaware that her brother Oreste (**bar**, Orestes) has killed her mother for murdering her father, has become a priestess. Arriving incognito, Oreste and his companion Pylade (**t**, Pylades) are arrested; Thoas (**b**) demands they be sacrificed. They are separated and Oreste loses his mind. Recovering, he reveals his family's misfortunes but not his identity, and secures Pylade's escape. Iphigénie recognizes Oreste just before sacrificing him. Pylade returns with soldiers, Thoas is killed and Diane (**s**, Diana) pardons Oreste.

CHARLES GOUNOD

Born Paris 1818, died St Cloud 1893. Gounod attended the Paris Conservatoire and in 1839 won the Prix de Rome. He concentrated at first on church music, and for a time his intention was to enter the priesthood. The moderate success of his first opera, *Sapho* (1851), brought him to the attention of the director of the Théâtre Lyrique in Paris, Léon Carvalho. It was he who commissioned *Faust*. The opera had 57 performances in its first season, 1859, and this was followed by successful productions all over Europe. After ballet was introduced and the spoken dialogue replaced the recitatives for the Paris Opéra production of 1869, it became more of a grand spectacle. Many of the tunes have retained something of their original popularity. Two of Gounod's later operas – *Mireille* (1864) and *Roméo et Juliette* (1867) – survive in the modern repertoire.

FAUST

Faust	tenor
Méphistophélès	bass
Marguerite	soprano
Valentin, her brother	baritone
Siebel, her admirer	mezzo-soprano

Germany, 16th century: Faust, granted a return to youth by the evil Méphistophélès, seduces and destroys the innocent Marguerite.

Jules Barbier's libretto is based on the early part of Goethe's dramatic poem, which he presents as a moral. The opera was first performed at the Théâtre Lyrique in Paris in 1859. The ballet at the beginning of Act V was added when it was produced at the Paris Opéra, where the inclusion of dance was a convention. *Faust*, sung in Italian, inaugurated the first season at the Metropolitan Opera House, New York, in 1883.

Faust's study

ACT I

Late at night, the elderly Faust reflects that he has lost his faith. He pours out some poison but pauses when he hears a chorus praising God. Faust sits back cursing his life and calling out for Satan. Immediately Méphistophélès appears. He can give Faust whatever his heart desires – riches, fame, power. It is youth that Faust asks for. Méphistophélès offers him a contract: youth in return for his soul. Faust hesitates and a vision of the beautiful Marguerite appears. He signs and is at once tranformed into a young man. They leave in search of pleasure.

A *moi les plaisirs* ('It's pleasure for me'): Faust's duet with Méphistophélès celebrating his return to youth

Outside the inn, The God Bacchus

Avant de quitter ces lieux ('Before I leave'): Valentin's aria praying for God's protection over Marguerite

Ainsi que la brise légère ('Like a gentle breeze'): the chorus of townspeople encouraging each other to join in the waltz

Marguerite's garden

Faites-lui mes aveux ('Let this be my avowal'): Siebel's confession of his love for Marguerite

Salut! demeure chaste et pure ('This blessed house'): Faust's soliloquy, watching the house where Marguerite lives out her innocent existence

Il était un roi de Thulé ('Once there was a king of Thule'): Marguerite's ballad about a king who died faithful to the memory of his love
Ah! je ris de me voir ('I am laughing with joy'): Marguerite's brilliant coloratura aria, the Jewel Song, a telling contrast to her previous simplicity

ACT II

A crowd of townspeople join together in a prolonged chorus celebrating the Kernis, or Easter fair. Valentin enters. He is a soldier and he asks Siebel to look after his sister Marguerite while he is away at the war, protected by the medallion that Marguerite has given him.

One of the students begins to sing a song about a rat but is interrupted by the appearance of Méphistophélès, who contributes his own song about Man's shameful worship of money.

Méphistophélès proceeds to read their palms. Siebel will never touch a flower without its fading. Valentin will be killed by someone he knows. With a flourish Méphistophélès conjures up some wine and proposes a toast to Marguerite. Valentin reacts by drawing his sword. But Méphistophélès has drawn a circle round himself and Valentin's sword breaks against the invisible barrier. Realizing his satanic force, they raise their swords in the sign of the Cross. Méphistophélès recoils, but recovers to assure Faust that he will possess Marguerite.

A crowd comes in singing and dancing for the Easter celebrations. Suddenly Faust sees Marguerite. Siebel takes a step towards her, but Méphistophélès gets in his way, giving Faust the opportunity to offer his arm to Marguerite. She modestly refuses. Méphistophélès continues to promise help to Faust, as the dance builds up to a climax.

ACT III

Siebel sings of his hope that Marguerite will understand how much he loves her. But when he picks her a flower, it withers as Méphistophélès had predicted. Then he remembers the font with holy water nearby. Dipping his fingers into this, he finds that the flowers can now survive his touch.

Faust and Méphistophélès watch Siebel leaving his flowers for Marguerite. While Méphistophélès goes to get a more tempting offering, Faust admires the scene and Marguerite's pure innocence. Méphistophélès returns with a box full of jewels. Faust has lost his enthusiasm to corrupt Marguerite. Méphistophélès scoffs at such scruples and drags Faust away to hide in the garden.

Marguerite appears. She settles down at her spinning wheel and sings a folk song. But all the time she is thinking about the handsome stranger (Faust). She finds Siebel's flowers. 'Pauvre garçon' ('That poor boy'). Then she sees the jewel box. Never in her life has she seen such riches. There is even a mirror, and she cannot resist adorning herself and approving the result. Her neighbour hurries in to admire the effect, too.

Méphistophélès and Faust come out of hiding and Méphistophélès tells the neighbour that her husband is dead. Far from being upset, she soon finds herself being led aside by this fascinating stranger, leaving Marguerite and Faust alone. Méphistophélès casts a spell over the garden, commanding the flowers to re-open so that their scent may intoxicate and confuse Marguerite.

O nuit, étends sur eux ton ombre ('Oh night, enfold them in your shade'): Méphistophélès rearranges nature to assist Faust
O nuit d'amour ('Oh night of love'): Faust's continued plea for Marguerite's love

Faust kneels before Marguerite, declaring his love for her. The couple express their love for each other until Marguerite modestly persuades him to leave until the morning. Faust, overwhelmed with happiness, begins to leave, but Méphistophélès makes him wait until they see Marguerite open her window. Thinking that she is alone, she pours out her love for Faust. Immediately Faust runs forward and, as she falls into his arms, Méphistophélès' laugh echoes in the distance.

Marguerite's room

Il ne revient pas ('He does not return'): Marguerite, sad and afraid, waits for Faust's return

Si le bonheur ('If ever happiness'): Siebel's aria telling Marguerite of his affection for her

The church

Marguerite. Sois maudite ('You are damned, Marguerite, you are going to hell'): Méphistophélès savagely discourages Marguerite's attempts at prayer

The street

Gloire immortelle ('Immortal glory'): the soldiers chorus

Vous qui faites l'endormie ('I know you're not asleep'): Méphistophélès makes fun of Marguerite's unhappiness

ACT IV

Marguerite is alone at her spinning wheel. Faust has long since disappeared and she can hear the girls outside laughing at her shame. She hopes, despairingly, for him to come back.

Siebel enters and offers to take revenge on Faust, repeating his love for Marguerite. She tells him that she still loves Faust and leaves for church to pray for the child that she is carrying. (This scene is sometimes omitted.)

Inside the church, Marguerite prays for forgiveness; Méphistophélès, seeking her soul, interrupts. He is assisted by a chorus of demons while the cathedral choir chants divine service. Marguerite's voice, praying for assistance, rings out over all. Méphistophélès' last words leave her fainting on the floor.

The soldiers have returned and, while Siebel tells Valentin that Marguerite is at church, the soldiers sing of the splendours of military life. Siebel tries to break the news to Valentin that Marguerite is expecting a child. Faust and Méphistophélès return. Méphistophélès insists on singing an insulting serenade.

Valentin comes out of Marguerite's house in a rage, determined to fight them. Faust is unwilling to cause further trouble but Valentin flings away the medallion that Marguerite had given him and, guided by Méphistophélès, Faust runs Valentin through with his sword. Valentin refuses Marguerite's help and renounces her in front of the gathering crowd, cursing her as he dies.

The Harz Mountains	**ACT V**

ACT V

The Harz Mountains

A scene of supernatural feasting and dancing takes place to celebrate Walpurgis Night, the Devil's festival.

The valley of the Brocken

Faust has a vision of Marguerite with a red line across her throat, like the cut of an axe, and he demands that Méphistophélès should take him to her.

The prison

Marguerite is in prison, having killed her baby, and she is to be executed the following morning. She is half demented and seems to be living in the past. Faust begs her to come with him, and Méphistophélès, too, urges her to escape through his powers. But Marguerite sinks to her knees, praying desperately for God to accept her soul. As she dies, a celestial choir can be heard welcoming her in Heaven, leaving Faust in the power of Méphistophélès.

Anges purs, anges radieux ('Oh shinging angels, pure at heart'): Marguerite's prayer as she rejects Faust's offer of escape

ROMEO ET JULIETTE
(ROMEO AND JULIET)

In five acts, text by Jules Barbier and Michel Carré, after Shakespeare. Premiere: Théâtre Lyrique, Paris, 1867. The tuneful if sentimental treatment keeps close to the original play.

Verona, 14th century: Capulet (**bar**) holds a masked ball at which his daughter Juliette (**s**) falls for Roméo (**t**) of the rival Montague clan. Roméo escapes when recognized by her cousin Tybalt (**t**) but later returns to her balcony; they are married by Frère Laurent (**b**), who hopes their families will thus be reconciled. Roméo is banished for killing Tybalt and the lovers part. Laurent give Juliette a sleeping potion to feign death and avoid the marriage arranged for her with Paris (**bar**). Thinking her dead, Roméo poisons himself. They are briefly reunited, before Juliette stabs herself. They die in each other's arms.

GEORGE FRIDERIC HANDEL

Born Halle 1685, died London 1759. Studying first as an organist, Handel went to Hamburg in 1703 and his first opera, *Almira*, was presented there in 1705. Four years in Italy followed and in 1710 he was appointed director of music in Hanover. In 1711 *Rinaldo* created a great impression – visual as well as musical – in London. When in 1714 his patron, the Elector of Hanover, ascended the English throne as George I, Handel settled in London. He spent the years 1720–28 writing and presenting operas, first for the Royal Academy of Music seasons at the King's Theatre and then for his own company, during which time he brought the *opera seria* form to a height. He was put out of business by John Gay's *Beggar's Opera* (1728), which had a more general appeal. His later operas include *Serse* (1738) and *Semele* (1744), but by then he was better known as a composer of oratorios such as the *Messiah* (1741).

GIULIO CESARE
(JULIUS CAESAR)

In three acts (11 scenes), with text by Nicola Francesco Haym. Premiere: Haymarket Theatre, London, 1724.

Egypt, 48 BC: at the battle of Pharsalus, Cesare (**c**, Caesar) has defeated Pompeo (Pompey), whose severed head is presented to him by Achilla (**b**) on the order of Tolomeo (**b**, Ptolemy), King of Egypt, who arranged the murder. Pompeo's widow Cornelia (**c**) is distraught, his son Sesto (**s** or **t**, Sextus) vows revenge. Cesare is angry. Cleopatra (**s**) resolves to woo Cesare so as to wrest control of Egypt from Tolomeo, her brother. At first disguised, Cleopatra reveals her identity to Cesare and begs him to flee; she is taken prisoner after losing a battle with Tolomeo. Cesare dives into the Nile and is presumed drowned, but seizes from Sesto the key to secret entry into the palace. While he frees Cleopatra, Sesto kills Tolomeo, whose crown Cesare then awards to Cleopatra.

SERSE
(XERXES)

In three acts, text by Nicola Minato (for Cavalli, 1654), revised by Silvio Stampiglia (for Bononcini, 1694). Premiere: Haymarket, London, 1738. Handel's most free-ranging, least rigid opera, blending elements of comedy and tragedy.

Court of Xerxes, Persia, 5th century BC: Serse (**ms**) and his brother Arsamene (**ms**) are both in love with Romilda (**s**), daughter of the bumbling army commander Ariodate (**b**). She prefers Arsamene, who is consequently expelled from Persia by Serse. (He is anyway betrothed to Amastre, **ms**.) Her sister Atalanta (**s**), who also loves Arsamene, hopes to get Romilda to marry Serse. After much intrigue, heightened by the comic servant Elviro (**bar**), all is happily resolved. Serse's aria 'Ombra mai fù' ('My welcome shade'), wholly parodistic and marked *larghetto*, is popularly known as Handel's Largo.

ENGELBERT HUMPERDINCK

Born Siegburg 1854, died Neustrelitz 1921. Humperdinck studied in Cologne and Munich, and in 1897 won a scholarship to Italy. There he met Wagner, who invited him to assist with the Bayreuth premiere of *Parsifal* (1882). He took up teaching positions in Barcelona and Frankfurt, and he was asked by Cosima Wagner to teach music to their son Siegfried. Humperdinck revered Wagner, like many composers of his time, and in *Hänsel und Gretel* (1893) he used Wagnerian harmonies, with their evocation of time and place, dotted with snatches of folk song to soften the harsh outlines of the Grimms' fairy tale: a story of poverty and fear brought to a happy close with a majestic chorale. He wrote six more operas, including *Königskinder* (1897), which was premiered at the Met, but none repeated the great, international success of *Hänsel und Gretel*.

HANSEL UND GRETEL

(HANSEL AND GRETEL)

Hänsel	mezzo-soprano
Gretel, his sister	soprano
Gertrud, their mother	soprano
Peter, their father	baritone
Sandman	soprano
Dew Fairy	soprano
Witch	mezzo-soprano

Germany, in legendary times: the Grimms' fairytale of the witch who lures Hänsel and Gretel into her gingerbread house in the forest.

The libretto is by the composer's sister, Adelheid Wette. The first performance at Christmas 1893 in Weimar was conducted by Richard Strauss.

The cottage

Brüderchen komm tanz' mit mir ('Little brother come and dance'): Gretel leads her brother in a dance

ACT I

In their cottage, Hänsel and Gretel keep their spirits up by dancing together, though racked by hunger.

Their mother returns. She is angry that they have not done more work and, in threatening to beat them, she knocks over a jug of milk. Hänsel laughs and Gertrud chases him out of the house with a stick, ordering them into the woods to find strawberries. She sinks into a mournful sleep and is woken by her jubilant husband. As he tries to kiss her, she reproaches him for spending all their money on beer. He shows her a basket full of eggs, sausages and coffee and makes her dance in celebration

Der Besen, der Besen
('Broomsticks'): the
broomstick maker explains
that there is another use for
broomsticks: to be ridden on
by witches

In the forest
Ein Männlein steht im Walde
('Stands a goblin in the
woods'): Gretel sings a folk
song as she makes a garland
Abends, will ich schlafen gehn
('When I lay me down to
sleep'): the children's beautiful
evening prayer, which precedes
the dream pantomime

The Witch's house
Der kleine Taumann heiss' ich ('I
am called the little Dewman'):
the Dew Fairy's song

Bei dunkler Nacht ('In the dark
night'): the Witch relishes her
power at night

Juchhei! Nun ist die Hexe tot
('Hurray! The Witch is dead'):
Hänsel and Gretel exult at their
success

for he has sold a large number of brooms. Suddenly he
notices that the children are missing. He is appalled that
she has not heard of the witch who lures children with her
sweets and then pushes them into her oven and cooks
them for herself. Distraught, mother and father set off in
search of their children

ACT II
During the Witch's Ride prelude, the curtain rises on
Hänsel looking for strawberries and Gretel playing with
some flowers. Night has fallen and Hänsel realizes he has
forgotten the way home. Suddenly they are scared. As
they hide together, they see a little man approaching. It is
the Sandman, who throws his sand into their eyes and
tells them to go quietly to sleep. The children kneel to say
their prayers, invoking the fourteen angels. As they fall
asleep, the angels appear.

ACT III
Dawn approaches and the Dew Fairy comes to wake the
children with dewdrops. Hänsel and Gretel tell each
other of the same dream – that they saw the fourteen
angels of their prayer. As they look around, they see and
smell the gingerbread house with a fence of gingerbread
figures. They tiptoe over and Hänsel breaks off a piece of
the house to eat. Immediately, they hear the voice of the
Witch asking who is nibbling at her house. She invites
them in, but Hänsel refuses. The Witch ties him up but he
frees himself and tries to lead Gretel away. The Witch
casts a spell over them both. Hänsel is imprisoned in her
cage and Gretel is sent off to do housework. The Witch
piles wood on the fire to heat her oven before dancing
wildly about on her broomstick to celebrate the coming
feast.

While the Witch feeds Hänsel to fatten him up, Gretel
manages to get hold of her magic wand. The Witch leads
them to the oven and Gretel shyly asks her to show them
how to climb in and see if the gingerbread is ready.
Believing them still to be bound by her spell, the
unsuspecting Witch climbs in. The children triumphantly slam the door behind her.

They rush about dismantling the gingerbread house
until suddenly the oven explodes and with this vanishes
all the Witch's power. The figures of the gingerbread
fence turn back into other little children. The Witch has
been turned into a huge cake and, as Hänsel and Gretel's
parents arrive, everybody unites in a hymn of thanks-
giving.

LEOS JANACEK

Born Hukvaldy 1854, died Ostrava 1928. Janáček studied in Prague, Leipzig and Vienna, founding a college for organists in Brno in 1881. His first opera was *Sárka*, written in 1887 but not produced until 1925. Collecting the folk songs of Moravia, he was influenced by their harmonic and melodic properties. He also attempted to echo the patterns of Czech speech by the use of musical phrases, or 'speech melodies'. *Její Pastorkyňa (Jenůfa)* was first performed in 1904, but it only achieved international success after it was produced in Prague in 1916. His gift for depicting characters can be heard in operas such as *Kat'a Kabanová (Katya Kabanova)*, premiered in 1921, and *Příhody Lišky Bystrovšky (The Cunning Little Vixen)*, of 1924. With *Věc Makropulos (The Makropulos Affair)*, 1926, and *Z mrtvého domu (From the House of the Dead)*, produced posthumously in 1930, his idiom is to be heard in its most concise and expressive form.

JEJI PASTORKYNA

(JENUFA)

Jenůfa	soprano
Kostelnička Buryjovka, her stepmother	soprano
Steva, the mill owner	tenor
Laca, his half-brother	tenor

The mill

Všeci sa ženija ('A choice between marriage or war'): the song of the recruits on their way home

Moravia, late 19th century: Jenůfa is scarred by Laca, jealous of Steva, his brother, whose child she bears. The murder of the child destroys the family.

The libretto is Janáček's, based on a controversial play by Gabriela Preissová. First performed at Brno in 1904, the opera was revised for the 1916 Prague production by Janáček's rival, Karel Kovařovic. It is usual now to revert to his original score.

ACT I

Two brothers are in love with Jenůfa: Steva, whose love she returns and whose baby she is secretly expecting, and Laca, who works at the mill.

Steva is being considered for conscription into the army. Jenůfa is worried that if he joins up he will not be able to marry her. Laca recognizes with bitterness that it is his brother whom she loves, but he tells the Foreman that he still hopes to succeed with Jenůfa.

The recruits return. Steva has not been conscripted but he is, as usual, drunk. Jenůfa's stepmother, the Kostelnička (sexton's wife) angrily forbids the marriage unless Steva can stay sober for a year. Because of the child, Jenůfa is anxious that they should get married. Steva boasts of being chased by other girls but says her beauty keeps him faithful to her. He has been given flowers by one of the girls and Laca picks these up when his brother has left and offers them to Jenůfa. He tries to kiss her, but she pushes him away. He slashes her on the cheek with his knife. Some think it is an accident, but the Foreman knows that he did it on purpose.

Stevo, Stevo: Jenůfa's anxious plea to Steva that he will marry her before the child is born

The Kostelnička's house five months later

Co jsem se namodlila ('How often I have prayed'): Jenůfa's stepmother prays for the death of the child that symbolizes Jenůfa's ruin

Já Pánabohu chlapce zanesu (I will take this child to God'): the stepmother's decision to kill Jenůfa's child and hide his body under the ice

Zdrávas královno ('Blessed Majesty, Holy Virgin'): Jenůfa kneels and prays for protection for her baby

ACT II

Jenůfa, still not married to Steva, has given birth to Steva's son, secretly concealed in her stepmother's house. Her neighbours believe that she has gone to Vienna to look for work. The Kostelnička tells her the child would be better dead. With Jenůfa asleep, the Kostelnička reluctantly decides that Steva had better marry her after all. When he arrives, Steva bluntly tells the Kostelnička that Jenůfa's disfigured face no longer pleases him. He intends to marry the mayor's daughter. Laca appears and is very willing to take care of Jenůfa, but he is angry to hear that Jenůfa has borne his brother's son. Desperate to win him over, the Kostelnička pretends that the child has died. Later, she snatches him up and takes him out into the wintry night.

Jenůfa wakes to find them both gone. Desperately she prays for her child before a picture of the Virgin Mary. When the Kostelnička returns, she tells Jenůfa that her child has died and reminds her of Steva's cruel rejection. Laca comes in and beseeches Jenůfa to marry him. Eventually she accepts. The storm outside blows the window open. The Kostelnička feels that Death itself is peering into the house.

The Kostelnička's house, three months later

Ej, mamko, mamko, maměnko moja! ('Oh mother, my mother!'): the village girls' wedding song
Ještě jsem tu já! ('You still have me to reckon with!'): the stepmother begins her confession

ACT III

Laca and Jenůfa are happy as they prepare for the marriage ceremony, but the Kostelnička is nervous and complains of sleeplessness. Jenůfa and Laca have forgiven each other for the pain they caused. The guests, including Steva, his fiancée and the mayor, are joined by village girls, who sing to celebrate the happy day.

The couple are blessed by Laca's grandmother. Before Jenůfa's stepmother can add her blessing, shouting announces that a dead child has been found under the ice. Jenůfa recognizes the child as her own since he still wears the bonnet that she made for him. The outraged villagers prepare to stone her. Then the Kostelnička comes forward and confesses her guilt.

V saňte, pěstounko moja ('Now you must rise again'): Jenůfa understands and forgives

Odešli. Jdi také! ('The others have gone. Now you must follow them'): Jenůfa encourages Laca to free himself from her troubles

In the crisis, Steva's fiancée rejects him; the tormented Kostelnička demands to be punished, and Jenůfa raises her to her feet and forgives her; Laca admits that his injury to Jenůfa is the cause of it all. Sadly, Jenůfa prepares to part from Laca since it seems inevitable that she will be put on trial. Laca, however, repeats his love and commitment to her and together they face the future.

PRIHODY LISKY BYSTROVSKY
(THE CUNNING LITTLE VIXEN)

Forester	baritone
Forester's wife	mezzo-soprano
Vixen	soprano
Fox	soprano
Cock	tenor
Hens	sopranos
Parson	bass
Schoolmaster	tenor
Poacher	bass

Moravia: a little vixen is captured by a forester. She escapes, takes over a badger's set, marries and breeds before being shot by a poacher. In a new generation of animals the forester seems to see the old. Throughout there are parallels between animals and humans.

Janáček wrote the libretto himself, basing it on Rudolf Těsnohlídek's story published in instalments in a Czech newspaper; this in turn was written around a series of drawings by the artist Stanislav Lolek. The premiere of the opera was in Brno in 1924.

The forest

ACT I
In a forest full of animals and insects, the forester, exhausted, settles down to sleep for the afternoon. A little vixen is playing in the sunshine. When she tries to catch a frog, it lands on the forester's face. He wakes up, sees the vixen and catches her, carrying her off for a pet.

Courtyard of the forester's lodge

Back home, the forester's wife gives her dachshund and the vixen some milk. The dog complains to the vixen about his love life. She tells the dog of scandal among the birds. She pushes him away when he gets interested in her. The vixen, pestered by the forester's son and school friend, snaps and is promptly tied up with a cord.

Bu! Bu! Ona mně užrala lýtko ('Oh, Oh, she's bitten my leg'): the schoolboy shouts when the vixen snaps at him

Night falls on the dejected vixen. The music builds up from her original desolation into a picture of warm eroticism. The vixen herself seems to turn into a gypsy girl and cries out in her sleep.

Bez kohóta? Bez kohóta? ('No cocks?'): the hens become hysterical at the thought of a feminist world

A badger's set

The inn

Bývalo, bývalo ('So long ago'): the forester mocks the schoolmaster's romance with a folk song about ageing lovers

The forest
O, ó, Terynko! Kdybych byl věděl ž vás tu potkám ('Oh, Oh, Terynka, if I'd thought to find you here'): the schoolmaster, half drunk, is overcome with nostalgia when he mistakes the vixen for his lost love

The vixen's earth
Co je na mně tak krásného? ('Am I really beautiful?'): the vixen basks in her suitor's admiration
Ta naša Bystrouška je jak ta nejhorši ('Our vixen's no better than the rest'): the owl is delighted to be the first with the news

The edge of a clearing
Déž sem vandroval ('When I'm on my way'): the poacher sings on his way through the forest

Běži liška ('Run little fox'): the fox cubs' gleeful song as they dance round the trap

Morning comes. The forester's wife comes out to feed her chickens. The vixen tries to stir them up with the rebellious idea of a better world, free from men and roosters. Irritated that they do not agree, she digs herself a grave and lies down as if to die. The chickens approach to inspect the 'corpse' and she kills them, one by one. When the furious forester and his wife come running out to beat her, the vixen bites through the cord and scampers off into the forest.

ACT II
Back in the forest, the vixen drives the badger away so that she can live comfortably in his set.

In the village, the forester is playing cards with the schoolmaster while the parson watches. The forester teases the schoolmaster about a girl. The schoolmaster retorts by teasing him about the vixen. The parson, drinking gloomily, warns them against women with a Latin quotation.

As they walk tipsily home, they catch a glimpse of the vixen. She calls to mind the schoolmaster's lost love, the delightful Terynka. Both the schoolmaster and the parson reflect individually on their past. The forester, infuriated, fires his gun at the vixen. This frightens his friend but has no effect on the vixen.

Safe in the forest, the vixen meets a fox, who offers to escort her. She impresses him with her description of being brought up in a human family and she is delighted with his compliments. He even brings her a rabbit for breakfast. They admit to each other that they have never found another creature worth loving. The more she asks why he loves her, the more intense he becomes. They scamper underground, scandalizing the birds, only emerging in order to be married by the woodpecker amid a blaze of forest celebration.

ACT III
The poacher sings cheerfully as he goes about his work. He is waylaid by the forester before he can pick up a hare that the vixen has killed. He tells the forester that he is about to get married to the celebrated Terynka and they leave after the forester has set a fox trap near the hare. The vixen's cubs come scampering out to laugh at the trap and ridicule the forester. The fox is eager for more cubs. They hear the poacher returning and the vixen warns her cubs to hide. When the poacher puts his basket down to try to

shoot the vixen to turn her fur into a muff for Terynka, he falls over the cubs as they raid his basket of chickens. While the vixen is complaining that people are always killing foxes yet object when foxes kill chickens, the poacher retrieves his gun and shoots her dead.

Garden behind the inn

In the village, Terynka and the poacher are getting married. The schoolmaster cannot hide his sadness. The forester reports that the foxes' earth is deserted. The parson has had to move on again.

The forest
Počké, tebe si drapnu jak tvoju mámu ('Hey, I'll catch you like your mother'): the forester's greeting to the new generation, promising to teach the little vixen to behave better than her mother

When the forester returns to the forest for a nap in the same glade, he seems to see the vixen's daughter – exactly like her mother. Another frog wakes him up, descendant of the earlier creature. Life in the forest continues in its eternal cycle.

KAT'A KABANOVA
(KATYA KABANOVA)

In three acts, text by the composer from Vincenc Cervinka's translation of Alexander Ostrovsky's *The Storm*. Premiere: Brno, 1921. Tightly-woven emotional conflicts are expressed in music both intense and lyrical.

Kalinov, on the Volga, *c.* 1860: Katerina (**s**, Katya) is unhappily married to Tikhon (**t**), son of the rich widow Kabanicha (**c**) who detests her. She secretly loves Boris (**t**) and after much soul-searching meets him in Tikhon's absence. During a violent thunderstorm, she confesses to Tikhon and his mother, and runs away, drowning herself in the river after a final rendezvous with Boris. In a sub-plot contrasting the emancipation of the younger generation, Vanya (**t**) has a parallel affair with Varvara (**ms**).

VEC MAKROPULOS
(THE MAKROPULOS AFFAIR)

In three acts, text by the composer after Karel Capek's play of the same name. Premiere: Brno, 1926. The complex fantasy is given unity by an unconventional central character. The 'case' is a secret formula for eternal life.

Prague, 1920s: because of an elixir, the singer Emilia Marty (**s**), née Makropulos, has lived over 300 years, changing identities every 70 years but retaining the initials E.M. At first frightened that its effects may wear off, she tries to find the formula from the papers of a lawsuit between Albert Gregor (**t**) and Baron Prus (**bar**). She later grows weary of life and eventually dies, giving the formula to Kristina (**ms**), who burns it.

FRANZ LEHAR

Born Komárom 1870, died Bad Ischl 1948. *Die Lustige Witwe* (*The Merry Widow*) is his best known operetta. Lehár studied at the Prague Conservatory, then, like his father, became a band leader in the Austro-Hungarian Army. He composed popular dances and marches, and in 1896 produced his first opera, *Kukuška*. Then, in 1905, came *Die Lustige Witwe*, with its brilliant waltzes and pastiche can-cans. *Der Graf von Luxembourg* (1909) and *Ziegeunerliebe* (1910) were well received, but by the end of World War I the genre seemed exhausted. However, works written for the famous tenor Richard Tauber brought renewed interest in Lehár and ensured reasonable popularity for his later works such as *Paganini* (1925), *Friederike* (1928) and *Das Land des Lächelns* (1929). This last, Tauber sang in a Broadway adaptation in 1946.

DIE LUSTIGE WITWE

(THE MERRY WIDOW)

Hanna Glawari	soprano
Baron Zeta, the Pontevedrian ambassador	baritone
Valencienne, his wife	soprano
Camille, her admirer	tenor
Count Danilo, an attaché	baritone

Paris, 19th century: love and intrigue are exposed at the Pontevedrian embassy, where the ambassador is desperate to find a suitable husband for the widow on whose wealth his country relies.

The plot was lifted from a French farce and the music was reluctantly entrusted to Lehár. Refusing to support the project with adequate rehearsals, costumes or scenery, the managers of the Theater an der Wien braced themselves for Lehár's latest flop. However, the rapturous enthusiasm of the audience made it an immediate triumph in 1905.

The salon of the Pontevedrian embassy in Paris

Ich bin eine anständ'ge Frau ('I am a respectable wife'): Valencienne's gentle protest that she is not free to return Camille's love

ACT I

In the embassy the assembled guests drink the health of Baron Zeta, their ambassador, while his wife Valencienne sits quietly with Camille, who loves her. Valencienne reminds him that she is respectably married; Camille declares that love conquers all.

The principal guest of the evening is Hanna Glawari, widow of Pontevedria's richest citizen. The ambassador is anxious to ensure that the widow's money remains in Pontevedrian hands and he wishes to promote a match between her and Count Danilo. Hanna arrives, an object of intense interest to all the bachelors. She proclaims that she is still very much a Pontevedrian and invites them all to a real Pontevedrian party.

Valencienne has the idea of encouraging Camille to improve his circumstances by marrying Hanna. At this point Danilo enters and reflects that he does not mind how hard he has to work for his country so long as he is free to enjoy himself at Maxim's in the evening. He is startled to hear that Hanna is at the embassy and tries to avoid her. When she finds him, it turns out that they had once hoped to marry but were prevented by his uncle's threat to disinherit him. She says that when a man tells her that he loves her it really means that he loves her money. Danilo replies that in that case he will never tell her that he loves her.

As soon as the ambassador finds Danilo he tells him that it his duty to marry Hanna to preserve her fortune for their country and to discourage foreign admirers. When Hanna asks for a dance from him rather than from any of her other admirers (who include Camille, encouraged by Valencienne), he offers to sell this pleasure for ten thousand francs for charity. The others withdraw. Then Camille steps forward and Valencienne, finding herself overcome with jealously, drags him away. Hanna tries to take back her offer to Danilo, but finally she gives in and compliments him on his dancing.

ACT II

Hanna amuses her guests by singing a song about a faithless nymph. When Hanna asks Danilo if he advises her to marry, he cannot hide his jealousy. Meanwhile Camille continues to court Valencienne and she is sufficiently carried away to agree to join him in the garden pavilion. The ambassador's attaché sees this just in time to prevent the ambassador from finding them together. The ambassador is delighted to think he has caught Camille with the married lady he is said to be in love with. Looking through the keyhole, he is appalled to recognize his own wife. She, however, is smuggled out at the back and walks in from another direction while Hanna, who has taken her place, now emerges from the pavilion with Camille. The confused ambassador needs reassurance, and Camille proclaims his love for Hanna so convincingly that Valencienne and Danilo are enraged. When Hanna names Camille as her future husband, the Pontevedrians are dismayed at the prospect of the ruin of their country's finances. Danilo steps forward and, after telling a story

Bin noch Pontevedrinerin ('I'm still a Pontevedrian'): Hanna proclaims that she has not turned her back on her homeland

Da geh' ich zu Maxim ('Then I'm off to Maxim's'): Count Danilo commends Maxim's as the best place to relax after a long day at the office

Damenwahl! ('Ladies' choice'): the next dance is announced to be one in which the ladies may choose their own partners

The garden of Hanna's house
Vilja, oh Vilja, du Waldmägdelein ('Vilja, oh Vilja, you nymph of the woods'): Hanna's folk song entertaining the guests at her party
Ja, das Studium der Weiber ist schwer ('Who knows women?'): Danilo and Hanna's admirers confess themselves puzzled by women

Wie eine Rosenknospe ('Like a rosebud'): Camille's song of love to Valencienne which he adapts when feigning love for Hanna

about a princess who let herself be seduced out of spite, marches indignantly off to Maxim's, leaving Hanna content in the knowledge that he loves her.

ACT III

Hanna's house

Auf dem Boulevard am Abend ('Up and down the boulevard'): Valencienne leads the chorus girls in a song about life on the street

It appears that Hanna has brought the whole of Maxim's to the party, with Valencienne dressed up as one of the dancing girls. The setting is a replica of Maxim's. As Hanna enters, Danilo goes up to her. He forbids her marriage for reasons of state. She explains that she had no intention of marrying Camille, and Danilo is overjoyed.

They break the news to the ambassador. He is intrigued by who it really was with Camille. At this very moment his attaché brings in Valencienne's fan, which has been found in the pavilion. Seeing the words *'Ich liebe Dich'* ('I love you') written on it, the ambassador angrily declares that he will divorce his wife. He proposes marriage to Hanna. She warns him that according to her husband's will she loses all her money on remarriage. Danilo, delighted with this news, repeatedly proclaims that he loves her. The news that her husband's will gives all the money to her future husband does not deter him. Meanwhile Valencienne has turned the fan over and shows her husband her written reply to Camille: *'Ich bin eine anständ'ge Frau'* ('I am a respectable wife'). Gratefully he kisses her hand as the opera ends with general agreement on the unpredictability of women.

Lippen schweigen ('Silent love'): Danilo's passionate outburst telling Hanna that he loves her

RUGGERO LEONCAVALLO

Born Naples 1857, died Montecatini 1919. Leoncavallo studied at the Naples Conservatory, subsequently making a living as a music teacher and as an accompanist. His first opera was *Chatterton* (1876). He came to the attention of the music publisher Ricordi, and he worked on the libretto of Puccini's *Manon Lescaut*. *Pagliacci*, the opera for which he is chiefly remembered, was written a short time after Mascagni's *Cavalleria Rusticana*, and it is with the latter that it is most often paired in performance. The first in a projected triology on the Medici was not well received; his *La Bohème* (1897) would have enjoyed greater success had Puccini's opera of the same name not appeared simultaneously. *Zazà*, about a music-hall singer and again set in Paris, is still staged occasionally.

PAGLIACCI

(CLOWNS)

Canio, head of a troupe of strolling players, Pagliaccio in the play	tenor
Nedda, his wife, Colombina in the play	soprano
Beppe, Arlecchino in the play	tenor
Tonio, Taddeo in the play	baritone
Silvio, a villager	baritone

Montalto, Calabria, 19th century: to Canio, leader of a group of *commedia dell'arte* players, the scene they enact on stage has an unbearable similarity to real life. A play within a play.

The libretto is the composer's. The first performance was given at the Teatro dal Verme, Milan, in 1892. A short opera, *Pagliacci* is frequently double billed with Mascagni's *Cavalleria Rusticana*.

PROLOGUE

Si può? Si può? Signore, Signori ('Ladies and Gentlemen, may I have your attention?'): Tonio announces that what the audience is about to see concerns real people

A group of travelling players has come to entertain the villagers. Tonio (dressed as Taddeo, the clown in the play) addresses the audience. He tells them that usually the emotions on stage are a reflection of real life but in this case they are about to see real passions and should remember that the lives of actors are not confined to the stage.

ACT I

At the edge of the village

Un grande spettacolo ('A show to remember'): Canio advertises the evening's performance

A chorus of villagers welcomes the troupe, which arrives with its leader Canio acting as salesman for the evening's performance. Canio's wife Nedda appears and Tonio, a hunchback, comes forward to help her, but her husband shoves him away roughly: the line dividing play-acting

Un tal gioco ('That sort of game'): Canio warns that the stage is not the same as real life

Qual fiamma avea nel guardo ('How fiercely he watches me'): Nedda is fearful of Canio

Stridono lassù ('Freely calling to each other'): Nedda's joy in living resembles the birds'

Nedda, Nedda: Silvio exhorts Nedda

Non mi tentar! ('Don't tempt me'): Nedda tries to resist

A stanotte, e per sempre tua sarò! ('At midnight I will be yours forever!'): Nedda succumbs to Silvio's plan to escape together

Vesti la giubba ('Put on the costume'): Canio's acceptance that the show must go on

O Colombina, il tenero fido Arlecchin ('O Colombina, your loving and faithful Arlecchino'): the voice of Arlecchino (Beppe) calling to Colombina (Nedda)

No, Pagliaccio non son ('No – I am not acting now'): Canio screams that he is no clown

La commedia è finita! ('Our comedy is over'): Canio's ironic ending

from real life is already becoming blurred. Tonio mutters revenge while Canio, taunted by one of the villagers, replies that only a fool would confuse true infidelity with play-acting. They all go off to church singing.

Nedda, left alone, reflects that Canio's jealousy is well-founded. Secretly she hates and fears him, and envies the swooping birds flying free above her. Tonio has been listening, and she makes the mistake of mocking him when he tries to seduce her. In a rage he grabs her, but she fights him off with Beppe's whip. Promising revenge, he leaves just as Silvio, Nedda's lover, makes his appearance. Silvio begs Nedda to run away with him.

They are so involved with one another that they do not realize Tonio has led her husband back to catch them. At last she agrees to leave with Silvio at midnight.

Suddenly hearing Canio, Silvio hastily leaves. Nedda refuses to tell her husband who was with her and he attempts to stab her. Beppe (now dressed as Arlecchino) stops him, announcing that the play must begin. The players depart to put on their costumes. Canio, now alone, persuades himself that the show must go on: even if the clown's heart is breaking he must play his part and make his audience laugh.

ACT II
Tonio (Taddeo) tries to get the audience seated. Nedda (Colombina), collecting the ticket money, tells Silvio that he was not recognized and that she will still meet him.

The play begins. Colombina encourages Arlecchino (Beppe) in the absence of her husband Pagliaccio (Canio). Taddeo the clown (Tonio), whose part in the play is to make unsuccessful advances to the girl as he does in real life, is sent off to keep watch. When Pagliaccio returns, her parting words to Arlecchino, disastrously, are the same as she used to Silvio: 'A *stanotte, e per sempre tua sarò!*' Pagliaccio asks the name of her lover, to which she replies '*Taddeo*'. Taddeo asserts her purity, and when the audience laughs he turns on them. '*Pagliaccio, Pagliaccio*', Nedda sings, calling him by his stage name. But his response '*No, Pagliaccio non son!*' shows that Canio's two roles are becoming confused and he is demanding the name of her real lover. Nedda tries, unsuccessfully, to bring him back to the play.

The crowd is impressed by the vehemence of his acting. Suddenly he draws his dagger. Arlecchino tries to intervene but Taddeo, intent on revenge for his treatment in real life, holds him back. As Canio kills Nedda, she calls out for Silvio. Her husband turns on him and kills him too. As the villagers rush to disarm him, Canio pronounces one of the most famous lines in opera.

PIETRO MASCAGNI

Born Livorno 1863, died Rome 1945. Mascagni studied at the Milan Conservatory, where he was a pupil of Ponchielli, leaving to take up work with travelling opera companies. He became known when *Cavalleria Rusticana* won the competition for a one-act opera organized by the music publisher Sonzogno in 1889. The opera was given its first performance in Rome the following year, receiving the highest acclaim. To this day it is regarded as a minor masterpiece, the epitome of *verismo*, rendering low life and the accompanying violent passions in a contemporary setting. Of his other operas, only *L'Amico Fritz* (1891) is known internationally. In 1929 Mascagni succeeded Toscanini as music director at La Scala, Milan. He became an enthusiastic supporter of Mussolini, writing *Nerone* (1935) in his honour. He died disgraced.

CAVALLERIA RUSTICANA

(RUSTIC CHIVALRY)

Santuzza, a village girl	soprano
Alfio, a village carter	baritone
Lola, Alfio's wife	mezzo-soprano
Turiddu, a young soldier	tenor
Mamma Lucia, Turiddu's mother	contralto

Sicily, late 19th century: Turiddu, finding his former love Lola married to Alfio, takes Santuzza as his mistress; but now, as Santuzza reveals to Alfio, Turiddu's love for Lola is rekindled. The vignette of village life concludes with a duel.

The libretto is by Giovanni Targioni-Tozzetti and Guido Menasci after a short story by Giovanni Verga. It won a competition in 1889 and was first performed at the Teatro Constanzi, Rome, in 1890.

A village square in Sicily
O Lola: Turiddu's opening aria serenading Lola, his neighbour's wife

Il cavallo scalpita ('The horse prances'): Alfio, Lola's husband, returns unsuspecting. He tells of the pleasures of life on the road with the faithful Lola waiting at home

Easter morning. Turiddu serenades his former love Lola while a chorus of villagers welcomes Spring.

As Mamma Lucia comes out of her house, Santuzza accosts her, looking for Turiddu with whom she has been having an affair. His mother says that he is not there, though she knows he was seen in the village the previous evening. Alfio, the husband of Lola, comes home. He is a travelling carter and he sings about his cheerful journeys and the joy of coming back to his faithful Lola. He has come to ask Mamma Lucia for some of her wine. When she tells him that Turiddu has gone off to get some more, he contradicts her. He says that he saw Turiddu near his own house earlier in the morning. Santuzza quickly warns Mamma Lucia not to show surprise.

195

Innegiamo, il Signor non è morto
('Let us sing, the Lord liveth'):
the Easter hymn

Alfio leaves and the villagers can be heard singing in church. Santuzza joins in. When Mamma Lucia asks why she told her to be quiet, Santuzza explains that Turiddu had promised eternal love to Lola before he went off to be a soldier and that when he came back and found her married to Alfio he tried to cure himself by seducing Santuzza, only to find that he was still enslaved by Lola: '*Lola e Turiddu s'amano io piango, io piango!*' ('Lola and Turiddu love each other and I am left weeping alone').

Mamma Lucia, appalled, hurries to the church. Santuzza, who has been excommunicated, waits for Turiddu. When he arrives, he is unwilling to talk to her. She tells him that he has been seen near Alfio's house and he asks if she means Alfio to kill him. He protests that he does not love Lola, but at that point she can be heard singing as she passes by to church, taunting Santuzza for not being allowed to join the congregation. When Santuzza implores him to be kinder to her, he throws her to the ground and rushes off after Lola into the church.

Alfio finds Santuzza and she tells him that his wife is betraying him with Turiddu. Immediately she regrets this, but it is too late. Alfio is already calling for a vendetta. After a short intermezzo that perfectly illustrates the story in music, the villagers can be heard coming home. Turiddu delays Lola and persuades his friends to join him for a drink.

Viva il vino spumeggiante
('Sparkling wine for all'):
Turiddu's triumphant joy leads
to his buying drinks for all his
neighbours

Alfio appears and when Turiddu offers him a drink he violently refuses. As others lead Lola away, Turiddu and Alfio prepare to fight, ritually embracing with Turiddu biting Alfio's ear. Turiddu admits that he is in the wrong but says he will fight to the death because he must live to look after Santuzza.

While Alfio goes to wait for him, Turiddu returns to his mother to ask her to bless him and to promise to be a mother to Santuzza. He kisses her and is gone before she understands. Santuzza rushes in, and, as the two women embrace, another can be heard calling out that Turiddu has been killed.

JULES MASSENET

Born Montaud 1842, died Paris 1912. Massenet dominated French opera at the end of the 19th century. An eclectic composer, he varied the subject and the style of his operas: *Manon* (1884), a pastiche of the 18th century; *Le Roi de Lahore* (1877), reflecting the current interest in the oriental and exotic; *La Navarraise* (1894), an example of *verismo*, the realism that became popular with Mascagni's *Cavalleria Rusticana*; *Le Jongleur de Notre-Dame* (1902), an expression of medievalism. Massenet had begun musical study at the Paris Conservatoire at the age of 11 in 1853. *Werther*, first performed in 1892, is with *Manon* (1884), the most frequently produced of his operas today. More than 20 of them won public favour at the time, in particular for their graceful melodies.

MANON

Manon Lescaut	soprano
Lescaut, her cousin, a soldier	baritone
Guillot, Minister of Finance	tenor
Chevalier des Grieux	tenor
Brétigny, Guillot's friend	baritone

France, 1721: Manon's dilemma, as she pursues love and money with one or other of her admirers, which leads to a tragic ending.

The libretto is by Henri Meilhac and Philippe Gille after the Abbé Prévost's novel *L'Histoire du Chevalier des Grieux et de Manon Lescaut*. To prevent Léon Carvalho, director of the Opéra-Comique, from interfering with his original composition, Massenet arrived at the first rehearsal with the score already printed. The first performance was in 1884.

An inn at Amiens

Je suis encore tout étourdie ('I am feeling so giddy'): Manon's enthusiasm for all the sights, dampended by thoughts of the convent where she is to spend the rest of her life

Ah! Voyons, Manon, plus de chimères ('Enough of my idle fancies'): Manon's reluctant acceptance of her future in the convent

ACT I
In the busy courtyard Guillot and Brétigny are enjoying themselves. The Arras stage-coach is due and Lescaut has come to escort his young cousin on her way to a convent. When the coach arrives, Manon, a beautiful 16-year old girl, greets Lescaut. She is full of excitement at what she has seen on the journey and regrets having to bury herself in a convent.

The elderly Guillot catches sight of Manon and immediately propositions her, explaining that he has a private coach and a casket of golds coins. Lescaut angrily intervenes, but soon leaves to go gambling. Manon again gives voice to regrets about the pretty clothes and all the other amusements she will be missing once she is locked away.

Manon suddenly finds herself face to face with the Chevalier des Grieux, who has missed the stage-coach. He is overcome by her beauty and she is far from unimpressed by him. A prolonged love duet leads to their commandeering old Guillot's coach to run away together to Paris. Lescaut accuses Guillot of abducting Manon and threatens to cause a scandal; the older man swears revenge for this slight.

Nous vivrons à Paris ('We'll go to Paris'): the love duet between Manon and Des Grieux draws to a close as they hear Lescaut and his companions returning

An apartment in Paris

ACT II

Des Grieux and Manon have taken an apartment in the rue Vivienne. He is writing nervously to explain to his father, but already they are quarelling because she has received flowers from an unknown admirer (Brétigny). Meanwhile, Lescaut has found out where they are living and, accompanied by Brétigny disguised as a soldier, he forces his way in, demanding to know whether Des Grieux intends to marry Manon. Manon is well aware of who sent the flowers and recognizes Brétigny, who tells her that Des Grieux's father has already arranged for his son to be abducted and taken home that night. She could warn him but Brétigny implores her not to: he is rich and Des Grieux has nothing. Manon admits to herself that she is torn between her two admirers. Preparing for dinner together, Manon is overcome with emotion at the thought that their idyll is over.

Adieu, adieu notre petite table ('Farewell to our simple life together'): Manon's sad acceptance that she will not prevent Des Grieux's abduction
En fermant les yeux ('When I close my eyes'): Des Grieux's beautiful aria describing his dream of how life will be for them together

When Des Grieux returns from posting a letter, he finds Manon in tears. He reassures her that all will be well and describes to her how happy they will be living quietly in the country. Suddenly, they hear someone outside. Frantically, Manon tries to stop him leaving. But he laughs at her fears and goes out. There is the sound of a struggle and then of a carriage driving away.

The fête in the Cours la Reine

ACT III

A vivid street scene brings together most of the characters: Lescaut is gambling again; Manon is showing off her latest dress, accompanied by Brétigny; Guillot remains intent on seducing Manon himself; and Des Grieux's father tells Brétigny and Manon that his son has decided to take holy orders and is even now at St Sulpice.

Je marche sur tous les chemins ('Every pleasure's worth a taste'): Manon's lively song about her new and extravagant life with Brétigny

Brétigny has refused to have the Paris Opéra perform at Manon's house so Guillot arranges to have the whole opera and ballet transported to perform for her in the street. She affects not to notice this grand gesture. She is overwhelmed with desire to see Des Grieux again and, encountering Lescaut, makes him take her to St Sulpice.

Reception room at St Sulpice

Quelle éloquence ('What a speaker'): the chorus of Parisian ladies, enthralled by Des Grieux's sermon

N'est-ce plus ma main? ('Have you forgotten?'): Manon's insistent reminder of their past happiness which leads to an impassioned love duet between her and Des Grieux

At the seminary, Des Grieux has been preaching and the congregation is full of praise for him. His father, after asking him to marry and become a father, respects his decision and promises to send him 30,000 livres as it is obvious he will be granted an abbey. When he is alone, Des Grieux tries to banish Manon from his memory forever.

Manon enters and prays that Des Grieux's heart may once more incline towards her, but on seeing her he begs her to go away and reproaches her for her faithlessness. She insists that she loves him and finally, despite a last prayer for strength, he falls into her arms and they leave together.

Hôtel de Transylvanie

Manon! Manon! Sphinx étonnant ('Manon, Manon, my enigmatic sphinx'): Des Grieux confesses that he will do anything for Manon in spite of her passion for pleasure and money

Ce bruit de l'or ('The clink of coins'): Manon celebrates the joys of gambling

ACT IV

Lescaut is gambling heavily and Guillot is surrounded by a flock of courtesans. Manon has brought Des Grieux, much against his will, because his money has again all been spent. Guillot proposes to play cards with Des Grieux, who proceeds to win a fortune. Guillot accuses him of cheating and denounces them both to the police. But while Des Grieux's father is there to rescue him and the family's name from dishonour, Manon is dragged away to prison.

On the road to Le Havre

ACT V

(In the original text, Act IV, Scene 2) Manon has been condemned as a prostitute. Des Grieux is waiting on the roadside to hear if Lescaut's gang have succeeded in rescuing Manon on her way to deportation. But they all behaved like cowards and ran away. Lescaut proposes that they bribe one of the soldiers, and a sergeant accepts Des Grieux's money. Manon appears, desperately ill and full of remorse. She begs for forgiveness for all the disgrace and unhappiness she has brought on him. She thinks she is dying. Together they remember their former happiness and look forward to the day when past joys will be reborn. As they kiss, she sinks back and dies.

Ah! je sens une flamme ('The warmth of love'): though dying, Manon sings with Des Grieux of their future happiness together

WERTHER

Werther, a poet	tenor
The Bailiff, a widower	baritone or bass
Charlotte, his daughter	mezzo-soprano
Albert, her fiancé	baritone
Sophie, her sister	soprano

Wetzlar, 1780s: Charlotte, rather than forget her duty to Albert, chooses to turn away from the intense adoration of Werther. Only when Werther commits suicide does she admit to her love for him.

The libretto is by Georges Hartmann, Paul Milliet and Edouard Blau after *Die Leiden des jungen Werthers* (*The Sorrows of the Young Werther*) by Goethe. The novel, published in 1774, was so influential throughout Europe that Goethe had to publish a denunciation of his hero to discourage emulation. The opera, rejected by the director of the Opéra-Comique, was given its first performance, sung in German, in Vienna in 1892.

Garden of the Bailiff's house in July

O Nature, pleine de grâce ('Oh graceful Nature'): Werther's famous soliloquy in praise of Nature
O spectacle idéal d'amour et d'innocence ('Oh perfect love and innocence'): Werther's expression of his growing love for Charlotte
Quelle prière de reconnaissance et d'amour ('My prayer of thanks and love'): Albert's aria in which he gives thanks that Charlotte has not forgotten him
A ce serment restez fidèle! Moi, j'en mourrai, Charlotte! ('You must keep that sacred promise, but it means death for me'): Werther cannot but accept her oath to her mother.

Wetzlar in September

ACT I

The Bailiff's younger children, though it is summer, are practising a carol. Two of his friends persuade him to join them for a drink, and they congratulate him on finding a perfect son-in-law in Albert for his daughter Charlotte. When they have gone, Werther appears. Before the house he sings dreamily of the beauties of Nature.

Charlotte has been dressing for a ball. When she comes down, her father notices Werther and introduces him to her. As she kisses the children goodnight, Werther watches with growing emotion. He takes her to the ball. Her father needs little encouragement to join his friends at the inn.

Night falls as Albert, Charlotte's fiancé, returns. He has been away for six months and wants to surprise Charlotte. Finding that she is not there, he plans to return in the morning.

Charlotte and Werther return from the ball. He pours out his love to her. Protesting that she hardly knows her, she is deeply moved but at the same time confused. As she begins to return to the house, they hear her father calling out that Albert is back. Charlotte explains that she promised her mother on her deathbed that she would marry Albert. Werther is left alone with his uncontrollable emotions.

ACT II

Charlotte and Albert have been married for three months and her father's friends comment on their obvious happiness. When Albert asks her if she is happy, Charlotte responds by asking why should she not be with

MASSENET

Un autre est son époux! ('She has
married another'): Werther
torments himself by dreaming
of how she might have been his

Du gai soleil ('From joyful
sunshine'): Sophie's song of the
radiance of Nature

*Lorsque l'enfant revient d'un
voyage* ('When a child returns
home early'): Werther
questions God's welcome
should he take his own life

**Albert's house on Christmas
Eve**
Je vous écris de ma petite chambre
('I am writing to you from my
little room'): Charlotte reads
from one of Werther's letters
Ah! le rire est béni ('Laughter is
blessed'): Sophie's
unsuccessful attempt to
brighten Charlotte's mood
Pourquoi me réveiller ('Why
must you wake me'): Werther
quotes from Ossian's poem of
despair

Werther's study

so perfect a husband. Werther, watching them from a
distance, is agonized by their intimacy one with the other.

Albert extends his friendship to Werther, knowing
that he had loved Charlotte, and Sophie tries to revive his
spirits. Werther decides to leave, but seeing Charlotte he
lacks the resolve. She tells him he must go; then,
weakening, invites him to return at Christmas. Werther,
alone, longs for death. When Sophie reappears to invite
him to join them, he abruptly takes his leave and runs off
down the road. Sophie, whose mood of joy vanishes,
tearfully breaks the news to Charlotte while an anxious
Albert looks on, comprehending at last Werther's true
feelings.

ACT III
Charlotte re-reads Werther's letters, confessing that he is
never away from her thoughts. One letter begs her to
mourn not blame him should he never reappear.

Her mood is interrupted by Sophie, who begs her to
rediscover the pleasure of laughter. Charlotte collapses in
tears when Sophie mentions Werther's name. After
Sophie has left, she prays to God for strength. Suddenly
Werther enters. She shows him that everything is as he
left it, including the poetry that he had been translating.
He seems to see that she loves him from her expression
and voice. She weakens for a moment when he takes her
in his arms, but freeing herself she quickly leaves.
Werther starts to follow her but stops. A sudden idea
enters his mind and he leaves the house.

When Albert enters, the room is empty. Calling for
Charlotte, he is worried by her agitation. A servant brings
him a letter from Werther explaining that he has gone on
a long journey and asking for the loan of his pistols.
Albert coldly orders Charlotte to send the pistols to
Werther. Mesmerized by her husband's grim stare, she
hands the pistols to the servant. As soon as Albert leaves,
she rushes out in despair: *'Dieu! Tu ne voudras pas que
j'arrive trop tard!'* ('Please God, let me be in time').

ACT IV
Charlotte enters to find Werther dying. He has shot
himself. He begs her forgiveness, as she begs his. He is
content to die, telling her that he loves her. Desperately
she tells him that she has loved him, too, and they kiss for
the first time. As the children can be heard singing their
carol, Werther falls into a trance. He tells Charlotte
where he wants to be buried and begs her to visit his
grave. He dies and Charlotte falls fainting over his body.
The opera ends as it began, with the sound of children
singing and laughing in the street outside.

LE JONGLEUR DE NOTRE-DAME
(OUR LADY'S JUGGLER)

In three acts, text by Maurice Lena, after a story in Anatole France's *L'Etui de Nacre*. Premiere: Monte Carlo, 1902. A charming parable of the monastic life.

Cluny, 14th century: after the Juggler, Jean (t), has put on a display outside the monastery, the Prior (b) upbraids him for his sacrilege and bids him enter the order. Entering reluctantly, but seemingly without an occupation, he encounters a poet, a painter, a musician and a sculptor, who suggest their own professions. Only the cook, Brother Boniface (bar), recommends humility. Donning his cap and bells, Jean performs in the chapel; Boniface restrains the Prior from punishing him. The Virgin's statue smiles and, exhausted, Jean falls dead.

DON QUICHOTTE
(DON QUIXOTE)

In five acts, text by Henri Cain after Jacques Le Lorrain's *Le Chevalier de la Longue Figure*, based on the novel by Cervantes. Premiere: Monte Carlo, 1910. A beautifully written work of late romanticism only partly derived from its famous original.

Medieval Spain: Don Quichotte (b) and his maverick henchman Sancho Panza (bar) engage in a series of madcap exploits, chiefly involving the courtesan Dulcinée (c), who is simultaneously trying to fend off four suitors. Quichotte eventually dies, dreaming of his beloved Dulcinée.

GIAN CARLO MENOTTI

Born Cadegliano 1911. Naturalized American operatic composer of Italian birth, he studied in Milan and at Philadelphia's Curtis Institute, where he later taught. His early *opera buffa*, *Amelia al Ballo* (*Amelia goes to the Ball*, 1937), was given at the Met. Writing his own librettos and employing a post-Puccini realism, he enjoyed enormous success in the two decades after World War II, notably with *The Medium* (1946), *The Telephone* (1947), *The Consul* (1950), the TV opera *Amahl and the Night Visitors* (1951) and *The Saint of Bleecker Street* (1954). He founded the Spoleto Festival of Two Worlds in 1958 and its American counterpart in Charleston, South Carolina, in 1977.

THE MEDIUM

In two acts, text by the composer. Premiere: Columbia University, New York, 1946. A concentrated thriller, often paired with Menotti's comedy *The Telephone*.

USA, the present: Madame Flora (c), with help from her daughter Monica (s) and the mute Toby (**dancer**), is a fraudulent medium known as Baba. Her confidence shattered by an imagined hand on her throat, she confesses; though disbelieved by her clients, she turns to drink and throws Toby out. In love with Monica, he returns and hides. Flora takes him for a ghost and shoots him dead.

THE CONSUL

In three acts, with text by the composer. Premiere: Philadelphia, 1950. This is Menotti's most successful work, almost more remarkable as drama than as opera, with a succession of relentless climaxes.

An unnamed police state in Europe, after World War II: Magda Sorel (s) is trying to obtain an exit visa for herself and her husband John (**bar**), an underground dissident who has been wounded by the secret police and is hiding in the mountains. The Consul's Secretary (**ms**) prevents several characters in the waiting-room including the magician Nika Magadoff (t) from seeing the Consul. When the Sorels' baby dies, John returns despite Magda's instructions to the contrary, just missing her; he is arrested. When the Secretary finally telephones to help, Magda does not answer but gasses herself. She dies dreaming of her family and the characters from the waiting room beckoning her over the frontier of death. The Consul never appears.

GIACOMO MEYERBEER

Born Berlin 1791, died Paris 1864. The foremost proponent of grand opera in 19th-century France, Meyerbeer was born into a wealthy and cultured German Jewish family. His early operas in German were received without enthusiasm. Then, in 1816, he went to Italy and achieved some success with a series of Italian operas in the manner of Rossini. *Il Crociate in Egitto* (1824) was put on in Paris in 1825, and it was then that he met Eugène Scribe and read the libretto of what was to be *Robert le Diable*. This was eventually produced at the Paris Opéra in 1831. Meyerbeer's collaboration with Scribe continued with *Les Huguenots* (1836), *Le Prophète* (1849) and *L'Africaine*, produced posthumously in 1865. The subject matter and the grand scale of these operas gave them a wide appeal and set the tone for contemporary – and later – productions at the Opéra.

L'AFRICAINE

(THE AFRICAN MAID)

Vasco da Gama	tenor
Don Diego, a member of the Royal Council	bass
Inès, his daughter	soprano
Don Pedro, president of the Royal Council	bass
Sélika, a slave girl	soprano
Nélusko, a slave	baritone

Lisbon, early 16th century: Vasco da Gama returns with two prisoners from an expedition. One of them, Sélika, is an Indian queen. After several mishaps and adventures it is she who saves Vasco so that he may be with the Portuguese Inès, whom he loves.

Meyerbeer and the librettist Eugène Scribe worked on *L'Africaine* for some 20 years and the composer had already died when it recieved its first performance at the Paris Opéra in 1865. A fabulous story of the exploits of Vasco da Gama and his arrival in India, the opera nonetheless retained the title of an earlier idea for a story about Africa.

Royal Council Chamber, Lisbon
Adieu, rive du Tage ('Farewell to the Tagus'): Inès repeats the song which Vasco sang the night that he left

ACT I
Inès is in love with Vasco da Gama, whose ship is reported to have sunk. The King and her father Don Diego wish her to marry Don Pedro, but even after two years she prefers to remain faithful to Vasco and hopes that he will return.

Inès' father begs her not to upset Don Pedro, who is himself very angry at his proposed bride's lack of enthusiasm. The members of the Council enter, led by the Grand Inquisitor, who is opposed to all voyages of discovery. Suddenly comes the news that three survivors, one of them a Portuguese officer, have appeared. They are Vasco himself with two slaves (unknown to all, Sélika is an Indian queen and Nélusko a member of her entourage who is in love with her). Vasco explains that they are living proof that there is land to be discovered and he begs the Council to support him. Don Pedro contrives to distort the evidence with the result that the Grand Inquisitor rejects the scheme. Vasco's indignant response, accusing them of blind stupidity, leads to his being imprisoned by the Council.

Tribunal aveugle et jaloux ('Judges too blind and jealous'): Vasco's outburst leads to a grandiose ensemble as he is sentenced to imprisonment

Prison of the Inquisition
Sur mes genoux, fils du soleil ('Kneeling by my Apollo'): Sélika's lullaby as she watches over the sleeping Vasco
Fille des rois, à toi l'hommage ('I bow to you my Queen'): Nélusko's powerful aria explaining his motives for trying to kill Vasco
Combien tu m'es chère, Ange tutélaire ('Teacher and angel'): Vasco's duet with Sélika recognizing the help she has given him

ACT II
In their cell, it is apparent that Sélika is in love with Vasco and that the jealous Nélusko intends to kill him. When Nélusko makes to strike the blow, Sélika intervenes. Nélusko tells her that the strength of his love for her is only equalled by the strength of his hatred of all Christians.

Sélika wakes Vasco. She shows him on one of his maps how to reach India. Gratefully he takes her in his arms just as Inès and Don Pedro enter. Inès informs the incredulous Vasco that he is to be freed. Vasco explains away Sélika as a mere slave girl, handing her over to Inès as a present. While Sélika mourns his ingratitude, Inès has to tell him that the price of his freedom was that she has married Don Pedro. Moreover, the expedition can now set forth but the King has decreed that Don Pedro will lead it. The wily Nélusko, who has stolen Vasco's maps, offers his services to Don Pedro as a pilot. This scene, which is partly unaccompanied, ends with Don Pedro leading Inès triumphantly away.

Don Pedro's ship
O grand Saint Dominique ('Greatest St Dominique'): the sailors' prayer for a safe voyage
Adamastor, roi des vagues profondes ('Adamastor, master of the deep'): Nélusko's sinister ballad invoking Adamastor

ACT III
While the sailors are singing a hymn to St Dominique, Nélusko changes course towards some rocks. Though plotting to cause the ship to be wrecked, he proclaims himself protector against Adamastor, God of Wrecks, who is credited with the loss of many ships.

Nélusko's plan is threatened when another Portuguese ship overtakes them. Vasco comes aboard to warn Don Pedro that he is heading for the same disaster as the previous expedition two years previously. Don Pedro insults him and Vasco draws his sword, giving Don Pedro the excuse to order him to be shot immediately. Inès and Sélika intervene, and Don Pedro orders Sélika to be

Brahma! Brahma!: the war cry
of the Indians as they overrun
the ship

Before a Hindu temple

Beau paradis sorti de l'onde
('Beautiful paradise appearing
through the waves'): Vasco's
excited aria on the discovery of
Hindustan and his own hopes
of fame

O Sélika, pardonne à ton époux!
('Oh Sélika, forgive the
husband who loves you'):
Vasco's commitment to Sélika
Adieu...rive du Tage ('Farewell
to the Tagus'): the song of Inès
and her companions, heard by
Vasco

The gardens of Sélika's palace
*D'ici je vois la mer, immense...et
sans limite* ('From here I can see
the infinite ocean'): Sélika's last
sad aria comparing the depth of
the sea to that of her own grief

chained and whipped. Just before Vasco is to be shot, a
storm engulfs the ship. As it strikes the rocks, Nélusko's
waiting comrades swarm up the side and massacre all
except a few who are saved when the Indians recognize
Sélika their queen.

ACT IV
To the sound of the Portuguese being tortured, Sélika is
crowned queen. She promises obedience to the gods of
Hindustan in a ceremony that is accompanied by an
Indian march and ballet. Meanwhile the Indians have
found another Portuguese survivor – Vasco himself.
While he sings excitedly about the wonderful new
country that they have discovered, the Indians prepare to
strike him down. The procession with Sélika, the High
Priest and Nélusko enters. Nélusko had decreed that the
Christian women should receive a merciful death. He
tells Vasco with relish that Inès is already dead and
Vasco, in despair, submits to his own execution. But
Sélika interposes, explaining that he saved her and
married her when she was enslaved abroad. She whispers
to Nélusko that if he does not support her, she will insist
on being killed with Vasco. Nélusko is aghast at what she
is asking of him. Singing sadly of his own lost hopes, he
reluctantly testifies that Vasco is indeed Sélika's husband.

Left together, Vasco reassures the anxious Sélika that
he does indeed love her, and this declaration is followed
by a long and moving duet. But just at the scene draws to a
close, he hears the voice of Inès and her companions, and
his heart is again changed in favour of Inès.

ACT V
Sélika has summoned Inès. She hears from Inès that
Vasco has told Inès he is married to Sélika and will never
see her again. Inès is content to die, but Sélika knows that
it is Inès whom Vasco truly loves. She orders Nélusko to
provide a ship to take Inès and Vasco back to Portugal
and settles herself beneath the manchineel tree, the scent
of whose leaves brings death. Sélika loses consciousness
and imagines herself in Vasco's arms. It is Nélusko who
comes to join her: '*Déjà sa main est froide et glacée! O
terreur! C'est la mort!*' ('Already her hand is as cold as ice,
Oh terror! It is death!') Sélika replies '*Non! c'est le
bonheur!*' ('No, it is happiness!') and together they die.

CLAUDIO MONTEVERDI

Born Cremona 1567, died Venice 1643. Monteverdi was an accomplished composer of polyphonic motets and madrigals in the employ of the Duke of Mantua when in 1607 he wrote *La Favola d'Orfeo*. This was the first opera in which the vocal line went beyond the type of heightened speech developed in Florence in the late 15th century, the music here serving to convey the thoughts and feelings of the characters. In 1608 he wrote *L'Arianna*, of which only the lament survives. In 1613 Monteverdi was appointed *maestro di capella* of San Marco, Venice, and produced a body of magnificent liturgical music. The opening of the first public opera houses in Venice in 1637 inspired him to write three operas, two of which survive: *Il Ritorno d'Ulisse in Patria* (1641) and *L'Incoronazione di Poppea* (1642).

LA FAVOLA D'ORFEO

(THE FABLE OF ORPHEUS)

Orfeo (Orpheus)	tenor or baritone
Euridice (Eurydice), his wife	soprano
Caronte (Charon), ferryman of the Dead	bass
Plutone (Pluto), King of the Underworld	bass
Apollo, father of Orfeo	baritone
Proserpina (Proserpine), Queen of the Underworld	soprano

Ancient Greece, in legendary times: amidst rejoicing over his wedding, Orfeo learns of the tragic death of Euridice. Journeying to the Underworld in search of his bride, Orfeo enchants all with his singing, but by disobeying Plutone's command he condemns Euridice to the Underworld forever.

Set to Alessandro Striggio's text of the Greek legend, *Orfeo* has the distinction of being the earliest opera still regularly performed. It was presented first to a small audience in the Palazzo Ducale, Mantua, in 1607. Although other works survive from the preceding 20 years, when music was moving from the wholly religious to the semi-secular, *Orfeo* may be seen as the foundation stone of Monteverdi's long career and of opera as drama

PROLOGUE
The Muse of Music announces that the power of singing to a golden lyre leads her to relate the legend of Orfeo.

Thrace

Rosa del ciel, vita del mondo
('Rose of heaven, life of the
world'): Orfeo's joyous aria in
praise of Euridice

ACT I

While nymphs and shepherds celebrate the wedding of
Orfeo and Euridice, Orfeo serenades his bride; she
responds that they are as one.

Thrace

Vi ricorda ('Do you
remember'): Orfeo compares
his former loneliness to his
present happiness

In un fiorito prato ('In a flowery
meadow'): Orfeo is told of
Euridice's death
Tu se' morta ('You are dead'):
Orfeo's despair on hearing of
Euridice's death

ACT II

Orfeo is encouraged by the chorus to play his lyre and
sing for them. This he gladly does, reflecting on his
sadness when he lived alone, changed now to joy by
Euridice.

A nymph comes with the tragic news that Euridice has
been bitten by a snake. She died calling for Orfeo. Orfeo
is overcome with grief and immediately determines to
follow her to the Underworld. He will either return with
her or remain in the Underworld. The nymphs and
shepherds bewail the tragedy and the precariousness of
mortal happiness.

Entrance to the Underworld

*Lasciate ogni speranza, voi
ch'entrate* ('Abandon hope, ye
who enter here'): Speranza
quotes the inflexible motto
inscribed on the entrance to
Hades
*Nulla impresa per uom si tenta
invano* ('Man's determination
conquers all'): the
encouragement given to Orfeo
as he crosses the River Styx

ACT III

Guided by Speranza, the Spirit of Hope, Orfeo reaches
the entrance to the Underworld. There she must leave
him. She warns that he will need great strength and all his
art in singing to succeed. Caronte, the ferryman, confronts him and Orfeo makes a passionate plea for help,
but Caronte cannot weaken. Orfeo lulls Caronte to sleep
with his lyre and his voice. He climbs into Caronte's boat
and crosses the River Styx, his courage applauded by a
chorus of spirits.

The Underworld

*Tue soavi parole d'amor l'antica
piaga* ('What pangs of love
your gentle words renew'):
Plutone's loving response to
his wife's sympathy for Orfeo

ACT IV

Proserpina, Queen of the Underworld, begs her husband
Plutone to release Euridice. He too has been moved by
Orfeo's singing. He commands that Euridice be released
providing that Orfeo does not give a single glance towards
her during their return to the world of the Living. His
generosity brings a renewal of love between him and his
wife.

Orfeo sings gratefully of his lyre's inspiration and
commits himself to obeying Plutone's condition. Suddenly he is startled by a noise. Fearing that Euridice is to
be snatched from him, he turns round to protect her.
Thus he loses her forever. Euridice is forced back,
lamenting that Orfeo has lost her through loving her too
much, and Orfeo is prevented from following. He is
rebuked by the spirits for not controlling his emotions.

Ah, vista troppo dolce ('Too
sweet a glance'): Euridice's grief
at the consequences of Orfeo's
backward glance

Thrace

Ma tu, anima mia ('But you, my very soul'): Orfeo's homage to his lost wife

Troppo troppo gioisti ('Too great your ecstasy'): Apollo blames his son for excessive emotion

ACT V

Back in the countryside where he had courted Euridice, Orfeo cries out his inconsolable sorrow, which is echoed among the trees. He contrasts the perfection of Euridice with the deceit of all other women, vowing that he will never give his heart to another.

Orfeo's plaintive song has reached Mount Olympus. His father Apollo comes down to scold him for being too extreme both in his love for his wife and in his grief at her death. He summons Orfeo to Heaven, where among the stars will be found the image of her beauty. Orfeo ascends with Apollo to a joyful chorus.

L'INCORONAZIONE DI POPPEA

(THE CORONATION OF POPPEA)

Poppea	soprano
Ottone (Otho), lately her lover	soprano
Nerone (Nero), Emperor of Rome	soprano
Ottavia, his wife	mezzo-soprano
Drusilla, her lady-in-waiting	soprano
Seneca, philosopher, statesman and Nerone's former tutor	bass

Rome, AD 65: love triumphs over morality as Nerone, ensnared by Poppea, crowns her empress.

The libretto is by G.F. Busenello. The opera was first performed in Venice in 1642. (The order of scenes may vary in today's productions, and it is sometimes performed in three acts.) In this magnificent piece of irreligious entertainment, written in his 75th year, Monteverdi disregarded the convention of a moral ending. Nerone and Ottone would originally have been sung by castrati.

PROLOGUE

The story of Nerone and Poppea is offered to illustrate the power of love.

Outside Poppea's palace

Sogni portate a volo ('Carry my sighs'): Ottone's aria, hopeful and then despairing as he realizes that Nerone is with Poppea

ACT I

Ottone has returned home to his mistress Poppea only to find the Emperor's guards outside. He imagines Nerone lying in her arms and cries out in anguish.

Dawn, and Poppea is reluctant to let Nerone leave. He promises to return and to put aside his wife in her favour. Poppea exults at the prospect of gaining the throne. She trusts in love, even though her old nurse warns her of the unexpected twists of fate.

Inside Nerone's palace
Disprezzata regina ('The Queen despised'): Ottavia's outburst at her husband's infidelity

Nerone's wife Ottavia, aware of his love for Poppea, is overcome with despair. Seneca joins Ottavia. He urges her to accept her suffering philosophically.

Seneca receives a heavenly warning that his end is near. When Nerone enters to tell him that he plans to marry Poppea, Seneca warns his former pupil not to outrage the Senate. After he has gone, Poppea turns Nerone against the old man. Nerone sends an order telling Seneca that he must die.

Ottone declares his love to Poppea; she tells him that she has greater ambitions. The Empress' lady-in-waiting, Drusilla, now offers her love to Ottone and he appears gratefully to return it. He admits to himself, however, that truly he still loves Poppea.

Garden of Seneca's villa
Sento un certo non so che ('What I feel is something new'): the young page feels the first pangs of love
Solitudine amata ('The joy of solitude'): Seneca's musings as he waits to hear his fate

A light-hearted love scene between two servants is enacted. Then there follows Seneca's resigned acceptance of Nerone's command. He bids goodbye to his pupils, ordering them to prepare his bath, in which he proposes to die by bleeding to death after cutting his wrists.

Nerone's palace
Cantiam di quel viso beato ('Let's sing of her lovely face'): Nerone and his poet celebrate Poppea's beauty

Adagiati, Poppea ('Lie quiet, Poppea'): Poppea's old nurse lulls her to sleep
Vivi, ma va ne' più remoti deserti ('Live on, but in the distant desert'): Nerone spares Ottone's life but exiles him from Rome
A Dio Roma ('Farewell to Rome'): Ottavia's parting salute to her homeland
Roma Hoggi sarà Poppea di Imperatice ('Today Poppea becomes empress of Rome'): Poppea's nurse looks forward to Poppea becoming empress
Pur ti miro, pur ti stringo ('Let me gaze at you as I take you in my arms'): the concluding love duet of Nerone and Poppea

ACT II

Rejoicing at Seneca's death, Nerone and his court poet improvise a duet in praise of Poppea's beauty.

The Empress Ottavia has summoned Ottone. She orders him to disguise himself as a woman and murder Poppea. Submitting unwillingly, he is helped by Drusilla, who dresses him in her own clothes. So disguised, he approaches Poppea, who, proclaiming her faith in love, has been soothed into sleep by her old nurse. As Ottone prepares to kill her, she is alerted by the Spirit of Love. His dress is recognized as Drusilla's and, as Drusilla waits to hear of Ottone's success, she is arrested. Nerone sentences her to prolonged torture and death but Ottone intervenes, proclaiming his own guilt. Nerone sends him into exile and pronounces that Ottavia too must leave Rome.

Ottavia sings a last farewell to her family and her native city. Poppea's nurse relishes the power that will be hers when Poppea becomes empress.

Nerone's subjects greet Poppea as their new empress. When they have all left, Nerone and Poppea turn to each other for a final ecstatic duet.

WOLFGANG AMADEUS MOZART

Born Salzburg 1756, died Vienna 1791. The son of
Leopold Mozart, a violinist and composer in the service
of the Prince-Archbishop of Salzburg, Wolfgang
Amadeus Mozart was already composing music by the
age of five. The child prodigy became the musical genius
of his age, and one of the most gifted and prolific
composers who has ever lived: in a life of 35 years
he wrote 41 symphonies, 36 violin sonatas and 27
piano concertos, 13 masses and nearly 20 operas and
operettas. From 1762 to 1766 he and his elder sister
Nannerl toured Europe, playing before the Empress
Theresa at the palace of Schönbrunn in Vienna, before
Louis XV at Versailles and at the court of George III in
London. In 1769 he went to Italy, where he acquainted
himself with Italian opera. While still very young he
wrote several stage pieces, among them Mitridate, Rè di

Ponto (1770), La Finta Giardiniera (1775) and Il Rè Pastore (1775). The first of his great operas
was Idomeneo (1781), written for the Elector of Bavaria. Dismissed from the court of
Salzburg, Mozart settled in Vienna and in 1782 married Constanze Weber, with whose sister
he had earlier been in love, and in that same year Die Entführung aus dem Serail received its
first performance. There followed the three Italian operas written in collaboration with the
poet and librettist Lorenzo da Ponte: Le Nozze di Figaro (1786), Don Giovanni (1787) and Così
Fan Tutte (1790). In these, drama and wit, contributed by da Ponte, were matched by the
brilliance of the score. In the last year of his life, in declining health, he completed La
Clemenza di Tito and Die Zauberflöte, and worked on the Requiem, which he left unfinished.
He was buried in an unmarked grave.

IDOMENEO

(IDOMENEUS)

Idomeneo (Idomeneus), King of Crete	tenor
Idamante (Idamantes), his son	soprano/ tenor
Ilia, a Trojan princess	soprano
Elettra (Electra), a Greek princess	soprano
Arbace (Arbaces), counsellor to Idomeneo	tenor

Ancient Crete: the mythological drama of
Idomeneo's appeasement of Neptune in
return for his safe landing in Crete, and his
mortification on discovering that his own
son Idamante is to be the sacrifice.

The libretto is by the Abbé Varesco after
the libretto by Antoine Danchet for an opera
by Campra. Idomeneo was first performed at
the Hoftheater, Munich, in 1781 and was
produced only once more during Mozart's
lifetime; the American premiere was not
until 1947. The title role was written for a
castrato.

211

Ilia's apartments in the royal palace

The seashore

Tutte nel cor vi sento ('The Furies tear my heart'): Elettra's rage at the prospect of her rival's triumph

Il padre adorato ritrovo e lo perdo ('My father, no sooner found than lost'): Idamante, ignorant of the vow, cannot understand his father's horror on seeing him

ACT I

Ilia, a prisoner of the Cretans, secretly loves Idamante, their King's son; and contrary to her fears he prefers her to Elettra.

A storm wrecks the ship of the King, Idomeneo, returning from the Trojan war. News of this enrages Elettra, who fears that the way will now be open for Idamante to marry Ilia. Idomeneo vowed to sacrifice the first person he meets if Neptune will save him. The sea god has granted his prayer. When the King arrives it is his son Idamante whom he sees, though they do not immediately recognize each other.

The royal apartments

Se il padre perdei ('One father I have lost'): Ilia's gratitude that Idomeneo is sparing his son, whom she loves

ACT II

Arbace advises the King to send Idamante away immediately, and it is decided that Idamante should escort Elettra back to Greece. Elettra rejoices at this, but when Idomeneo learns from Ilia of her grief at losing Idamante (and of her gratitude in finding in Idomeneo a new father), he realizes how much suffering is caused by his vow.

The port of Sidon

Placido è il mar, andiamo ('Come, the sea is calm'): the chorus of farewell

Corriamo, fuggiamo ('Quick, away!'): the crowds are scattered by the God's anger

The people assemble to wish them a safe journey. As Idomeneo says goodbye to his son and Elettra, a storm erupts and a monster rises up out of the sea, demonstrating Neptune's anger with the King. Idomeneo admits his guilt as all flee.

The royal garden

Zeffiretti lusinghieri ('Carry my love'): Ilia's wistful prayer to the wind

Andrò ramingo e solo ('I leave if I must'): Idamante, ordered by his father to leave, consents in a scene of deep sorrow for all

The temple of Neptune

ACT III

Ilia, alone in the garden, can think only of Idamante. He joins her and the two declare their love for each other. Elettra, angry, and Idomeneo, distraught at having to tell his son never to return, enter. All contribute to Idamante's sad farewell.

The High Priest calls on Idomeneo to fulfil his oath. Idamante returns, having killed Neptune's monster. On learning of his father's vow, he prepares to offer himself on the altar. Ilia begs that she be allowed to take his place. But the voice of the God proclaims the triumph of love: Idamante shall take the throne from Idomeneo with Ilia as his bride. The anguish of Elettra is submerged in the general rejoicing.

Torna la pace ('Let peace extend'): Idomeneo presents his son to the Cretans as their new king and Ilia as his queen

DIE ENTFUHRUNG AUS DEM SERAIL

(THE ABDUCTION FROM THE SERAGLIO)

Konstanze (Constanze), a Spanish lady	soprano
Blondchen (Blonde), her maid	soprano
Belmonte, a Spanish nobleman	tenor
Pedrillo, his servant	tenor
Osmin, keeper of the harem	bass
Pasha Selim	speaking part

Turkey, 18th century; Belmonte's attempt to abduct Konstanze from Pasha Selim's harem, and his servant Pedrillo's to rescue Blondchen, succeeds despite the efforts of the comic villain Osmin.

The libretto is by Gottlob Stephanie, based on a play by Christoph Friedrich Bretzner. The premiere was at the Burgtheater, Vienna, in 1782. Mozart had had to overcome the opposition of those Viennese who supported only Italian opera.

Outside the harem

Wer ein Liebchen hat gefunden ('Anyone who has a woman'): Osmin's aria on women, sung to himself.

O wie ängstlich, o wie feurig ('So anxiously, so ardently'): Belmonte's ringing aria about his desperate search for Konstanze
Ach, ich liebte ('Oh, I loved'): Konstanze reveals that her love is pledged to another
Marsch! Trollt euch fort ('Get out of it!'): Osmin tries to prevent Belmonte and Pedrillo from entering

ACT I

Belmonte, searching for his lost love Konstanze, comes upon Osmin, overseer of the Pasha Selim's harem, who sings about the need to keep women under lock and key. Belmonte asks if he is near the Pasha's palace. Osmin confirms this and Belmonte asks about his former servant Pedrillo (of whom Osmin is furiously jealous), now in the Pasha's service. As soon as Belmonte has left, Pedrillo himself arrives, perfectly happy to make peace with Osmin. Osmin will have none of this, however.

Belmonte returns and is overjoyed to find Pedrillo, who tells his former master that Konstanze is in the palace and remains faithful to him despite the Pasha's persistent attentions. Her ship had been captured by pirates but by good fortune she, with Pedrillo and her maid Blondchen, were all bought by the Pasha who, unusually, would rather win her love than force it from her.

Pedrillo suggests introducing Belmonte to the Pasha as a well-known architect. Belmonte is overcome at the thought of seeing Konstanze again. Pedrillo hears the Pasha and his entourage returning and Belmonte quickly hides.

The Pasha is questioning Konstanze as to whether she can bring herself to love him. She is shy about admitting that she swore to be true to the one she loved. Separation has brought her great sorrow. Her strength of mind only makes her the more desirable to the Pasha. At this point Pedrillo successfully introduces Belmonte as a young architect, much to the disgust of Osmin.

The palace garden

Durch Zärtlichkeit und Schmeicheln ('With gentleness'): Blondchen attempts to teach Osmin some European manners
Traurigkeit ward mir zum Lose ('Sorrow has become my lot'): Konstanze's yearning for Belmonte
Martern aller Arten ('Every sort of torture'): Konstanze again defies the Pasha
Welche Wonne, welche Luste ('What overwhelming rapture'): Blondchen's joy at bringing news of Belmonte's arrival to Konstanze
Wenn der Freude Tränen fliessen ('When the tears of joy are falling'): the blissful reunion of Belmonte and Konstanze

Outside the harem at midnight

Ich baue ganz auf deine Starke ('Love's strength sustains me'): Belmonte's aria as he prepares to rescue the captives
O, wie will ich triumphiren ('Now I will have satisfaction'): Osmin's triumph at catching the four as they are about to escape

ACT II

Outside Osmin's house, Blondchen has been fighting off Osmin's boorish attentions. She claims that English women are used to more delicate handling and drives him demented with her disdain.

Konstanze is still aching with love for Belmonte and sings sadly about the bitterness of being apart. Proudly she tells the Pasha that he can try every sort of torture before she will consent to be untrue.

Pedrillo tells Blondchen that Belmonte is nearby with a ship. The plan is to drug Osmin and escape by ladder. Blondchen is ecstatic. Pedrillo prepares himself for the night's ordeal.

Once Osmin's Moslem scruples have been overcome, he drinks the drugged wine given to him by Pedrillo. With Osmin asleep, Belmonte returns and is reunited with Konstanze. Their love is echoed by that of Pedrillo and Blondchen. Both men suddenly admit suspicions about the fidelity of their loves. Konstanze weeps while Blondchen slaps Pedrillo's face. Thus reassured, the men prepare for escape.

ACT III

Pedrillo and Belmonte have the ladder in place. While Belmonte sings of love's persuasive power, Pedrillo's serenade serves as a signal to Blondchen. She and Konstanze are about to be freed when Osmin, recovering from the drug, is in time to have them all seized.

Konstanze explains to the Pasha that Belmonte is the man to whom she was promised. Belmonte introduces himself as the son of the Commandant of Oran, who, it transpires, is the Pasha's most hated enemy. The four helpless conspirators prepare to die; but the Pasha returns and says that he does not wish to sink to the level of his old enemy and will release Belmonte with Konstanze. Pedrillo asks that he and Blondchen should be set free too, to which the Pasha agrees despite Osmin's protests. In the finale the four captives give thanks to the Pasha for his generosity, while Osmin lists the particular tortures that he thinks each of them has deserved and the janissaries renew their hymn of praise to the Pasha.

LE NOZZE DI FIGARO

(THE MARRIAGE OF FIGARO)

Figaro, servant to Count Almaviva	bass
Susanna, maid to Countess Almaviva	soprano
Dr Bartolo	bass
Marcellina, originally his housekeeper	soprano
Cherubino, page to the Countess	soprano
Count Almaviva	baritone
Countess Almaviva, his wife	soprano
Don Basilio, their music master	tenor
Barbarina, Susanna's cousin	soprano

Near Seville, 1780s: the humorous and continuously changing relationship between the Count and Countess Almaviva and their servants, Figaro and Susanna, to which Cherubino the page makes a light-hearted contribution.

The libretto, which represents Lorenzo da Ponte's first collaboration with Mozart, is based on Beaumarchais' play, which had been banned in Paris and Vienna for exposing and ridiculing the upper classes. The play was a sequel to one about Figaro, *Il Barbiere di Siviglia*, which had already been translated into opera by Giovanni Paisiello (Rossini's version was not produced until 1816). *Le Nozze di Figaro* received its first performance in 1786 at the Burgtheater in Vienna, where it had only a moderate success.

Early morning in a half-furnished room in Count Almaviva's castle

Cinque, dieci ('Five by ten'): Figaro measures the proposed bedroom
Se vuol ballare, Signor Contino ('If you want a dance, your Lordship'): Figaro's angry diatribe on learning his master has designs on Susanna

La vendetta ('Vengeance'): Dr Bartolo is set upon revenge against Figaro

Non so più ('Lost in a cloud'): Cherubino's first song of love

ACT I

The Count is beginning to regret that he renounced the *droit du seigneur*, according to which his predecessors had enjoyed the first embrace of every village girl before her wedding. It is the wedding day of Figaro and Susanna, and Figaro is measuring the room that they will occupy. This is close to the Count's apartments, and Susanna draws attention to how easy it would be for the Count, by sending Figaro on an errand, to get her on her own. Figaro accepts the challenge, confident that he can outwit the Count.

Enter Dr Bartolo, the Countess' erstwhile guardian, summoned by Marcellina, his ex-housekeeper. Bartolo nurses a grudge against Figaro (see *Il Barbiere di Siviglia*) and is still seeking revenge. Figaro has borrowed money from Marcellina and the contract stipulates that he must marry her if he does not repay the capital. Susanna returns and exhibits a sarcastic deference to Marcellina's age before finding herself alone with Cherubino, the Countess' page and godson. Captivated by a ribbon belonging to the Countess, Cherubino sings of the love which fills his heart for every woman in the place.

The Count comes in and Cherubino has to hide. The Count's renewed approaches to Susanna are interrupted by Don Basilio, and the Count hides too. When Basilio talks about Cherubino's obvious infatuation with the Countess, the outraged Count comes out of hiding to hear more. Only the day before, the Count had found Cherubino hiding in the bedroom of Barbarina the gardener's daughter. As he describes the scene, he once again discovers Cherubino hiding in the chair. The Count is at first furious and then, remembering his own conversation, embarrassed. Instead of dismissing Cherubino altogether, the Count nominates him for a commission in his regiment. Figaro warns the reluctant recruit that his days of love are over.

Non più andrai ('No longer like a butterfly'): Figaro's aria preparing Cherubino for the life of a soldier

The Countess' boudoir, later that morning

Porgi amor ('O God of Love'): the Countess' lament on her husband's infidelity

Voi, che sapete ('You, who understand'): Cherubino's second love song, this time to the Countess herself

Giudizio! ('Take care!'): the Count and Countess rebuke each other in an accelerating argument, each fearing a scandal

Nudo il petto? ('Bare-chested?'): the Count's exclamation of disbelief on being told by the Countess that Cherubino will emerge from the locked room half-dressed

ACT II

The Countess reflects on the disappointment of her marriage. Figaro arrives ready with a plan: the Count is to receive a note telling him that the Countess has an assignation that evening; also, Susanna is to agree to meet her master in the garden, and Cherubino will be there, dressed as Susanna. Cherubino enters with a song dedicated to the Countess. While expressing delight, they proceed to dress him in Susanna's clothes, locking the door to prevent discovery.

Suddenly the Count arrives. Why is the door locked? Cherubino, hidden in the next room, knocks something over, and the Count finds yet another locked door. His wife says it must be Susanna, who at this moment is returning from the other direction and has just time to hide. The Count rushes to fetch a crow-bar, taking the Countess with him and locking the door to the servants' quarters. Cherubino jumps out of a window, and Susanna takes his place. Back come the Count and Countess, and she starts to confess, begging forgiveness for an innocent Cherubino even if he is half-dressed. Half-dressed! The Count loses all control. But it is Susanna who is discovered. Both the Count and the Countess are stunned, the latter quickly recovering and pretending it was all a joke. But then the gardener arrives to complain about flowers which Cherubino broke in his fall. The others claim he is drunk, but the gardener insists he saw a man running off. Figaro owns that it was he. The gardener then produces the paper dropped by the fugitive. The Count, suspicious, seizes it, and there follows a game of cat and mouse, with Figaro trying to guess what it is. With a little help, he identifies Cherubino's army commission which the boy gave him because it had no seal.

Now Marcellina (supported by Dr Bartolo and Don

Basilio) arrives to claim Figaro as her husband in accordance with the contract. The act ends with Figaro's plans in total disarray.

A few hours later in the hall of the castle

Hai già vinto la causa! ('We have won our case!'): Susanna's aside to Figaro which is overheard by the Count and rekindles his anger

ACT III

The Count is confused. Susanna leads him on to believe that at last she will accommodate his desires. Impatiently he awaits the evening, but as she leaves him she tells Figaro (a little too loudly) that their plans are now secure. The Count overhears and determines to punish them. Why should Figaro, his servant, enjoy what Susanna withholds from him?

The notary arrives to deliver the judgment that Figaro must indeed marry Marcellina. Figaro counters that he cannot marry without his parents' consent. He cannot tell where they are. When he mentions his birthmark, it is enough to identify him as the long-lost illegitimate child of Dr Bartolo and Marcellina.

Dove sono ('Those happy days'): the Countess mourns past happiness before planning her revenge

Figaro's marriage to Susanna may proceed, and Marcellina agrees to marry Bartolo. The Countess has decided to go herself to her husband's rendez-vous disguised as Susanna. She dictates a letter to the Count, as if from Susanna, fixing the assignation. The letter is sealed with a pin.

Cherubino (disguised as a village girl) comes in to pay his respects but is unmasked. Susanna seizes this opportunity to pass the note. The Count pricks his finger on the pin and Figaro, noticing this, rightly deduces that his master has received a *billet doux*.

Evening in the garden of the castle

ACT IV

Figaro discovers that the pin (and thus the *billet doux*) came from Susanna and suspects that she is planning to deceive him after all. Having at last a mother to turn to, he confides in Marcellina; Marcellina is less willing to mistrust Susanna and decides to warn her. Figaro complains that already he is discovering a husband's miseries.

Aprite un po' quelgl' occhi ('Open your eyes'): Figaro's aria on the deceit of women
Deh vieni, non tardar ('Come now without delaying'): Susanna's aria pretending (because she knows Figaro is listening) to be longing for the Count's arrival

Susanna and the Countess, each disguised as the other, arrive with Marcellina. Susanna pretends to sing dreamily of her approaching surrender to bliss while Figaro, his worst fears confirmed, can hardly restrain his fury.

Cherubino arrives, sees the Countess and approaches, believing her to be Susanna. Amidst general confusion, the Count drives the page away and begins to entice 'Susanna' towards some suitable hiding place. Figaro joins 'the Countess' and enlists her aid in catching their erring partners. Inadvertently speaking in her own voice, she is recognized by Figaro, but for a time he deceives her into thinking that she has deluded him.

The Count comes back to find his wife (as he thinks) in Figaro's embrace. Cherubino, Barbarina and Marcellina are dragged forward, and finally 'the Countess'. The latter kneels and asks for his forgiveness, which he utterly refuses. But then 'Susanna' appears to intercede. As 'Susanna' is revealed as his wife, the Count, deeply ashamed, can only kneel in penitence. The Countess forgives him and the opera ends with the whole household calling for a party to round off this day of follies.

DON GIOVANNI

Don Giovanni, a young nobleman	baritone
Leporello, his servant	baritone
Donna Elvira, a lady of Burgos	soprano
Donna Anna	soprano
Commendatore, her father	bass
Don Ottavio, her betrothed	tenor
Masetto, a peasant	baritone
Zerlina, his betrothed	soprano/ mezzo- soprano

Seville, 17th century: the philanderings of Don Giovanni, a fearless libertine, are finally punished by the statue of one of his victims.

Don Giovanni was first performed in 1787 in Prague, and it followed Mozart's and Da Ponte's original success there the year before with *Le Nozze di Figaro*. The subject was well known, mainly from the two plays *El Burlador de Sevilla* by Tirso de Molina and *Le Festin de Pierre* by Molière.

The palace garden

ACT I
Leporello, Don Giovanni's servant, complains as he waits for his philandering master. The Don's escape is delayed by Donna Anna, who wishes to identify the masked man, and the noise alerts her father. In the ensuing struggle the Commendatore is killed. Donna Anna and her intended, Don Ottavio, are left to mourn and vow revenge on the unrecognized intruder.

The street
Ah! Chi mi dice ('Who can help me!'): Donna Elvira bewails the disappearance of her former admirer
Madamina ('Madam'): Leporello catalogues the Don's many conquests

Leporello rebukes his master but the Don is unrepentant. Donna Elvira makes her appearance. Don Giovanni consoles her as she sings of her search for her vanished love, but, recognizing her as someone he has himself deserted, loses no time in evading her again. He leaves Leporello to explain how many and varied are her rivals.

In the country

Là ci darem la mano ('Give me
your hand'): Masetto departs
and Don Giovanni makes
overtures to Zerlina
Ah! fuggi il traditor ('Beware
this wicked man'): Donna
Elvira's warning to Zerlina

Or sai chi l'onore ('Honour
demands revenge'): Donna
Anna's aria having recognized
Don Giovanni as her father's
murderer

A ballroom

Batti, batti ('Punish me'):
Zerlina's attempt to make
peace with Masetto

The street

Deh, vieni alla finestra ('Come
to the window'): Don Giovanni
serenades Donna Elvira's maid
Vedrai carino ('You will see,
beloved'): Zerlina's aria
promising to take care of
Masetto

A dark courtyard

Il mio tesoro in tanto ('My
treasure'): Don Ottavio's aria
swearing to defend and console
his love

This is the day of Zerlina and Masetto's wedding. Their celebrations are interrupted by Don Giovanni, who insists that they all accept his hospitality. Having despatched the guests and an increasingly angry bridegroom, he prepares to lead Zerlina to a secluded spot, promising her a more glittering marriage if she will accept his love. This plan is thwarted by the reappearance of Donna Elvira, who warns the girl of her escort's doubtful reputation. Hardly can he recover from this before the Don is confronted by Donna Anna and Don Ottavio. Pledging himself to help them track down the murderer, he is again harassed by Donna Elvira, who, finding him with yet another woman, denounces him to his astounded friends. His explanation (that Donna Elvira is mad) fails because Donna Anna suddenly recognizes his voice as that of her masked companion of the previous night. Aghast, she calls for vengeance against him. Don Ottavio, alone, pledges to prove that she was mistaken or else avenge her.

Don Ottavio, Donna Anna, and Donna Elvira disguise themselves to watch what happens at the party Don Giovanni has arranged. This is to be a great test of the Don's resourcefulness. Suspected by all, yet still intent on succeeding with Zerlina, matters become increasingly confused. When his attempt to blame Leporello for an unsuccessful assault on Zerlina's honour fails, he has to escape the general outrage as best he can.

ACT II
Don Giovanni is reunited with Leporello, who again tries to leave his service and is again persuaded to stay. The Don, interested in Donna Elvira's maid, commands Leporello to exchange clothes with him. While Leporello, in the guise of his master, pays court to Donna Elvira, Don Giovanni serenades the maid from beneath her bedroom window. This time he is interrupted by Masetto's gang who intend murdering him; but since he is dressed in Leporello's cloak, he succeeds in sending them off in all directions before beating Masetto half senseless. His victim is found and comforted by Zerlina.

Leporello's masquerade is less successful. Exhausted by Donna Elvira, his attempts to escape detection are foiled first by the arrival of Donna Anna and Don Ottavio, and then by Zerlina and Masetto. Unmasked, and threatened by all, he manages to escape only with difficulty. There is a moment of calm while Don Ottavio reflects on Donna Anna and his need to avenge her distress. In a variation of the original order of performance, Donna Elvira again bewails Don Giovanni's betrayal of her love.

A churchyard	Don Giovanni is now in hiding. He infuriates Leporello by boasting of his success with a woman in the street who mistook him for Leporello. But now a voice from out of the darkness is heard. To Leporello's terror it appears to come from the monument to the Commendatore. Don Giovanni, undismayed by the words inscribed in the marble, insists on inviting the statue to dine with him, and the invitation is accepted.
A room in Donna Anna's house *Non mi dir* ('Do not speak of marriage'): Donna Anna rejects Don Ottavio's attentions till her father's death is avenged	Don Ottavio, anxious about the constantly delayed engagement, again asks Donna Anna to accept him and again she rebuffs him saying that she can think of nothing but revenge for her father's murder.
A banqueting hall *Vivan le femmine! Viva il buon vino! Sostegno e gloria d'umanità* ('Long live women. Long live wine. The strength and glory of mankind'): Don Giovanni's motto	Don Giovanni prepares for dinner with the Commendatore watched, enviously, by Leporello. Donna Elvira comes to make a desperate last plea to the Don to change his ways – in vain, for he replies that his life is dedicated to wine and women. Disconsolate, she leaves, but comes back screaming with terror. Leporello, sent to investigate, also returns in panic, fleeing from some fearful apparition. The Commendatore has come to accept Don Giovanni's invitation and to issue a matching summons which Don Giovanni's code requires him to accept. Pressed to repent, Don Giovanni resolutely stays firm to his principles and goes to his death without flinching, while those left behind reflect on the moral of his fate.

COSÌ FAN TUTTE

Fiordiligi	soprano	Naples, 18th century: Guglielmo and Ferrando, confident of the faithfulness of Fiordiligi and Dorabella, are challenged by the cynical Don Alfonso to put the constancy of their betrothed to the test.
Dorabella, her sister	soprano	
Despina, their maid	soprano	
Ferrando, Dorabella's betrothed	tenor	*Così Fan Tutte* was the third in Mozart's wonderful collaboration with the librettist Lorenzo da Ponte. The first performance was at the Burgtheater, Vienna, in 1790. The story is supposed to have been based on a contemporary Viennese scandal; and Mozart himself had a comparable experience, loving one sister before marrying another. The original custom of casting Guglielmo as a bass and Don Alfonso as a baritone is nowadays reversed.
Guglielmo, Fiordiligi's betrothed	baritone	
Don Alfonso, an old philosopher	bass	

A square with a view of the sea

E la fede delle femmine ('Women's faith is as rare as the phoenix'): Don Alfonso's cynical advice to his friends

Ah guarda, sorella ('Sister, look at this'): Fiordiligi and Dorabella's duet congratulating themselves on their suitors

Soave sia il vento ('Let the wind blow softly'): the trio between Don Alfonso and the two sisters as they wave goodbye to the soldiers

An apartment

Smanie implacabili ('Implacable desires'): Dorabella's impassioned aria giving in to hysteria
In uomini, in soldati ('Fidelity in men, in soldiers'): Despina's incredulous outburst at the sisters' trustfulness

Come scoglio ('Like a rock'): Fiordiligi's aria in which she maintains her faithfulness to the absent Guglielmo

Un aura amorosa ('The scent of love'): Ferrando's affectionate aria placing love before food

ACT I

Guglielmo and Ferrando, two young soldiers, are convinced that their fiancées are incapable of deception, and they threaten to fight anyone rash enough to doubt them. Don Alfonso, older and more experienced, reflects that for women solitary devotion is as rare as the mythical phoenix. The young men insist, and he bets them a hundred gold pieces that he will be proved right if they will let him use them to play a trick on the two sisters, Fiordiligi and Dorabella. They readily agree and begin to plan how to spend the money – Ferrando by serenading Dorabella, Guglielmo by giving a banquet in Fiordiligi's honour.

The two sisters are praising their lovers' portraits. They too believe in unalterable affection and foresee marriage near at hand. But Don Alfonso arrives with bad news: he tells them that the regiment has been summoned away and that their lovers are here to say goodbye. They do so tragically, the two soldiers secretly confident that the sisters will wait faithfully for their return. The sisters get some final encouragement from their men, who leave to the sound of martial music and promises of daily letters. Those left behind pray for good weather at sea. Don Alfonso, alone, ridicules the simplicity of those who place confidence in a woman's heart.

Despina, the sisters' maid, brings in their morning chocolate and finds the young ladies in despair. Dorabella gives vent to the terrible longings brought on by separation. To their horror Despina advises them to welcome the situation as a chance to divert themselves and then warns them not to waste time looking for faithfulness in men, least of all in soldiers. When the sisters leave to consider this, Don Alfonso arrives to enlist Despina's help, with the aid of a bribe, in introducing her mistresses to two lovesick Albanian friends of his. Guglielmo and Ferrando come in, disguised, and Despina fails to recognize them. Soon the sisters discover their presence and demand the ejection of these strange young men. That they dare to court their young hostesses gives rise to Fiordiligi's indignant insistence that her heart is as firm as a rock. Don Alfonso asks them to be polite to his foreign friends, and Guglielmo sets out to commend himself and his companion to the outraged sisters; but in vain. The ladies withdraw and the men are left triumphant, demanding that Don Alfonso's debt be paid. Not yet, he replies, and while they laugh with relief, he too is laughing at what the end must be. Guglielmo is already concerned about lunch, but as they leave Ferrando sings beautifully of the refreshment that comes from true love.

Ah! Che tutte in un momento
('Oh how suddenly'): the
sisters exclaim in a duet how
their fate has changed in a
single moment

The two sisters have retreated to sing of how their peace of mind has been affected dramatically in so short a time. They are interrupted by the two Albanians, waving bottles of poison and apparently determined to die from unrequited love. Don Alfonso tries to prevent these 'suicides' - but too late! They drain the poison. As they appear to draw their last gasps, they implore compassion from the hard-hearted girls. In the ensuing confusion, Despina arrives disguised as a doctor with a miraculous cure – a magnet.

Slowing reviving, the pitiful sufferers believe themselves in heaven, attended by two angels. They demand a reviving kiss (*'un bacio'*) and the two sisters, becoming suspicious of this part of the charade, withdraw with what little dignity is left amid general hilarity. The identity of the Albanians is still safe, but their ardour has been decisively rejected.

The apartment
Una donna ('Any young girl'):
Despina encourages a flirtation

A garden
Secondate, aurette amiche ('Let
friendly breezes aid our cause'):
the Albanian suitors invoke
assistance in their courting

ACT II
Despina complains to her two employers that they are far too choosy. She sings of the need for all young ladies to know how to deal with men.

The two Albanians returning to their task, serenade the sisters. Encouraged by Don Alfonso and Despina, the two young couples begin, after initial awkwardness, to converse. It is here that the sisters' different characters are especially noticeable. Dorabella, carried along by her own artlessness, soon finds herself exchanging her medallion (which contains Ferrando's portrait) for the disguised Guglielmo's heart-shaped locket. (Thus she chooses to receive the attentions of her sister's lover.) Half appalled by what he has achieved, he sings with her of their hearts beating in unison, echoed in the palpitating music. Fiordiligi rejects absolutely Ferrando's enthusiastic wooing, though once alone she admits to burning with passion. Nevertheless, she remains true to her absent Guglielmo and, in the opera's greatest aria, she asks his forgiveness, wherever he may be.

Per pietà, ben mio, perdona ('Pity
me, my darling one'):
Fiordiligi's prayer that her
absent lover would understand
her predicament

The square
Donne mie ('Women'):
Guglielmo's diatribe against
the perfidy of women

While Guglielmo is congratulated by Ferrando on Fiordiligi's chastity, he has no such reassurance to offer in return. Ferrando is filled with jealously. Guglielmo tries to console him by reciting all the many ways in which women, while full of grace, charm and beauty, invariably deceive those who most readily defend them.

The apartment
Fra gli amplessi ('In Guglielmo's
arms'): Fiordiligi's aria
declaring devotion to

The watching Guglielmo commends himself on Fiordiligi's strength. She orders Despina to allow no-one in and prepares to set off after her betrothed and join him on the battlefield. But Despina, bribed now by Ferrando, has

Guglielmo which turns into a
duet yielding to Ferrando

Tutti accusan le donne
('Everybody blames women'):
Don Alfonso excuses the
frailty of women

Un contratto nuziale! ('A
marriage contract'): the
soldiers' pretended indignation
at finding the document

smuggled him into the house. He comes forward to plead further with her. At last, they admit to their love for each other.

Guglielmo and Ferrando reflect on the day's developments, with Don Alfonso countering their outrage by excusing the fickleness of women as an unavoidable habit. He makes the two young men repeat the lesson they have learned at such cost: *'Così fan tutte'* ('All women are alike in this'), the theme of the overture.

The wedding hour of the Albanians and the sisters approaches and Despina (now disguised as a notary) arrives to perform the ceremony. Just as they all prepare to sign, martial music announces the return of the regiment. The Albanians quickly hide next door and soon Guglielmo and Ferrando, restored to normal appearances, enter to embrace their stricken fiancées. The soldiers appear puzzled by the confusion. Finding a marriage contract, they affect rage and are unmoved by the sisters' attempt to blame the two impresarios: Don Alfonso and Despina. Don Alfonso takes the soldiers next door to meet their rivals and they come back all smiles, carrying with them their former disguises. Each deception is exposed in turn to the increasingly thunderstruck girls. To Don Alfonso, the whole thing is a splendid joke, but as they all sing of the need to take life as it comes, it seems that Fiordiligi and Ferrando are more affected by what they have undergone than it would at first appear.

LA CLEMENZA DI TITO

(THE CLEMENCY OF TITUS)

Tito (Titus), Emperor of Rome	tenor
Vitellia, daughter of the deposed Emperor	soprano
Sesto (Sextus), Roman patrician	mezzo-soprano
Servilia, his sister	soprano
Publio (Publius), captain of the guard	bass
Annio (Annius), Sesto's friend	mezzo-soprano

Rome, 79–81 AD: the clemency of the Emperor is illustrated first in his treatment of Servilia, to whom he is betrothed, and then of Vitellia and Sesto.

The libretto was adapted by Caterino Mazzolà from one of an earlier and simpler form by Pietro Metastasio. Mozart wrote the opera in about 50 days, the recitatives being left to his pupil Süssmayr. Commissioned to celebrate the coronation of Leopold II, it was first performed in Prague on 6 September 1791, less than a month before Die Zauberflöte.

ACT I

Vitellia, whose father was deposed, is anxious to see his successor, Tito, overthrown – not least because he has chosen a foreign wife instead of her. Sesto, who loves her, is unwilling to take part in the scheme because of Tito's heroic qualities. This excites Vitellia further, for she believes that Tito deliberately deceived her into falling in love with him. Sesto eventually accepts her instructions with the promise of marriage to her.

Annio brings news that the foreign bride has been sent home. Vitellia, her hopes aroused, orders Sesto to delay the uprising. He angers her with his obvious jealousy. Annio wants to marry Sesto's sister Servilia and now asks Sesto to seek imperial consent for their engagement. The two friends pledge mutual support.

Surrounded by his subjects, Tito is greatly praised. Vesuvius has recently erupted and he asks that the money set aside by the Senate to build a temple in his honour be spent instead on helping the victims. He tells Sesto that, having managed to overcome his love for the foreign princess, he has now decided to marry Sesto's sister Servilia. There is the pretence of great joy, even from Annio. Tito tells them that the only real pleasure in power is in rewarding friends.

Annio's unhappy task of telling Servilia of Tito's intentions is made worse by her joy at seeing him. She neither understands nor welcomes the honour, and being together strengthens their love for each other.

Servilia confesses to Tito that her heart belongs to Annio. Tito, overwhelmed by her simple honesty, releases her. As she leaves, she is met with sarcastic reverence by Vitellia. Servilia's remark tells Vitellia nothing. Sesto enters and admits that the plot is no further forward. Inspired by Vitellia's words, Sesto leaves to carry out her orders. Publio and Annio arrive to tell Vitellia that she has been chosen as Tito's wife and empress.

Sesto is uneasy. He has given the order and the Capitol is seen to be on fire. There is tremendous uproar and then Sesto returns from the Capitol with the news that Tito is dead.

ACT II

Annio tells Sesto that he is wrong: Tito has survived. Sesto plans immediate flight, though Annio tries to persuade him to remain and make amends. Vitellia hastens in, anxious that he escape before her own guilt be discovered. But immediately Publio arrives to arrest Sesto, who is taken away to be tried before the Senate.

The Roman people greet their emperor, but he is

Vitellia's apartments

Come ti piace imponi ('Order me as you will'): duet between Sesto and Vitellia in which he agrees to her every wish
Deh, se piacer mi vuoi ('If you want to please me'): Vitellia tells Sesto to cast aside his suspicions having ordered the uprising to be delayed

The Forum

Del più sublime soglio ('Of absolute power, the one reward'): Tito's reflections on rewarding merit and virtue
Ah perdona al primo affetto ('Forgive through former love'): Annio's love for Sevilia overcomes his sense of duty to Tito

The Emperor's palace
Ah, se fosse intorno al trono ('If every monarch could rely'): Tito's dignified renunciation of Servilia on hearing of her love for Annio
Parto, ma tu ben mio ('I go at your command'): Sesto's commitment to carry out Vitellia's wishes in return for her love

The Emperor's palace

Tu fosti tradito ('You were indeed betrayed'): Annio's last attempt to persuade Tito to look with mercy on Sesto

Deh per questo istante solo ('Grant that once again'): Sesto's last request is to kiss the hand of his friend, the Emperor

Non più di fiori ('No more bouquets'): Vitellia finally admits to herself her guilt

A square outside the arena

Tu, ancora? ('You too?'): Tito is astounded by another admission of betrayal, this time from his betrothed

preoccupied with Sesto's trial, refusing to believe that Sesto could have betrayed him. Annio comes to beg for mercy for Sesto as Publio returns to say that Sesto has admitted his guilt. The sentence – that he be thrown to the lions – needs only the Emperor's signature. Annio tries again to save his friend and then Tito is left alone to sign the warrant. He decides to confront the traitor. When Sesto is brought before him, Tito is amazed at how his face has been transformed by guilt. Sesto confesses to betraying Tito, but to protect Vitellia will say no more. Tito angrily condemns him. Sesto asks as a last favour that he may kiss his emperor's hand. Tito is confused by his friend's submissiveness. He signs the death warrant; Then, tearing it up, he summons the people to the arena.

Vitellia believes that Sesto is to be killed and that he has betrayed her. Then Annio tells her that the wedding is to take place and she realizes that Sesto has kept her secret. At last Vitellia must face the truth. She is preparing to marry the man whose murder she plotted, using Sesto's love for her, and she is letting Sesto be sacrificed for her amibition. Reluctantly, she accepts her guilt.

The people are assembled. Vitellia hurriedly enters and confesses her guilt to the astonished Tito. He feels that the stars are conspiring to make him cruel but he is determined to deny them this triumph. He orders the release of Sesto and the conspirators, and all join in a hymn of praise to his clemency.

DIE ZAUBERFLOTE

(THE MAGIC FLUTE)

Queen of the Night	soprano
Pamina, her daughter	soprano
Tamino, an Egyptian prince	tenor
Papageno, the Queen's birdcatcher	baritone
Sarastro, High Priest of Isis and Osiris	bass
Monostatos, his servant	tenor
Papagena	soprano

Egypt, in legendary times: Tamino undergoes tests of will in his bid to win Pamina, daughter of the Queen of the Night, from the High Priest Sarastro. Papageno, the Queen's birdcatcher, is appointed his companion.

Die Zauberflöte was written at the instigation of Mozart's friend and fellow freemason, Emanuel Schikaneder. Schikaneder wrote the libretto and took the role of Papageno. The first performance, with Mozart conducting from the keyboard, was in Vienna in September 1791 and the opera was an immediate success. But the unique formula – a fairy tale set to sublime music – was never to be repeated as within two months he was dead.

A rocky landscape

Der Vogelfänger bin ich ja ('I am a birdcatcher'): Papageno introduces himself as the Queen's birdcatcher
Dies Bildnis ist bezaubernd schön ('Her portrait is so lovely'): Tamino's aria on first seeing Pamina's portrait

Sarastro's domain

Bei Männern ('The man who loves'): the duet between Pamina and Papageno

A grove with three temples

O Isis und Osiris ('O Isis and Osiris'): Sarastro's prayer to the gods of Egypt

A forest of palm trees

Court of the temple

ACT I

Tamino, an Egyptian prince, faints while trying to escape from a snake. Rescued by the Three Ladies of the Queen of the Night, who rules this land, he recovers to find a strange figure: Papageno, the Queen's birdcatcher. Papageno claims the credit for saving Tamino but the Ladies return and punish him for this lie by sealing his mouth. They show Tamino a portrait of Pamina, the Queen's daughter, with whose beauty he immediately falls in love. The Queen herself now appears to tell him that Pamina has been stolen from her by the wicked Sarastro. Tamino must rescue her, and the Ladies return to give him a magic flute to help him. They free Papageno and order him to accompany Tamino as his servant, giving him some silver bells as additional protection.

Pamina is in the amorous clutches of Sarastro's servant Monostatos. Faced with death or dishonour, she chooses death, but Monostatos is scared away by the sudden arrival of Papageno, each mistaking the other for the Devil. Papageno tells Pamina that he has come to rescue her. They sing together of the healing power of love.

Tamino has arrived with his guides, and they leave him with the warning that he must try hard and bear all things patiently and in silence. Faced with the three doors of Wisdom, Reason and Nature, Tamino learns that Sarastro is in truth a leader dedicated to furthering the holy Brotherhood of Man. Playing his flute, he is answered by Papageno's pipe; but they miss each other, and Papageno and Pamina are captured by Monostatos. This time it is the silver bells which subdue even the wild animals; but hardly have they evaded Monostatos before his master Sarastro appears. Pamina explains why she was trying to escape. When Monostatos appears, with a captive Tamino, he is sent off to be whipped, while Sarastro orders Tamino and Papageno to be brought to the temple to test their true worth. In a beautiful prayer, Sarastro introduces Tamino to the gods as the man destined to marry Pamina if he is found to be worthy to acquire the order's inner truth.

ACT II

The speaker of the temple informs Papageno that he too may win a young and beautiful partner, named Papagena, if he survives the trials which both are warned may bring death if they fail.

The first test is Silence. The Queen's Ladies return and urge flight, but Tamino helps Papageno keep their vow.

A garden

Der Hölle Rache kocht in meinem Herzen ('Revenge is boiling in my heart'): the Queen of the Night urges Pamina to kill Sarastro

In diesen heil' gen Hallen ('In these sacred halls'): Sarastro's song of forgiveness

In the temple

Ach ich fühl's es ist verschwunden ('Ah, it is gone, gone forever'): Pamina's loss of confidence faced with Tamino's apparent indifference

Monostatos is pursuing his attempts to conquer Pamina. This time he is scared away by her mother, who gives Pamina a dagger to kill Sarastro. Monostatos has overheard and now threatens to denounce Pamina if she will not yield to him. Again she prefers death; but this time it is Sarastro himself who saves her. When she pleads for mercy for the Queen, he tells her that in God's temple there can be no talk of vengeance.

It is time for a second test of Silence. First an old woman appears, claiming to be the 18-year-old lover of Papageno. This greatly encourages him to keep silent. But soon it is Pamina's turn and she, knowing nothing of the ordeals, mistakes Tamino's silence for indifference. She is heartbroken and decides to kill herself since she believes she has lost Tamino's love. Papageno is wilting also for lack of affection – he is even prepared to swear fidelity to the old crone. Suddenly she turns into a young girl; then, just as suddenly, she is snatched from him as he is not yet worthy of her.

Pamina prepares to die, but at last the reason for Tamino's silence is explained to her as he himself is made ready for the final test of Fire and Water. This they face together, playing the magic flute that Pamina's father himself made for her. Triumphantly they pass through to gain Sarastro's approval.

Papageno, however, is sunk in despair. Everything seems black without the support of his adored Papagena. He too decides to kill himself; then, summoned by his silver bells, Papagena comes to him.

Pa, pa, pa, pa: the duet between Papageno, finally united with his Papagena

A last bid by Monostatos, who has bargained with the Queen of the Night for possession of her daughter, fails. The opera ends with Tamino and Pamina united and safe.

LA FINTA GIARDINIERA
(THE BOGUS GARDEN-GIRL)

In three acts, text by Marco Coltellini taken from Raniero da Calzabigi's libretto for a 1774 Anfossi opera. Premiere: Assembly Rooms, Munich, 1775. A tortuous, mainly comic tale of mistaken identities wrapped in an enchanting score.

Countess Violante Onesti (s), believed dead at the hands of her lover Count Belfiore (t), is in fact searching for him, disguised as a gardener, Sandrina. She is amorously pursued by her employer, Don Anchise (t), whose servant Serpetta (s) is a rival for his love. Angered by discovering Belfiore wooing Arminda (s), Anchise's niece, Sandrina succeeds in having him arrested and reveals her identity, though later pretending not to be the Countess. All is happily resolved in the end.

MODEST MUSSORGSKY

Born Karevo 1839, died St Petersburg 1881. Mussorgsky's first music lessons were with his mother before, aged ten, he entered the St Petersburg military academy. Serving with a guards regiment, he met several young composers whose enthusiasm for Russian nationalist music fired his imagination. He resigned his army commission to devote himself to music. Already in his early songs he was attempting to set to music the sound of the Russian language. While earning a living as a civil servant, his family's fortunes having collapsed, he began work on *Boris Godunov*. Completed in 1869, the opera was rejected. Mussorgsky revised it and it was rejected again. Then several scenes were produced and eventually, in 1874, the entire work was staged. Meanwhile he had started *Khovanshchina* and *Sorochintsy Fair*. He worked on both intermittently, but completed neither. After Mussorgsky's death, Rimsky-Korsakov made two new editions of *Boris*.

BORIS GODUNOV

Boris Godunov, Tsar of Russia	bass
Xenia, his daughter	soprano
Fyodor, his son	mezzo-soprano
Prince Shuisky	tenor
Grigori, later pretending to be Dimitri	tenor
Pimen, an old monk	bass
Marina Mnishek, a Polish princess	soprano
Rangoni, a Jesuit priest	bass

Russia and Poland, 1598–1605: episodes in the rise and fall of the Tsar, Boris Godunov, all in some way dependent on his having murdered the rightful heir to the throne of Russia.

Adapted from a chronicle play by Pushkin and Karamazin's *History of the Russian State*, the libretto is the composer's. Originally rejected by the Imperial authorities, a new version was given its first performance in St Petersburg in 1874. The opera was twice revised by Rimsky-Korsakov after Mussorgsky's death.

The Monastery of Novodevichy, 1598

Zhivi i zdrástvuy ('Long life to the Tsar'): the people's anthem to their new ruler

PROLOGUE
Boris Godunov has had Dimitri, the heir to the throne, murdered. A crowd, orchestrated by the police, is calling on Boris to accept the throne. He refuses; but when the people reassemble it is to hear that Boris has at last consented.

A monastery cell, 1603

Nye syetúy, brat ('Without regret, brother'): Pimen quietly rebukes Grigori for missing the drama of the outside world

An inn on the border with Lithuania
Kak vo górodye bílo vo Kazáni ('And this was what we did at Kazani'): one of the drunken monks reminds the other of the slaughter in Kazan planned by Ivan the Terrible

The Tsar's palace, 1604

Dotíg ya víshey vlásti ('I hold great power'): Boris' great monologue on supreme power, addressed to his son, which is overcast by guilt

Uf, tyazheló! Day dukh pyeryevyedú ('I am stifling, I cannot breathe'): Boris is overcome by paroxysms of remorse for murdering the Tsarevitch Dimitri

The Castle of Sandomir, Poland
Skúchno Marínye, akh kak skúchno-to! ('I, Marina, am so desperately bored'): the Princess expects her boredom with life at court to vanish in joining with Dimitri, the pretender, to seize the Russian throne

ACT I

Pimen, an ancient monk, has almost completed his chronicle. The young monk Grigori has been sleeping, troubled by the same dream as before: that he is perched on a tower being mocked by all below before falling. He asks Pimen about the murdered Tsarevitch and is told that he would have been the same age as himself. So is planted the seed of an idea.

While the hostess of the inn is singing, she hears visitors arriving. It is two disreputable monks travelling with Grigori, who has escaped from the monastery. They drink and reminisce, but Grigori is interested only in finding out the quickest route to the border. Soldiers arrive with a description of the fugitive and Grigori tries to incriminate one of the others. When this fails he runs off.

ACT II

Boris' daughter Xenia is mourning the death of her betrothed. Her nurse sings her a gloomy folk song about a gnat; her brother Fyodor tries to cheer them up. Boris enters and Fyodor shows him that he has been studying the geography of their kingdom. Boris is oppressed by guilt. His six years of peace seem only to have increased Russia's poverty. His sleep is constantly interrupted by the spectre of the child he murdered. Fyodor amuses his father with a song about his parrot before the arrival of Prince Shuisky, who has come to tell him that a pretender (Grigori, calling himself Dimitri) has gained support from the King of Poland. Having sent his son away, Boris asks Shuisky whether he is certain it was Dimitri who was killed. The Prince affirms that it was; he adds that he stayed with the body for five days and that whereas the other corpses from the massacre began to decay, the boy's face remained serene and unaltered. Shuddering, Boris dismisses Shuisky, whom he suspects of being a traitor, and sinks into a trance in which he again sees the bloodstained child. Falling to his knees, he prays for forgiveness.

ACT III

Marina Mnishek, flattered by her attendants, is interested only in glory for Poland. Sending them away, she reflects on her decision to seduce the pretender in order to join him on the throne of Russia. Rangoni, a Jesuit priest, wishes her to seduce the pretender but for the altogether different purpose of bringing Russia under the rule of the Vatican. In the altercation that follows, Marina curses Rangoni before complying.

The false Dimitri, in love with Marina, is waiting for

O, tsaryevich, umolyáyu ('Oh, Tsarevitch, forget these words'): having provoked the pretender to further her ambitions, Marina declares her love for him

her. The wily Rangoni persuades 'Dimitri' to accept him as mentor and tells him to hide as Marina passes with a crowd of admirers. His jealousy aroused, 'Dimitri' determines to leave. Then Marina re-enters the garden. By spurning his simple declarations of love, she makes him vow to overcome Boris and win for her, as Dimitri's wife, the throne of Russia. Rangoni watches triumphantly as his ambitions, too, are served.

ACT IV
The mob threatens one of Boris' noble supporters and some boys tease a holy simpleton. The two vagrant monks who had accompanied 'Dimitri' proclaim the arrival of the true Tsarevitch, the crowd having seized and bound a pair of chanting Jesuit priests. Only the simpleton foresees the darkness of the days to come. (There is a variant to this scene, which Mussorgsky himself planned as the conclusion to the opera.)

The Tsar's palace

The assembled Russian nobles are discussing what is to be done about the pretender. Shuisky tells them that Boris seems to have lost his mind. At this, Boris enters, his state according with the Prince's description. Shuisky introduces Pimen, who tells of a blind shepherd whose sight was restored at the tomb of the murdered Tsarevitch. Boris collapses, calling for his son to come to him. Advising Fyodor on how to rule the country fairly, he gathers his strength for one last moment, proclaiming that he is still their tsar and naming his son as his successor.

Syeychás ti tsárstvovat' nachnyósh ('Farewell Tsarevitch, I am dying'): Boris' long helpless farewell to his son, warning him not to trust his treacherous noblemen

KHOVANSHCHINA
(THE KHOVANSKY RISING)

In five acts, text by the composer and Vladimir Stasov. Premiere: Kononov Theatre, St Petersburg, 1886. A moody, atmospheric tale of political strife, completed/orchestrated after Mussorgsky's death by Rimsky-Korsakov and in 1959 by Shostakovich.

In or near Moscow, 1682–89: the Streltsy (musketeers) under Prince Ivan Khovansky (b) and the Old Believers under Dosifey (b) are chafing under the new regime of Peter the Great. They are opposed by Prince Golitsin (t) and the Boyar Shaklovity (bar), who murders Khovansky. A sub-plot links Khovansky's son Andrey (t) with the young widow Marfa (ms). Both die when the Old Believers immolate themselves rather than surrender to the Tsar's troops.

JACQUES OFFENBACH

Born Cologne 1819, died Paris 1880. The composer of nearly 100 stage works, whose witty and sophisticated operettas epitomize the French Second Empire, was brought to Paris in 1833 to study at the Conservatoire. He played in the orchestra of the Opéra-Comique and conducted at the Théâtre Française before opening his own theatre, the Bouffes Parisiennes, in 1855. There, for 11 years, he premiered his operettas, among the best known of which are *Orphée aux Enfers* (1858), *La Belle Hélène* (1864) and *La Vie Parisienne* (1866). Using popular dance rhythms, in particular the can-can, the infectious musical line is radiant with impudent charm. When a later theatrical venture failed, Offenbach toured the USA in the hope of regaining his fortune. Back in Paris, he expected to see his only opera, *Les Contes d'Hoffmann*, produced at the Opéra-Comique, but he died before he had time to complete it.

ORPHEE AUX ENFERS

(ORPHEUS IN THE UNDERWORLD)

Orphée (Orpheus), a famous musician	tenor
Eurydice, his wife	soprano
Pluton (Pluto), God of the Underworld, who in human guise as Aristée (Aristaeus) courts Eurydice	tenor
Jupiter, King of the Gods	baritone

Ancient Greece, in legendary times: a comic variation on the classical tragedy of Orphée (Orpheus) and his deceased wife Eurydice. In this they are only too pleased to be parted, as is revealed amidst much tomfoolery on the part of the gods of Olympus.

The libretto is by Hector Cremieux and Halévy; the premiere was at the Bouffes Parisiens in 1858. Some of the critics were offended by his ludicrous portrayal of the usually solemn subject of Ancient Greece; others thought they saw too close a comparison between Jupiter and Napoleon III. It was, however, generally acclaimed, and the Emperor himself attended the 228th and last performance of the original production.

The countryside near Thebes

ACT I

Nymphs, shepherds and town councillors sing a chorus. An unfamiliar character in the shape of Public Opinion introduces herself. Her role is to regulate the behaviour of the principal characters.

When Eurydice appears, she confides to the audience

La femme dont le cœur rêve ('A woman in love'): Eurydice's dreamy soliloquy about her new lover

Moi, je suis Aristée ('I call myself Aristée'): Pluton introduces himself as Aristée, a simple shepherd

La mort m'apparaît souriante ('Death seems such fun'): Eurydice is far from heartbroken at leaving the world
Libre! ô bonheur! ô joie extrême! ('Free!, Oh joy! What utter bliss'): Orphée learns that his wife is dead

Mount Olympus

Eh hop! Eh hop! Place à Mercure ('Hop, hop, make way for me'): Mercure's jaunty description of his adventures as he hops and skips about the stage
Pour séduire Alcmène la fière ('To seduce proud Alcmène'): Diane's song about how Jupiter seduced a wife by turning himself into – of all unlikely ruses – her husband

that she is in love with a local shepherd and every day brings him flowers without her husband's knowledge. Her husband Orphée (Orpheus) appears while her back is turned and for a moment he thinks she is the nymph he fancies. Each is startled to recognize the other. Eurydice tells him that she is bored by his music and admits to being consistently unfaithful to him. In revenge, he threatens to play her his latest concerto. She begs the goddess Vénus to be kind and arrange that they may part. Orphée agrees that he, too, would be willing to separate, but he warns her that he has hidden a surprise for her shepherd in the cornfield.

After they have left, the chorus celebrates with country dancing until the sound of a flute announces the arrival of Aristée (Aristaeus).

When the others leave, Eurydice approaches. She warns Aristée not to go into the cornfield where she believes her husband has released some snakes. Aristée pretends not to mind and runs into the corn. Eurydice, greatly impressed, joins him and is immediately bitten. Aristée gathers her in his arms and reveals that he is Pluton, God of the Underworld. Eurydice is surprised that she feels no pain. She is entirely content to accompany her lover, pausing only to leave a last light-hearted message on the door for Orphée.

When Orphée returns, he is delighted to read her message. But just as he is about to go to break the good news to his nymph, a highly critical chorus backed up by Public Opinion insists that he must make some effort to get his wife back by pursuing her into the Underworld.

ACT II

The sun has not yet risen and one by one the gods creep in from their individual excursions, each believing that his absence has not been noticed. A ballet heralds the day and then a hunting horn is heard which wakes Jupiter and the other gods. It is Diane (Diana) the Huntress complaining that she could not find her lover Actéon. Jupiter announces that he has turned the boy into a stag because Diane's behaviour was becoming a scandal. He is interrupted by his wife Junon (Juno), who reproaches him for his own constant infidelities and accuses him of kidnapping Eurydice. This he indignantly denies. He is supported by Mercure (Mercury), who has seen Eurydice with Pluton.

Pluton is full of elaborate compliments, but he is cut short by Jupiter insisting that his guilt is known. At that there is general revolt among the gods and goddesses, who turn on Jupiter and repeat the songs they sing about his philanderings.

Orphée and Public Opinion arrive together, Orphée increasingly angry at what he is being forced to do against his will. Reluctantly, Orphée strikes up Gluck's immortal tune and Jupiter solemnly decrees that he himself will go down to Hades to make Pluton return Eurydice to her dismayed husband. This sounds so fascinating that all the other gods decide to go with him.

Gloire, gloire à Jupiter ('Glory to great Jupiter'): one of Offenbach's most exhilarating ensembles, sung by the gods

Pluton's abode

Personne encore! ('No-one yet!'): Eurydice's chagrin at being left by herself

ACT III

Eurydice, alone because of Pluton's summons to Mount Olympus, complains of boredom. There follows a scene of Eurydice with John Styx (a character inserted especially for a celebrated comedian of the day). Now Pluton's butler, he sings her a ditty about when once he was a king and generally pesters her until at last his master returns. Pluton is accompanied by Jupiter, some judicial advisers and Cerbère (Cerberus). They are joined by Cupidon (Cupid) re-inforced by a chorus of policemen.

Nez au vent ('With our noses in the air'): Cupidon's policemen describe their familiarity with the guiles of love

Jupiter still cannot find Eurydice but thinks she may be behind the locked door. Cupidon proceeds to metamorphose Jupiter into a fly, thus enabling him to pass through the keyhole. He makes up to Eurydice with surprising success. When she catches the fly and kisses it, Jupiter reveals himself as the King of the Gods. Eurydice is enchanted and readily agrees to a rendez-vous.

Hades

J'ai vu le Dieu Bacchus ('I saw the god Bacchus'): Eurydice's sparkling hymn to the God of Wine

ACT IV

Pluton is giving a splendid party for Jupiter and all the gods. Egged on by Cupidon, Eurydice (disguised as a bacchante) sings a song in praise of Bacchus. As the other goddesses join in, Pluton introduces a ballet.

Ce bal est original ('This is a new dance'): the gods throw themselves into the Infernal Gallop

Jupiter dances an elaborate caricature of a minuet with Eurydice, still in disguise (though already recognized by Pluton), and the admiring gods are swept into a splendid gallop to music usually connected with the can-can. The party is interrupted by Orphée and Public Opinion. Jupiter very reluctantly agrees that Eurydice should be returned to Orphée, but on one condition: Orphée must not look back at his wife while they are on their way back to Earth. The disconsolate Eurydice leaves, with her husband. But Jupiter has a plan. Suddenly he hurls a thunderbolt which so startles Orphée that he turns round involuntarily. The pact is ended and Jupiter pronounces that Eurydice is now free to remain for ever a bacchante. The opera ends with her rejoicing with all the gods at this happy conclusion.

LES CONTES D'HOFFMANN

(THE TALES OF HOFFMANN)

Hoffmann, a poet	tenor
Nicklausse, his companion	mezzo-soprano
Stella, a prima donna	
Olympia, a doll	soprano
Giulietta, a courtesan	
Antonia, a young girl	
Lindorf, a rival for Stella	
Coppélius, an optician	baritone
Dappertutto, a sorcerer	
Dr Miracle, a doctor	
Spalanzani, an inventor	tenor
Pittichinaccio, an admirer of Giulietta	tenor
Schlemil, Giulietta's lover	bass
Crespel, Antonia's father	baritone

Nuremberg, 19th century: the romantic drama of the poet Hoffmann's love for an opera singer reflects facets of three previous infatuations. Each of these had been frustrated by a sinister interloper.

Although he had had numerous successes with operetta, Offenbach always wanted to produce a full-scale opera. By the time he died he had completed the piano score for *Hoffmann* and the orchestration for the Prologue and Act I to the libretto of Jules Barbier and Michel Carré. This is after their play based on the stories of E.T.A. Hoffmann. When the opera was presented four months later, in 1881, at the Opéra-Comique, Ernest Guiraud had completed the orchestration. However, changes crept in, both then and at later presentations: for instance, the dialogue was extended into recitative and the order changed. The sequence given here is as it is usually performed today.

Luther's tavern, next door to the opera house

PROLOGUE

The Muse of Poetry complains that the poet Hoffmann has deserted her for Stella, an opera singer who is appearing in *Don Giovanni*. Lindorf also desires Stella and he intercepts a letter in which she promises to meet Hoffmann. The tavern fills with students calling for wine. Hoffmann comes in accompanied by Nicklausse. Pressed by the enthusiastic crowd, he sings them a popular song about a dwarf. He recognizes an old adversary in Lindorf and to illustrate his bad luck tells them the stories of the three women he has loved.

Spalanzani's house in Paris

Laisse, laisse ma flamme ('Let the flame of my love'): Hoffmann's ecstatic avowal of love for the motionless Olympia

ACT I (Olympia)

Spalanzani has invented a mechanical doll, Olympia, to help him recoup the fortune he has lost through a banker's failure. Hoffmann, believing that the doll is Spalanzani's daughter, finds her apparently asleep and falls in love with her despite Nicklausse's attempts to disillusion him. Coppélius joins them. He has provided the eyes for the doll and wants to share Spalanzani's profit. Spalanzani buys him off with a bill drawn on the bankrupt banker. Coppélius then suggests that Olympia should be married to Hoffmann.

A party is given to introduce Olympia to the public. When she begins to sing, there is obviously something wrong with her mechanism. Since her vocabulary consists only of the word 'yes', Hoffmann makes considerable progress with her while the others are at dinner. When they return to dance, Olympia waltzes at such speed that there are fears for Hoffmann's safety. Eventually the inventor is able to stop her and takes her next door while Hoffmann recovers. But Coppélius has discovered that the banker's bill is worthless and he forces his way into the doll's bedroom and smashes her, leaving the heartbroken Hoffmann ridiculed by all.

Les oiseaux dans la charmille ('Birds in the bower'): Olympia's mechanical song

Elle danse! ('She can dance!'): the guests are amazed at Olympia's versatility

ACT II (Giulietta)

Nicklausse sings a barcarolle in duet with Giulietta, a courtesan, to which Hoffmann responds. Of Giulietta's other admirers, Schlemil currently holds the key to her bedroom while Pittichinaccio acts as her jester. Nicklausse is worried that Hoffmann is about to fall in love again, but Hoffmann rashly says that the devil may have his soul if he can tempt him to fall in love with a harlot. At this, Dappertutto introduces himself. When Hoffmann has gone, he produces a magnificent diamond.

Giulietta, mesmerized, asks him for her orders. She has captured Schlemil's soul through his shadow; this time it is to be by Hoffmann's reflection. She tells Hoffmann that she loves him, but Schlemil intervenes. When he draws his sword, Dappertutto gives Hoffmann his. In the succeeding duel Hoffmann kills Schlemil. Nicklausse urges him to leave Venice immediately, but Hoffmann cannot bear to leave Giulietta. She insists, however, asking only to keep something of his: his reflection. She produces the magic mirror. Although Hoffmann is uneasy, she leads him on in a rapturous duet to do what she asks. The loss of his reflection leaves him exhausted and barely conscious.

Dappertutto returns to gloat over his success and leaves a poisoned drink for Nicklausse, who still hopes to rescue Hoffmann. Giulietta returns with Pittichinaccio and they laugh at the enfeebled Hoffmann. She drains the drink; as she falls dead in Hoffmann's arms, Pittichinaccio runs off with the diamond and Dappertutto mocks her mistake. (In an alternative ending to Act II, the duel with Schlemil follows the loss of Hoffmann's reflection, providing a delay which gives Pittichinaccio a chance to carry Giulietta off in a gondola.)

A palazzo in Venice
Belle nuit, ô nuit d'amour ('Oh lovely night, Oh night of love'): the famous barcarolle sung by Nicklausse and Giulietta

Scintille, diamant ('Flashing diamond'): Dappertutto's aria explaining how the diamond will help him use Giulietta to capture Hoffmann's soul

O Dieu! de quelle ivresse ('Oh God, what exhilaration'): Hoffmann's passionate lyrical declaration of love for Giulietta

Crespel's house in Munich

Elle a fui, la touterelle ('Your turtle dove has flown away'): Antonia's song about her forced separation from Hoffmann

C'est une chanson d'amour ('It's our song of love'): Hoffmann's reminiscence of Antonia's favourite song becomes a duet when she joins him

Chère enfant ('Darling child'): the trio between the ghost of Antonia's mother, Dr Miracle and Antonia herself, which, as her voice rises, leads to her death

Luther's tavern

ACT III (Antonia)

Crespel's daughter Antonia, in love with Hoffmann, sings of her sorrow that they have been parted by her father. Crespel rushes in to tell his daughter to stop singing. Her mother, a great mezzo-soprano, had died, worn out by singing and consumption, and he is afraid that Antonia will follow her. He orders his deaf servant Frantz not to admit anyone, but when Hoffmann and Nicklausse arrive they make their way in without difficulty. Antonia is overjoyed to see her lover and they plan to marry the following day. Hoffmann has to hide when her father returns and Frantz then announces Dr Miracle, the very man who visited Antonia's mother on the day she died. Crespel orders that he should not be admitted, but Frantz mishears and the doctor enters. He has heard of Antonia's danger and, ignoring Crespel's protests, he proceeds with an imaginary examination of Antonia even though she is not actually in the room. When Crespel has dragged the doctor out into the street, Hoffmann begs Antonia never to sing again. She promises, but after Hoffmann has gone Dr Miracle reappears and tries to poison her mind against Hoffmann, encouraging her to sing. She refuses to listen to him, but her mother's portrait also encourages her. She cannot resist singing together with her mother, and the two are eagerly accompanied by Dr Miracle urging them on with a violin. When Crespel returns, it is to find his daughter dying. Poor Hoffmann runs in, only to be blamed by Crespel. He calls for help and it is Dr Miracle who pronounces that the girl is dead.

EPILOGUE

Back in Nuremberg, Hoffmann has been drinking heavily as he relives these past disasters. It is all too much for him and he says he has had enough of love. He wants to return to the Muse of Poetry and she welcomes him back. When Stella arrives, she finds Hoffmann incoherent. She is lured away by the wily Lindorf as the customers call for more wine.

AMILCARE PONCHIELLI

Born Paderno Fasolaro 1834, died Milan 1886. The composer of several operas, only *I Promessi Sposi* achieved success, in its revised form (1872), apart from *La Gioconda* (1876), which is his one lasting monument. Among his pupils at the Milan Conservatory in the 1880s were Puccini and Mascagni.

LA GIOCONDA

In four acts, text by 'Tobia Gorrio' (alias Arrigo Boito) after Victor Hugo's drama *Angelo, Tyran de Padoue*. Premiere: La Scala, Milan, 1876. A dramatic work in Verdian style, it is famous for its Dance of the Hours; Callas made her Italian debut in the title role in Verona in 1947.

Venice, 17th century: Enzo Grimaldo (t), a Genoese nobleman disguised as a sea captain, has returned illegally from exile. He is loved by La Gioconda (s), a street singer, but prefers Laura (ms), wife of Alvise (b), a leader of the Inquisition. Out of revenge for Gioconda's disdain at his advances, Barnaba (bar), a spy, has her mother La Cieca (c) arrested; and he denounces Enzo. Laura arranges Cieca's release. In return, Gioconda warns her of the danger to Enzo; she also substitutes a sleeping potion for poison Alvise had ordered Laura to take. Promising herself to Barnaba in exchange for Enzo's safety, she takes the poison as Barnaba arrives to claim her.

FRANCIS POULENC

Born Paris 1899, died Paris 1963. One of the group known as 'Les Six', he composed in a wide variety of forms – orchestral, chamber, choral and solo vocal – often in a religious vein. His first operatic success was the satirical farce *Les Mamelles de Tirésias* (1944). Apart from *Dialogues des Carmélites* (1957), he is also known for *La Voix Humaine* (1959), a dramatic monologue for soprano.

DIALOGUES DES CARMELITES
(DIALOGUES OF THE CARMELITES)

In three acts (twelve scenes), text from George Bernanos' play, inspired by Gertrude von le Fort's novel *Die Letzte am Schafott* and a film scenario by Rev Fr Bruckberger and Philippe Agostini. Premiere: La Scala, Milan, 1957. A minutely observed, insistent drama that testifies to Poulenc's own religious renewal.

The convent in Compiègne and in Paris, April 1789 – Summer 1792: the aristocratic but neurotic Blanche de la Force (s) joins the Carmelite order. Her co-novice Sister Constance (s) has a premonition that they will die together, which is strengthened by the dying prioress, Mme de Croissy (c). When a revolutionary mob attacks the convent, now under Mme Lidoine (s), all the sisters decide on martydom – except Blanche, who escapes. Coaxed by Mother Marie (ms), a pivotal figure in her life, Blanche relents and joins the sisters as they go peacefully to the guillotine.

SERGEI PROKOFIEV

Born Sontsovka 1891, died Moscow 1953. The child of well-to-do and cultured parents, Prokofiev showed early and prodigious musical talent. While still at the St Petersburg Conservatory, where he studied under Rimsky-Korsakov, he wrote the first two of his piano concertos. Remaining in Russia during the revolution, he wrote among other works the opera *The Gambler* (first performed, after revisions, in 1929). In 1920 he went to the USA, where he wrote *L'Amour des Trois Oranges* (*The Love for Three Oranges*) for Chicago, the sharp rhythmic style well suited to the bizarre and lively plot. During a period of years spent in Europe he wrote the opera *The Fiery Angel* (not performed until 1955, after his death), re-using part of the music in his Third Symphony. He returned to Russia in 1934. *War and Peace*, based on Tolstoy's novel, was written during World War II but later revised to satisfy the Soviet authorities.

L'AMOUR DES TROIS ORANGES

(THE LOVE FOR THREE ORANGES)

King of Clubs	bass
Prince, his son	tenor
Clarissa, the King's niece	contralto
Truffaldino, the court jester	tenor
Tchelio, the King's magician	bass
Morgana, a witch	soprano
Léandre, the Prime Minister	baritone
Sméraldine, his accomplice	mezzo-soprano
Farfarello, a devil	bass
Princess Ninette	contralto

A fantasy, watched by a vociferous stage audience, in which a hypochondriac prince is cured of his illness by love for three oranges and the princess who emerges from one of them.

Prokofiev based his libretto on Carlo Gozzi's comedy *Fiaba dell'Amore delle Tre Melarance*. The commission was given to him in 1921 by Chicago Opera on the condition that he completed the opera that year. Working desperately against the deadline, he was struck down by scarlet fever, then by diptheria. Forbidden to work, he wrote part of it underneath the blankets in his hospital room.

PROLOGUE

A performance is about to start and the stage audience is variously composed of those who prefer tragedies, comedies, romances and farces. Then comes the announcement that they are about to see something altogether new.

The King's palace

ACT I

The King of Clubs is worried about the threat to his throne caused by the illness of his son and heir. The doctors diagnose incurable hypochondria. The King is so overcome with despair that some in the audience think he is in danger of overplaying his part. The only hope of a cure would be if the Prince could be made to laugh. The King summons his Prime Minister Léandre, who is not keen for the Prince to recover: he is plotting the Prince's death so that the woman he loves, the King's niece Clarissa, may ascend the throne.

Je le nourris de prose extra-tragique ('I will feed him on deeply tragic prose'): the Prime Minister's dastardly scheme is applauded by the supporters of tragedy in the audience

The witches' domain

The magician Tchelio is working to support the King, while the witch Morgana is against him, siding with Léandre and Clarissa. This time it is Morgana who wins at cards.

The King's palace

Léandre is promised marriage by Clarissa if he succeeds in gaining the kingdom for her.

The Prince's chamber

ACT II

Truffaldino, the court jester, tries in vain to amuse the Prince. To a splendid march, he drags the Prince off to watch an entertainment. The witch Morgana staggers in to keep an eye on the proceedings. When Truffaldino tries to push her out, she falls over with her legs in the air and the Prince laughs. Everyone is delighted. The witch places a curse on the Prince: that he will fall in love with three oranges.

Il faut que tu soubisse l'amour des trois oranges ('You shall fall in love with three oranges'): the witch Morgana casts a spell on the Prince

The spell takes immediate effect and the Prince announces his departure to free his beloved oranges from the clutches of the wicked Créonte, a giant cook. The King tries to stop him. When the alternative is shown to be even deeper depression for his son, the King sends him off with the reluctant Truffaldino, both blown on their way by the devil Farfarello armed with bellows.

The desert

ACT III

Tchelio tries to protect the Prince from Farfarello; but by losing at cards, he has lost his power. He warns them that the cook is murderous and tells them that the oranges must only be cut open near water. He gives Truffaldino a magic ribbon.

Créonte's castle

Qui piaille ici? ('Who's that I hear?'): the terrifying cook discovers the presence of Truffaldino and the Prince

The desert
Comment, pourrais-je dormir? ('Sleep! How can I sleep?'): Truffaldino sings that he is too thirsty for sleep

Non rien ne pouvait m'arrêter ('Nothing now can keep me from you'): the Prince's pledge of love

The witches' domain

The throne room
Gloire à notre Roi! ('Praise to the King'): the chorus of courtiers prepares for the ceremony

Spurred on by the orchestra and by Farfarello's bellows, the two adventurers find themselves at the castle. Terrified of the cook's legendary ladle, they hide; but the cook spots Truffaldino. As she is about to kill him, she sees the ribbon. While Truffaldino gives it to her, the Prince is able to snatch up the oranges.

The Prince falls asleep, leaving the oranges in the care of the thirsty Truffaldino. When Truffaldino cuts one open, he finds instead of juice a princess. She too is desperately thirsty. He cuts open a second orange and out steps another princess. Both of them die at his feet and he runs away.

The Prince awakes to find one orange and two dead princesses. Four soldiers march past and the Prince orders them to bury the princesses. Then he opens the third orange and finds the answer to his dreams: the beautiful Princess Ninette. She is dying of thirst as well. This is too much for the audience and a bucket of water is produced. The two pledge eternal love and the Prince goes to fetch the Princess a suitable royal gown. As she waits for him, Sméraldine, Morgana's black servant, is persuaded to prick Princess Ninette with a needle. The Princess is turned into a rat. The royal party returns, the Prince insisting that Sméraldine is not Ninette but an imposter. She however protests that the Prince had promised to marry her. The King orders his reluctant son to lead her into the palace.

ACT IV
Tchelio and Morgana accuse each other of cheating in the battle of wills over the royal succession. Suddenly the audience takes a hand, pushing Morgana into one of the castle turrets.

The courtiers are preparing to celebrate the Prince's marriage. A huge rat is discovered sitting on the Princess' throne. Soliders are summoned as Tchelio tries to break the spell. The soldiers open fire, the magician disappears and the rat turns back into Princess Ninette. There is general rejoicing, but the King wants to know who the other 'princess' is. Truffaldino arrives to identify her as Sméraldine, known to be an associate of the Prime Minister. Despite their protests, the King sentences Sméraldine, the Prime Minster Léandre and his niece Clarissa to be hanged. As they try to escape, the witch Morgana breaks out of her turret and leads them through a convenient trap-door amid flames and clouds of smoke. 'Long live the King! Long live the Prince and Princess!' All rejoice at the happy ending.

GIACOMO PUCCINI

Born Lucca 1858, died Brussels 1924. The creator of several of the most popular operas in the international repertoire, Puccini was born into a family with long-established musical connections. Having decided to devote himself to the composition of opera, he entered the Milan Conservatory in 1880, where he was taught by Ponchielli. His first opera, *Le Villi*, had been written for a competition and it had failed to win, but with the help of Arrigo Boito (Verdi's librettist) it was successfully produced at the Teatro dal Verme, Milan, in 1884. It came to the attention of the music publisher Giulio Ricordi, who commissioned Puccini's next opera, *Edgar* (1889), and became his lifelong friend and mentor. In 1891 Puccini bought a house at Torre del Lago, where most of his work was written. With *Manon Lescaut* (1893), which brought

him international acclaim, he began the practice of using a believable libretto, and his music became an inspired reflection of the dramatic content. Luigi Illica drew up the scenarios and Giuseppe Giacosa took charge of the versification of the text. *Manon Lescaut* was the first of a series of moving love stories, followed by *La Bohème* (1896), *Tosca* (1900) and *Madama Butterfly* (1904) in which he incorporated Japanese folk tunes. His career was halted by scandal in 1908, when his wife Elvira, mistakenly jealous, drove a servant girl to suicide. In 1910 he completed *La Fanciulla del West*, and, after his three stylistically separate one-act operas, known collectively as *Il Trittico* (1918), Puccini started work on his most ambitious project: *Turandot*. No other opera caused him so much effort and so many problems, yet it prompted some of his most glorious music. Puccini died of cancer of the throat before completing the opera. At the La Scala premiere in 1926 Toscanini, conducting, finished where the original manuscript ended; the following evening it was performed with Franco Alfano's conclusion. Mussolini refused to attend the premiere because Toscanini would not play the Fascist anthem.

MANON LESCAUT

Manon Lescaut	soprano
Chevalier des Grieux, a student	tenor
Edmondo, a student	tenor
Lescaut, Manon's brother	baritone
Geronte, an elderly admirer	bass

France, second half of the 18th century: another adaptation to opera (see Massenet, *Manon*) of the Abbé Prévost's novel about a fickle, pleasure-loving young woman and her irresistible fascination to a young nobleman and to his wealthy and ageing rival.

In Massenet's version, Manon dies before boarding the convict ship; here, she reaches America before dying. Puccini's librettists were Marco Praga, Domenico Oliva, Giulio Ricordi, Luigi Illica and Giuseppe Giacosa. The premiere at the Teatro Reggio, Turin, in 1893 established Puccini overnight.

Amiens, near the Paris Gate

('*Donna non vidi mai* ('Never have I seen'): Des Grieux's excitement is aroused by talking to Manon

Vedete? Io son fedele ('You see? I am faithful'): Manon comes looking for Des Grieux, and they exchange confidences

Geronte's house in Paris

In quelle trine morbide ('In this gilded cage'): Manon's aria complaining of being confined to luxurious isolation

Vieni, colle tue braccia stringi Manon che t'ama! ('Hold Manon who loves you in your arms!'): Manon and Des Grieux's duet as they embrace *Ah! Manon, mi tradisce il tuo folle pensier* ('Your empty thoughts betray us'): Des Grieux rebukes Manon for her love of the gilded life

ACT I

It is evening, and a crowd of students led by Edmondo are laughing and singing in the street when Des Grieux passes by. His serious mood suggests a love affair, and to satisfy his friends he serenades a group of girls. The stage-coach arrives and among the passengers is Manon with her brother and the elderly Geronte. Des Grieux, overcome by Manon's beauty, asks her name. She tells him that she is to enter a convent the following day and that it is her father's will.

Geronte and Lescaut return, Lescaut explaining that he is a soldier, reluctantly doing his duty by escorting his sister. Geronte reveals that he is a collector of taxes. Lescaut gets involved in a card game and Geronte in a low voice orders a coach with fresh horses to be ready in one hour. He is overheard by Edmondo, who warns Des Grieux that his new love is about to be abducted. Manon appears, looking for Des Grieux. He tells her of Geronte's intention and implores her to flee with him. At last she agrees, just as Geronte returns to carry her off. Edmondo informs Geronte that Manon has already left. While the old man rages, Lescaut coolly predicts that the student's money will soon run out and that then Manon will be happy to accept Geronte's protection.

ACT II

Lescaut has been proved right and Manon is now installed with Geronte; but, surrounded by servants, she is bored. She longs for news of Des Grieux. Lescaut reveals that Des Grieux is always asking after her and is trying to make money at cards, as instructed by him. Musicians and then a dancing master are brought in to try to entertain her. They leave and Des Grieux appears at the door. She is overcome with happiness until she perceives his bitterness at her desertion. She begs for his forgiveness. He is completely won over by her, but suddenly they are interrupted by Geronte. Cruelly, she hands Geronte a mirror to compare himself with Des Grieux and herself. He goes out as Des Grieux tells Manon to make haste and leave with him.

Lescaut rushes in: the old man has denounced her as a harlot and the soldiers are on the way to arrest her. As they leave, Manon loses precious moments collecting an emerald and emptying some boxes. Already the house is surrounded. As Manon dashes across the room, soldiers enter. Des Grieux draws his sword but Lescaut holds him back, warning that he can be more use to Manon free than in prison.

Le Havre

E Kate rispose al Re ('And Kate's reply to the King'): the nightwatchman's ballad as dawn breaks

ACT III

Des Grieux and Lescaut are waiting near the harbour, determined to rescue Manon before she is deported to America. One of the soldiers has been bribed to help, and they are able to speak to Manon in prison. She and Des Grieux comfort each other while a nightwatchman sings a ballad.

As Manon prepares to escape, a shot is heard and soon guards are everywhere, frustrating any hope they had. Immediately, the women prisoners are brought out and the roll is called with the townspeople looking on. Des Grieux and Manon try to say goodbye. The captain, taking pity on the desperate couple, permits Des Grieux to join the ship as cabin boy.

A desert in Louisiana

Sola, perduta, abbandonata ('Lost and alone'): Manon's despairing aria as she thinks on the cause of their predicament

ACT IV

Manon, in rags, can scarcely walk. She is seriously ill but there is no water and nowhere to rest. She urges Des Grieux to go and look for shelter. Left alone, she is full of self-reproach. Des Grieux returns and she collapses, telling him again and again how much she has always loved him: '*Le mie colpe – travolgerà l'oblio – ma l'amor mio – non muor*' ('My guilt goes with me but my heart remains with you'). In his arms Manon dies.

LA BOHEME

(THE BOHEMIAN GIRL)

Rodolfo, a poet	tenor
Marcello, a painter	baritone
Colline, a philosopher	bass
Schaunard, a musician	baritone
Mimi	soprano
Musetta	soprano
Benoit, the landlord	bass
Alcindoro, Musetta's elderly admirer	bass

Paris, c. 1830: Mimi and Rodolfo's love for each other blossoms in the cold and misery of Christmas in Montmartre. Rodolfo's jealousy drives them apart, and fear that in his penniless state he cannot support her in her illness. They are, however, reunited before she dies.

Based on Henry Murger's novel *Scènes de la Vie de Bohème*, the libretto is by Luigi Illica and Giuseppe Giacosa. The first performance was given at the Teatro Regio, Turin, in 1896, conducted by Toscanini.

ACT I

An artist's studio in Montmartre, Christmas Eve

Marcello and Rodolfo, one working on a painting, the other writing, are cold and hungry. Restraining his friend from burning a chair, Rodolfo sacrifices the manuscript

243

of his play, act by act. Colline enters, having failed to pawn some books. Just as the fire is dying down a huge supply of provisions is to their astonishment brought in. Schaunard has been hired to play for an Englishman. As they celebrate, the landlord knocks. He has come to ask for the rent, three months overdue. They ply him with drink; Marcello teases him for being caught with a woman, at his age, and they pretend great indignation on behalf of his wife. Soon he is confused with wine and embarrassment, and they bundle him out of the door. Rodolfo stays behind to work on an article and the others disappear.

There is a knock at the door. Mimi, who lodges below, has come to ask for a match. Out of breath with coughing, she faints. Rodolfo revives her with some wine. He lights her candle for her but she comes back after realizing she has left her key behind. Her candle blows out again and so does his, and he contrives to hide her key while appearing to look for it. Taking her hand, he is amazed by how cold she is. He tells her that he loves his carefree Bohemian existence; she reveals that she works at embroidery and confides that she loves poetry. The others call up from the street saying that they are off to the Café Momus, leaving Rodolfo and Mimi in each other's arms.

Che gelida manina ('Your tiny hand is frozen'): Rodolfo's aria as he and Mimi rise from searching for her key
O soave fanciulla ('A beautiful girl like you'): Rodolfo's ringing declaration of love

Quartier Latin

ACT II

The street is full of bustle. Mimi and Rodolfo are together, and he buys her a pink bonnet. He introduces her to his friends. Marcello tells of his bitterness that the girl he loves, Musetta, has moved on to someone else. She has just seated herself at a nearby table, dogged by the elderly Alcindoro, who is embarrassed by her skittishness. Rodolfo warns Mimi that he could never forgive infidelity and she reassures him that there is no need.

Quando m'en vo ('When I go for a walk'): Musetta's brazen song about the attention she attracts

Musetta sings an outrageous song about how much she enjoys being desired, directed at the sulking Marcello. When she thinks that she has gone far enough, she pretends that her shoe is hurting her and sends Alcindoro to fetch her another pair. As soon as he is gone, she makes up to Marcello and all is forgiven. The bill comes and she gets the waiter to add all their bills on to that of the absent Alcindoro. When he eventually makes his way back through the crowd, he finds that she has gone and he is left with an immense account to pay.

Barrière d'Enfer, February

ACT III

People pass in the snow through the customs post at the Paris Gate. Mimi has come to find Marcello and Musetta. Her cough is worse and she explains that Rodolfo's crazy jealousy is driving them apart. Marcello says that he and

Musetta take things very light-heartedly and advises Mimi that she is probably better off away from Rodolfo. He is asleep next door, having stumbled back in the middle of the night. At that moment Rodolfo wakes up, and Mimi hides. He tells Marcello that he is bored with Mimi because she is just a flirt. Rebuked by Marcello, he admits that he is really desperately worried that her illness can only get worse living in poverty with him. Love is not enough to save her. She coughs and he realizes that she has been listening, until then unaware that she is dying. Musetta can be heard laughing with a man next door and Marcello leaves hurriedly.

Donde lieta uscì ('Back from where I came'): Mimi's farewell to Rodolfo as she plans to return to her old lodgings

Mimi says goodbye to Rodolfo, explaining that she is going back to her lonely room. She asks him to send her things but to keep the bonnet as a memento. Distraught at the prospect of parting, they are interrupted by Marcello and Musetta having a row. As those two separate, Rodolfo and Mimi agree to stay together until the Spring. The act ends with Mimi wishing that Winter would last for ever.

The studio

ACT IV

Marcello and Rodolfo pretend indifference as they discuss seeing Musetta and Mimi in comfortable circumstances. Both fall to gloomy reminiscence. Schaunard and Colline appear with some bread: money is short again but they joke until suddenly Musetta enters. She has brought Mimi, who is ill and too weak to climb the stairs. Rodolfo carries her to the bed. Musetta tells how she found Mimi stumbling through the streets saying that she wanted to die with Rodolfo. In familiar surroundings Mimi feels secure. Musetta gives her earrings to Marcello to pay for something to drink and for a doctor. Colline sacrifices his overcoat to raise more money, and he and Schaunard leave so that Mimi and Rodolfo can be alone together. He assures her that she is still beautiful and they remember how happy they were when they first met. The others come back with medicine and a muff, which Mimi thinks Rodolfo has given her. As Musetta starts to pray, Mimi's voice fades into silence. The others realize that she is dead, but Rodolfo believes her to be resting until he sees their expressions. He calls our her name for the last time.

Vecchia zimarra ('Goodbye, old friend'): Colline's parting with his overcoat to raise money for Mimi
Sono andati? ('Have they gone?'): alone together, Mimi and Rodolfo begin their last duet

TOSCA

Tosca, an opera singer	soprano
Cavaradossi, a painter	tenor
Scarpia, chief of police	baritone
Angelotti, a conspirator	bass
Spoletta, a police agent	tenor

Rome, 1800: playing on Tosca's jealousy and her love for Cavaradossi, Scarpia, the chief of police, makes her reveal the hiding place of the escaped political prisoner, Angelotti. Tosca's murder of Scarpia does not alter the final tragedy.

The libretto is by Luigi Illica and Giuseppe Giacosa after the play by Sardou, which was written for Sarah Bernhardt. The premiere of the opera was at the Teatro Constanzi, Rome, in 1900. Later, Maria Callas was to be particularly associated with the role of Tosca.

The church of Sant' Andrea

Recondita armonia di bellezze diverse! ('The hidden harmony of differing beauties'): Cavaradossi's aria contrasting different types of feminine beauty
Non la sospiri ('Don't you desire'): Tosca and Cavaradossi's love duet, marred by the distraction of his hidden friend
Qual' occhio al mondo ('What other eyes'): Cavaradossi's aria reassuring Tosca of his wholehearted devotion

ACT I

Angelotti, a republican on the run from Scarpia's agents, hurries in and finds the key to the chapel hidden by his sister. Cavaradossi is working on a painting of a fair-headed Mary Magdalene, based on a regular visitor to the church (Angelotti's sister). While he compares this to the miniature of his dark-haired mistress, Tosca the opera singer, Angelotti returns and the two men embrace. The sound of Tosca approaching sends Angelotti hurrying back into hiding with Cavaradossi's basket of food.

Tosca's jealousy is her weakness. She suspects Cavaradossi of whispering with another woman, reproaches him for lack of enthusiasm and then rages at recognizing Cavaradossi's sister in the portrait. At last he persuades her of his love. She leaves to take her part in a performance as Angelotti re-emerges. Cavaradossi helps Angelotti, telling him to hide in his well.

The sound of a cannon signals that the prisoner's escape has been discovered and Angelotti runs off. The sacristan bustles in with the news that Napoleon's army has been defeated. As the church is prepared for a triumphal *Te Deum* one of the great villains in the operatic repertory, Baron Scarpia, appears. His assistant Spoletta and other agents search the building for the escaped Angelotti. They find the open chapel, the empty basket and Angelotti's sister's fan. Recognizing her likeness in the portrait, Scarpia is immediately able to deduce all that has happened. He himself desires Tosca and knows that Cavaradossi is her lover. He realizes he can use her to reach his prisoner. When she returns, he contrasts her

Va, Tosca! Nel tuo cuor s'annida Scarpia ('Go, Tosca, Scarpia has a place in your heart'): after Tosca has left, Scarpia contemplates her betrayal of her lover, opening the way for Scarpia

piety with the lust of painter and sitter, using the fan to convince Tosca that her lover has made off with Angelotti's sister. In an agony of jealousy, she leaves to confront Cavaradossi, and Scarpia sends Spoletta with other men to follow her. As the *Te Deum* resounds throughout the church, he rejoices at the prospect of possessing Tosca himself: '*Tosca, mi fai dimenticare Iddio!*' ('Tosca, the thought of you hides even God').

Scarpia's apartment in the Palazzo Farnese

ACT II

Scarpia is dining while waiting for news of the outcome of his scheme. He reflects that conquest is more satisfying than affectionate surrender. Spoletta returns to say that they found Cavaradossi alone in his house and no sign of Angelotti.

When Cavaradossi is brought in for questioning, both men can hear Tosca singing in the concert below. Cavaradossi denies all knowledge of Angelotti. Tosca arrives and he is able to warn her before being taken next door for further interrogation. Alone with Scarpia, Tosca laughs off her earlier jealousy until she hears the awful sounds of her lover being tortured. He shouts to her to keep silent, but Cavaradossi's cries and Scarpia's laughter finally overwhelm her and she tells Scarpia to look in the well. Cavaradossi, released, curses her weakness; but suddenly the three of them are interrupted with fresh news that the Battle of Marengo has been won by Napoleon's armies and the royalists have fled. Cavaradossi's jeers of triumph are cut short: Scarpia orders him to be taken out and executed. Settling down to resume his dinner, he smilingly invites Tosca to join him, murmuring that there is a price for saving Cavaradossi.

Vissi d'arte, vissi d'amore ('I have lived for art and for love'): Tosca's tragic prayer for pity reminding God of her piety

Scarpia tells Tosca that he has often imagined her suppleness and desires it for himself. Her outraged rejection of him coincides with the sound of preparations for the execution. Sinking to her knees, she begs for pity, but he is unmoved. Spoletta returns to report that Angelotti has killed himself and that all is prepared for Cavaradossi. As the two men watch, Tosca hides her face and nods her submission to Scarpia. Scarpia tells Spoletta that Cavaradossi's execution must be faked. The two men understand each other, however. Spoletta leaves and, as Scarpia approaches her, Tosca asks first for a safe conduct for herself and Cavaradossi by way of Civitavecchia. While he writes, she picks up a knife. As he opens his arms to her, she plunges the knife into his chest.

Questo è il bacio di Tosca ('This is Tosca's kiss'): Tosca's revenge: the highlight of a scene of immense power

As her tormentor expires, Tosca exults at his efforts to call for help. Once he is still, she extracts her safe conduct from his fingers; then takes the candles and stands them on either side of his head, carefully placing a crucifix on his chest: '*E avanti a lui tremava tutta Roma!*' ('And once he frightened all Rome!').

Castel Sant' Angelo
E lucevan le stelle ('In the starlight'): Cavaradossi remembers his midnight meetings with Tosca
O dolci mani ('With these sweet hands'): Cavaradossi marvels at his mistress' courage

ACT III

As a shepherd sings in the distance, Cavaradossi bribes his jailer with a ring to let him write a last letter to Tosca. Suddenly Tosca is brought in with news of his pardon and tells him secretly of the murder. She explains that the execution will be only a pretence: he must fall down when the shots are fired and stay still until the soldiers have left. Joyfully they plan the future together, and he takes his place after her last caution that he must not laugh. The firing squad forms up, they fire and Spoletta prevents their sergeant from delivering the *coup de grâce*.

The soldiers leave. Tosca urges Cavaradossi to stay still a moment longer and then rushes forward, only to find that he is truly dead. It was Scarpia's last trick. But already shouts show that the murder has been discovered. As Spoletta and others rush in to seize her, she flings herself over the parapet into the courtyard below.

MADAMA BUTTERFLY

Cio-Cio-San, known as Madama Butterfly	soprano	
B.F. Pinkerton, US Navy lieutenant	tenor	
Sharpless, US consul	baritone	
The Bonze, Butterfly's uncle	bass	

Japan, 1900s: Butterfly's marriage to Pinkerton is seen by the American lieutenant as a temporary arrangement, but not so by his Japanese bride. Her heart is broken when he returns to America.

Puccini was recommended David Belasco's play *Madam Butterfly* and at once saw it as a suitable story to set to music; the libretto is again by Luigi Illica and Giuseppe Giacosa. The audience barracked throughout the premiere, which was at La Scala, Milan, in 1904. A year later a radically revised version achieved in Brescia the huge success that it retains to this day.

A house near Nagasaki

ACT I

Pinkerton, a naval lieutenant on foreign service at Nagasaki, is being shown round the house he is renting for his Japanese bride, the geisha known as Madama

Dovunque al mondo ('Wherever one happens to be'): Pinkerton's boastful aria on taking whatever is offered, the motif based on the *Star Spangled Banner*

Spira sul mare ('The breath of Spring'): Butterfly's entrance

Dolce notte! ('This beautiful night'): duet heralding Butterfly's brief period of happiness

Inside Butterfly's house, three years later

Un bel dì vedremo ('One fine day'): Butterfly's aria expressing confidence in her absent husband

Butterfly. The marriage broker has everything in hand. Sharpless, the American consul, calls and is not impressed by Pinkerton's selfish attitude, taking whatever presents itself and then moving on. In Puccini's Japan the contract for both houses and wives may be cancelled subject only to one month's notice. Indeed, Pinkerton is already looking forward to the day when he marries a proper American wife.

Sharpless' rebukes are interrupted by the sound of Butterfly and her friends approaching. When she tells the consul that she is only 15, Sharpless tries to impress upon Pinkerton the responsibility of taking care of her. Her relations bicker about the wedding preparations and the wine. Butterfly has brought with her all her possessions, of which the most precious is a knife, the present the mikado gave her father when instructing him to commit hara-kiri.

The marriage proceeds but is immediately followed by the outraged interruption of the Japanese priest, the Bonze, who drives her family away because Butterfly has renounced her traditional religion for her husband.

Alone and blissfully happy together under a perfect starlit sky, Pinkerton encourages Butterfly to yield to him, while she begs him to take care of her: Butterflies are notoriously fragile, and already she draws the awful analogy of being fixed by a pin on display.

ACT II

Pinkerton has been gone for some time and Butterfly, alone with their son and her faithful maid, is now short of money. The maid warns her that he will not return, for foreign husbands never do, but Butterfly replies that he arranged for locks on her doors and for the consul to pay her rent. Furthermore, when he left he promised he would come back to her when the robins nest again.

The consul visits her with a letter. Timidly she asks him whether robins nest less frequently in America. They are interrupted by the marriage broker, who is trying to sell her to a rich prince. They maintain that Pinkerton's desertion has set her free. When she tries to persuade Sharpless to support her, he very reluctantly reads Pinkerton's letter asking him to pay her off. Heartbroken, she calls for Pinkerton's son: either she must go back to dancing to support them both, or die. Sharpless leaves, promising to explain all this to Pinkerton. Suddenly a cannon is fired. An American ship has sailed into the harbour and it is Pinkerton's. Wild with happiness, Butterfly sends her maid to pick all the flowers in the garden and the three of them settle down 'as quiet as mice' ('*come topolini*') to watch for his return.

Dawn

ACT III

They are still waiting and finally the exhausted Butterfly falls asleep. Pinkerton and Sharpless creep in. They have a third companion, Pinkerton's American wife, who waits outside in the garden. Too late, Pinkerton realizes the consequences of his selfishness, and leaves his wife and the consul to face Butterfly. Through the maid, Pinkerton's wife offers to take care of the child and Butterfly agrees, asking for a last half-hour alone with him. When they have gone, she prepares for a ritual death with her father's knife. Just as she is about to use it, the little boy comes in and she sings a last farewell. Giving him an American flag to play with, she goes behind a screen to complete her task. As she staggers back to die beside him, Pinkerton's voice can be heard calling for her as he and the consul return for the boy.

Tu, piccolo iddio! ('You are the idol of my life!'): Butterfly's farewell to her son

TURANDOT

Turandot, Princess of Peking	soprano
Timur, exiled King of Tartary	bass
Calaf, his son	tenor
Liù, a slave girl	soprano

Peking, in legendary times: Calaf, exiled and unrecognized Prince of Tartary, solves the three riddles that will win him the hand of the beautiful Princess Turandot, and with magnanimity offers to release her from the oath if she can discover his name. The slave girl Liù, refusing to disclose the secret, dies for her devotion to Calaf. Finally, Turandot reveals her true feelings.

Puccini did not live to finish this, his last and most exotic opera, the libretto of which is by Giuseppe Adami and Renato Simoni after a fable by Carlo Gozzi. It was completed, using Puccini's drafts, by Franco Alfano. The premiere was at La Scala, Milan, in 1926.

The Imperial City

ACT I

Turandot, daughter of the Emperor of China, will marry any man of royal blood who can answer three riddles; any man who fails must be beheaded. A mandarin announces that her latest suitor has failed. Among the crowd are Timur, exiled King of Tartary, and Liù, the slave girl who helped him to escape. They are found and recognized by Calaf, Timur's son. Liù loves Calaf because one day in the palace he smiled at her.

The executioners sharpen their blades in preparation as the crowd calls on the legendary Turandot to show herself to them. She appears briefly in the moonlight,

Lascia le donne! ('Leave women alone!'): Ping, Pang and Pong, the Emperor's ministers, advise giving up women or keeping a harem
Signore, ascolta! ('Listen, my Lord!'): Liù begs Calaf not to break her heart

A pavilion
Ho una casa nell'Honan ('I have a country home in Honan'): Ping longs to leave the Violet City of Peking and return to Honan

A square within the palace

In questa reggia ('In this same palace'): Turandot's revengeful description of how a princess of long ago was overcome

Mi vuoi nelle tue braccia a forza? ('Must you take me by force?'): Turandot's demand, which is met by Calaf's magnanimous answer that he only wants her of her own free will

The garden of the palace

Nessun dorma ('No-one shall sleep'): Calaf looks forward to telling the secret of his name to Turandot

---

gesturing that her latest victim should be executed. Calaf is bewitched by this brief sight of Turandot and determines to win her for himself. Everyone tries to discourage him, including the Emperor's ministers, but he insists. As Calaf prepares to strike the gong which announces a new suitor, Liù confesses her love for him, but Calaf directs her to look after his ailing and distraught father. With that he rushes forward and strikes the gong three times.

ACT II
The three ministers are ruminating on the confusion caused by the endless round of executions; the crowd meanwhile can be heard calling for more blood.

When the Emperor arrives, he reveals that he himself is sick of the ritual. Calaf persists, however. Turandot comes to meet him, repeating the story of her ancestress, whose cruel abduction she continues to avenge. No-one shall ever possess her and she asks her first riddle: 'What phantom, much desired, dies every morning but is born again every night?' 'It is Hope' ('*Speranza*') replies Calaf. The scroll is opened and he is shown to be right. Turandot immediately asks the second riddle: 'What burns like a flame but dies down in idleness and grows cold in defeat?' 'Blood' ('*Sangue*') he replies, correctly. The crowd are exultant. Turandot orders the people to be beaten and she towers over Calaf, demanding the answer to the third riddle: 'What is like ice but gives off fire?' Calaf triumphantly confronts her with the answer: 'Turandot'. For the third time the ancient scrolls show him to be right. Turandot begs her father to break his oath and not to hand her over to Calaf. Taking pity on her, Calaf proposes that if she can find out his name before dawn he will die like the others. She accepts the challenge as the Emperor and all the court sing of their hope that she will be unsuccessful.

ACT III
Heralds can be heard announcing that Turandot has forbidden anyone to sleep until the stranger's name has been discovered. Calaf himself looks forward to the moment when he can unlock her love by telling her his name himself. The desperate ministers offer Calaf every inducement to tell them his name and, when he refuses, they seize his father and Liù who had been seen talking to him. To spare Timur, Liù admits that she alone knows the answer. Tortured but still refusing to reveal his name,

Tanto amore, segreto e inconfessato ('Great love, so secret and concealed'): Liù's expression of the power of love *Tu, che di gel sei cinta* ('Icy, as you are'): Liù's final words before stabbing herself

she is asked by Turandot what gives her the courage to keep silent. 'Love' is the reply. The crowd calls for the executioner. Liù, prophesying that Turandot will before dawn be thawed by Calaf's love, seizes a soldier's dagger and kills herself. Timur falls to his knees beside her, begging her to rise. As her body is carried away, he walks beside it still holding her hand. (This is the end of Puccini's completed score. What follows is by Alfano, working from Puccini's sketches and notes).

Calaf and Turandot remain, alone. He reproaches her for her cruelty and, despite her protests, takes her in his arms and kisses her. Her anger turns to passion and she sheds her first tears. She begs him to leave her alone with her shame and admits to feelings of love and fear from the first. Believing that he has won her, he reveals his name to her just before the trumpets announce the deadline set for his riddle. His life is in her hands.

Del primo pianto ('These unfamiliar tears'): Turandot's admission that she both loved and hated him from the first

Outside the palace

She leads him before the crowd and announces that she knows the name of the unknown prince. His name is Love.

LA FANCIULLA DEL WEST
(THE GIRL OF THE GOLDEN WEST)

In three acts, text by Guelfo Civinini and Carlo Zangarini after David Belasco's play *The Girl of the Golden West*. Premiere: Metropolitan, New York, 1910. This is Puccini's tribute to American frontiersmen, in which lyricism plays second fiddle to atmosphere.

A mining-camp in the Cloudy Mountains of California, 1849–50: Minnie (**s**), the girl of the title, owns The Polka, a saloon where she is mother-figure to miners of the Gold Rush. She falls for Dick Johnson (**t**), alias the notorious bandit Ramerrez, who is wanted by Sheriff Rance (**bar**). Shot by the Sheriff's posse, Johnson hides in Minnie's loft. Bargaining her life for Johnson's safety in a game of poker with Rance (who also loves her), Minnie cheats and wins. Captured later, Johnson is about to be hanged: '*Ch'ella mi creda libero*' ('Let her believe me free'). Then Minnie rides up and successfully pleads for his release. They leave to start a new life together.

GIANNI SCHICCHI

In one act, text by Giovacchino Forzano after an episode in Canto XXX of Dante's *Inferno*. Premiere: Metropolitan, New York, 1918. The comic third part of Puccini's *Trittico* (triptych) – after *Il Tabarro* (The Cloak) and *Suor Angelica* (Sister Angelica) – is the composer's only light opera, and shows his orchestration at its finest.

Florence, 1299: the relatives of the recently deceased Buoso Donati are gathered round his deathbed to hear his will read, worried that he is leaving everything to a monastery. Rinuccio (**t**) suggests bringing in Gianni Schicchi (**bar**), wily father of his sweetheart Lauretta (**s**). Schicchi devises a plan: with the body hidden, he will impersonate the dying man and revise the will. All plea for special consideration, offering him bribes. But Schicchi, after announcing insignificant legacies to the others, keeps the plums for himself. Chasing the furious relatives from the house, now his, he turns to the audience and pleads extenuating circumstances.

HENRY PURCELL

Born, probably London, 1659, died London 1695. The outstanding English composer of the Baroque period. A chorister of the Chapel Royal until 1673, he became organist of Westminster Abbey in 1679, moving to the Chapel Royal three years later. Apart from anthems, odes, solo songs and harpsichord music, he leaned most strongly towards music for the theatre, writing incidental music to 43 plays and five semi-operas (with masques and ceremonial scenes), including *King Arthur* (1691) and *The Indian Queen* (1695). His masterpiece was *Dido and Aeneas* (1689), his only real opera.

DIDO AND AENEAS

In prologue and three acts, with text by Nahum Tate after Virgil's *Aeneid IV*. Premiere: Josias Priest's Boarding School for Girls, London, 1689. The first major opera in English, full of dramatic invention and beauty, with a prominent role for the chorus.

Carthage, after the Trojan War: Dido (s), Queen of Carthage, is tormented by her love for the Trojan prince Aeneas (t). Her lady-in-waiting Belinda (s) persuades her to yield to Aeneas' pleas and marry him. There is general rejoicing. A Sorceress (ms) concocts a plan with her witches to destroy Dido's court: after she has disrupted the royal hunt with a storm, one of her assistants will appear as Mercury and persuade Aeneas to leave. As Aeneas prepares to sail, the witches rejoice. Fearing that she is being betrayed, Dido is unimpressed by his decision to defy Mercury and stay, and dismisses him. In desolation she prepares for death with her famous lament, '*When I am laid in earth*'.

MAURICE RAVEL

Born Ciboure, Basses Pyrénées, 1875, died Paris 1937. Of Swiss-Basque descent, he grew up in Paris. The success of his early piano works was increased by his imaginative orchestrations of several of them.

Polished colourings abound in his largely impressionistic orchestral works and in his two operas, *L'Heure Espagnole* (1911) and *L'Enfant et les Sortilèges* (The Child and the Magic, 1925).

L'HEURE ESPAGNOLE (THE SPANISH HOUR)

In one act, text by Franc-Nohain after his own comedy. Premiere: Opéra-Comique, Paris, 1911. Gallic wit and Spanish atmosphere combine here in elegant impudence.

Toledo, 18th century: the absent-minded clockmaker Torquemada (t) goes off to wind the municipal clocks, leaving the muleteer Ramiro (bar) in his shop to wait for his return. This inconveniences Concepción (s), Torquemada's wife, who counts on this weekly hour to meet her lovers; she sets him to carry a grandfather clock upstairs. The poet Gonsalve (t) arrives to see her, but babbles unsatisfactorily; the banker Don Inigo (b) also leaves her frustrated. Each in turn is hidden in a clock. Finally Concepción, admiring Ramiro's strength, takes him up to her room. Torquemada returns and makes quick sales to the two admirers he finds 'examining' clocks.

NIKOLAI RIMSKY-KORSAKOV

Born Tikhvin, Novgorod region, 1844, died Lyubensk, St Petersburg region, 1908. He began composing while still a naval officer. His First Symphony earned him a professorship at St Petersburg Conservatory. A country childhood had exposed him to folk song, and all but two of his 15 operas are on Russian nationalistic themes. An inspired orchestrator, he was the leading theorist among the Russian group of composers, including Mussorgsky, known as 'The Five'.

ZOLOTOY PYETUSHOK (LE COQ D'OR/THE GOLDEN COCKEREL)

In three acts, with text by Vladimir Bielsky after Pushkin's poem. Premiere: Solodovnikov Theatre, Moscow, 1909. Rimsky-Korsakov's spectacular last opera, premiered after his death because the censor found elements parodying the Tsar's court, this subtle score requires its principals to dance.

In and near King Dodon's palace on the Southern Steppes, in legendary times: worrying over military strategy with his sons, Princes Guidon (t) and Afron (bar), the ageing Dodon (b) is given by the Astrologer (t) a miraculous Golden Cockerel (s), which crows at imminent danger. The Astrologer at first refuses payment for it. After two warning cries from the Cockerel, Dodon goes to war and encounters the seductive Queen Shemakha (s): she sings her famous Hymn to the Sun and agrees to marry him. When the Astrologer demands the Queen as payment for the bird, Dodon kills him. But the Cockerel kills Dodon and, together with the Queen, disappears.

GIOACHINO ROSSINI

Brought up in a theatrical milieu, Rossini at 14 entered the Bologna Liceo Musicale. His early operas, beginning with *La Cambiale di Matrimonio* (1810), were one-act farces in the *opera buffa* style. Their success brought a La Scala commission, *La Pietra del Paragone* (1812), in which the 'Rossini crescendo' was first heard. *Tancredi* (1813), his first serious opera, followed by the comic *L'Italiana in Algeri* (1813), launched him on a major career. His first of many operas for Naples, *Elisabetta, Regina d'Inghilterra* (1815), was written for the diva Isabella Colbran, later his wife. *Il Barbiere di Siviglia* (1816) was scorned by the Roman audience at its premiere, but other productions soon bought it great popularity and it remains a universal

favourite. The flowing melody, felicitous harmonies and dramatic ensembles create rounded characters, unlike the stock *commedia* figures of *opera buffa* or the shallow ones of *opera seria*. From 1824 Rossini was based in Paris: *Guillaume Tell* (1829) found him at the height of his powers. At the age of 37, the outstanding composer of opera of that time, he produced no further work of this kind.

IL BARBIERE DI SIVIGLIA

(THE BARBER OF SEVILLE)

Figaro, a barber	baritone
Count Almaviva	tenor
Rosina	mezzo-soprano
Dr Bartolo, her guardian	baritone
Don Basilio, a music master	bass
Berta, Dr Bartolo's maid	soprano

Seville, 17th century: the ingenious Figaro helps Count Almaviva to rescue Rosina from her scheming guardian Dr Bartolo and to marry her.

The libretto is by Cesare Sterbini, based on the first of three plays about Figaro by Beaumarchais. (Mozart's *Le Nozze di Figaro*, though written earlier, relates to the second play.) The first performance of the opera, which had been composed in less than three weeks, was at the Teatro Argentina, Rome, in 1816.

Outside the house of Dr Bartolo
Largo al factotum della città ('Make way for the factotum of the city'): Figaro's famous song of self-congratulation

ACT I

Almaviva and the chorus are serenading Rosina as Figaro, Seville's ubiquitous barber, appears. Recognizing the Count, he immediately offers to assist his suit. Rosina herself appears, holding a note. She is followed closely by Dr Bartolo. When he asks what she is holding, she says it is a song, 'The Useless Precaution', and promptly drops it. The Count swiftly retrieves it so that when Bartolo reaches the spot it has apparently been blown away. Figaro warns the Count that Bartolo plans to marry her as soon as possible – in fact the next day. Bartolo leaves and the Count calls out to Rosina that he is a poor student called Lindoro who loves her desparately. Encouraged by her reply, he engages Figaro to outwit Bartolo. The first plan is to disguise the Count as a soldier billeted on Bartolo's household; Figaro's additional idea is that the soldier should pretend to be drunk.

A room in Dr Bartolo's house
Una voce poco fa ('A voice in the distance'): Rosina reflects on her attraction to 'Lindoro'
La calunnia è un venticello ('Slander is a powerful weapon'): Basilio plans a whispering campaign against the Count
Dunque io son? ('It is I he loves?'): Rosina learns that her love is reciprocated by 'Lindoro'
A un dottor della mia sorte ('To a doctor as clever as I'): Dr Bartolo warns Rosina that he is not to be deceived

Rosina, alone, sings of how 'Lindoro' has touched her heart. Figaro arrives and is about to tell her the plan when, hearing Bartolo, he has to hide. Bartolo is joined by Don Basilio, the music master, who proposes to unleash a hurricane of malicious rumours about the Count. Figaro, who has overheard it all, warns Rosina, and he tells her that 'Lindoro' is in love with her. She is delighted, and Figaro asks her to write a letter to him. Despite pretended reluctance, she has a letter already prepared.

Bartolo returns and immediately sees that she has been writing and that a sheet of paper is missing. Brushing aside her ingenious explanations, he warns her that she needs to be more subtle to trick him. A knocking is heard: it is a drunken soldier (the Count). Bartolo tries to deny him lodging. Rosina arrives and he tries to slip her a note while Bartolo is looking for the papers which exempt him from military billets. Bartolo sees the note and, although Rosina gets it first and substitutes the laundry list, a quarrel ensues involving successively Berta, his housekeeper, Don Basilio and Figaro. It is only resolved when an officer of the watch arrives to investigate the racket. He prepares to arrest the soldier, who secretly shows him proof that he is a nobleman and thus above the law. All are amazed at the turn of events, and there is general agreement that their heads are spinning with the day's confusion.

Fredda ed immobile ('As still as a statue'): a sextet centering on Bartolo's surprise at the soldier's immunity from arrest

A room in Dr Bartolo's house

ACT II

Bartolo is worried that the soldier may have been an agent of Count Almaviva. More knocking announces the arrival of a new music master (the Count again) standing in for Don Basilio, who is said to be ill. His elaborate politeness arouses Bartolo's suspicions but, when he produces Rosina's letter, claiming to have acquired it from another of the Count's lovers and suggesting that it is used to show Rosina that the Count is playing with her affections, Bartolo's confidence in the 'music master' is established.

Contro un cor che accende amore ('Against a heart inflamed by love'): with her new music master seated at the piano, Rosina has a singing lesson

Rosina recognizes the new arrival immediately and in her music lession sings of how feeble tyranny becomes when faced with true love. This inspires Bartolo to sing himself. Figaro returns and insists on shaving Bartolo to give the lovers a chance to plan their escape. Figaro succeeds in getting the key to Rosina's balcony; but suddenly Don Basilio arrives. Eventually the Count manages to confuse Bartolo and persuade Basilio that he really is ill and must go back to bed at once, assisted by a purse.

Alone at last, the lovers arrange to elope at midnight, but Bartolo is on the alert. Overhearing them, he throws the conspirators out of the house before the Count can explain to Rosina the trick of giving her letter to Bartolo to disarm his suspicions. Berta, on her own, reflects on the contrast with her own single state. Meanwhile Basilio is back, and Bartolo, realizing that the 'music master' must have been the Count, decides to act at once. Despatching Basilio to fetch a lawyer, he shows the letter to Rosina, suggesting that her young man is working for Count Almaviva. She is appalled. With sorrow she agrees to marry him and confesses the plan to elope that night. Thus, when midnight comes, with a storm raging outside, the conspirators are met by a furious Rosina. At once the Count reveals that Lindoro and Almaviva are one and the same. All is well, and they fall into each other's arms while Figaro tries to hurry them away. But then they discover their ladder has gone. Trapped, they decide to brazen it out. Basilio and the notary arrive and are swiftly persuaded (with a jewel backed up by a loaded pistol) to join with the Count. By the time Bartolo returns, the young lovers are married and he is too late. Indeed, as Figaro points out, removing the ladder was a useless precaution.

LA CENERENTOLA

(CINDERELLA)

Cenerentola (Cinderella)	contralto (or mezzo-soprano)
Prince Ramiro	tenor
Dandini, a courtier	baritone
Don Magnifico	bass
Clorinda } daughters of	soprano
Tisbe } Don Magnifico	mezzo-soprano
Alidoro, Prince Ramiro's tutor	bass

Italy: Rossini's version of the story of Cinderella, in which the Prince is assisted in his search for a bride by his servant Dandini and tutor Alidoro, who escorts Cenerentola (Cinderella) to the ball. The next day the Prince recognizes her by her bracelet.

The libretto is by Jacopo Ferretti; the opera was premiered at the Teatro Valle, Rome, in 1817.

Don Magnifico's palace

Una volta c'era un rè ('Once upon a time there was a king'): Cenerentola's sad folk song describing her drudgery

Un soave non so che ('What lovely eyes'): Cenerentola and Prince Ramiro's love duet

Come un'ape ne giorni d'aprile ('As bees in springtime'): Dandini's extravagant overplaying of his role as the Prince
Là del ciel nell' arcano profondo ('Hidden in heaven'): Alidoro's comforting prophesy that Cenerentola's lot will improve

Prince Ramiro's palace

Mi par d'essere sognando ('Like a dream'): the expression of incredulity and wonder at the appearance of Cenerentola

Prince Ramiro's palace

Sia qualunque delle figlie ('Whichever gains the throne'): Magnifico's anxiety to be recognized as the power behind the throne whichever of his daughters is chosen by the Prince

Un segreto d'importanza ('Let me explain'): the comic duet between two buffoons, Magnifico and Dandini

Don Magnifico's palace

ACT I

In their father's battered palace, Clorinda and Tisbe are trying on hats and practising dancing while Don Magnifico's stepdaughter Cenerentola (Cinderella) gets on with the housework. She welcomes a beggar (Alidoro in disguise), though her stepsisters try to throw him out. The announcement that Prince Ramiro is coming to deliver an invitation to a ball is greeted with great excitement.

The Prince arrives, disguised as his valet, as devised by Alidoro, and is enchanted by Cenerentola. She has to attend to her work, and the Prince, alone, wonders why she is so poorly dressed. Dandini, his real servant, arrives, delighted to play the part of the Prince. His ridiculous grandeur creates a fine impression. Don Magnifico indignantly refuses to allow Cenerentola to join the party and when Alidoro returns, not in disguise, to enquire about the third sister listed in the social register, Magnifico pretends that the missing girl has died. Once the others have gone, Alidoro promises Cenerentola that she will go to the ball and that he will provide her with a dress and jewels.

Dandini, as the Prince, has appointed Magnifico chief wine-taster; the two elder sisters wrangle over the Prince. The Prince, advised that he should marry one of Magnifico's daughters, is confused to learn from Dandini that both are frightful. Suddenly a new guest is announced: Cenerentola appears, gorgeously dressed and wearing a pair of matching bracelets. There follows an ensemble in which everyone joins in, with conflicting sentiments.

ACT II

Magnifico and his two daughters, despite the arrival of the beautiful stranger, are confident that one of the sisters will capture the Prince. Meanwhile, Dandini has fallen for Cenerentola. When she turns him down, confessing that she loves his servant, she is overheard by the Prince, who joyfully comes forward to claim her. But he too is spurned. She gives him one of the two bracelets and promises to be his only if he seeks her out and repeats his proposal in whatever circumstances he finds her.

The Prince resumes his proper role and Dandini reverts to being his valet. When Magnifico returns to ask which of his daughters Dandini has chosen, it takes time for the hoax to be explained to him.

Cenerentola is back in rags, still wearing the second bracelet, when Magnifico and his daughters return. A storm, reflected in the music, leads the Prince and Dandini to take shelter under Magnifico's roof. When Cenerentola is ordered to bring a chair, she and the Prince recognize each other. He sees the bracelet, and the story is complete. An intricate ensemble gives the characters in turn an opportunity to express their feelings.

Prince Ramiro's palace
Nacqui all'affanno ('Born to sadness'): Cenerentola extends her happiness to the rest of her family

Back in the palace, the opera finishes with Cenerentola's sparkling *rondò*, in which she forgives her stepfather and her stepsisters while the others admire her generosity.

L'ITALIANA IN ALGERI

(THE ITALIAN GIRL IN ALGIERS)

In two acts (eight scenes), with text by Angelo Anelli, originally written for Luigi Mosca. Premiere: Teatro San Benedetto, Venice, 1813. A genial comedy that sparkles with youthful promise, it was written in four weeks by the 21-year-old Rossini.

The Bey's palace, Algiers: the lady in question, Isabella (**ms**), has travelled widely in her search for her lover Lindoro (**t**), who has been enslaved by the Bey of Algiers, Mustafà (**b**). Escorted by her elderly admirer Taddeo (**bar**), whom she passes off as her uncle, she has been shipwrecked and taken to the palace, where she recognizes Lindoro. Mustafà offers Lindoro his freedom if he marries Elvira (**s**), the wife he no longer loves. Isabella promises Mustafà her affection if he will join the order of 'Pappatacci' (their rule: 'eat and keep quiet'). With the help of her compatriots at the palace, he is 'initiated' and they all escape by sea. Realizing his mistake, Mustafà returns to Elvira.

SEMIRAMIDE

In two acts, with text by Gaetano Rossi, after Voltaire's tragedy *Sémiramis*. Premiere: La Fenice, Venice, 1823. One of Rossini's grander tragedies, its title role was written for the Spanish soprano Isabella Colbran, Rossini's first wife.

Ancient Babylon: Semiramide (**s**), Queen of Babylon, with the help of Prince Assur (**bar**) who wants her hand and the throne, has murdered her husband Nino. She has meanwhile fallen for the Assyrian commander Arsace (**c**), not realizing he is her son. The high priest Oroe (**b**), who alone knows this, tells Arsace, who loves Princess Azema (**s**). When Semiramide declares her intent to marry Arsace, Nino's ghost (**b**) announces Arsace as his successor – after crimes have been expiated. Angry at this, Assur follows Arsace back to Nino's tomb, intending to kill him. Semiramide is now aware that Arsace is her son and warns him against Assur. Coming between the two men, she receives the death blow Arsace intends for Assur. (In a revised version, Arsace kills Assur). Arsace ascends the throne.

LE COMTE ORY
(COUNT ORY)

In two acts, with text by Eugène Scribe and Charles-Gaspard Delestre-Poirson, based on an old Picardy legend. Premiere: Opéra, Paris, 1828. Rossini's only comic opera in French, it elegantly re-uses several numbers from his unsuccessful *Il Viaggio à Reims* (*The Journey to Rheims*).

Touraine, during the Crusades: the decadent Count Ory (**t**) and his friend Raimbaud (**bar**) attempt to win over the Countess Adèle (**s**), who has forsworn the company of men during her brother's absence on the Crusades. Her companion Ragonde (**c**) consults a 'hermit' – in reality Ory – over the Countess' depressed state. The Count's tutor (**b**) and his page Isolier (**m-s**), who also loves the Countess, devise a plan to enter her castle dressed as pilgrims. Not to be outdone, the Count goes in as the Mother Superior of a group of nuns, who raid the cellars. The crusaders return just as the revels are getting out of control, and the Count and his cronies escape.

GUILLAUME TELL
(WILLIAM TELL)

In four acts, with text by Etienne de Jouy, Hippolyte-Louis-Florent Bis and Armand Marast, after Schiller's drama. Premiere: Opéra, Paris, 1829. This is Rossini's ambitious final opera, in Parisian grand opera style, with the most famous Italian overture ever written.

Switzerland, under Austrian rule, 13th century: while Tell (**bar**) wants to liberate Switzerland, the young Arnold (**t**), also Swiss, is in love with Mathilde (**s**), sister of the hated Austrian governor Gessler (**b**). The Austrians seize and kill Arnold's father Melcthal (**b**) in exchange for an escaped prisoner: Arnold's patriotism hardens. Tell and his son Jemmy (**s**) refuse to acknowledge Gessler's hat; he is forced to shoot an apple on his son's head. Despite succeeding, he is arrested on confessing that the next arrow was destined for Gessler. Jemmy sets fire to Tell's house as a signal that the rebellion has begun. Allowed to pilot a boat carrying Gessler in a storm, Tell escapes ashore and shoots Gessler when he lands. The Swiss are victorious.

CAMILLE SAINT-SAENS

Born Paris 1835, died Algiers 1921. A child prodigy, Saint-Saëns gave his first public performance at the piano aged ten. After studying at the Paris Conservatoire with Halévy, he became organist of the church of La Madeleine in 1857. Musicologist, piano virtuoso and conductor, he taught and also wrote plays, poetry and music criticism; and he was interested in astronomy and archaeology. Through the Société Nationale de Musique, which he joined in 1871, he encouraged the performance of new music by the younger generation. Only one of his operas remains in the modern repertoire: *Samson et Dalila* (1877). It was successfully premiered at Weimar under the aegis of his friend Liszt, but there was no major production in Paris until 1892.

SAMSON ET DALILA

(SAMSON AND DALILA)

Dalila, a Philistine	mezzo-soprano	
Samson, leader of the Hebrews	tenor	
Abimélech, the Philistine Satrap of Gaza	bass	

Palestine, Old Testament times: Dalila seduces Samson, leader of the Hebrews. Dramatically, he avenges her betrayal of his love, as recounted in *The Book of Judges*.

The libretto is by Ferdinand Lemaire. Destined for the Paris Opéra, the Franco-Prussian War interrupted completion of the work. Promoted by Liszt, it was given its first performance at the Hoftheater, Weimar, in 1877.

A square in Gaza

Arrêtez, ô mes frères ('Stop complaining, comrades'): Samson's stern reproach to the Hebrews
Qui donc élève ici la voix? ('Who dares to raise their voice?'): Abimélech's attempt to restore order, ending in his death at the hands of Samson
Maudite à jamais soit la race ('Eternal anathema'): the High Priest's dreadful denunciation of Israel

ACT I

Gathered in front of the temple of Dagon, the Hebrews bewail their oppression by the Philistines. From among them Samson at last stirs them to action, urging them to pray to Jehovah the Lord of Hosts. The unaccustomed noise of their fervour brings Abimélech, the local leader of the Philistines, to investigate. He taunts the Hebrews with the weakness of their god as compared with the redoubtable Dagon. Samson rouses the crowd still more. Abimélech attacks him and Samson seizes the sword and slays the Philistine. At this, the High Priest of Dagon comes out of the temple. He pronounces a grand and solemn curse on the Hebrews, predicting that their leader will be betrayed by a faithless woman.

As the Philistine men take to the hills, their women, among them the enchanting Dalila, come to pay homage

261

Je viens célébrer la victoire ('Come celebrate your victory'): Dalila makes no secret of her feelings
Printemps qui commence ('With the coming of Spring'): Dalila's seductive aria which wins Samson's heart

The valley of Sorek
Il faut, pour assouvir ma haine ('To gratify my hate'): Dalila plans to seduce Samson only in order to find a way of destroying him

Mon cœur s'ouvre à ta voix ('My heart opens to the sound of your voice'): Dalila, in her deceit, begs Samson to stay with her forever

In the prison
Vois ma misère, hélas! ('You see my distress Oh Lord'): Samson's groans under the weight of his despair

In the temple of Dagon

Laisse-moi prendre ta main ('Do let me take your hand'): Dalila's aria mocking her blinded victim
Gloire à Dagon vainqueur ('Glory to all-powerful Dagon'): the High Priest and Dalila's hymn to Dagon

to Spring and to their new masters. Dalila reminds Samson that she waits for him with open arms. An old Hebrew warns Samson to ignore her dangerous offer. As she launches into the opera's most famous and beautiful aria, Samson succumbs.

ACT II
At her home, Dalila is waiting to ensnare Samson, whom she once loved. She greets the High Priest of Dagon and is able to reassure him that her power over Samson is as strong as ever. He offers her money to betray him. She scornfully rejects this, saying that she herself longs to see him in chains. But they have yet to discover the secret of Samson's exceptional strength. After the priest has left, Samson is drawn back to Dalila against his better judgement. Overcoming her true feelings of hatred, she passionately embraces him.

Dalila knows that some vow which Samson has made to Jehovah gives him his strength and she now asks him to confide this in her as proof of his love. He refuses and she reproaches him for not trusting her. She runs into her house and, after a moment of terrible indecision, he runs in after her. Philistine soldiers quietly encircle the house. Suddenly Dalila throws open the window with a triumphant cry. Samson is caught.

ACT III
Samson, chained, blinded and with his hair shorn, is forced to work the grindstone. In the background can be heard the voices of the Hebrews reproaching him for betraying his god and his people. He prays to Jehovah to accept his life by way of atonement.

Samson is led in by a child to a scene of the Philistines feasting and dancing. The High Priest ironically welcomes Samson and encourages Dalila to make fun of him. She dances up to him and playfully reminds him of her successful trap. His desperate prayers serve to encourage the Philistines' taunts, and Dalila and the High Priest launch themselves into an ecstatic hymn to Dagon.

The High Priest orders the child to lead Samson to the centre of the temple and Samson, pleading for inspiration, asks to be placed between the pillars. As the celebration reaches its height, Samson offers up a final prayer. Bowing himself, with all his might, he pulls down the pillars and the whole temple collapses, crushing all within.

ARNOLD SCHOENBERG

Born Vienna 1874, died Los Angeles 1951. After teaching in Vienna and Berlin, he was forced out by the Nazis and moved to California in 1934. At first composing in late Romantic style, he gradually moved to atonality before inventing serialism (giving equal prominence to all 12 semitones in the scale). He wrote four operas: *Erwartung* (*Expectation*, 1909), *Die Glückliche Hand* (*The Lucky Hand*, 1913), *Von Heute auf Morgen* (*From One Day to the Next*, 1929) and *Moses und Aron* (1957).

MOSES UND ARON (MOSES AND AARON)

In three acts, with text by the composer derived from The Bible (*Exodus 3, 4* and *22*). Premiere: Stadttheater, Zurich, 1957. A powerful exploration of the difficulties of communication between God and Man; its third act, left uncomposed, is sometimes spoken over other music by Schoenberg.

Egypt and the Sinai desert, 14th century BC: Moses (**b, speaking role**), a thinker but inarticulate, is appointed by God to be leader of the Israelites; his brother Aron (**t**) will act as his spokesman. Encouraged by miracles, the people pledge allegiance to God. In Moses' long absence on Mount Sinai receiving the Ten Commandments, Aron encourages the construction of a Golden Calf, which reflects the people's wavering faith. There is an extended erotic orgy (The Dance before the Golden Calf). Furious with Aron on his return, Moses destroys the Calf and smashes the tablets of stone he has brought down from Sinai. Aron, in chains, attempts to defend himself; released by Moses, he falls dead.

DMITRI SHOSTAKOVICH

Born St Petersburg 1906, died Moscow 1975. He became a member of the Leningrad avant-garde in his twenties, after the success of his First Symphony, and wrote his first opera, *The Nose* (1928), a satirical comedy. The core of his output is his fifteen symphonies and string quartets. Apart from a musical comedy about Moscow and orchestrations of Mussorgsky's *Boris Godunov* (1940) and *Khovanshchina* (1959), his only other complete operatic work is *Lady Macbeth of the Mtsensk District*.

LEDI MAKBET MTSENSKOVO UYEZDA
(LADY MACBETH OF THE MTSENSK DISTRICT)

In four acts (nine scenes), with text by the composer and A. Preis, after N. Leskov's story. Premiere: Maly Theatre, Leningrad, 1934. This acidly cutting parody of bourgeois morality earned Shostakovich official discredit until it was (slightly) revised much later.

Kursk Gubernia, Russia, *c.* 1865: bored with her sterile marriage to Zinovy (**t**), Katerina (**s**) has a passionate affair with the feckless Sergei (**t**), a recent recruit to the family business. She poisons her father-in-law Boris (**b**) when he punishes Sergei. She later strangles Zinovy with Sergei's help. The lovers marry. Returning from the wedding, they are arrested. On their way to exile in Siberia, Sergei flirts with Sonyetka (**c**), a convict. Katerina is furious, grabs her and jumps off a bridge with her into a river, where they drown.

BEDRICH SMETANA

Born Litomyšl, Bohemia, 1824, died Prague 1884. Smetana is regarded as the founder of Czech nationalist music, his comic masterpiece *Prodana Nevesta* (*The Bartered Bride*, 1866) celebrating Bohemian village life and his cycle of symphonic tone poems *Má Vlast* (1874–79) creating a portrait in music of his country. As a boy he displayed formidable musical talent. He became a virtuoso pianist and composed music for the piano. After teaching and conducting in Sweden, from 1856 to 1861, he returned to Prague, determining to write operas for the new Provisional Theatre. *The Brandenburgers in Bohemia* was performed there in 1866, the same year as *The Bartered Bride*. This last, with its infectious comic spirit and folk-like melodies is today a popular opera in the international repertoire, but Smetana's later operas, such as *Dalibor* (1868) and *Libuše* (1881) are rarely heard outside Czechoslovakia.

PRODANA NEVESTA

(THE BARTERED BRIDE)

Mařenka	soprano
Jeník, her suitor	tenor
Vašek, his half-brother	tenor
Kečal, a marriage broker	bass
Esmeralda, a circus girl	soprano

Bohemia, 19th century: the village marriage broker thinks that he has persuaded Jeník to exchange Mařenka, who has promised to be his bride, for money; and so for a time does Mařenka.

The libretto of *The Bartered Bride* (*Prodaná Nevěsta*) is by Karel Sabina. The first performance of the opera, conducted by the composer, was given in Prague in 1866.

A village green

Věrné milování ('Faithful at heart'): Mařenka and Jeník sing of their love

ACT I

The villagers are enjoying the fair but Jeník and Mařenka are in despair: she has been promised by her parents to the son of a rich neighbour. They pledge to be faithful to each other, but Mařenka worries that Jeník's reticence about his past may conceal another woman.

Mařenka's parents are negotiating with Kečal, the marriage broker. They are agreed that Mařenka should marry one of their neighbour's sons: the elder one was chased out of the house by his stepmother, and that leaves Vašek. When they break the news to Mařenka, she retorts that she has already sworn to be faithful to Jeník. Kečal believes that he can overcome any obstacle. Meanwhile, life in the village proceeds with a festive polka.

A village inn

To pivečko ('Heavenly beer'): the villagers' hymn to beer

ACT II

The villagers sing a splendid chorus in praise of beer. They warn Jeník against Kečal before dancing a furiant. The simpleton Vašek approaches, muttering his misgiving at being pushed into marriage by his mother. Mařenka realizes who he is, though he does not recognize her. She warns him that everyone knows that the flighty Mařenka is in love with somebody else and would probably poison him to get his money after the wedding. She tells him that there is another girl who loves him dearly. 'If she is like you', he replies, 'I would certainly marry her'. Mařenka promises that she will love him if he swears not to marry Mařenka; this he haltingly does.

Kečal is trying to divert Jeník either with a rich bride or with money. Jeník maintains that Mařenka is the only bride for him.

Jak možná věřit ('Who would ever believe'): Jeník is as amazed that anyone could believe that he could barter Mařenka for money, and he is delighted by his trick

After some hard bargaining, Jeník agrees to renounce Mařenka for three hundred crowns (paid for out of Kečal's fee); but only if she marries the rich neighbour's son. When Kečal goes off to get witnesses, Jeník congratulates himself on a bargain – he is, of course, the missing elder son. Kečal returns with the villagers, who are dismayed that Jeník can forsake Mařenka and outraged that he should have bartered her for money. Even Mařenka's father is angered by Jeník's apparent greed.

The village green

ACT III

Vašek is still worrying about being poisoned by the bride his parents have chosen. A group of comedians enters and the leader announces that the highlight of the fair will be the beautiful Esmeralda dancing with a bear. Vašek is stunned by Esmeralda's beauty. When it emerges that the man who plays the bear is drunk, Esmeralda promises to marry Vašek if he will put on the bearskin and dance.

Milostné zvířátko ('A perfect bear'): Esmeralda and the chief comedian encourage Vašek to join their troupe

When Vašek's parents arrive, they are astonished to hear that two strange women have each promised to marry Vašek and that nothing would induce him to marry Mařenka. After he has left, Mařenka rushes in. She refuses to believe that Jeník has bartered their happiness, even when she is shown his signature on the contract.

Ten lásky sen ('My dream of love'): Mařenka's disbelief that Jeník has abandoned her

Believing that Jeník has deceived her, Mařenka will not let him explain. His laughter only infuriates her the more. Everyone assembles and Jeník reveals that he, too, is a son of Vašek's father, as specified in the contract, and that Mařenka must choose between the two. With the marriage broker's reputation in ruins, the two lovers are reunited. But suddenly there is an uproar. A bear is loose in the village. When it turns out to be Vašek, his parents are persuaded that he is still a little boy and give their blessing to the marriage of Jeník and Mařenka.

JOHANN STRAUSS

Born Vienna 1825, died Vienna 1899. The son of a leading Viennese conductor and composer of waltzes (Johann Strauss the elder), he had founded his own small orchestra by the age of 19. His compositions – polkas, gallops and quadrilles, as well as waltzes – were so popular throughout Europe in the 1860s that he became known as the 'King of Waltzes': the *Blue Danube* was written in 1867. With *Die Fledermaus* (1874), Strauss composed some of the most sparkling and delightful melodies of his career. He had been inspired by the success of Offenbach's operettas in Vienna and encouraged to emulate them by the directors of the Theater an der Wien. Of Strauss' 17 other stage works, only *Der Zigeunerbaron* (1885) continues to be performed. *Fledermaus* moved from the theatre to opera house when it entered the Staatsoper repertoire in 1899, with Strauss conducting the overture at the premiere.

DIE FLEDERMAUS

(THE BAT)

Rosalinde	soprano
Adele, her maid	soprano
Eisenstein, her husband	tenor
Alfred, her lover	tenor
Prince Orlofsky	mezzo-soprano
Dr Falke	baritone
Frank, the prison governor	baritone

Vienna, c. 1850: Dr Falke takes revenge on his friend Eisenstein with an elaborate practical joke.

The libretto is by Carl Haffner, following the plot of the farce *Le Réveillon* by Meilhac and Halévy. The first performance was on Easter Sunday 1874, with Marie Geistinger as Rosalinde. She had recently had a great success with a *csárdás* written by Strauss for her to sing at a charity concert in aid of the Hungarians. The national song is heard in Act II, where Rosalinde pretends to be a Hungarian countess.

A room in Eisenstein's house

ACT I

Three years before, Dr Falke, disguised as a bat (*Fledermaus*) for a fancy dress ball, was made to walk home in broad daylight as a joke by his friend Eisenstein. Ever since, he has been plotting his revenge. He arranges for Eisenstein to attend a party where his behaviour will be watched by his wife, in disguise.

Outside Eisenstein's house Alfred, Rosalinde's former lover, has returned to serenade her. Inside, the maid

Adele has received a letter, apparently from her sister Ida (in fact forged by Dr Falke), inviting her to a masked party if she can take the evening off.

Rosalinde is excited that Alfred is back, but at first she deals with Adele, denying her permission to visit an (imaginary) ailing aunt. Entranced by his singing, she agrees to let Alfred return later and then hears from her husband that his lawyer Blind has so mishandled a lawsuit for a minor offence that he has to leave immediately for a prison sentence that has been extended to eight days. Dr Falke arrives and whispers an invitation to Eisenstein to call in at a party for delicious young ballerinas on his way to prison. Eisenstein enthusiastically accepts, concealing it from his wife, and husband and wife part painfully – he rushing off to the party as the 'Marquis Renard' and she finally agreeing to give Adele the evening off so that she can receive Alfred alone.

Alfred, wearing Eisenstein's dressing-gown, is trying to make Rosalinde forget she is married when Frank, the prison governor, arrives to arrest her husband. He mistakes Alfred for Eisenstein, and Rosalinde covers up Alfred's denial by insisting that of course he is her husband. Who else would be dining alone with her? Alfred reluctantly falls in with the deception, going off to prison after a prolonged farewell.

ACT II
Prince Orlofsky, a Russian roué, is host at the party. Adele's sister Ida is surprised to see Adele there (having no knowledge of Dr Falke's invitation). Orlofsky is bored and Dr Falke amuses him with the details of his joke. The 'Marquis' (Eisenstein) arrives and Orlofsky explains that the only demand he makes of his guests is that they match his appetite for wine or get thrown out. It is just a custom: 'chacun à son gout'

Eisenstein is astounded to see Adele but she makes fun of him saying she is called Olga and is surely prettier than any lady's maid. The prison governor, appears, also with a pseudonym: 'Chevalier Chagrin'. Eisenstein and Frank do their best to carry off the parts that Dr Falke has given them as Frenchmen.

They are waiting for only one more guest, a Hungarian countess (Rosalinde, summoned by Dr Falke). She arrives, masked, and Eisenstein immediately pursues her, using the little pocket watch which he claims makes any woman his within ten minutes. Rosalinde recognizes him and is not amused. She contrives to make off with the watch just as Eisenstein believes her to be ready to yield to him. She quells any doubts that she is truly Hungarian by singing the celebrated csárdás.

Komm mit mir zum souper ('Come and dine'): Dr Falke's invitation to Eisenstein to join him at a party
Trinke, Liebchen, trinke schnell ('Drink up, my darling'): Alfred's duet with Rosalinde in which he encourages her to enjoy herself in Eisenstein's absence
Mein Herr, was dächten Sie von mir ('Dear Sir, what do you mean'): Rosalinde's insistent false declaration that Alfred is indeed her husband Eisenstein

Prince Orlofsky's villa
Ein Souper heut uns winkt ('A supper party is planned'): the opening chorus at Orlofsky's party
Ich lade gern mir Gäste ein ('My guests must expect'): Orlofsky's aria about what he expects of his guests.

Mein Herr Marquis ('My dear Marquis'): Adele's aria pretending to object to being taken for a lady's maid

Die Klänge meiner Heimat ('The song of my homeland'): Rosalinde sings a Hungarian national song in praise of her native countryside

Brüderlein und Schwesterlein ('Brotherhood and sisterhood'): Dr Falke leads the chorus in praise of companionship

The prison governor's office

Spiel' ich die Unschuld vom Lande ('I can play the part of a country girl'): Adele's aria displaying her talents as an actress

So rächt sich die Fledermaus! ('This is the bat's revenge'): the chorus celebrating the bat's triumph

Dr Falke and Eisenstein are persuaded to tell the story of the bat, and Orlofsky, enchanted, leads the whole party in a song about the delights of champagne. Dr Falke follows this with a song about companionship. Eisenstein is now determined to see his companion's face. Suddenly the clock strikes six: it is morning, and he has to hurry off to prison.

ACT III
The jailer Frosch is having difficulty with a merry Alfred (supposedly Eisenstein and still wearing Eisenstein's dressing-gown). The governor returns, befuddled, from the party. He is delighted when Olga (Adele) turns up with Ida to ask him to help her train for a career on the stage. She admits that she really is a lady's maid but his outrage that she allowed him to kiss her hand is silenced by her pointing out that he had no such complaints about kissing her lips. She then proceeds to show him how well she can act any role, whether a peasant girl, a queen or an erring lady of Paris.

At this point the real Eisenstein is announced. Eisenstein is amazed to find that his friend from the previous evening is in fact the prison governor, and he has difficulty in convincing Frank that he is in truth Eisenstein since there is already a prisoner by his own name who was arrested while dining alone with his wife. Disguising himself in the lawyer Blind's wig, he cross-questions Alfred and Rosalinde, Alfred having sent for a lawyer. When he finally reveals in a rage who he is, Rosalinde counters his accusations by producing his little pocket watch. Dr Falke arrives with Prince Orlofsky to explain that it is all a joke and his revenge for the incident of the bat. Fortunately Eisenstein takes this to include Alfred's visit.

RICHARD STRAUSS

Born Munich 1864, died Garmisch-Partenkirken 1949. The son of a horn player, Strauss began to write music while still pursuing his academic studies. His acquaintance with Hans von Bülow introduced him to conducting, and in 1889 his symphonic tone poem *Don Juan* established his reputation for symphonic composition. The two early operas *Guntram* (1894) and *Feuersnot* (1901) in no sense anticipate the spectacular harmonic inventions of *Salome* (1905) and *Elektra* (1909). The operas' decadence made him notorious. *Elektra* was written with the poet and playwright Hugo von Hofmannsthal, and their collaboration – on six major works which included *Ariadne auf Naxos* (1912) and *Arabella* (1933) – was to last for twenty-five years. Their most famous joint creation was *Der Rosenkavalier* (1911), with its captivating Viennese waltzes, and acute portraits of the leading characters. In his later years his style became leaner and more in the manner of Mozart, as in his last opera *Capriccio* (1942).

SALOME

Salome, Princess of Judea	soprano	
Jochanaan (John the Baptist)	tenor	
Herod, King of Judea	tenor	

Galilee, c. AD30: Herod's infatuation with Salome is used by her to procure the head of Jochanaan (John the Baptist).

The libretto was adapted by Strauss from Oscar Wilde's erotic play based on the New Testament story. The opera was premiered at the Court Opera, Dresden, in 1905. At the Met, New York, in 1907 *Salome* was banned after the first performance.

The terrace of Herod's palace at Tiberias Galilee

Ich will deinen Mund küssen, Jochanaan ('I am going to kiss your mouth, Jochanaan'): Salome's lust for Herod's captive
Ah! Du wolltest mich nicht deinen Mund küssen lassen, Jochanaan ('You wouldn't let me kiss your mouth, Jochanaan'): Salome's ecstasy in contemplating the severed head

The officer of the watch is in love with Salome, daughter of Herod's wife, Herodias; but Salome is intrigued by the voice of Jochanaan (John the Baptist) prophesying from the dungeon below. She persuades the officer to bring the prisoner up. Though he denounces Salome's mother, her lust for the prisoner grows to the point of madness. He utterly rejects Salome.

Herod propositions Salome, his stepdaughter, and she agrees to perform the celebrated Dance of the Seven Veils for him in return for his agreeing to anything she desires. At the conclusion of the dance, she demands the head of Jochanaan. The King begs her to change her mind. When Jochanaan's gory head is brought to her on a silver dish, her mad, erotic incantations so disgust Herod that he orders Salome's immediate execution.

ELEKTRA

Klytemnästra (Klytemnestra), widow of Agamemnon		mezzo-soprano
Elektra	⎫ her daughters	soprano
Chrysothemis	⎭	soprano
Orest (Orestes), her son		baritone

Mycenae, in legendary times: Agamemnon's children, Elektra and Orest, avenge their father's murder.

Strauss saw Hugo von Hofmannsthal's play based on Sophocles' tragedy and initiated the idea of their partnership. Both composer and librettist concentrated more on the stark savagery of Ancient Greece than on the more conventional simplicity expressed, for example, in Gluck's *Orfeo ed Euridice*. The contrast between Elektra's sensuality, Chrysothemis' gentle femininity and their mother's tortured guilt produced the first of Strauss' celebrated combinations for two or three women's voices. *Elektra* was premiered at the Court Opera, Dresden, in 1909.

Courtyard of the palace of Mycenae

Agamemnon! Wo bist du, Vater? ('Agamemnon, where are you my father?'): Elektra's daily cry of grief for her murdered father
Ich hab's wie Feuer in der Brust ('My breast contains the fire of life'): Chrysothemis' craving for a normal life

Ich habe keine guten Nächte ('My sleep is never undisturbed'): Klytemnästra's complaint that her rest is plagued by nightmares

Klytemnästra and her lover Aegisth murdered her husband Agamemnon (by throwing a heavy net over him and slaughtering him in his bath) when he returned from the Trojan War. His son Orest fled abroad but his daughters Elektra and Chrysothemis remained.

The servants comment on Elektra's continuing grief for her father and her ill-treatment by his usurper Aegisth. Elektra enters. This is the very hour of her father's murder and she promises that his three children will unite to butcher his betrayers and dance on their bodies. She is joined by Chrysothemis, her sister. Chrysothemis does not share her sister's obsessions. She wishes to have children and to escape from the grim atmosphere of fear that Elektra creates around her. Chrysothemis warns her sister not to cross their mother that day.

Klytemnästra appears, lame and grotesquely depraved in appearance. Though asking why she is cursed with such a daughter at Elektra, she is nevertheless eager to talk to her about her nightmares. Elektra advises that a sacrifice is needed to bring her sleep. 'A virgin or an experienced woman?' 'Very experienced' is her daughter's reply.

Klytemnästra is confused by her daughter's riddles. She refuses to speak about the missing Orest and, when Elektra accuses her of trying to have Orest murdered, Klytemnästra responds by threatening to have Elektra tortured until she reveals the identity of the necessary

Was bluten muss? ('Whose blood?'): Elektra's gleeful portrayal of her mother's approaching fate

sacrifice . Elektra is only too happy to explain the secret. It is Klytemnästra's blood that must flow to appease the gods. Revelling in her spite, she describes her mother's dying moments to her. As Klytemnästra cowers in fear, a whispered message revives her. She staggers back into the palace as Chrysothemis appears with the news that Orest is dead. Distraught, Elektra demands that her sister help her to slay their mother and Aegisth. But Chrysothemis is incapable of this and, breaking free, leaves Elektra clawing dementedly in the ground for the axe that killed Agamemnon, watched by a silent stranger.

Orest! Orest! Orest!: the return of Orest arouses Elektra's tender sisterly love

The stranger is one of the bringers of the news of Orest's death. The woman's grief is such that he questions its cause. He discovers with astonishment that she is Elektra. He then reveals himself to be Orest, her brother, returning secretly to avenge their father. He goes into the palace to kill Klytemnästra. The servants are aroused by her dying screams and Elektra blocks the door. Aegisth, knowing nothing, approaches. Elektra offers to assist him into the palace, dancing round him. No sooner inside than he shouts for help and his face appears at the window. Demanding to know whether any man can hear him, the reply comes from Elektra that Agamemnon can hear him clearly.

Ob ich nicht höre? ('Can I hear it?'): Elektra hears in her mind the music of her triumphant dance of death

The women of the palace, Chrysothemis among them, hasten to salute the triumphant Orest. Elektra, her head full of supernatural music, celebrates the slaughter with a frenzied dance that ends with her death.

DER ROSENKAVALIER

(THE CAVALIER OF THE ROSE)

The Marschallin	soprano
Baron Ochs auf Lerchenau, her cousin	bass
Octavian	mezzo-soprano
Herr von Faninal	baritone
Sophie, his daughter	soprano

Vienna, mid-18th century: the end of Octavian's affair with the Marschallin as, wisely and painfully foreseen by her, he falls in love with a younger woman.

Written to a libretto by Hofmannsthal, the nostalgic portrait of 18th-century Vienna was premiered in Dresden in 1911. Not since *Figaro* had the classic combination of love, intrigue and humour been brought together to such effect. As in *Figaro*, the composer's instructions are crucial to the success of a production: the Marschallin is to be beautiful and 32, Baron Ochs 35 and Octavian 17.

STRAUSS, R.

The Marschallin's bedroom

Wie du warst! Wie du bist!
('What you were and are'):
Octavian and the Marschallin's
duet as morning light streams
into the room

Di rigori armato il seno
('Armoured against love'): the
Italian tenor shows off his voice
with a song about the
inadequacy of any defence
against love

Wo ist sie jetzt? ('Where is she
now?'): looking in the mirror
the Marschallin recalls her
childhood
Die Zeit im Grunde ('Time, in
the end'): the Marschallin
ponders on the passage of time
Heut' oder Morgen ('Today or
tomorrow'): sad in her
wisdom, she predicts the
inevitable end of their affair

Herr von Faninal's house

ACT I

After an erotic prelude, the Marschallin and Octavian, her lover, greet the morning with regret. He has to hide when her black page brings in her breakfast, and they quarrel briefly when she admits that she dreamed of her husband during the night.

Confused sounds warn them that something is wrong. For a moment she thinks it is her husband but it is the Marschallin's rustic cousin, Baron Ochs. As the Baron forces his way in, Octavian quickly dresses himself as her maid. Ochs is much distracted by the alluring result.

Baron Ochs has come to ask his cousin's advice about the presentation of the silver rose (a ceremony specially devised for this opera) to mark his engagement to Sophie von Faninal, the daughter of a rich army contractor.

While the Marschallin prepares for her levée, Ochs tries to make an assignation with her 'maid', boasting of his success with the women on his estate.

In come the day's attendants and supplicants: orphans, a man selling animals, a singer and a pair of Italian intriguers offering gossip. Ochs is engrossed in drawing up an unusual and advantageous marriage settlement when the hairdresser's lack of succes causes the Marschallin to send them all away. She promises to arrange the presentation of the silver rose for Ochs and he leaves after recruiting the Italians to promote his pursuit of the mysterious 'maid'.

Left alone, the Marschallin sings sadly of how she, too, once was forced into a similar marriage. She wishes that God would not let her see herself in old age so plainly. Octavian returns, in his own clothes, and tries to cheer her up. She reproaches him for being like all other men and prophesies that he will leave her. Having made him sad and jealous, she wryly reflects that now it is up to her to soothe the lover who will one day desert her – today or tomorrow. This stimulates a passionate contradiction from Octavian.

She, however, tells him that love must be taken lightly if one is to escape disaster and sends him off so that she may go to church. After he has left, she realizes that she forgot to kiss him. The footmen hurry after him, but it is too late. So she sends her page to follow him with the Baron's silver rose.

ACT II

There is great excitement as the bearer of the silver rose is awaited. Faninal is being directed by his majordomo. Sophie's chaperone describes the scene outside from the window. Sophie herself, alone since her mother's death, prays for guidance and for protection against pride.

272

Mir ist die Ehre widerfahren ('I have the honour'): Octavian's presentation of the silver rose to Sophie

Mit mir keine Kammer dir zu klein ('With me no room is too small'): Ochs' breezy waltz song assuring Sophie that no night with him would seem too long

A chambre séparée at an inn

Nein, nein, nein, nein! I trink' kein Wein ('No, no, no, no, I'll drink no wine'): the 'maid' spurns the Baron's pressing offer of wine

Papa! Papa! Papa!: the Baron's privacy is disturbed by screaming children and mysterious strangers

Octavian, splendidly dressed in white and silver, presents Sophie with the silver rose – ceremonial symbol of her engagement to Baron Ochs.

Sophie is overcome by the appearance of Octavian. He is amazed at her beauty, too, and there follows a long duet during which she admits she has been reading all about him in the court almanac. They are interrupted by her father introducing her future husband – an unpleasant shock, not improved by Ochs' elaborate condescension, battered complexion and open lust. His attempts to woo her with a cheerful song only make matters worse. When he goes next door to discuss the contract, Octavian and Sophie fall into each other's arms. They are caught and held by the two Italians, who release them to Ochs.

Ochs is not particularly worried, but Octavian insists on a duel, in which the former receives a slight scratch. In the subsequent uproar, Ochs' servants run amok and Sophie is ordered to her room. The Baron himself is restored by wine and, even more, by a note saying that the Marschallin's 'maid' will meet him for supper.

ACT III

Octavian, who has now recruited the Italians himself (Ochs was too mean), prepares an extensive tease on the Baron, hiding various people in and around the room, which is well furnished with trap doors and sliding panels. While the 'maid' scrutinizes her appearance in the mirror, the Baron blows out some of the candles and checks the bed behind a curtain in the alcove. Sending the waiters away, he tries to encourage his companion to drink. When he tries to kiss 'her', he is startled by the resemblance to Octavian. The 'maid' appears quite skittish but suddenly one of the hiding men appears and the Baron begins to show alarm. As he begins to undress the 'maid', and takes off his wig, another face appears; then the Italian woman bursts in pretending to be his wife, accompanied by screaming children, several waiters and the anxious landlord. There is so much noise that a police commissioner is brought in. The Baron tries to pass off the 'maid' as his fiancée, Sophie Faninal, a great mistake as Herr von Faninal has been tricked into coming to the house. As the children claim the Baron as their father, Sophie arrives to find her fiancé wigless and at the centre of a major scandal.

At this point Octavian takes charge and explains the joke to the commissioner before disappearing behind the curtain. Ochs, believing he is losing the 'maid', is further agitated by her clothes being thrown out one by one from behind the curtain. Suddenly the Marschallin is announced. Now dressed as himself, Octavian reappears and is amazed at the unexpected arrival of the Marschallin. Advising the Baron to leave, the Marschallin explains that it was all just a Viennese masquerade. While Sophie thinks this over, the Baron slowly grasps the truth, staring at Octavian and remembering how he first met the 'maid'. Suddenly he finds himself bowled over by a wave of creditors and screaming children, and hastily departs with his son, leaving the Marschallin alone with Octavian and Sophie.

Hab' mir's gelobt ('I promised'): the Marschallin's opening words of the famous trio illustrating Octavian's triangle of love

'Was it all just a farce?' asks Sophie as she sees Octavian beside the Marschallin. He hesitates between the two, but the Marschallin commands him to go to the younger woman, reminding herself that she always vowed to bear the inevitable with calm. Sophie and Octavian admit their love for each other and the final trio ends with the Marschallin slipping away as Octavian takes Sophie in his arms.

Ist ein Traum ('Just like a dream'): Sophie and Octavian's final duet, reassuring each other that their love is eternal

They break apart when Faninal returns with the Marschallin. '*Sind halt aso, die jungen Leut*' ('What it is to be young') he says to her. '*Ja, ja*' she nods, as the opera ends with a last duet for Octavian and Sophie. They kiss and run out. She has let slip her handkerchief. The Marschallin's page comes back to collect it and this suggests that the Marschallin's influence is by no means over.

ARIADNE AUF NAXOS

(ARIADNE ON NAXOS)

Composer		soprano
Ariadne, the heroine of his opera		soprano
Zerbinetta	characters in	soprano
Harlequin	the harlequinade	baritone
Bacchus		tenor

Vienna, probably 18th century: at the whim of a wealthy patron, a serious opera and a comic opera are to be performed together. Thus, the frivolous Zerbinetta and her four suitors interpose in the rendering of the story of Ariadne on the island of Naxos.

With a libretto by Hofmannsthal, the opera was written to honour the producer Max Rheinhardt. It originated as an interlude to *Le Bourgeois Gentilhomme* by Molière and as such was premiered in Stuttgart in 1912. The revised version of 1916 – without the play – is the one now generally performed.

A room being prepared as a theatre

PROLOGUE

There is confusion in the palace of 'the richest man in Vienna'. A serious opera that has been commissioned for the party is to be followed by a comic harlequinade, and

Eselsgesicht! ('You silly ass'): the Composer's diatribe against the servants in the house where he is trying to present his great work *Süsses, unbegreifliches Mädchen!* ('You are so sweet and energetic'): the Composer falls for Zerbinetta's charms

The island of Naxos

Ein schönes war ('How beautiful he was'): Ariadne's lament *Grossmächtige Prinzessin* ('All powerful Princess'): Zerbinetta's aria reminiscing about her many love affairs *Männer! Lieber Gott, wenn du wirklich wolltest, dass wir ihnen widerstehen sollten, warum hast du sie so verschieden geschaffen?* ('Men! Dear God, why if you meant us to resist them did you make them all so different?'): Zerbinetta justifies coquetry

the young Composer is distraught. He fears that his beautiful music will be made fun of by the comedians, who include the beautiful Zerbinetta; she thinks her act should come first. Then comes the news that their patron wishes them to present the two performances simultaneously so as not to delay the fireworks. While everyone haggles over how to combine and reduce each other's parts, the Composer first loves and is then enraged by Zerbinetta.

Ariadne, observed by nymphs, is bemoaning her desertion by Theseus. The comedians try to revive her spirits without success. Ariadne longs to escape from the misery of her life. Zerbinetta takes it upon herself to persuade Ariadne that men are naturally faithless and woman must adapt as best they can. Ariadne withdraws to her cave and Zerbinetta teases three of her admirers before disappearing with Harlequin.

The nymphs reappear to herald the arrival of the god Bacchus. He has escaped from Circe and is looking for a new love. Ariadne believes him to be the God of Death. When he kisses her, she forgets Theseus with the start of a new passion. As they leave together, Zerbinetta comments *Kommt der neue Gott gegangen, hingegeben sind wir stumm* ('When a new god comes, we go without a word').

ARABELLA

Arabella	soprano
Zdenka, her sister	soprano
Graf Waldner, their father	baritone
Gräfin Waldner, their mother	mezzo-soprano
Graf Elemer, one of Arabella's suitors	baritone
Mandryka	bass
Matteo	tenor

A hotel in Vienna

Vienna, 1860s: Mandryka, the stranger to whom Arabella has been attracted, asks for her hand in marriage; but matters are complicated by her sister Zdenka being dressed as a boy.

The same combination of Strauss' music and Hofmannsthal's words failed to achieve the success of some of their earlier works when *Arabella* was given its first performance in Dresden in 1933. Hofmannsthal had in fact died before the opera was presented on stage.

ACT I

Graf Waldner has gambled away his money and he relies on his elder daughter Arabella making a good marriage. Zdenka, the younger daughter, is dressed as a boy – and passed off as one – in order to save money. Zdenka welcomes Matteo, who is an admirer of Arabella. He has received an encouraging letter, apparently from Arabella though in fact from Zdenka, who is secretly in love with him.

Arabella, discussing the various suitors from among whom she must make her choice, muses on a stranger who has caught her attention. Graf Waldner returns in deeper difficulty: even the hotel where they are staying will not serve him on credit. He had hoped for help from an old comrade named Mandryka.

A young man enters and explains that he is Mandryka, the nephew and heir of Waldner's friend. He has fallen in love with the picture of Arabella which Waldner had sent to his uncle and he asks for Arabella's hand. He offers to lend Waldner some money.

Matteo is told by Zdenka to expect another letter. Arabella again considers the men hoping to claim her hand, among them Graf Elemer, who has arrived to take her for a sleigh ride.

Aber der Richtige ('The right man will appear'): Arabella is confident that one day she will find a man she can love

Mein Elemer ('My own Elemer'): Arabella considers Elemer as a husband, but her thoughts return to the stranger

The ballroom

Der Richtige – so hab' ich still zu mir gesagt ('It is right'): the duet between Mandryka and Arabella seals their engagement

ACT II
Arabella is introduced by her father to Mandryka, who, it transpires, is the stranger himself. She is happy to agree to their engagement, ritually signified by his offering her a glass of water.

Arabella parts from the rest of her admirers and goes to dance. Matteo receives from Zdenka a key, which he believes to be to Arabella's bedroom. Mandryka, overhearing, thinks Arabella is already betraying him.

By the hotel staircase

Sie gibt mir keinen Blick ('She never even glances'): Mandryka fears that he many have offended Arabella irreparably

ACT III
As Matteo comes dancing down the staircase, he is astonished to meet Arabella. She is as puzzled by his open affection as he by her confusion. Mandryka arrives. He and Matteo prepare to duel, ignoring Arabella's protestations. Zdenka, now dressed in female attire, comes down and reveals that the key was to her room. Mandryka's apologies are spurned by Arabella.

Waldner agrees to Zdenka's engagement to Matteo. Arabella ascends the stairs, having told Mandryka that matters between them must be resolved in the morning. Suddenly she reappears with a glass of water in her hand. The renewal of their engagement is celebrated in a final duet.

DIE FRAU OHNE SCHATTEN
(THE WOMAN WITHOUT A SHADOW)

In three acts, with text by Hofmannsthal based on his own story. Premiere: Staatsoper, Vienna, 1919. This is an exotic, highly symbolic score on the theme of procreation as the ultimate expression of married love.

In legendary times: The Empress (s), a supernatural being, has no shadow because she is infertile, despite her marriage to the Emperor of the South Eastern Islands (t). She is warned that the Emperor will be turned to stone if she remains childless. She and her Nurse (ms) descend to Earth to buy a shadow. In disguise, they visit the hut of the dyer Barak (bar) and his wife (s), also childless. The wife agrees to exchange her prospects of motherhood for great wealth. Barak's family and hut are swallowed into the earth in a storm. Seeing their misery in a subterranean vault, the Empress feels remorse and refuses to acquire a shadow. The spirit-world rewards her with one. Both couples are offered the prospect of children.

CAPRICCIO

In one act (but full-length), with text by the composer and Clemens Krauss, derived from Salieri's *Prima la Musica e poi le Parole*. Premiere: Staatsoper, Munich, 1942. Strauss' last opera, this conversational comedy about the primacy of words or music in opera is set at the time of Gluck's operatic reforms.

A chateau near Paris, *c.* 1775: the poet Olivier (bar) and the composer Flamand (t) are both wooing the Countess Madeleine (s), a young widow, using arguments about the supremacy of their respective professions in the making of opera. She warns her brother, the Count (bar), not to get carried away by his mistress, the famous actress Clairon (c). A theatre director, La Roche (b), puts a strong case for drama. The Countess asks Flamand and Oliver to collaborate – on an opera – involving all sides of the argument heard during the day. She eventually realizes that any decision between her suitors or their skills will seem trivial.

IGOR STRAVINSKY

Born Oranienbaum, Russia, 1882, died New York 1971. The son of a well-known operatic bass, Stravinsky studied composition with Rimsky-Korsakov after leaving university. His early successes were three ballet scores for Diaghilev's Ballet Russe. *The Rite of Spring* (1913), with its dissonant, almost barbaric music, caused one of the most famous scandals in musical history at its premiere in Paris. His short opera, *The Nightingale*, written in an exotic and brilliant musical language, was performed as part of the Ballet Russe season of 1914. Exiled from Russia after World War I, Stravinsky began to experiment with older, classical forms, as in his opera-oratorio *Oedipus Rex* (1927). This was modelled on Handel but used modern dissonance. Also classical in style is his opera deriving from the 18th-century series of engravings by Hogarth, *The Rake's Progress* (1951). Later in the 1950s, by then a US resident, Stravinsky turned to 12-tone music, and several of his works were used as ballet scores by Balanchine's New York City Ballet.

THE RAKE'S PROGRESS

Trulove	bass
Anne, his daughter	soprano
Tom Rakewell, her admirer	tenor
Nick Shadow	baritone
Baba the Turk, a bearded lady	mezzo-soprano

England, 18th century: a morality play portraying the decline of Tom Rakewell, who is led on by the satanic Nick Shadow, though loved to the last by the faithful Anne Trulove.

Inspired by *The Rake's Progress*, a series of engravings by William Hogarth, the words are by W.H. Auden and Chester Kallman. In the music, too, there are echoes of the 18th century, in particular of Mozart and Gluck. The opera was first performed at La Fenice in Venice in 1951.

The garden of Trulove's cottage

Since it is not by merit we rise or we fall: Tom's aria rejecting Trulove's offer of work and entrusting himself to fortune

ACT I

Trulove's daughter Anne and her suitor Tom Rakewell welcome Spring. Trulove, in the background, hopes that his doubts about Tom are unfounded. When his daughter leaves, he offers Tom a job in the City which is carelessly rejected. Tom believes that chance rules everything and decides to live by his wits.

As Tom expresses his longing for money, Nick Shadow appears with news of a fortune left to him by an unknown uncle. Tom asks Shadow what wages he would expect as his servant. The sinister arrival replies that the account should be settled in a year and a day, when Tom may decide for himself what is just. Shadow leads Tom towards London, before he leaves turning to the audience to announce 'The progress of a rake begins'.

Mother Goose's brothel, London
Love, too frequently betrayed: Tom's aria reveals a serious side to his nature in the unlikely company of whores and 'roaring boys'

Shadow has introduced Tom to the brothel. Tom enters into the spirit of the place, though the word 'love' disturbs him. He sings of the tragic vulnerability of love before succumbing to the advances of Mother Goose, who takes him away.

Trulove's garden
I go to him. Love cannot falter: Anne's cabaletta announcing her decision to go to London to find Tom

Anne, who has heard no word from London, is torn between devotion to her father and her loving concern for Tom. But all at once she decides. Tom is the weaker character of the two and it is he who needs her most.

A room in Tom's house in London
That man alone his fate fulfils, for he alone is free who chooses what to will, and wills: Shadow's aria luring Tom further into the abyss

ACT II
Tom reflects on the disappointments of his self-indulgent life. He dares not think of his one pure love. For the second time he expresses a wish, this time for happiness. Immediately, Shadow is beside him, urging him to marry Baba, the bearded Turkish woman, as someone he neither desires nor is obliged to. Tom sees this as a good joke and they leave together.

Outside Tom's house
Could it then have been known: Anne and Tom voice their despair in a trio with Baba, who is complaining about being kept waiting

Anne, standing in the street, sees with trepidation the busy preparations being made. Tom appears and he gently holds her away from himself. He tells her to forget him and return home. Baba angrily interrupts. Understanding at last that this exotic figure is Tom's wife, Anne leaves hurriedly.

The room in Tom's house, now full of clutter
Come, sweet, come. Why so glum?: Baba's attempts to make up to her husband

Tom sits silently while his wife chatters. He rejects her caresses and she storms about, smashing the ornaments. He covers her face with a wig and sinks into a mournful sleep. Shadow enters and, uncovering a bizarre machine, proceeds to turn loaves of bread into china ornaments. Tom makes another wish in his sleep (he has dreamed of a magic machine that converts stones to bread). Tom is elated as the machine is demonstrated.

The same room, in complete disarray
Ladies, both fair and gracious: the auctioneer opens the sale

ACT III
The house is unkempt and the contents up for sale. The auctioneer arrives and the bidding begins. One hundred pounds is given for an unidentifiable object, which is Baba, still sitting with the wig over her face. As he shouts 'Gone', he snatches off her wig. Furious, she tries to

I go to him: Anne, encouraged by Baba, determines to save Tom

A churchyard

Renew my life, O Queen of Hearts again: thoughts of Anne prompt Tom to guess that Shadow has tried to outwit him by using the Queen of Hearts twice

Bedlam

Gently, little boat: Anne's lullaby to calm the demented Tom

throw them all out. Seeing Anne, she admits that it is Anne whom Tom loves, not her, his wife, and she warns her against Shadow, who can be heard singing with Tom. Baba urges Anne to save Tom and makes as dignified an exit as she can manage.

Shadow announces that the year and a day of their original bargain has passed. Tom protests that he is now a pauper. Shadow states that his price is Tom's soul and that he must kill himself on the stroke of twelve; but, as the clock begins to strike, he offers Tom an alternative. Stopping the clock in mid-strike, he promises Tom his freedom if he can name three hidden cards. For a moment Tom loses heart but then, calling Anne's name, he guesses each card correctly. As Tom collapses with relief, Shadow rages at his own defeat and condemns Tom to insanity.

In the madhouse, the other inmates are making fun of Tom. Anne appears to rescue him. He believes that she is Venus and he Adonis and, after singing him to sleep, she is led away by her father. Awaking and finding himself alone, Tom dies of grief.

EPILOGUE
The characters return to remind everyone that for idle hands and hearts and minds the Devil finds work to do.

PETER ILYICH TCHAIKOVSKY

Born Kamsko-Votkinsk 1840, died St Peterburg 1893. In 1862 Tchaikovsky began to study musical composition at the newly founded St Petersburg Conservatory. He relinquished a minor government post to devote himself to music and was appointed professor of harmony at the Moscow Conservatory. His early operas are imbued with Russian nationalism, but in *Eugene Onegin* (1879) he fused the folk idiom with Western elements. Tchaikovsky's short and disastrous marriage to a music student infatuated with him seems to be echoed in part in Tatyana's position in *Eugene Onegin*. Fourteen years of patronage by Madame von Meck (who stipulated that they should never meet) ended in 1890. By this time the popularity of his music, especially his ballet scores and symphonic music, and the chilling and powerful opera *Pikovaya Dama* (*The Queen of Spades*, 1890), had made him financially secure. He died of cholera soon after the premiere of his Sixth Symphony, the *Pathétique*.

EUGENE ONEGIN

Tatyana	soprano
Olga, her sister	mezzo-soprano
Lensky, Olga's suitor	tenor
Eugene Onegin, his friend	baritone
Prince Gremin	bass

Russia, 1820s: the vain and self-important Onegin loses Tatyana with his first rejection of her love and later kills his greatest friend in a duel.

The libretto is by Konstantin Shilovsky and the composer, after the poem by Pushkin. *Eugene Onegin* was first performed by students from the Imperial College of Music in Moscow in 1879. Later, performed professionally, it was recognized as the most compelling of Tchaikovsky's eight operas.

The Larins' garden
Slikháli-l vs za roǐchei ('Did you hear behind the trees?'):
Tatyana and Olga sing a duet, overheard by their mother
Bólát mǒyí skóri nózhenki só pǒkhódushki ('How my poor feet ache'): the peasants celebrate the end of the harvest
Yá dǒzhdalás ('I have waited'): the quartet when Tatyana first meets Onegin

ACT I
The two sisters, Tatyana and Olga, are singing. Their mother, making jam, listens to them and remembers how she used to sing.

Tatyana is always lost in daydreams, while Olga is naturally bright and gay. Their neighbour Lensky is in love with Olga. He has come to visit her and brings with him his friend Eugene Onegin. As soon as she sees him, Tatyana recognizes him as the man for whom she has been waiting. When Lensky leads Olga away, Onegin condescends to walk with Tatyana. Lensky and Olga return, and he declares his love for her.

Tatyana's bedroom
Puskái pŏgíbnu yá ('Even if it kills me'): Tatyana determines to tell Onegin by letter of her consuming passion

Tatyana's head is spinning with fantasies of love. She cannot restrain herself from writing to Onegin and gets her nurse's grandson to deliver the letter.

A corner of the garden the following morning

While the girls on the estate are picking berries, Onegin comes to see Tatyana. He lectures her on the decline of his own ardour and his inability to match her youthful enthusiasm. As she sinks into embarrassed misery, he warns her to be careful and have more control over her emotions.

A room in the Larins' house some months later
Nó sĕvódnă uznál yá ('Now I know the truth'): Lensky's jealous outburst leads to an ensemble in which Onegin reproaches himself, too late, for his malice while the women mourn men's natural inclination to quarrel

ACT II
The girls' mother is giving a grand party to celebrate Tatyana's name day. Lensky again brings Onegin, who is angered by the neighbours' gossip about him. Blaming his friend that he came, he flirts with and monopolizes Olga. When Lensky protests, Olga only infuriates him by objecting to his jealousy. A quarrel breaks out between the two friends. Neither can control his temper and, despite general protest, they commit themselves to a duel.

On the banks of a river at dawn
Kudá, kudá, kudá vĭ udalílis ('Where, oh where are they?'): Lensky's deeply moving aria, expecting the worst

The following morning, Lensky and his second are waiting. He muses on his lost youth and approaching fate, and wonders whether Olga will remember him. At last Onegin approaches. While the seconds decide on the details, the two friends ignore each other. The pistols are loaded, the ground paced out and the two young men take their places. They raise their pistols and Onegin shoots Lensky dead.

A nobleman's house in St Petersburg four years later
I zdés mné skúchnŏ! ('No respite here!'): Onegin's despair at being unable to escape from his own conscience
Lubví vsé vózrastï pŏkornï ('Love conquers all'): Prince Gremin expresses love for Tatyana
Uzhél tá sámaya Tatyána ('Can that be the same Tatyana?'): Onegin is filled with hope at the thought of regaining Tatyana's love

ACT III
Onegin has returned to St Peterburg after prolonged and miserable wanderings. At a ball, the elderly Prince Gremin leads in his beautiful young wife. She is much admired. Onegin recognizes her as Tatyana. She has recognized him, too, and is greatly agitated by her own feelings.

The Prince tells Onegin of the depth of his love for his young wife. He presents Onegin to her. She immediately says she is tired and they leave together, watched by Onegin. He is overcome by a passion for Tatyana which fills him with new hope, and he runs away from the party.

Prince Gremin's house

Tatyana is crying over a letter from Onegin. He rushes in and falls at her feet, but she will not accept his frenzied apologies for spurning her original declaration. He begs

Onégin! Yá tŏgdá mŏlózhe ('Onegin! When I was just a girl'): Tatyana's gentle reminder of the reason for their present situation

her for pity. She cries out that she loves him. He takes her in his arms, but she breaks free and repeats, despite his anguished protests, that they must part. For a moment it seems that she will weaken but, regaining her resolution, she quickly departs, leaving him with the realization that he has lost her forever.

PIKOVAYA DAMA
(THE QUEEN OF SPADES/PIQUE DAME)

In three acts, with text by Modest Tchaikovsky and the composer, after Pushkin's story. Premiere: Maryinsky Theatre, St Petersburg, 1890. This is a strongly flavoured tale of violent emotions.

St Petersburg, late 18th century: Herman (t), an impoverished young officer, despairs on discovering the girl he loves is Lisa (s), fiancée of Prince Yeletsky (bar); she is also grand-daughter of the old Countess (ms), once known as the 'Queen of Spades' for her winning formula at gambling. Obsessed with obtaining this secret so as to win enough to marry, he declares his love for Lisa. She responds with a key to her apartments. On his way, Herman begs the old woman for her secret, but she dies of fright; he learns the formula ('3, 7, Ace') from her ghost, who advises marriage to Lisa. When he insists on gambling, Lisa drowns herself. At the gaming club, he wins twice and stakes all on the final 'Ace' – which is the Queen of Spades. Ruined and deranged, he kills himself.

SIR MICHAEL TIPPETT

Born London, 1905. A late developer as a composer, he worked as a teacher, becoming director of music at Morley College, London (1940–51). His earliest success was the oratorio *A Child of Our Time* (1944), in which the idea of reconciliation between the light and dark sides of human nature – which permeates much of his work – is first explored. His output, which spans all musical genres, includes four symphonies. Since his first opera, *The Midsummer Marriage*, he has written *King Priam* (1961), *The Knot Garden* (1969), *The Ice Break* (1976) and *New Year* (1989).

THE MIDSUMMER MARRIAGE

In three acts, with text by the composer. Premiere: Covent Garden, London, 1955. This 'quest' opera examines the problems of modern marriage, using mystical elements in similar fashion to *Die Zauberflöte*.

The present. An engaged couple, Mark (**t**) and Jenifer (**s**), are to get married on Midsummer Day but she draws back, unhappy at her lack of self-knowledge. When she disappears into the hillside, he follows suit, taking a different entrance. They are pursued by her father King Fisher (**bar**), a businessman who puts obstacles in their path, and by his secretary Bella (**s**) and her boyfriend Jack (**t**), whose relationship is less complicated, more intuitive. After several encounters with mythological elements involving the clairvoyante Sosostris (**c**), the Ancients (**b** and **ms**), and the famous Ritual Dances, along with the death of King Fisher, they emerge with a better understanding of each other, ready for marriage.

KING PRIAM

In three acts, with text by the composer after Homer's *Iliad*. Premiere: Coventry Theatre, 1962. In spare, tight and condensed textures, Tippett reflects on the timeless problem of moral choice through the heroes of antiquity.

Ancient Troy: Hecuba (**s**) dreams that her son Paris (first **s**, later **t**) will kill his father Priam (**b-bar**). They agree to have him killed, but are relieved when he reappears alive. Priam takes Paris and his elder son Hector (**bar**) to Troy, where the two sons quarrel and Paris falls for Helen (**ms**). Paris chooses Aphrodite (sung by Helen) in his famous Judgement. As war follows, Achilles (**t**) sulks, but, when the Trojans appear to prevail, he stops them with a chilling warcry. He later kills Hector, who has slain his friend Patroclus (**bar**). Priam sends off Paris to kill Achilles, while he himself dies at the hands of Achilles' son.

GIUSEPPE VERDI

Born Roncole 1813, died Milan 1901. The giant of 19th-century Italian opera, Verdi was born into a family of modest means. A merchant from nearby Busseto, noting the boy's talent, encouraged him and paid for his musical tuition in Milan. Verdi's first opera, *Oberto*, produced at La Scala in 1839, brought him a contract to compose three operas. The first, the comic *Un Giorno di Regno* (1840), written while Verdi was suffering after the tragic death of his wife and child, failed so disastrously that Verdi vowed never to write another opera. However, the libretto of *Nabucco* fired the young composer, its story of the captive Hebrews echoing nationalist sentiments over the Austrian subjugation of northern Italy. The opera received a triumphant premiere at La Scala in 1842. During the next decade, succeeding operas established Verdi's masterly use of music to portray character and situation. *Macbeth* (1847) was the first of his operas with a Shakespearean theme, the libretto by Francesco Maria Piave. The three great operas, *Rigoletto* (1851), *Il Trovatore* (1853) and *La Traviata* (1853) brought international acclaim. With *Les Vêpres Siciliennes* for the Paris Opéra in 1855, to a Scribe libretto, his talents widened to encompass the grand opera style demanded by the Parisians. *Simon Boccanegra* (1857) and *Un Ballo in Maschera* (1859), continuing in this grand manner, showed his ever-increasing powers to depict character, using the orchestra to reinforce the drama. With *La Forza del Destino* (1862), *Don Carlos* (1867) and *Aida* (1871), he reached new heights of dramatic expression. Verdi retired to his estate near Busseto with his second wife, the former soprano Giuseppina Strepponi, the original Abigaille of *Nabucco*. The publisher Ricordi eventually persuaded Verdi to work again. With Arrigo Boito's libretto to inspire him, he produced in *Otello* (1887) a supreme work, its seamless flow of glorious sound carrying the drama inexorably forward. With Boito again as librettist, the comic masterpiece *Falstaff* was produced in 1893, when Verdi was 80.

NABUCCO

(NEBUCHADNEZZAR)

Nabucco (Nebuchadnezzar), King of Babylon	baritone
Fenena, his daughter	mezzo-soprano
Abigaille (Abigail), a slave, believed to be his daughter	soprano
Ismaele (Ismael), Prince of Jerusalem	tenor
Zaccaria (Zechariah), High Priest of Jerusalem	bass
High Priest of Baal	bass

Jerusalem and Babylon, 6th century BC: the Old Testament story of the victory of Nabucco (Nebuchadnezzar) over Israel. Disaster follows when he proclaims himself God: only by turning to Jehovah does he regain his throne and save his daughter Fenena.

Nabucco, with a libretto by Temistocle Solera, is an example of a one-aria opera, in this case the Hebrew slaves' song in Act III. Perhaps the most famous chorus ever written, it was used to inspire Italian dreams of self-government. The opera, written shortly after Verdi's wife had died and as he prepared to give up composing opera altogether, was his first real success and established him as Bellini's successor. It was premiered at La Scala, Milan, in 1842.

The temple of Solomon in
Jerusalem

Sperate, o figli ('Keep up your
hopes'): the High Priest's grand
solo giving encouragement to
the Hebrew faith

Nabucco's apartments in
Babylon
Anch' io dischiuso un giorno
('My heart once opened also'):
Abigaille fiercely contrasts her
present position of loveless
power with the happiness she
once hoped for through loving
Ismaele
Non son più Re, son Dio! ('Not
just a king, I am God!'):
Nabucco's fateful claim that
brings down a thunderbolt

The Hanging Gardens of
Babylon

The banks of the Euphrates
Va, pensiero, sull'ali dorate ('Let
my thoughts fly back to
Jordan'): the song of the
Hebrew slaves

An apartment in the palace

The Hanging Gardens
Oh, dischiuso è il firmamento!
('Heaven opens for me'):
Fenena's prayer as she prepares
to be sacrificed to Baal

ACT I
The Hebrews have captured Fenena, the daughter of
Nabucco. Fenena loves Ismaele, as does the slave girl
Abigaille, who is believed to be her sister. Nabucco's
armies have conquered the Hebrews. Zaccaria leads the
Hebrews in prayers for the safety of the temple. Nabucco
arrives as the High Priest prepares to sacrifice Fenena, but
she is saved by Ismaele and delivered to her victorious
father.

ACT II
Abigaille finds a paper proving that she is not after all the
daughter of Nabucco. The High Priest of Baal, outraged
that the King's real daughter is planning to free the
Hebrew captives, encourages Abigaille to seize her
'father's' throne. He has already spread it abroad that
Nabucco is dead. Ismaele is still blamed by his compatriots for saving Fenena and, as they argue, Abigaille
arrives to claim the crown from Fenena. She is however
closely followed by the returning Nabucco. His arrogant
claim to be God brings down a thunderbolt which knocks
off his crown (a testing detail in any production), and he
becomes insane.

ACT III
Abigaille has taken the throne. Approached by the ailing
Nabucco, she tricks him into signing the death warrant
for all the prisoners, including Fenena. When the ram-
bling Nabucco searches for the paper which disproves
Abigaille's royal birth, she tears it up in front of him. She
taunts him when he begs for Fenena's life.

The Hebrew slaves, held in chains, sing longingly of their
homeland, echoing the words of Psalm 137: 'By the
waters of Babylon we sat down and wept'. Zaccaria
furiously denounces the impious values of their Assyrian
masters.

ACT IV
Nabucco is still a prisoner and anxious to save Fenena.
With sudden inspiration, he kneels to pray to Jehovah.

Thus restored to strength, he leads his newly trusting
soldiers to save Fenena just as she is about to be sacrificed
before the statue of Baal. The idol falls over of its own
accord. Abigaille, who has poisoned herself and is dying,
joins in the final submission to Jehovah as Nabucco sends
the Hebrews back to Israel to rebuild their temple.

MACBETH

Lady Macbeth	soprano	
Macbeth	baritone	
Banco (Banquo)	bass	
Macduff	tenor	
Malcolm, son of Duncan King of Scotland	tenor	

Scotland and the Borders, 11th century: the Shakespearean tragedy of the ambition which leads Macbeth and Lady Macbeth to murder their king.

The libretto is by Francesco Maria Piave. The opera was first performed in Florence in 1847 and substantially revised for Paris in 1865.

A wood

ACT I
Macbeth and Banco (Banquo) first encounter the Witches (who prophesy wealth and the crown for Macbeth now and, after, for Banco's descendants). Then a messenger brings news that Macbeth has been granted the Cawdor estates.

Macbeth's castle
Or tutti sorgete ('Come you spirits'): Lady Macbeth's prayer for more than mortal strength
Mi si affacia un pugnal ('Is this a dagger'): Macbeth's vision

Lady Macbeth, reading of this in her husband's letter, realizes that Duncan's life is all that stands in the way of the second half of the prophecy. When the King's visit is announced, she plans immediate action. Macbeth agrees; but whereas he can, and does, murder the King, it is left to his wife to smear the blood on the hands of the sleeping attendants.

The castle
La luce langue ('As darkness comes'): Lady Macbeth's aria, added for the Paris revision, illustrates her fierce ambition

ACT II
Duncan's murder has been blamed on Malcolm, who has fled to England. Lady Macbeth sends her husband to murder Banco in order to secure the crown against the Witches' prophecy.

A park
Sparve il sol ('The sun is set'): the murderers' chorus as they lie in wait for Banco.

In the dark, the assassins, on the orders of Macbeth, lie in wait for Banco and his son. Banco is murdered, though his son escapes.

The castle

At the banquet, Banco's ghost unnerves Macbeth. His wife attempts to distract the guests with a toast.

A dark cavern

ACT III
Macbeth seeks out the Witches, who warn him to beware of Macduff. Lady Macbeth joins him and he recovers from the visions of Banco's royal descendants. Together they determine to triumph over Macduff and Banco's son.

Ora di morte e di vendetta ('Death and revenge'): the Macbeths' duet of defiance

The Borders

Ah, la paterna mano ('As an absent father'): Macduff bitterly mourns the death of his children

The castle

Una macchia ('Out damned spot'): Lady Macbeth's mad scene

ACT IV

Macduff and Malcolm have brought an army to avenge the murders. Malcolm commands his men to cover themselves with branches for their advance on Dunsinane.

Sleepwalking, Lady Macbeth confesses her guilt. Even when news reaches Macbeth that she has died, he still defies the triumphant Macduff. Macbeth's death is greeted with a rousing chorus.

RIGOLETTO

The Duke	tenor
Rigoletto, his jester	baritone
Gilda, Rigoletto's daughter	soprano
Sparafucile, a professional assassin	bass
Maddalena, his sister	contralto
Count Ceprano, a nobleman	bass or baritone
Countess Ceprano, his wife	mezzo-soprano

Italy, 16th century: Rigoletto, the hunchbacked jester, encourages the Duke to dishonour the wives and daughters of his courtiers; but then his own daughter becomes ensnared.

Piave's libretto is based on Victor Hugo's play *Le Roi s'amuse*, written in 1832. Set at the court of François I, the play's theme is the abuse of royal power, and it was banned as subversive after one performance. Venice, where the opera was to receive its premiere in 1851, was ruled from Vienna by the Habsburgs. To appease the censors, important changes were made which included demoting the King to the rank of duke and giving the opera the name of the Duke's jester. The traditional setting for the opera is Mantua in the 16th century but producers have introduced variations such as America during Prohibition and Nazi Germany.

The Duke's palace

Questa o quella ('This one or that one'): the Duke's first important aria, sung as he surveys the ladies of his court

ACT I

While a party is taking place, the Duke tells of his dual pursuit of Countess Ceprano and an unknown girl whom he sees every Sunday in church. Cuckolded by the Duke, Count Ceprano's frightened anger is increased by the hunchbacked jester. It is Rigoletto who suggests that the Count be imprisoned or beheaded. The courtiers' fear of the Duke is matched by their hatred of his procurer, Rigoletto. Hearing that Rigoletto has a woman hidden in the suburbs, they plan to abduct her. Suddenly Count Monterone bursts in and reproaches the Duke for

Sii maledetto ('You are cursed'): Count Monterone puts a curse on the Duke and Rigoletto

The street

Pari siamo ('He and I are alike'): Rigoletto's observation on the similarity between Sparafucile and himself
Figlia! Mio padre! ('My daughter! My child!'): duet between Rigoletto and Gilda
Veglia o donna, questa fiore ('Take care of my precious child'): Rigoletto's command to Gilda's guardian, who has already betrayed his trust
Caro nome ('Dearest name'): Gilda repeats the name assumed by the Duke, 'Gualtier Malde'

The palace

Passente amor mi chiama ('Love's power is with me'): the Duke's second great aria, as he contemplates his love for Gilda

Piangi, fanciulla ('Weep, my child'): duet by Rigoletto and Gilda as the Duke's deceit is described
Sì, vendetta, tremenda vendetta ('Yes, vengeance, fearful vengeance'): Rigoletto vows revenge on the Duke on his own and the Count's behalf

Sparafucile's inn a month later

La donna è mobile ('Women's hearts cannot be trusted'): the Duke's famous aria on the fickleness of women

dishonouring his daughter. Mocked by Rigoletto, the Count curses them both. The Duke laughs and orders his arrest; but Rigoletto is terrified.

In the street between the Palazzo Ceprano and his own house Rigoletto is approached by a stranger, Sparafucile, who offers his services as an assassin. Rejecting the offer, Rigoletto ponders on the likeness between them: he is as much an assassin with his tongue as Sparafucile with his dagger. He is met by his daughter Gilda, whose mother, now dead, was the only woman to have loved him. He orders Giovanna, her guardian, to take special precautions; but the Duke is already in the garden, delighted to learn that his next quarry is actually Rigoletto's daughter. By bribing Giovanna, he is able, in the guise of a student, to make advances to Gilda before being interrupted by the courtiers who have come to abduct her. Alone, Gilda speaks lovingly the Duke's assumed name, 'Gualtier Malde'. The conspirators are disturbed by Rigoletto. They persuade him to help them by pretending that they intend to carry off not Gilda but Countess Ceprano, duping him into wearing a mask which blindfolds him. Too late he discovers the truth. Count Monterone's curse has begun to take effect.

ACT II
The Duke is in despair, having returned to Gilda's house and found her gone. His lament is cut short by the arrival of the courtiers, who tell him that they have brought Rigoletto's mistress for his entertainment. Realizing her identity, the Duke is overjoyed and hurries to join her. Rigoletto enters, trying to make light of his desperate search for Gilda. When the Duchess' page inadvertently reveals that she is in the Duke's bedroom, he breaks into a rage at first and then pleads for the courtiers to help him. Despite the news that Gilda is his daughter, they remain unmoved. At last Gilda herself appears. As the truth emerges, Rigoletto's obsessive pride in his daughter's purity is destroyed.

The procession leading Monterone to the scaffold passes by. He, another outraged father, pauses to reflect that the Duke is untouched by the curse. As it moves on, Rigoletto calls out that he will avenge them both.

ACT III
Rigoletto has brought Gilda to watch what is happening at Sparafucile's inn. The Duke, again in disguise, is pursuing Maddalena, the assassin's sister. Gilda observes that the Duke uses the same technique as with her. The Duke sings that since a woman's heart is forever chang-

Bella figlia dell'amore ('Beautiful daughter of love'): quartet sung while the Duke courts Maddalena

ing, only a fool places any hopes in her constancy. Gilda, though consumed with jealousy, finds that she still loves the Duke. Rigoletto sends her off while arranging with Sparafucile for the Duke's murder that night. Maddalena, in love with the Duke, persuades her brother to kill a substitute if one can be found before midnight. Gilda, returning and overhearing this, forces herself to come forward as a beggar needing shelter. A moment's preparation, and Sparafucile's knife is in her back.

Midnight, and Rigoletto has come to claim his master's body. The sack is handed over and the balance of the money paid. He gloats, with one foot on his victim's body.

Suddenly, he can hear the Duke's voice singing again the words of the aria 'La donna è mobile'. Rigoletto, terrified, opens the sack and finds his own daughter. She is dying and he begs her not to leave him. Monterone's curse has struck home.

Ah, la maledizione ('Ah, the curse'): as Gilda dies, Rigoletto recalls the curse

IL TROVATORE

(THE TROUBADOUR)

Leonora, a lady-in-waiting	soprano
Azucena, a gypsy	mezzo-soprano
Manrico, a troubadour	tenor
Ruiz, his aide	tenor
Count di Luna	baritone
Ferrando, captain of the palace guard	bass

Spain, 15th century: the Count di Luna and Manrico, the troubadour (il trovatore), are rivals in war and for the hand of Leonora. A crucial part in the complicated plot is played by Azucena, a gypsy whose mother had been burned as a witch.

Adapted from a play by García Gutiérrez, the libretto is by Salvatore Cammarano. The opera, today one of the most universally popular, was first performed at the Teatro Apollo, Rome, in 1853.

The palace of Aliaferia, Saragossa

ACT I

The Count di Luna is in love with Leonora, a lady-in-waiting to the Princess of Aragon, but she in turn loves a troubadour (trovatore) who serenades her at night. The opera begins with the Count's officer Ferrando telling the guards how the Count's brother was stolen from his cradle and burned by a gypsy woman to avenge her mother, who had been burned as a witch. Ferrando saw her at the time and believes he would recognize her again.

The palace gardens
Tacea la notte placida ('One peaceful night'): Leonora's aria describing how she first knew that the troubadour loved her

Leonora, listening for the troubadour, tells her maid how they first met at a tournament.

The Count is watching for Leonora. Suddenly, he hears the troubadour. The troubadour identifies himself as Manrico, a follower of the enemy, in the angry trio that

Di geloso amor sprezzato ('The agonies of jealousy'): a spirited trio between the defiant troubadour, the jealous Count and the distraught Leonora

A gypsy camp on a mountainside in Biscay
La Zingarella! ('A gypsy girl'): the gypsies' chorus

Stride la vampa! ('The flames are roaring!'): Azucena's dramatic description of the pyre on which her mother was burned

Mal reggendo ('Overcome by my attack'): Manrico remembers how he felt unable to kill the Count in a duel

Perder quell' angel! ('To lose that angel'): Manrico cries that, whatever the call of duty, he would risk anything rather than lose Leonora

The convent
Il balen del suo sorriso ('Her lovely smile'): a famous baritone aria in which the Count celebrates his love for Leonora

The Count's camp

follows. The two men prepare to fight. Leonora, begging the Count to let his fury fall on her, faints as they disappear into the darkness.

ACT II
Among the gypsies, Manrico is resting with his mother Azucena. In the Anvil Chorus, the gypsies' song is of how their ceaseless hard work is cheered by thoughts of gypsy girls.

Azucena, from beside the fire, tells the terrible story of her mother's execution. After the other gypsies have left, Manrico asks her to tell him the whole story. She recounts how, to avenge her mother, she stole one of the old Count di Luna's sons. She took the child to the flames and later found that, in terrible confusion, she had thrown her own child into the fire. Thus, it is suddenly revealed to Manrico that he is the present Count di Luna's brother. But then she contradicts herself. Was it just a dream?

Reassuring Azucena that she has always been a tender mother to him, Manrico nonetheless tells her that when he overcame the Count in combat he felt unable to kill him because of some supernatural force. Azucena, remembering her mother's last cries for revenge, makes him swear that next time he will kill the Count. They are interrupted by orders that Manrico must supervise the defence of the Castle of Castellor, and the messenger tells him that Leonora, believing him to be dead, is about to enter a convent. Azucena tries to stop him but he hastens to join Leonora.

The Count believes that Manrico is dead and he is waiting to kidnap Leonora on her way to the convent near the Castle of Castellor. While the nuns sing a welcome, Leonora prepares to enter. As the Count interrupts, Manrico also arrives, and in the general turmoil Manrico and Leonora escape.

ACT III
The Count's soldiers, led by Ferrando, are preparing to attack the castle as Azucena, who has been found wandering nearby, is brought in. Ferrando recognizes her as the murderess of the child. The Count orders that she be burned. In her terror, she calls for her son, Manrico, so telling the Count that he has his rival's mother as hostage.

Inside the castle

Ah sì, ben mio, coll'essere ('I am yours'): the love duet of Manrico and Leonora

Di quella pira ('Those terrible flames'): Manrico commits himself to rescuing Azucena

Outside the castle

Non ti scordar ('Remember me'): the duet between Manrico in the cell and Leonora outside, backed by the monks' chorus

In a dungeon

Ai nostri monti ('Back to our mountains'): the nostalgic duet of Manrico and Azucena awaiting execution

Sei vendicata, o madre! ('Mother you are avenged!'): Azucena's triumphant cry of revenge

Leonora and Manrico are about to be married in the chapel of the Castle of Castellor. Then comes the shocking news that a pyre is being built for his mother below the castle walls. Determined to save her, Manrico leads his men out of the safety of the castle.

ACT IV

Manrico has been captured and Leonora has come to beg for his release. She hears the monks chanting a *Miserere* for the dying and then, above their voices, Manrico singing farewell to her. This develops into a duet between the two of them.

The Count appears and Leonora comes forward asking for mercy for Manrico. The more she pleads, the angrier the Count becomes. Finally, she offers herself to the Count in return for Manrico's life. He accepts. Swearing to be his, she secretly drinks the poison concealed in her ring.

Manrico and Azucena prepare themselves for death with a duet dreaming of their mountain home. Leonora comes in to tell Manrico he is saved. He refuses to leave without her, immediately suspecting the price. He curses her for selling her love, but, as the poison begins to take effect, he begs her forgiveness. The Count arrives to find Leonora dying. On his orders, Manrico is dragged out and executed. As the final revelation, Azucena tells the Count that Manrico was his brother.

LA TRAVIATA

Violetta Valery, a courtesan	soprano
Alfredo Germont, her lover	tenor
Giorgio Germont, his father	baritone
Baron Douphol, Alfredo's rival	bass
Flora Bervoix, Violetta's friend	mezzo-soprano
Annina, Violetta's maid	soprano

Paris, 1850: the romantic tragedy of the love between a courtesan and the son of a respectable family.

La Traviata (often translated as *The Fallen One*) is based on the play *La Dame aux Camélias* by the younger Dumas (itself inspired by Dumas' own summer idyll with the dying courtesan Marie Plessis). The libretto is by Piave. The premiere of the opera was at the La Fenice, Venice, in 1853.

Violetta's apartment

Libiamo ('Let us drink'): a toast
sung by Alfredo and taken up
by Violetta
Un di felice ('That happy day'):
the duet between Alfredo and
Violetta which is to haunt her

E strano! E Strano! ('How
strange'): Violetta reflects on
her feelings for Alfredo

Sempre libera ('Always free'):
the motto of a courtesan

A house in the country

De'miei bollenti spirito ('In the
heat of passion'): Alfredo's
ecstatic depiction of their life
together

Pura siccome un angelo ('Pure as
an angel'): Alfredo's father
explains to Violetta that his
innocent daughter's
engagement is at risk

Di Provenze ('In the country of
Provence'): Alfredo's father
gives comfort with thoughts of
the simple life at home

Flora's apartment in Paris

ACT I

Among the guests at a party in Violetta's apartment are
her friends Gaston and Flora, and her current protector
Baron Douphol. Gaston has brought with him the young
Alfredo Germont. The latter proposes a toast to Violetta
and to love. As the guests move next door, Violetta half
faints from the effects of consumption. The others
depart, but Alfredo stays and sings of how, a year ago, he
first fell in love with her.

Before he goes, she gives him a camellia, telling him that
he may return when it is withered. Rapturously he leaves,
knowing he can be back the next day. The party breaks up
and Violetta is left alone to sing of how strange it is for her
to be an object of affection rather than just a pleasant
reason for extravagance. Her song begins to echo Alfredo's own loving declaration, but with a cry of exaspera-
tion she declares that it is her nature and her fate to
pursue only pleasure.

ACT II

Alfredo and Violetta have now become lovers, leaving
Paris for an idyllic summer in the country. Alone,
Alfredo sings of their ecstatic happiness. Annina, Violet-
ta's maid, comes in. When pressed, she admits that she
has been to Paris to raise money secretly by selling
Violetta's horses and jewellery.

Violetta returns to find an invitation from Flora, which
she casts aside. A visitor arrives. It is Alfredo's father,
come to rebuke her for living off Alfredo's money. When
she shows that this is the reverse of the truth, he still begs
her to give up Alfredo lest the scandal affect the
fashionable marriage of Alfredo's sister.

Feeling that her happiness has been undeserved, she
agrees to give up his son forever. Germont asks her what
he can do for her in return and she asks that Alfredo
should be told only after her death of the sacrifice she has
made. He agrees. Left alone, Violetta writes first an
acceptance to Flora's invitation and then a farewell note
to Alfredo. He returns and for a moment she weakens;
then, crying, she begs him to remember her as she is at
that moment.

Alfredo, confused by Violetta's emotional behaviour,
receives a note from her saying that she has returned to
Paris and to Baron Douphol. His father is at hand, ready
to comfort him, begging him to return home. Alfredo,
swearing revenge on Violetta, pursues her to Paris.

Alfredo arrives at Flora's party, followed by Violetta on
the arm of Baron Douphol, who orders her to ignore her
former lover.

At the card-table, Alfredo wins. He calls out that he expects Violetta's return. The Baron joins the game and loses heavily. Supper is announced. Presently Violetta hurries back. She has asked Alfredo to follow her and, when he comes, tells him to leave Paris at once. She is afraid Douphol means to challenge him. When pressed, she admits she has sworn never to return to him. 'Who by?' 'By someone who has the right to ask it.' 'Douphol?' '...Yes.' 'So you love him?' 'Yes.' Enraged, Alfredo calls the others in and flings the money he has won in her face, saying that he has now repaid all that she has spent on him. Her friends are appalled by this insult; even his father now turns against him, uncomfortably aware of the depth of the misunderstanding.

Violetta's bedroom several months later

ACT III

Violetta is dying. The doctor calls and warns Annina that there is little time left. Violetta reads again a letter she has received telling her that Alfredo, having fled abroad after wounding Douphol in a duel, now knows the truth of her apparent betrayal and is on his way back to her. Looking in the mirror, she realizes that her life is over and sings of her hope that God will pardon her.

Addio, del passata ('Farewell to the past'): Violetta sings of her approaching death

Suddenly Alfredo is with her, begging forgiveness and singing of their future together. Tenderly she responds, but then collapses. Annina rushes for the doctor, while the lovers try to comfort each other. Alfredo's father arrives, reproaching himself. Violetta begs Alfredo to find a new love, untainted by the world's miseries, and to remember that she will be praying for them both in heaven.

Parigi, o cara, noi lasceremo ('To Paris together'): the tragic duet in which Violetta and Alfredo half believe that they have a future together in Paris

The bystanders give way to grief. Suddenly Violetta revives for a moment. Her youth returns. Then, with a last cry, it is over. '*La traviata*' is at rest.

SIMON BOCCANEGRA

Simon Boccanegra, Doge of Genoa	baritone	
Amelia, his illegitimate daughter	soprano	
Gabriele, her suitor	tenor	
Fiesco, her grandfather	bass	
Paolo, leader of the plebeian party	bass	

Genoa, 14th century: as Doge of Genoa, Simon Boccanegra finds himself caught up in political intrigue. The rivalry for his daughter's hand precipitates tragedy.

The libretto is by Piave. The plot of *Simon Boccanegra* remains very complicated, even after the considerable revisions made by the composer Boito and by Verdi himself. Indeed, the composer was still tinkering with it 25 years after its initial failure in Venice in 1857.

A square in Genoa

PROLOGUE

Simon Boccanegra has become a hero of Genoa through his success in driving away pirates. He had a child by the daughter of the Doge Fiesco and this child has been lost. Boccanegra, though a plebeian, is elected to the office of doge just as Fiesco's daughter dies.

The garden of the Grimaldi palace

ACT I

Twenty-five years later, Amelia (unknowingly the lost daughter of Boccanegra) is the cause of rivalry between her lover Gabriele and Boccanegra's chief supporter Paolo. Fiesco, her guardian (in fact, her grandfather) is now plotting secretly with his fellow patricians and supports Gabriele. When Boccanegra comes to visit Amelia, the truth about her birth is accidentally discovered, and father and daughter rejoice at finding each other.

Figlia, a tal nome ('Daughter, that precious word'): Boccanegra's discovery that Amelia is his daughter

The council chamber of the Doge's palace

Boccanegra now supports Gabriele's efforts to claim Amelia's hand, but Paolo plans to kidnap the girl. During a council meeting, a riot is provoked by Gabriele killing one of Paolo's servants in defence of Amelia. When Gabriele, a patrician, turns against Boccanegra, supposing he has ordered her kidnap, it is only Amelia's intervention that forestalls disaster. She rightly suspects Paolo. Boccanegra forces all (including the horrified Paolo) to pronounce a curse on the man responsible for the attempted abduction.

Plebe! Patrizi! ('Plebeians! Patricians!'): Boccanegra attempts to restore order

The Doge's apartments

ACT II

Paolo, having poisoned Boccanegra's wine, tries to bribe Fiesco. Then he taunts Gabriele, suggesting that Amelia is Boccanegra's mistress: she is living in his house, and their true relationship is still being concealed. Boccanegra drinks the poisoned wine. When Gabriele enters intending to kill him, Amelia is just in time to prevent this. The two men join forces, Gabriele volunteering to quell a further patrician uprising and Boccanegra agreeing to his marriage to Amelia.

Perdon, Amelia ('Forgive me, Amelia'): the trio between Boccanegra, his daughter and Gabriele bringing peace between them

A room in the palace

ACT III

Paolo has been captured fighting for the rebels. On the way to his execution he tells Fiesco that he has poisoned Boccanegra. When Boccanegra enters, Fiesco announces his fate. Before dying, Boccanegra is able to reveal Amelia to Fiesco as his long-lost grand-daughter, to bless her marriage with Gabriele and finally to commend Gabriele as his successor.

Un velen ('A poison!'): Paolo triumphantly tells Fiesco that he has poisoned Boccanegra, just before he himself is dragged off to execution

UN BALLO IN MASCHERA
(A MASKED BALL)

Gustavus, King of Sweden	tenor
Oscar, his page	soprano
Captain Anckarstroem, the King's secretary	baritone
Amelia, Anckarstroem's wife	soprano
Mlle Arvidson, a fortune-teller	contralto

Sweden, 18th century: King Gustavus is in love with Amelia, wife of his secretary. He is murdered by her husband even though he had arranged that they part.

Gustavus III's assassination at a masked ball at the Stockholm opera house in 1792 was the event on which a libretto by Eugène Scribe was based. It was from this that Antonio Somma's libretto for *Un Ballo in Maschera* in turn derived. The opera was first performed at the Teatro Apollo, Rome, in 1859. Since anything that threatened the concept of monarchy was proscribed in Italy, Verdi was forced (as with *Rigoletto*) to alter the setting. He transferred the action to America, substituting Richard, Earl of Warwick, governor of Boston (Riccardo), for the Swedish King and Renato for Anckarstroem. Modern producers almost invariably re-set the action in Sweden, as described here.

ACT I

The hall of the royal palace
La rivedrò nell'estasi ('Found again in ecstasy'): the King's joy at having the chance to see the woman he loves
Volta le terrea ('Turn to the stars'): Oscar's aria defending the fortune-teller against threats of banishment

The court of King Gustavus is divided between those who enthusiastically support him and those who plot his assassination. The King is in love with Anckarstroem's wife Amelia, and he is more interested that he will see her at his masked ball than in her husband's warning of a plot against him.

Oscar defends the reputation of an old fortune-teller and this encourages the King to visit her incognito.

Mlle Arvidson's hut

E scherzo ed è follia ('What a joke'): the King scorns the prophecy of his murder

While there, Gustavus overhears Amelia confessing her love for him. The fortune-teller predicts his imminent murder at the hand of the next friend to greet him. When the others draw back, it is Anckarstroem who hurries in and takes the King's hand. At this, the King reveals his identity and laughs off the prophecy.

ACT II

Outside the city at midnight
Oh, qual soave ('How wonderful'): the love duet between the King and Amelia

The King and Amelia (in disguise) meet, but they are interrupted by her husband who has come to warn the King against the conspirators. Gustavus manages to persuade his friend to escort the heavily veiled woman to safety without trying to discover her identity. Anckarstroem, now wearing the King's cloak, is ambushed by the conspirators. He is unable to prevent them unveiling his companion, so revealing that it is his own wife.

The Anckarstroem's house

Eri tu ('It was you'): the King's
portrait provides a focus for
Anckarstroem's bitterness and
jealousy

The royal palace

ACT III

Having decided against killing his wife, Anckarstroem
and two other conspirators place their names in an urn to
decide who will kill the King. It is her husband's name
that Amelia draws, unaware of its import.

At the masked ball that night, the King meets Amelia and
tells her that he has decided to send Anckarstroem as
ambassador to Finland with Amelia to protect his
friend's marriage. Meanwhile, her husband has succeeded in discovering from Oscar his master's disguise.
As Amelia parts sadly from the King, her husband steps
forward and stabs him.

DON CARLOS

Elisabetta di Valois	soprano
Princess Eboli	mezzo-soprano
Filippo II	bass
Don Carlos, Filippo's son	tenor
Rodrigo, his friend	baritone
Grand Inquisitor	bass
Friar	bass

France and Spain, mid-16th century: Don
Carlos and Elisabetta di Valois fall in love
before his father, Filippo II, claims her as
wife. Don Carlos is also in opposition to his
father over conditions in Flanders.

The libretto is by Joseph Méry and Camille du Locle. Verdi wrote his great political
work, which deals with the struggle between
Church and State, for the Paris Opéra,
where it was first performed in 1867. It was
originally in five acts with a ballet, and the
story is set out here as in the original. Since
this can last over four hours in performance,
some cutting and rearrangement is normal.

The Forest of Fontainebleau

*Fontainebleau! Foresta immensa e
solitaria!* ('Fontainebleau! Vast
and lonely forest'): Don
Carlos' aria as he surveys the
beautiful forest
Di qual amor ('So much
happiness'): the young lovers'
duet before their dream is
shattered

ACT I

Don Carlos, Infante of Spain, has come to France to meet
Elisabetta, whom he is to marry as part of a peace treaty.
During the hunt, Don Carlos celebrates the beautiful
forest where he has already fallen in love with the young
princess from a distance. She, lost, meets him, and
gradually he wins her confidence before revealing that he
is also her future husband. Their love duet is interrupted
by the news that his father, Filippo II of Spain, has
decided to marry her himself. They part in despair as she
is hailed as queen.

**The monastery of San Giusto,
beside the tomb of Carlos V,
Don Carlos' grandfather**

ACT II

While the monks sing a hymn to Carlos V, a solitary friar
reflects that the King ruled with an earthly pride and that
God alone is great. Don Carlos has come to the

monastery to try to forget Elisabetta. He remembers the rumour that his grandfather is in truth still alive and living there as a simple monk. His friend Rodrigo, Marquis of Posa, arrives to ask him to help free the Flemish people enslaved by Spain. Carlos confides in Rodrigo his passion for Elisabetta just as she arrives with his father. The two vow perpetual friendship in the cause of liberty.

Dio, che nell' alma infondere ('Oh God who promotes love and hope'): Don Carlos and his friend Rodrigo pledge faithful support to each other

In the monastery garden
Nei giardin ('In a garden'): the Veil Song has unintentional irony for Princess Eboli herself

While the ladies of the court are resting, Princess Eboli tells them the story of a Moorish king who tries to seduce a veiled almah, only to find it is his wife. Elisabetta, queen now, returns, and Rodrigo brings her a letter from her mother together with a note from Don Carlos, which she reads secretly. Rodrigo loves Princess Eboli but she in turn loves Don Carlos. She understands his words to mean that Don Carlos returns her feelings.

Perduto ben, mio sol tesor ('Lost love, my only treasure'): Don Carlos' increasingly amorous approach to his stepmother, Elisabetta

Don Carlos arrives to ask the Queen to promote his being sent as viceroy to Flanders. Once alone with her, he pours out his love. The King, arriving to find the Queen alone, dismisses her French companion for neglecting her. Seeing Rodrigo, the King asks where he has been and Rodrigo replies that he has been in Flanders, where the people are unjustly oppressed by the Inquisition. The King retorts that the Spanish people are happy enough within their religious peace. This peace Rodrigo, however, likens in Flanders to the peace of death. At this, the King warns him to beware of the Grand Inquisitor. The King's further confidences, about his suspicions concerning his wife, encourage Rodrigo to believe that he will be able to guide the King in the future and thus further his own and Don Carlos' purposes.

The Queen's garden at night during a masked ball

Io t'amo, io t'amo – Ciel! Non è la Regina ('I love you. Oh heavens, you are not the Queen'): Don Carlos mistakes Princess Eboli for the Queen, echoing the mistake told in her song

ACT III
Don Carlos has received a note from Elisabetta agreeing to meet him by the fountain. A woman dressed like the Queen enters and he rushes to embrace her, only to find that it is Princess Eboli, who thus discovers his secret. Rodrigo intercedes to calm her anger, but without success. When she threatens to reveal all, Rodrigo draws his dagger, but Don Carlos stops him from killing her and she escapes. Rodrigo persuades Don Carlos to let him have any secret papers about Flanders in case the King orders his son's arrest, and they part with renewed commitment to each other.

A square in Madrid

The crowds have gathered to watch Flemish Protestants being burned at the stake. As they and the monks rejoice at this festival, the King and Queen lead the procession towards the church. They are interrupted by Don Carlos and six Flemish deputies who have come to beg for clemency. The King rejects their appeal even though the Queen, his son and Rodrigo join in. At last his son demands that he be allowed to go and rule the Flemish. The King refuses. Don Carlos draws his sword and promises freedom for the Flemish when he becomes King. This is treason, and when no-one will obey the King's order to disarm Don Carlos, the King seizes a soldier's sword himself. At this, Rodrigo goes forward and takes Don Carlos' sword, to the latter's dismay. Conferring a dukedom on Rodrigo for his loyalty, the King orders the burnings to proceed amid wild rejoicing, while a voice from heaven can be heard welcoming the souls of the dying.

The King's study
Ella giammai m'amò ('She has never loved me'): A famous bass aria. Filippo reflects that his wife has never loved him and that her heart has always been closed against him

ACT IV
At daybreak, Filippo reflects that his wife has never loved him. The Grand Inquisitor is announced. He is old and blind. The King has asked whether the Church would absolve him if he had his son beheaded. To this, the Inquisitor assents, asking in turn that Rodrigo should be handed over to the Inquisition. The King refuses. The Inquisitor threatens the King and, turning to go, asks why he was brought there in the first place.

The Queen arrives to complain that her jewel box has been stolen. The King returns it to her and asks her to open it. When she refuses, he forces it open and finds his son's portrait. She explains that she loved him when they were betrothed but has been faithful to her husband. He accuses her of adultery so violently that she faints. As others help her, Rodrigo rebukes him for being in control of half the world and yet unable to control himself.

The Queen is alone with Princess Eboli. When the latter admits that it was she who alerted the King, the Queen banishes her to a convent. The Princess welcomes her sentence, cursing her own vanity and asking for one day of freedom to help save Don Carlos.

O don fatale ('The fatal gift of beauty'): Princess Eboli denounces the gift that has destroyed her and the man she loves

A dungeon

When Rodrigo visits Don Carlos in prison, it is to tell him that by being in possession of the secret papers he has taken the blame on himself for the future of Flanders. A shot rings out. It is Rodrigo who is the victim. He tells Don Carlos that the Queen will be waiting for him at the monastery next day. As he dies, the King enters to return his son's sword. Overcome, Don Carlos reveals that Rodrigo's self-accusation was false. Meanwhile, a riot has broken out and a mob storms the prison calling for Don Carlos. As the King offers to release him, the Grand Inquisitor returns. He silences the crowd, giving back the King his authority only after the King acknowledges his allegiance to God.

**At the monastery of San
Giusto**
Tu che la vanità conoscesti ('You
who know the emptiness of
earthly power'): the Queen's
piteous aria, asking for help at
the tomb of Carlos V

ACT V

The Queen, alone in front of the tomb of Carlos V, prays
that he will intercede for her in heaven. Don Carlos joins
her and they share a long duet reassuring each other of
their love. Both realize that Don Carlos is doomed. When
the King and the Grand Inquisitor arrive to arrest them,
the friar emerges from the tomb in his imperial robes and
the Grand Inquisitor hears in his voice that of Carlos V.
As the others fall back, the figure of his grandfather leads
Don Carlos out of sight.

AIDA

Aida, an enslaved Ethiopian princess	soprano
Amneris, an Egyptian princess	mezzo-soprano
Radames, an Egyptian army captain	tenor
Amonasro, the Ethiopian King and Aida's father	baritone
Ramfis, High Priest of Egypt	bass
King of Egypt, Amneris' father	bass

Memphis and Thebes, in the time of the
Pharaohs: Radames, an officer in the Egyptian army, loves the enslaved Ethiopian,
Aida; he is indifferent to the affection of
Princess Amneris. Radames' passion leads
him to betray his country to Aida's father,
and tragedy is inevitable.

The plot was devised by Auguste
Mariette; the libretto was written in French
by Camille du Locle and translated into
Italian verse by Antonio Ghislanzoni. Commissioned by the Khedive of Egypt, *Aida*
was first performed in Cairo in 1871. Verdi
was not present at the world premiere, but at
its first performance in Milan the following
year the composer received 32 curtain calls.

**Hall in the King's palace at
Memphis**

Celeste Aida ('Heavenly Aida'):
Radames' hymn to Aida

ACT I

Ramfis, the High Priest, tells Radames, the captain of the
guard, that Ethiopian forces are again threatening the
valley of the Nile and that the goddess Isis will name the
new leader of the Egyptian army. Radames goes to tell the
King. He hopes to be given the command so that he may
win the love of Aida, an Ethiopian princess held as a
slave.

The King's daughter Amneris, who is in love with
Radames, joins him, and they talk of the coming battle.
Each is concerned to hide her true feelings from the other;
but when Aida enters, Amneris suspects Radames' love
for Aida from his expression. The King enters with
Ramfis and others to hear the latest news of the Ethiopian
invasion. He announces that Isis has named Radames as

Ritorna vincitor! ('Return as conqueror!'): Aida urges on Radames even though he marches against her compatriots

general. Amneris presents him with a banner as he leads the people into the temple.

Aida is in a dilemma. She returns Radames' love and wants him to succeed, but the invaders are led by her father, the King of the Ethiopians. Victory for one means defeat for the other.

Inside the temple of Phtha

Ramfis and the assembled priests and priestesses invoke the God of Fire. While the priestesses perform the ritual dance, Radames is handed the sword which will give him divine power.

Amneris' apartment

ACT II
Amneris, preparing for the victory celebrations, pretends sympathy with Aida, who is worried about her father and brothers. To test her suspicions, Amneris tricks Aida by telling her that Radames has died leading his troops. When Aida breaks down, Amneris immediately accuses her of being her rival; and Aida, overwhelmed by the news that Radames is alive, admits her love. Amneris threatens to have her killed. Aida asks simply for pity so that she may die in peace.

Pietà ti prenda ('Have pity'): Aida's plea in the face of Amneris' jealous hatred

By the temple of Ammon in Thebes

The tremendous review of the victorious Egyptian army, to the accompaniment of a glorious march precedes the return of Radames. While Amneris gives him the victor's crown, her father promises to grant him any request. The prisoners are brought in, among them Aida's father, Amonasro. When questioned, Amonasro pretends that the Ethiopian King is dead and that he is just one of the officers. He asks for mercy for his soldiers. Ramfis and the priests demand their execution though the King would prefer to spare them. At last Radames intervenes and asks, as his favour, that the Ethiopian prisoners be freed. The crowd is delighted, but Ramfis, though believing that Amonasro was killed, warns both King and general to beware of mistaken generosity. The High Priest suggests that Aida and her father remain as hostages for peace. This the King accepts, granting also the hand of his daughter to the startled and unwilling Radames.

The banks of the Nile at night

ACT III
Ramfis has brought Amneris to the temple to pray for the love of her future husband; Aida is also there, ready to drown herself in the Nile should her lover intend to turn away from her. She remembers happier days in her own country. Suddenly, her father enters. He knows of her love and tells her that he can unite her with Radames and take them both home if only she can persuade him to betray his soldiers by revealing his battle plan. She resists and Amonasro imagines for her the destruction of their

O patria mia ('O homeland'): Aida thinks back to her days of freedom in Ethiopia

cities and the spectre of her mother cursing her for abandoning them. At least Aida agrees, and her father draws back into the shadows.

Radames appears, and finds her alone and in despair. He tries to cheer her with the thought that further victories will give him the right to claim her as his bride. She, however, persuades him to desert and follow her to Ethiopia and, as they plan their escape, she asks which route his army will follow so that they can avoid it. He tells her, and her father triumphantly repeats his words. He reveals himself to be Amonasro, the King. As Radames reproaches himself for betraying his country, Amneris comes out of the temple having overheard everything that was said. Amonasro moves to stab her, but Radames stops him and surrenders himself to Ramfis as Aida and her father escape.

Fuggiam gli ardori inospiti ('Let us escape the scorching heat'): Aida's plea that Radames should run away with her
Le gole di Nápata ('The pass at Napata'): with these fatal words, Radames betrays his army

The King's palace

ACT IV
Amneris is torn between rage at Radames' love for Aida and her wish to save the man she loves. The guards bring him in. Radames tells her he will not defend himself because life without Aida is unbearable to him. Amneris tells him that Amanasro was killed and that Aida has disappeared. She begs Radames to forget Aida and let her save him, but he remains resolute. As he is taken before the priests, she curses the jealousy that has rebounded against her. She can hear the accusations, to which Radames gives no response, thus condemning himself. The priests commit Radames to entombment beneath the altar. Leaving, they ignore Amneris' desperate cries.

Inside the temple
O terra, addio ('O Earth, farewell'): the dying duet between Aida and Radames developing into a trio with Amneris waiting above, joined by the chorus of priestesses

Sealed in the tomb, Radames hears a sound. Aida, guessing his fate, has managed to hide beneath the altar and they are trapped there together. As the priestesses with Amneris pray for peace and forgiveness for Radames, he and Aida sing a last duet of love.

OTELLO

Otello (Othello), a Moorish general in the Venetian army	tenor	
Desdemona, his wife	soprano	
Emilia, her maid	mezzo-soprano	
Iago, Emilia's husband and Otello's aide	baritone	
Cassio, Otello's lieutenant	tenor	
Roderigo, a Venetian gentleman	tenor	

Cyprus, 15th century: Shakespeare's tragedy, the plot revolving round Otello's terrible jealousy, which leads him to act upon Iago's treacherous insinuation of Desdemona's guilt.

Fifteen years after *Aida*, and having apparently given up operatic composition, Verdi was persuaded to set Arrigo Boito's libretto to music. The collaboration resulted in a masterpiece. *Otello* was first performed at La Scala in 1887.

Outside the castle

Esultate! ('Rejoice'): Otello celebrates his victory over the enemies of Venice

Inaffia l'ugola! ('Quench your thirst!'): Iago's drinking song, intended to make Cassio drunk
Già nella notte densa ('Hidden in the night'): the love duet between Otello and Desdemona

A room in the castle

Credo in un Dio crudel ('I believe in a God of cruelty'): Iago's creed glorifying evil

Dove guardi splendono ('Where'er you look'): the delightful chorus of Desdemona's companions in the garden

ACT I

The opera opens to a colossal storm. Cassio and others assembled can see Otello's ship approaching the harbour and in great trouble. They pray for its safety, all except Iago and Roderigo, who hope for its destruction: Shortly afterwards, Otello leads his crew triumphantly up to the castle. Roderigo and Iago are left sour and disappointed. Roderigo desires Desdemona, Otello's wife; Iago is angry that Otello has promoted Cassio instead of himself. Iago advises Roderigo to be patient, saying that Desdemona will soon tire of 'black embraces'. Encouraging Cassio to get drunk, Iago is able to provoke him into fighting with Roderigo. Otello intervenes. He demotes Cassio, giving the command to Iago. When the others depart, Otello is left alone on the ramparts with Desdemona, and there follows a splendid love scene between husband and wife.

ACT II

Iago, pretending to help Cassio, suggests he should wait in the garden and ask Desdemona's help in regaining his command. When Cassio has gone, Iago sings a ringing celebration of the power of evil.

Cassio is with Desdemona. Seeing Otello approaching, Iago utters the words 'Ciò m'accora' (How upsetting'). Subtly he attempts to poison Otello's mind by pretending to try to hide his suspicions about Desdemona's faithfulness. Desdemona comes back through the garden, surrounded by children – the very image of innocence. Otello's delight at this happy scene serves to increase Iago's determination to shatter their contentment.

Desdemona joins her husband and her first words are about Cassio. She is amazed when Otello angrily refuses

Dammi la dolce e lieta parola ('Say that you forgive me'): Desdemona's request for forgiveness if she has unwittingly annoyed her husband

Ora è per sempre addio ('Farewell to all joy'): Otello's bitter renunciation of happiness

Sì, pel ciel ('By the heavens above I swear'): Otello and Iago pledge themselves to destroy Desdemona and Cassio

The hall of the castle

E un dì sul mio sorriso ('Smiling only yesterday'): Desdemona reflects sadly on their lost happiness amidst a scene of gathering violence

to discuss him. When she pulls out her handkerchief to soothe his brow, he throws it to the ground and Emilia picks it up. In the quartet that follows, Desdemona reiterates her love for Otello while Otello sings of the loss of his dream of love. Meanwhile, Iago persuades the apprehensive Emilia into giving him Desdemona's handkerchief.

When the women have left, Otello is tortured by his own suspicions. He bitterly reproaches Iago for disturbing his peace of mind; then, turning on Iago, Otello demands proof. With the handkerchief still to be used as evidence, Iago tells Otello that he heard Cassio murmuring about Desdemona in his sleep. Lying side by side, Cassio embraced Iago, thinking that he was Desdemona. At this, Otello loses all restraint and, in a fierce duet, he and Iago vow to take revenge on the guilty lovers.

ACT III
As the vessel belonging to the envoy from Venice is sighted, Otello is preoccupied with Iago's plan to lead Cassio into further indiscretions. Apparently as an afterthought, Iago suggests that Otello ask his wife to show him the handkerchief he gave her. Desdemona enters and soon returns to the subject of Cassio. Offering him a handkerchief to soothe the burning pain in his forehead, she is asked for the one Otello gave her when they first met. When she cannot find it, Otello warns her that it contains a spell which will bring ruin if she has given it away. Desdemona promises to go and find it later, and a quarrel ensues. She swears that she is faithful to him, but Otello insists that she is no better than a whore and sends her from the room. Iago brings in Cassio and, while Otello hides, Iago encourages Cassio to speak unguardedly about the girl (Bianca) whom he loves. Otello is led to believe Cassio is speaking of Desdemona. When Cassio produces the handkerchief, which he says someone left in his room, the last piece of Iago's plot fits into place.

For Otello the only decision now is how to kill his wife. The envoy from Venice appears with many compliments for both Otello and Desdemona. All are startled by Otello's cruelty towards his wife. Otello reads to the assembly the Doge's decree: Otello is to be recalled to Venice and Cassio given command of Cyprus. Suddenly, Otello in a fury flings his wife to the ground. As the whole assembly breaks up in scandalized confusion, Iago counsels Otello to kill his wife as soon as possible and plots with Roderigo to murder Cassio that night. A crowd outside choruses its praise of Otello, the living

Ecco il Leone ('Here is your Lion'): Iago's ironical comment as he looks at Otello, slumped on the floor

Lion of St Mark; but Otello, in his agitation, falls senseless to the ground, where Iago points to him in a gesture of triumph.

Desdemona's bedroom

O Salce! Salce! Salce! ('Oh willow! willow! willow!'): Desdemona's tragic song
Ave Maria: Desdemona's last prayer

ACT IV

Desdemona has been ordered to wait for Otello in their bedroom, their bridal sheets upon the bed. She remembers that her mother told her of a girl deserted by her lover who sang a willow song. She sings it now for Emilia and, as her maid leaves her, the song ends on a piercingly beautiful note of farewell.

Desdemona kneels to pray and, afterwards, lies down on the bed to sleep. Her husband enters silently and, after watching her for a moment, bends over to kiss her. When she wakes, he tells her that he has come to kill her. She protests her innocence, imploring him to ask for proof from Cassio. Otello tells her that Cassio is already dead. She begs to be allowed to live a little longer or at least to say a last prayer. In vain. Otello strangles her as, too late, a knocking on the door brings help. Cassio has killed Roderigo, who confessed Iago's plot. As Emilia reveals the truth about the handkerchief, Iago flees. Otello is left to face the truth. He crosses to the bed and stabs himself with a dagger.

Un bacio ancora ('One last kiss'): Otello's dying words

FALSTAFF

Sir John Falstaff	baritone
Alice Ford	soprano
Ford, her husband	baritone
Nannetta, their daughter	soprano
Fenton, her suitor	tenor
Mistress Quickly, a neighbour	contralto
Bardolfo (Bardolph) ⎫ Falstaff's	tenor
Pistola (Pistol) ⎭ friends	bass

Windsor, during the reign of Henry IV: the amorous intrigues of the bibulous Sir John develop into a series of comic schemes directed against him.

Falstaff is Verdi's last opera and it is partly due to the ingenious encouragement of Arrigo Boito, who wrote the libretto, that he began in his late 70s to work on it. Based principally on Shakespeare's *The Merry Wives of Windsor*, elements from *Henry IV* and *As You Like It* were assimilated into the plot. The first performance of the opera was given at La Scala in 1893.

The Garter Inn

ACT I

Falstaff, after promising Dr Caius that he will try to drink less (except in good company), complains to Pistola and

L'onore! Ladri! ('Damn your honour!'): Falstaff's splendid tirade on the subject of the honour which prevents Pistola and Bardolfo delivering his letters

The garden of Ford's house

Quell'otre! quel tino! ('That barrel of sack!'): a quartet of outraged women giving tongue

The inn

E sogno? o realtà? ('Is this a dream? or is it really true?'): Ford's disbelief at his wife's deceit

A room in Ford's house

Quand'ero paggio ('The Duke of Norfolk's page was I'): Falstaff's vision of himself in slimmer days, intended to excite Alice Ford

The inn

Versiamo un po' di vino nell'acqua del Tamigi ('Thames water will be much improved by pouring in some wine!'): Falstaff's self-pity is greatly enlivened by the offer of some wine

Bardolfo that his income cannot support them and his belly. He has fallen for two well-heeled wives of Windsor but his friends refuse to carry his love-letters. Chasing them away, he gives the letters to a page.

Mistress Ford and Mistress Page have received the letters and are comparing them: they are identical. While Nannetta Ford flirts with Fenton, her father is learning the unwelcome news that Falstaff has designs on his wife. The act ends in a complicated ensemble as all Windsor unites in its outrage at Falstaff's presumption.

ACT II

Mistress Quickly is introduced by Pistola and Bardolfo (now in Ford's pay) to tell Falstaff that Alice Ford will receive him between 2 and 3 o'clock but that Meg Page is too closely guarded by her husband to receive him. He is overcome with excitement. They then produce 'Mister Fountain' (Ford in disguise). He pretends also to be unsuccessfully in love with Alice Ford. Falstaff cannot help boasting that he, on the contrary, has an assignation with her in half an hour and will willing pass her on to 'Fountain' in return for money. After cheerfully abusing Ford (to his face), Falstaff leaves the wretched husband in an agony of jealousy.

Ford wants his daughter to marry old Dr Caius, but her mother is sympathetic to her love for Fenton. Falstaff arrives. He has hardly begun to serenade Alice Ford before they are interrupted with news that her husband is returning. He has to be squeezed behind a screen and then bundled into a laundry basket full of dirty clothes. When Ford hears a kiss behind the screen, he becomes convinced of his wife's guilt, but, when he pulls it aside, he finds his daughter and Fenton. The women throw the laundry basket out of the window into the Thames. Alice shows her husband the remarkable sight of Falstaff swimming to the bank.

ACT III

Poor Falstaff needs more wine. Mistress Quickly returns. This time he is less inclined to listen and follow the instructions in Alice's letter. But told that she loves him, he does agree to go to Herne's Oak in Windsor Great Park at midnight disguised as the Black Huntsman. The others are all listening, and Ford is still trying to arrange the marriage of his daughter.

Windsor Great Park

With his neighbours all suitably disguised as supernatural phantoms and hiding among the trees, Falstaff arrives, horned and cloaked and ready for love. Alice comes towards him. She tells him that Meg Page is also coming, and his enthusiasm is heroically redoubled. However, they are interrupted by fearsome noises and visions. Nannetta, disguised as the Faerie Queen, appears with an enchanting chorus.

Sul fil d'un soffio etesio ('Born by the breeze'): Nannetta, dressed as the Faerie Queen, calls her followers to dance through the moonlit forest

Tutto nel mondo è burla ('All the world's a stage'): the thoughtful finale to the hilarity

More and more interlopers confuse the unhappy Falstaff until the joke is revealed. He claims to have at least provided them all with comic relief and, after further confusion, Ford finds that he has inadvertently agreed to his daughter marrying Fenton. The fugue which ends the opera restores to Windsor a sense of calm, its opening words coming from a speech in *As You Like It* of more sombre mood.

ATTILA

In a prologue and three acts, text by Temistocle Solera, after Zacharias Werner's play *Attila, König der Hunnen.* Premiere: La Fenice, Venice, 1846. A robust drama of vivid contrasts, its dashing momentum is typical of Verdi's earlier works.

Italy, mid-5th century: Attila (**b**), King of the Huns, has invaded Italy and taken Aquileia. Against his orders, some of the women, led by Odabella (**s**), have been saved; he admires her but she swears vengeance upon him with the sword he gives her. Attila rejects an offer from Ezio (**bar**), a Roman general, to rule the world but leave him Italy. Despite omens to the contrary, he invites Ezio to a banquet. Odabella prevents her lover, Foresto (**t**), from poisoning Attila with wine, wanting to exact her own vengeance; she persuades Attila to spare Foresto. Attila claims her in marriage but, when he finds her in Foresto's arms, she stabs him to death.

LA FORZA DEL DESTINO
(THE FORCE OF DESTINY)

In four acts, with text by Francesco Maria Piave, after Angel de Saavedra, Duke of Rivas' play *Don Alvaro o La Fuerza del Sino* and scenes from Schiller's play *Wallensteins Lager.* Premiere: Imperial Theatre, St Petersburg, 1862. Despite its diffuse libretto, this stirring drama contains some of Verdi's finest tunes, beginning with the impassioned overture.

Spain and Italy, mid-18th century: Don Alvaro (**t**) accidentally kills the Marchese di Calatrava (**b**), father of Leonora (**s**), with whom he is trying to elope. They are pursued by her brother Don Carlo (**bar**), who hopes to exact vengeance. Leonora, disguised as a man, is taken into a monastery by Padre Guardiano (**b**). Joining the army, Alvaro saves Carlo in battle. They become firm friends, until Carlo discovers Alvaro's true identity and challenges him to a duel. Alvaro escapes to Guardiano's monastery, where Carlo tracks him down. They fight. Leonora prays for peace ('*Pace, pace, mio Dio*'), but is stabbed by Carlo, himself already mortally wounded. Comic colour is added by the gypsy Preziosilla (**ms**) and the monk Fra Melitone (**bar**).

RICHARD WAGNER

Born Leipzig 1813, died Venice 1883. With his radical approach to opera as music drama, Wagner raised the melodic and harmonic style of German music to an emotional summit. He became committed to opera after seeing a performance of Beethoven's *Fidelio*. His own first complete opera, *Die Feen*, was finished while he was chorus master at Würzburg in 1834, though not performed until 1888. He was his own librettist and this practice he was to continue for the rest of his life. He held appointments in Magdeburg, Königsberg and Riga, and in 1839 fled with his first wife, the actress Minna Planer, to Paris to escape creditors. Living there in penury and helped by Meyerbeer, he completed *Rienzi* in 1840 and wrote *Der Fliegende Holländer* in 1841. Productions of these in Dresden led to his appointment as *Kapellmeister* to the Saxon court. His romantic fascination with Germanic legend inspired *Tannhäuser* (1845) and *Lohengrin* (1850). A focal point of his operatic career was reached while holidaying in Marienbad in 1845. He had his first premonition of *Die Meistersinger*, read the poems that led to *Tristan und Isolde* and the *Ring*, and started work on *Lohengrin* while also ruminating on the legend of Parsifal. Caught up in the revolutionary movement of 1848, Wagner again fled, settling in Zurich. During his 15-year exile he wrote the essays expounding his ideas on operatic reform and worked on *Der Ring des Niberlungen*, completing the libretti of the four operas in the cycle and some of the music. A love affair with Mathilde Wesendonk interrupted his efforts and he wrote *Tristan und Isole*, with its theme of redemption through love. This was first performed in 1865 at the instigation of Ludwig II of Bavaria, who also was responsible for the premiere in Munich of *Die Meistersinger von Nürnberg* in 1868. Wagner's relationship with Ludwig was regarded as scandalous by the King's ministers, and he moved to Lake Lucerne with Cosima, daughter of Liszt and wife of Hans von Bülow, the conductor. He married Cosima in 1870. The Festspielhaus in Bayreuth was built with the help of Ludwig and it was in this theatre, designed specially for the performance of Wagner's work, that *Der Ring* was premiered in 1876. His last work, *Parsifal*, received its premiere at the second Wagner festival in 1882.

DER FLIEGENDE HOLLANDER

(THE FLYING DUTCHMAN)

Daland, captain of a Norwegian ship	bass
Senta, his daughter	soprano
Erik, her suitor	tenor
Der Holländer (the Dutchman)	bass-baritone

Norway, 18th century: the legendary Flying Dutchman believes Senta to be the woman who will be true to him until death and thus save him from damnation. Overhearing the words of her suitor, Erik, he departs, to be reunited with her as they die together.

Wagner's libretto, based on a legend recounted in an article by Heinrich Heine, was coloured by his own experience of fleeing from Riga by sea: caught in a storm, his ship sought shelter in a Norwegian fjord. This, Wagner's first successful opera, was first performed in Dresden in 1843.

The coast of Norway

Mit Gewitter und Sturm ('Through storm and tempest'): the steersman tries to stay awake by singing
Die Frist ist um ('Another phase completed'): the Dutchman's aria despairing of finding the salvation that he seeks

ACT I

Daland's ship has been driven off course into the creek near Sandviken. He goes below to rest leaving his steersman singing to try to stay awake.

As silence falls, the mysterious black ship of the Flying Dutchman heaves to. While his crew works in silence, the Dutchman himself goes ashore. He reflects that once again the seven-year cycle is complete. Death has always evaded him.

Daland comes back on deck and rebukes his steersman for not noticing the other ship. He commiserates with the fellow captain and the Dutchman offers him some of his treasure in return for hospitality. Learning that Daland has a daughter, he seeks her hand in marriage. Daland is overwhelmed with excitement, while the Dutchman's hopes are also aroused.

Daland's house

Joho hoe!: Senta's ballad of the Flying Dutchman

ACT II

Senta, Daland's daughter, listens dreamily to her companions as they sit spinning, singing of their lovers away at sea. She herself has been much affected by the legend of the Flying Dutchman, condemned by Satan to sail the seas forever as punishment for a foolish oath unless he can find a woman faithful to him until death. He is permitted to anchor every seventh year to search for her. Senta determines to be the woman who will redeem him.

Senta's suitor, Erik, is distressed by her indifference to him. He has dreamed of losing her to a sinister stranger. His warnings increase her desire to drown with the legendary mariner. As Erik leaves, her father brings in the man she immediately recognizes to be the Dutchman in

Wie aus der Ferne ('As from the furthest regions'): the Dutchman believes Senta to be the woman for whom he has been waiting so long

A rocky bay, the two ships moored side by side

Willst jenes Tag's ('But what of that day...?'): Erik reminds Senta of her past affection for him

the portrait on her wall. He exhorts her to greet the homeless and wealthy stranger as her bridegroom. At first they are lost in contemplation of each other. Senta pledges herself to the Dutchman until death and her father blesses their union.

ACT III

On Daland's ship there is much rejoicing but the Dutchman's ship is silent. The Norwegian sailors' invitations seem to be ignored. Suddenly the sea around the dark ship begins to swell; elsewhere the water remains calm. The ghostly chorus of the Dutchman's crew terrifies Daland's men. As the wind drops, they are mocked by the Dutchmen.

Erik has returned to reproach Senta for being untrue to him. The Dutchman, overhearing, believes he has lost his chance of salvation. Senta tries to hold him back and he reveals to her the extra penalty. Not only is he damned until he finds a faithful woman, but any woman who joins him and then proves inconstant is herself condemned eternally. To save her, he jumps aboard his ship and departs.

As the ship heads out towards the open sea, Senta reaches the edge of the cliff and throws herself into the sea, proclaiming her constancy. At this, the Dutchman's ship disappears beneath the waves. As the sun rises, the spirits of Senta and the Dutchman appear together, transfigured.

TANNHAUSER

Tannhäuser, a minstrel knight	tenor	
Hermann, Landgrave of Thuringia	bass	
Elisabeth, Hermann's niece	soprano	
Venus, Goddess of Love	soprano	
Wolfram, a knight	baritone	

The Venusberg

Thuringia, 13th century: at the minstrels' song contest at the Wartburg, Tannhäuser makes his final choice between profane and sacred love – sensuality and spirituality.

Wagner combined a historical figure with a medieval legend to create the libretto of *Tannhäuser*. The opera was first performed in Dresden in 1845.

ACT I

The scene opens in the interior of the Venusberg, legendary home of the goddess who has ensnared Tannhäuser on his travels. Tired of her demands, he is

Naht euch dem Strande ('Come here to me'): the opening chorus of the Venusberg, the legendary mountain of Love

anxious to return home. She seeks to keep him with her, while the luring calls of the nymphs can be heard. As he calls on the Virgin Mary, the Venusberg dissolves and he finds himself in a beautiful valley near the Wartburg, the castle of the Landgrave Hermann.

The valley of the Wartburg

A shepherd is singing of the glories of Spring and pilgrims pass on their way to Rome, when, with the sound of a horn, the Landgrave and his minstrel knights (*minnesänger*) ride up. Tannhäuser had left them some years before because of a quarrel. After not recognizing him at first, they welcome him back. He wishes to travel on, but when his friend Wolfram mentions the name of Elisabeth (whom Wolfram himself has always loved) he falters. Wolfram tells him that however much he offended the others with his outspokenness, he won the heart of Elisabeth. Hearing this, he joyfully agrees to follow them back to the castle.

The Singers' Hall in the Wartburg
Dich, teure Halle ('This blessed room'): Elisabeth's aria expressing her joy at Tannhäuser's return
Gepriesen sei die Stunde ('This glorious moment'): their loving duet convinces Wolfram that his chance of gaining Elisabeth's love is lost

ACT II

Elisabeth rejoices at Tannhäuser's return in the room where she last saw him so long ago. Tannhäuser is led in by Wolfram. Tannhäuser avoids telling her where he has been and they rejoice at the miracle that has brought them together again; meanwhile, Wolfram reflects on the uselessness of his love for Elisabeth. The Landgrave joins his niece. She is unwilling to speak of her love for Tannhäuser but delights him by showing new interest in the song festival. As the contestants and audience appear, he compares the coming battle through music to their past battles in war. Elisabeth will grant the prize to he who sings most worthily of Love, the subject of the competition.

The contest begins with a song about Love as a clear fountain that must never be muddied with wicked boldness. Tannhäuser reacts fiercely, saying that a fountain that may not be approached is unlikely to quench the thirst. Elisabeth wishes to applaud, but the other listeners are shocked. Tannhäuser replies again with frank praise of sensual pleasures. He is immediately challenged, and the knights demand permission to slay him. Wolfram demands the prize. Tannhäuser persists in taunting those unaware of the joys of Venus. As they all rush upon Tannhäuser, Elisabeth protects him. She pleads that, though he has greatly offended, yet he should have the chance of God's mercy. All, including Tannhäuser, are shamed by her. The Landgrave decrees that he must join a pilgrimage to Rome to seek absolution. Tannhäuser willingly departs, while Elisabeth remains to pray for him.

The valley of the Wartburg

O du, mein holder Abendstern
('O dearest star of evening'):
Wolfram's aria as he loses
Elisabeth

ACT III

An orchestral prelude illustrates Tannhäuser's pilgrimage. Wolfram finds Elisabeth waiting in prayer for news from Rome. Pilgrims can be heard returning, but there is no sign of Tannhäuser. In despair, Elisabeth prays to the Virgin that she might be allowed to take on herself the sins of Tannhäuser and by dying win his salvation. As she rises, Wolfram approaches. She motions him away. Watching her for the last time, he greets the evening star, symbol of his hopeless love.

Night is falling and a single pilgrim enters. Wolfram does not at first recognize Tannhäuser, who is pale and exhausted. Now on his way back to the Venusberg, Tannhäuser warns Wolfram to keep away from one who is irredeemably cursed. He tells his friend of his long and devout pilgrimage; of how the Pope, absolving thousands, withheld his blessing from Tannhäuser saying that he had no greater chance of redemption than had the papal staff of sprouting leaves. Thus rejected, he seeks the sympathy of Venus, and while they speak she can be heard welcoming him back. As Tannhäuser is about to throw himself into Venus' arms, Wolfram again invokes the name of Elisabeth. At that moment the minstrels announce her death. Venus, disconsolate, disappears as Elisabeth's coffin is carried past. Tannhäuser kneels to ask her to intercede for him and at that moment another group of pilgrims arrives with the news that the Pope's staff is covered with leaves. As Tannhäuser dies, there is rejoicing at his salvation.

LOHENGRIN

Elsa, Princess of Brabant	soprano
Friedrich von Telramund, her uncle and guardian	baritone
Ortrud, his pagan wife	mezzo-soprano
Heinrich, King of Germany	bass
Lohengrin	tenor

Brabant, 10th century: a knight in shining armour appears to champion Elsa's innocence. In submitting to the evil influence of Ortrud and persuading him to reveal himself as Lohengrin, a knight of the Holy Grail, Elsa loses Lohengrin forever.

Wagner's libretto links the legendary knights of the Holy Grail with the historical character of Heinrich I of Germany. The first performance of the opera, at Weimar in 1850, was conducted by Liszt.

The banks of the Scheldt, near Antwerp

ACT I

Germany is threatened with invasion by Hungary and King Heinrich has come to Brabant seeking military aid.

There, the young Duke of Brabant has mysteriously disappeared while in the care of Elsa, his sister. Friedrich, urged on by his wife, accuses Elsa of murdering him and claims the dukedom for himself. The King, having sent for Elsa, is confused by Elsa's trancelike state as she relates her dream of a knight in shining armour. He rules that her fate shall be decided by combat. The herald calls for a knight to step forward and champion her, but in vain. Then a silver knight appears in a boat being drawn towards the river bank by a swan.

Lohengrin offers himself to Elsa as her champion and future husband. She accepts and promises to obey his solemn instruction that she must never ask him his name or origin. All stand back in preparation for the fight. Lohengrin defeats Friedrich but spares his life, urging him to devote his remaining years to repenting of his false accusation.

Nun sei bedankt, mein lieber Schwan! ('My gratitude, O noble swan!'): Lohengrin regretfully bids the swan depart

ACT II

Friedrich, disgraced, bitterly reproaches his wife for encouraging him to accuse Elsa. Ortrud had persuaded him that her pagan family was destined to regain the dukedom of Brabant. She tells him that there are two ways of destroying Lohengrin's power: by tricking Elsa into asking him his name or by wounding him, cutting off even the tip of one of his fingers.

Elsa appears, singing of her happiness. Ortrud calls out to her for pity and Elsa readily agrees to take her in. Ortrud prays to her gods Wotan and Freia to help her. Alone with Elsa, she tries subtly to undermine Elsa's trust in Lohengrin. Friedrich comes forward and declares his intention to murder Lohengrin.

The people of Brabant are celebrating the accession of Lohengrin as their leader and the coming war against Hungary. Four of the nobles, however, are secretly disturbed at the threat to their own power and prosperity, and they conceal the banished Freidrich. Ortrud again taunts Elsa, casting doubts about Lohengrin's past. When the King and Lohengrin appear, on their way to the cathedral, Friedrich steps forward with loud accusations about Lohengrin's mysterious powers. The crowd sets on him, but Elsa's faith has been disturbed.

Antwerp, outside the castle and the cathedral
Der Rache Werk sei nun beschworen ('Together now, revenge's work'): Friedrich and Ortrud together pledge vengeance on Elsa and Lohengrin

Entweihte Götter! ('You gods whom others have profaned!'): Ortrud's hopes that her ancient gods will triumph over Christianity

O König! Trugbetörte Fürsten! Haltet ein! ('Stop, O King and Princes!'): Friedrich's dramatic interruption of the wedding procession

The bridal chamber
Treulich geführt ('Faithfully guided'): the wedding chorus as Lohengrin and Elsa are conducted to their room

ACT III

After their marriage, Lohengrin and Elsa are escorted to the bridal chamber. Alone together they sing of their love for each other, but soon Elsa cannot resist gently enquiring his name. Lohengrin tries to deflect her, but

Atmest du nicht mit mir die süssen Düfte ('Is not the fragrance of these flowers?'): Lohengrin tries to distract Elsa from her questioning

again and again she reverts to his secret despite his reminder of her promise.

Suddenly Friedrich and his supporters break in. Elsa gives Lohengrin his sword and he instantly kills Friedrich. Elsa sinks unconscious to the ground. The nobles kneel in fear before him. Lohengrin announces that all must meet before the King to hear the answer to Elsa's fateful question.

The banks of the Scheldt

In fernem Land ('In a distant country'): Lohengrin's mystical monologue telling of the knights of the Holy Grail, who are ruled by his father, Parsifal

The King and his followers are assembled with the citizens of Brabant. They proclaim Lohengrin's right to have killed Friedrich. He tells them that he can no longer lead them and that Elsa has broken her promise not to ask him who he is. He discloses that he is one of the knights who guard the Holy Grail, that he is Lohengrin, son of their king, Parsifal.

Lohengrin foretells that King Heinrich will defeat the Hungarians. The swan returns. Lohengrin leaves his sword, horn and ring for Elsa's brother, should he return, and at that Ortrud comes forward to tell them that the swan which draws Lohengrin's boat is Elsa's brother. Because of Elsa's disobedience, he will never now escape Ortrud's spell. Lohengrin kneels in prayer. A dove shows the Divine presence and, as the swan disappears, Elsa's brother is restored to life. With this, Ortrud falls dead. All rejoice, but, when Elsa looks again, Lohengrin is vanishing. With a cry of despair, she slowly sinks to the ground in her brother's arms and dies.

Mein Gatte! Mein Gatte! ('My husband! My husband!'): Elsa's last cry of despair as Lohengrin passes into the distance

TRISTAN UND ISOLDE

Marke, King of Cornwall	bass
Tristan, his nephew	tenor
Isolde, Princess of Ireland	soprano
Melot, a knight of Cornwall	tenor
Kurwenal, Tristan's comrade	baritone
Brangäne, Isolde's companion	mezzo-soprano

Aboard ship, Cornwall and Brittany, in legendary times: the passionate love of Tristan and Isolde for each other, revealed to them through Brangäne's potion, attains fulfilment in darkness and death.

The libretto of the music drama was written by Wagner himself, and the first performance was given in Munich in 1865 under the patronage of Ludwig II of Bavaria

ACT I

The King of Cornwall paid tributes to Ireland. Then Morold, betrothed to the Irish princess Isolde, was sent to exact the tributes and was killed by Tristan. His severed head, still containing a fragment of Tristan's sword, was sent back to Ireland. Tristan was wounded in the conflict and, crossing to Ireland in disguise, sought to be healed through the magical powers of Isolde. Matching the fragment with the Cornish knight's sword and realizing that he must be Tristan, Isolde had intended to kill him but found herself incapable of doing so. Tristan, conquered by the same instantaneous passion, is now carrying Isolde back to Cornwall to become the bride of his king.

The deck of Tristan's ship
Westwärts schweift der Blick ('My eye roves back to the West'): the sailor's eerie song, which arouses Isolde
Mir erkoren, mir verloren ('Chosen for me, lost to me'): Isolde's anguished cry that she and Tristan were destined for each other but are divided by fate
Rache! Tod! Tod uns beiden! ('Revenge! death! Death to us both'): Isolde's curse on Tristan and on herself for sparing the traitor

Following the haunting prelude, the voice of a sailor is heard, aboard the ship in which Tristan is bringing Isolde to Cornwall.

Isolde confides in Brangäne her companion, and tells her to summon Tristan.

Kurwenal, Tristan's comrade, gives an insolent reply to Brangäne.

Isolde now relates how she healed Tristan and confesses to Brangäne her love for him. Brangäne has brought with her the magic potions handed down from Isolde's mother and offers the one which inspires love. Isolde, however, orders her to prepare the draught of death. Kurwenal comes to announce that land is in sight, and she demands that Tristan seek her forgiveness. The young knight enters and she reminds him of his debt to her. He offers her his sword. Instead, she proposes that he drink what is being prepared. Accepting this to be poison, he takes the cup and they drink together as the sailors bring the ship into port. As the potion takes effect, they surrender to the freedom of declaring their love for each other. Brangäne warns them of the arrival of the King and, failing to stir them, admits to having administered the draught of love. (In Wagner's version of the myth, the love potion serves only to free Tristan and Isolde to admit their existing love for each other; in other versions it is the love potion itself that precipitates their passion.)

Wie sich die Herzen wogend erheben! ('Our hearts surge and swell together'): Tristan and Isolde, their reserve broken by Brangäne's potion, pour out their love for each other

King Marke's castle

O sink' hernieder, Nacht der Liebe ('May this night of love enfold us'): the love duet between Tristan and Isolde
O ew'ge Nacht, süsse Nacht! ('Eternal night, sweetest of nights!'): the lovers' exaltation of night

ACT II

Isolde, now queen, waits impatiently for the end of the day. The orchestra indicates the twilight departure of the King's hunting expedition which will free the lovers to meet. Brangäne warns Isolde to beware of Melot. Isolde disregards her and Brangäne puts out the flame which is the signal for Tristan to come. As soon as the torch is extinguished, Tristan joins her and they embrace rapturously. To the lovers, night and death are as one, and oblivion the only path to undisturbed eternal union.

But it was a trap, and Kurwenal warns them as Melot leads in the King. Tristan covers Isolde with his cloak,

Wozu die Dienste ohne Zahl
('What was the point of all
your devotion?'): King Marke
sorrowfully asks why Tristan
served him so faithfully if all
was to end in dishonour

Tristan's castle in Brittany

Der einst ich trotzt' ('She whom I
once defied'): Kurwenal
promises his master that Isolde
will come to him if she is still
living
*Mein Kurwenal, du trauter
Freund!* ('My Kurwenal, my
closest friend'): Tristan's
gratitude to his faithful
companion

Mild und leise ('Softly,
quietly'): Isolde joins Tristan in
death through love (*Liebestod*)

while the King is overcome with grief at Tristan's
treachery.

Tristan asks Isolde if she will accompany him to the
land where sunlight never shines. Willingly, she agrees to
follow him. Melot draws his sword and Tristan, knowing
that it is Melot's love for Isolde that has driven him to
betray them both, prepares to fight.

ACT III
Kurwenal and a shepherd are watching the empty sea.
Tristan, wounded by Melot, is in a trance. As Tristan
revives, Kurwenal explains that he is back home, carried
from the ship on Kurwenal's shoulders. Tristan yearns
for Isolde. Kurwenal tells him that word has been sent to
bring her to him in order once again to heal his wound.

Tristan imagines that he sees Isolde's ship. His mind
wanders back, to how his mother died giving birth to him
and to his father's death when he was a child; then to the
love potion.

There at last is Isolde's ship, with the flag of Cornwall
flying from its mast. It passes the rocks and Kurwenal
reports that Isolde has leaped ashore. Tearing off his
bandages, Tristan raises himself to greet her. She rushes
to him and at once he falls into her arms and dies, calling
out her name. Isolde sinks unconscious over him.

Another ship brings King Marke, Melot and Brangäne.
Kurwenal kills Melot before being struck down himself,
falling beside his master. The King has learned of the
potion from Brangäne, and he comes to bring peace and
to unite the lovers. But Isolde, deaf to his words, is in a
state of ecstasy. As the music swells to a climax, she sings
of her passion for Tristan before sinking lifeless on to his
body.

DIE MEISTERSINGER VON NURNBERG

(THE MASTERSINGERS OF NUREMBERG)

Veit Pogner, a goldsmith	bass
Eva, his daughter	soprano
Magdalene, her nurse	mezzo-soprano
Walther von Stolzing, her suitor	tenor
Sixtus Beckmesser, the town clerk and Walther's rival	baritone
Hans Sachs, a cobbler and poet	baritone
David, his apprentice	tenor

Nuremberg, 16th century: Walther, to win the hand of Eva, must prove himself worthy of becoming a Mastersinger (*Meistersinger*) and triumph in the St John's Day song contest. With his dream-song and with the help of Sachs' cunning, he eventually succeeds, defeating his rival Beckmesser.

Die Meistersinger is a love story and a comedy, set against the background of the town and its people; an allegory of Wagner's struggle for recognition for his style of composition. It was premiered in Munich, in 1868.

St Catherine's Church, Nuremberg

ACT I

Walther von Stolzing, recently arrived in Nuremberg, has fallen in love with Eva, daughter of the goldsmith Pogner, with whom he is staying. Eva is drawn to him. She is promised to the member of the Guild of Mastersingers who wins the forthcoming song contest. David, apprenticed to Sachs the cobbler-poet, explains the rules of the guild to Walther.

Walther is invited by Pogner to take part in a trial. The Marker, who writes the mistakes of an aspiring Mastersinger on a slate, failing him on the eighth, is Beckmesser. He, too, desires to marry Eva, though suspects, rightly, that she dislikes him. Pogner announces the contest to be held on the following day, St John's Day, and after some dissent among the Masters it is concluded that Eva may reject the winner.

Am stillen Herd ('Quietly by the hearth'): Walther describes how he learned to sing from an ancient book and from the sounds of nature

Walther presents his credentials as a poet and singer, and begins his song. Numerous faults are soon shown on Beckmesser's slate and the song is condemned by all except Sachs, who is intrigued by its novelty. Walther is rejected for membership.

The street outside Pogner and Sachs' houses

Was duftet doch der Flieder ('The fragrance of the lilac fills the air'): Sachs reminds himself of how much Walther's song pleased him

ACT II

The apprentices sing a Midsummer's Day song. Eva is determined to marry Walther and to have nothing to do with Beckmesser. Pogner is adamant that Eva must marry a Mastersinger. Sachs, at his workbench, muses on Walther's song. Eva seeks help from Sachs. Throughout the opera there is a delicate suggestion that Sachs also loves Elsa but is too wise to respond to her gentle coquetry. Here, and later, the score specifically quotes from *Tristan*.

Walther appears, angry and disappointed. He and Eva plan to elope, Eva having already decided to disguise herself from Beckmesser by exchanging clothes with her nurse, Magdalene. Sachs, who has overheard their conversation, forestalls their escape by allowing his lamp to light up the street.

Beckmesser arrives to serenade Eva – in truth Magdalene dressed as Eva – but his song is drowned by Sachs' hammering as he mends Beckmesser's shoes. Sachs marks Beckmesser's serenade with blows of the hammer as on the slate in the trial. David, finding Beckmesser paying attentions to Magdalene, whom he loves, attacks him, and a fight breaks out. Then the nightwatchman's horn is heard and the crowd vanishes.

ACT III
David sings the song he has been writing, by mistake to Walther's music. He leaves after encouraging Sachs to marry again and to compete for Eva's hand. Alone, Sachs reflects on the madness of the world and especially of the previous evening, for today is St John's Day.

Walther enters and tells Sachs of the dream he had. Sachs writes it down and helps him to arrange it in a manner that will appeal to the Mastersingers. When they go to dress for the song contest, Beckmesser slips in. He sees the piece of paper with Sachs' writing on it and believes it to be Sachs' song, addressed to Eva. Sachs allows him to take it and use it in the song contest, knowing that Beckmesser could never give a good interpretation of Walther's style.

Eva, pretending that her shoe hurts, comes to the cobbler's shop and there meets Walther, who sings her the third verse of his song. Sachs deals tactfully with the situation, and Eva shows him gratitude for his protective love. The three of them, and David and Magdalene, celebrate the birth of Walther's song.

Members of the various guilds assemble to a march. One of Sachs' own poems is sung, and he steps forward to announce the competition.

Beckmesser is the first contestant. He makes nonsense of Walther's song and turns in humiliation on Sachs as its creator. Sachs proposes that its real creator should sing it. Walther's version strikes all with its beauty. Eva places the winner's wreath on his head. Pogner is about to invest Walther as a Mastersinger, but he declines. Then Sachs intervenes. He persuades Walther to accept, in recognition of the honourable traditions of the Mastersingers and of German art.

Jerum! Jerum! Hallahallohe!: Sachs' noisy song about Adam and Eve, an oblique reference to Eva

Inside Sachs' workshop
Am Jordan Sankt Johannes stand ('On Jordan's bank the Baptist's cry'): David's song for the St John's Day
Wahn! Wahn! Überall Wahn! ('Illusion! Nothing is what it seems'): Sachs' reflections
Morgenlich leuchtend ('Glowing in the dawn'): Walther recites his dream-poem and Sachs writes it down

Selig wie die Sonne ('Blessed as the sun'): the quintet celebrating the birth of Walther's song

A meadow

DER RING DES NIBELUNGEN

(THE NIBELUNG'S RING)

The immense music drama comprises three operas and a preliminary one, to be presented on consecutive days: *Das Rheingold* (*The Rhinegold*), *Die Walküre* (*The Valkyrie*), *Siegfried* and *Götterdämmerung* (*Twilight of the Gods*). It tells of Nibelungs (Dwarves), Gods and Men, their loves and their greed for power. Wagner wrote the libretto and the music, and the plots of the four operas are linked not only by the story but by the recurrence of musical themes, *leitmotifs*.

The operas are based on legend, existing in Germany as an epic poem, the Nibelinglied, and in various versions and other forms in northern Europe. No other work of fiction so perfectly illustrates the saying that the building of a vast central headquarters is the sign of the decay of an organization. From the moment Wotan promises to hand over Freia in return for the giants' building Val-halla, the whole structure of the gods' power is doomed to extinction. The traditional setting is on the Rhine, nears Worms, an ancient Burgundian city.

Wagner began with the death of Siegfried, and by 1848 had completed an opera. He then decided to deal with preceding events in the story. He wrote the complete libretto in reverse chronological order and some of the music before breaking off in 1857 for 12 years. During that time he wrote *Tristan und Isolde*. *Rheingold* and *Die Walküre* were performed separately, in 1869 and 1870, under the patronage of Ludwig II of Bavaria. And it was Ludwig who helped him with the building of the Festspielhaus, the festival opera house, in Bayreuth. The foundation stone was laid on Wagner's 59th birthday in 1872. In 1876 the King arrived by special train to attend the first four-day performance.

DAS RHEINGOLD

(THE RHINEGOLD)

Alberich } Mime	Nibelungs (Dwarves)	bass-baritone tenor
Wotan } Loge	Gods	bass-baritone tenor
Fricka } Freia } Erda	Goddesses	mezzo-soprano soprano contralto
Fasolt } Fafner	Giants	bass-baritone bass

Part I of *Der Ring*: The Nibelung Alberich steals the Rhinegold and has fashioned from it the all-powerful Ring. Overcome by the god Wotan, he lays a curse on the wearer of it. The magic headpiece, the Tarnhelm, and the Ring come into the possession of the giant Fafner, exchanged for the goddess Freia who was the promised reward for building Wotan's castle, Valhalla.

The riverbed of the Rhine

So verfluch ich die Liebe! ('I curse love'): Alberich's first curse, renouncing love

SCENE I

The Rhinemaidens guard the sacred gold, but in teasing Alberich, a Dwarf, they reveal that whoever renounces love and makes a ring from the gold can rule the world. Alberich, cursing love, steals the gold and, laughing, vanishes back to his lair.

The meadows below Valhalla

SCENE II

Wotan (Ruler of the Gods), protector of contracts, is woken by Fricka his wife (Goddess of Marriage). Wotan has bribed the Giants, Fasolt and his brother Fafner, to build a magnificent castle (Valhalla) in return for giving them his sister-in-law Freia (Goddess of Love), forgetting that the Gods' youthfulness depends upon her golden apples. Loge, the devious Fire God, has promised to extricate Wotan from the contract. The Giants appear, demanding the girl as their reward, but Wotan, encouraged by the other Gods, wins a delay to steal and pay over the Rhinegold, now in Alberich's possession, as an alternative prize. The Giants seize Freia as a hostage, and immediately the Gods grow pale without her presence. The inevitability of their decline is already apparent. A mist begins to cloud the brightness of the Gods.

Vollendet das ewige Werk ('The eternal work is complete'): Wotan's pride in the new symbol of his power, to the majestic Valhalla theme

Hieher, Maid! In unsre Macht ('Here, my girl, you belong to us'): the Giants seize Freia as a hostage

The Nibelungs' cavern

SCENE III

The music follows Wotan and Loge down past Alberich's busy slaves to where his brother Mime has forged the Tarnhelm, a magic headpiece that permits whoever wears it to take any form. Alberich, who already possesses the Ring described by the Rhinemaidens, seizes the Tarnhelm and beats his brother. Loge pretends to doubt the powers of the Tarnhelm and Alberich eagerly turns himself first into a dragon and then into a toad, at which he is seized by Wotan and dragged in chains back past his slaves to the surface of the earth.

Dort die Kröte, greife sie rasch! ('Now he's a toad, trap him!'): Alberich's boastfulness leads to his capture by Wotan and Loge

The meadows below Valhalla

SCENE IV

Alberich uses the Ring's power to purchase his release by handing over his accumulated gold. But when Wotan demands the Ring as well, Alberich curses it, that it shall destroy all who wear it.

Fasolt and Fafner return with their hostage Freia to claim the Rhinegold. Fasolt would rather keep the girl and asks that the gold be piled up to hide her. This gives them the chance to demand the Tarnhelm and the Ring. Wotan refuses to deliver the Ring, but Erda (Goddess of Earth) persuades him to add it to the pile. Freia is freed. Immediately, Alberich's curse claims its first victim: Fasolt is murdered by his brother in front of the Gods in a quarrel over who shall have the Ring.

Wotan's attention turns to Valhalla. A rainbow bridge leads the Gods across to their new citadel. Their dignified ascent is accompanied by Loge's cynical prediction of coming disaster and by the Rhinemaidens' pathetic lament at the loss of the Rhinegold.

Verflucht sei dieser Ring! ('Cursed be this Ring!'): Alberich, dispossessed of the Ring, curses whoever holds it

Weiche, Wotan, Weiche! ('You must yield'): Erda's warning to Wotan not to keep the Ring

Ihrem Ende eilen sie zu ('They hurry to their doom'): Loge ironically observes the Gods, consumed with their own vanity

DIE WALKURE

(THE VALKYRIE)

Sieglinde } Walsings, the mortal twin daughter and son of Wotan	soprano	
Siegmund	tenor	
Hunding, Sieglinde's husband	bass	
Wotan, Ruler of the Gods	bass-baritone	
Fricka, his wife	mezzo-soprano	
Brünnhilde, eldest Valkyrie, daughter of Wotan and Erda	soprano	

Part II of *Der Ring*: Sieglinde and Siegmund, the mortal twins born to Wotan, discover each other. In providing for Siegmund the magic sword Nothung, Wotan is accused by his wife Fricka of deceit in influencing the course of their lives. Wotan, as protector of contracts, cannot himself take back the gold, contractually handed over to Fafner. This can only be justly achieved without his influence. Wotan agrees that Brünnhilde, eldest of the Valkyries, should go to the defence of Hunding, Sieglinde's husband; but Brünnhilde defies him. Siegmund dies and Brünnhilde is banished.

The forest dwelling of Sieglinde and Hunding

ACT I

An exhaused and unarmed fugitive (Siegmund) staggers into a rough hut, home of Sieglinde and Hunding. Sieglinde welcomes him, but on her husband's return it is revealed that there is a blood-feud between the two men which must be settled in the morning. The unhappy wife drugs her husband and then learns that Siegmund is her missing brother. She was carried off by Hunding and their mother killed while Siegmund and their father Wälse (one of Wotan's incarnations) were away hunting. Their love for each other is aroused by a breeze entering the hut, and their thoughts of Spring. Once Siegmund has found and drawn the sword (Nothung) that a disguised Wotan has left for him in the ash tree, round which the hut is built, they run away together into the night.

Ha, wer ging? Wer kam herein? ('Who had left? who had entered?'): the door blows open, startling Siegmund and Sieglinde

Among the mountains

ACT II

Just as Wotan, as a man, had fathered Siegmund and Sieglinde, so too, as a god, he had fathered the nine Valkyries. Their mother is Erda and their role is to bring dead heroes to help guard Valhalla. His favourite is Brünnhilde.

Wotan orders Brünnhilde to save Siegmund. But Fricka, Wotan's wife, advances and demands vengeance for Hunding, the wronged husband, she being the Goddess of Marriage. When Wotan protests that the marriage was forced on Sieglinde, Fricka asks whether he is now condoning incest. With pain, Wotan concedes that his earthly son should die.

Hojotoho! Brünnhilde's battle cry

Was deinem in Worten ich künde
('Never have I spoken of this
before'): Wotan's explanation
to Brünnhilde of the history of
the Ring and the reason why
Siegmund must die

To Brünnhilde, in a sustained monologue, Wotan reveals how he pledged first Freia and then the fated Ring to pay for Valhalla. In despair he tells her that the mortal Siegmund is the only one who could regain it and protect the Gods. Fricka has uncovered his deceit in leaving the magic sword Nothung for him and thus interfering in the affair. He commands Brünnhilde, contrary to his emotions, to conquer Siegmund.

Sieglinde, meanwhile, imagines that she hears Hunding's horn. Brünnhilde comes to warn Siegmund that he will die and promises to care for Sieglinde and their unborn child. Then, suffering a change of heart, she defies Wotan, committing herself to protecting Siegmund. Sieglinde wakes as Siegmund and Hunding begin to duel. Siegmund is about to deal the death blow to his rival when Wotan appears. The God shatters Nothung with his spear, at which Hunding kills the unarmed Siegmund. Brünnhilde snatches up the prostrate Sieglinde and disappears. At a gesture from Wotan, Hunding falls to the ground dead.

The Valkyries' rock
The Ride of the Valkyries

*Lebe, O Weib, um der Liebe
willen!* ('You must live for the
sake of love'): Brünnhilde's
inspiration to Sieglinde to live
for the sake of Siegmund's
child

ACT III
The Valkyries assemble, having carried out their business of ferrying dead heroes to Valhalla. Brünnhilde rides in carrying Sieglinde and seeking sanctuary from their father's vengeance, to the dismay of the Valkyries. Sieglinde begs them to let her die. When Brünnhilde tells her that she is carrying Siegmund's child, Sieglinde is inspired with new hope. She escapes to where Fafner, changed into a dragon by the Tarnhelm, guards the gold. Brünnhilde gives her the shattered fragments of Siegmund's sword and pronounces that the child, as yet unborn, shall be named Siegfried.

Brünnhilde remains, and is confronted by the angry Wotan. His sentence is that she shall be a Valkyrie no longer. She is to be left to sleep, a prey to the first man to find her. Pleading that she was carrying out his deepest and most secret wish in giving her support to Siegmund, she begs him to protect her from all but a great hero. This he does by surrounding her with fire. To music of great depth and sadness, Wotan parts forever from his favourite child.

*Leb wohl, du kühnes, herrliches
Kind* ('Farewell sweetest,
bravest child'): Wotan's
parting from Brünnhilde

ROFIELD

SIEGFRIED

Siegfried, son of Siegmund and Sieglinde	tenor
Mime	tenor
Alberich } Nibelungs	bass-baritone
Wanderer (Wotan in disguise)	bass-baritone
Dragon (Fafner in disguise)	bass
Erda, Goddess of Earth	contralto
Brünnhilde, eldest Valkyrie, daughter of Wotan and Erda	soprano

Part III of *Der Ring*: Siegfried, son of Sieglinde and Siegmund, refashions the sword, broken by Wotan. He slays the dragon (Fafner), who is hoarding the Rhinegold. Disposing of Mime and then evading the Wanderer (Wotan), Siegfried claims Brünnhilde as his wife.

Mime's workshop in the forest

ACT I

Mime, who joined Sieglinde and brought up Siegfried after Sieglinde died giving birth to him, is trying yet again to forge a sword that Siegfried cannot break. The latter, returning from the forest with a bear, taunts the Dwarf, whom he despises, and tries to learn more about his birth.

Wotan, disguised as a wanderer, comes in. Mime asks him about the races: his own Nibelungs beneath the earth, Fafner's Giants upon the earth and Wotan's Gods among the mountaintops. In return, Wotan asks Mime about Siegfried's parents and the shattered sword Nothung, the fragments of which Mime has kept. The last question, about who can weld the pieces together, defeats Mime since he himself has failed, and it signals his doom.

Notung! Notung! Neidliches Schwert! ('Nothung! Nothung! Sword desired by all'): Siegfried's triumph as he succeeds in welding the shattered sword

Siegfried returns, fearless and thus invulnerable, and proves himself by successfully welding Nothung. Mime plans to lead him to the dragon's cave, and to drug and murder him once Fafner is dead so that he can take the Ring for himself.

Fafner's cave

ACT II

Alberich has been watching and plotting to regain the Giant's hoard. Wotan, the Wanderer, makes his appearance. Both seek the Ring. Abusing each other, they wake Fafner to warn him that he can only save his life by handing over the Ring. The dragon Giant yawns.

Aber – wie sah meine Mutter wohl aus? ('I wonder how my mother looked'): Siegfried's poignant thoughts of his dead mother

Mime leads Siegfried, carrying the newly made Nothung, to the cave and leaves him there pondering on his mother, listening to the murmurs of the forest and the beautiful call of a forest bird. The dragon returns and is

Hei! Siegfried gehört nun der Niblungen Hort! ('Hi! Now Siegfried holds the Niblungs' gold'): the bird's song can suddenly be understood by Siegfried, having tasted the dragon's blood

killed by Siegfried. Splashed with the dragon's blood, he can suddenly understand the forest bird's song telling him about the Nibelungs' hoard in the cave and Mime's design.

After arguing with his brother Alberich, Mime now returns to carry out his plan to poison Siegfried and obtain the Ring and the Tarnhelm. He, betrayed by his own words, is killed by his intended victim, Siegfried. Bearing the Tarnhelm and the Ring, the hero is led by the forest bird towards the mountain where Brünnhilde lies sleeping, surrounded by flames.

On the mountainside

Um der Götter Ende grämt mich die Angst nicht ('The downfall of the Gods no longer troubles me'): Wotan's weary acceptance of the inevitable, having listened to Erda

Das ist kein Mann! Brennender Zauber zückt mir ins Herz ('My heart is filled with mystical pain'): Siegfried stands astonished at Brünnhilde's beauty as she lies asleep on her rock

ACT III

The Wanderer summons Erda to ask her advice as to whether the Gods' downfall can be averted. She cannot help. Siegfried arrives, rudely challenging the stranger (who, unknown to him, is his grandfather). Taunted by the arrogant young man, Wotan tries to bar his way with his spear, but Siegfried shatters it with Nothung. Wotan, his power ended, disappears.

Now at last there is a hero whose will is proved independent of the Gods. Reaching the summit and passing unafraid through the flames, he finds a figure in heavy armour. Cutting it loose, he is amazed to find a beautiful woman. Waking her with a kiss, they find that their love for each other overcomes even Brünnhilde's fear for the Gods' destruction.

GÖTTERDÄMMERUNG

(TWILIGHT OF THE GODS)

Gunther, King of the Gibichungs	baritone
Gutrune, his sister	soprano
Hagen, son of Alberich by their mother	bass
Alberich, his father	bass-baritone
Siegfried	tenor
Brünnhilde	soprano
Waltraute, her sister	mezzo-soprano

Part IV of *Der Ring*: Hagen, son of Alberich, conspires with the Gibichungs Gunther and Gutrune. His intention is to gain the Ring. Siegfried and Gunther are killed by him and, as he is about to claim the prize, Brünnhilde intervenes. The Ring returns to the Rhinemaidens and Alberich's curse is laid to rest as Valhalla passes away

The Valkyries' rock

Zu neuen Taten ('New triumphs'): Brünnhilde urges her lover to new deeds of glory, and this leads to an ecstatic duet

The Hall of the Gibichungs

Siegfried, der Wälsungen Spross ('Siegfried, son of Wälse'): Hagen explains to Gunther that only Siegfried was brave enough to win Brünnhilde

Hier sitz ich zur Wacht ('I need only sit here and wait'): Hagen's glee as he thinks of possessing the Ring, the Nibelung treasure

The Valkyries' rock

Höre mit Sinn ('Listen carefully'): Waltraute's description of Wotan's preparations for the end of the power of the Gods

PRELUDE

The three Norns (the mythical Fates) reminisce while spinning the sacred rope which weaves the destiny of the world. Suddenly the rope breaks and the Norns vanish in despair.

Siegfried and Brünnhilde emerge from their cave. He gives her the Ring as a token of his love for her; in exchange she gives him Grane her horse to accompany him on his travels until he has proved his heroism further and can return to her again.

ACT I

An orchestral interlude depicts Siegfried's journey to the Rhine. Gunther feels that his standing is insufficiently noble and Hagen suggests that it would be enhanced if he were able to win Brünnhilde. The Gibichung family's renown would be still greater if Gutrune (Gunther's sister) could for her part win Siegfried as her husband. While brother and sister lament that they cannot aspire to such success, Hagen (Alberich's son by Grimhilde, the mother of Gunther and Gutrune, thus, their half-brother) reminds Gutrune that he has a love potion which will bewitch anyone who drinks its. Siegfried is known to pass often on the Rhine and just then they hear his horn. He enters and they greet him. Hagen already knows well the significance of the Tarnhelm and the Ring, which he learns from Siegfried is now on Brünnhilde's finger. When Gutrune brings Siegfried a drink, he raises the cup in honour of Brünnhilde. As soon as he drinks, he falls under the spell, declaring his love for Gutrune. Gunther offers her to Siegfried as wife if he will win Brünnhilde for Gunther. Siegfried offers to transform himself into the likeness of Gunther by means of the Tarnhelm, using his own courage to pass through the flames into Brünnhilde's cave. Sealing this pact with their blood, Siegfried hurries off on his errand, leaving Hagen delighted at his own success and eagerly awaiting the Ring.

The Ring is precious to Brünnhilde as a memento of Siegfried. Her sister Waltraute approaches. Waltraute describes Wotan's decline. She paints a vivid picture of Wotan with all the Gods grouped around his throne. The Valkyries sit at his feet and the heroes have heaped up timber into a pyre to consume them all. To save Valhalla, the fateful Ring should be returned to the Rhinemaidens thus removing the curse. But Brünnhilde, herself now a victim of the curse, will not relinquish it and sends her sister back empty-handed.

A stranger steps through the flames encircling her and pulls the Ring from her finger, dragging her into a cave for the night. It is Siegfried (disguised by the Tarnhelm as Gunther), and, because she has not renounced love, the Ring gives her no protection. He spends the night in the cave with her, though separated by his sword.

On the banks of the Rhine
Schläfst du, Hagen, mein Sohn?
('Are you sleeping, Hagen my son?'): Alberich appears to his son to encourage the plan and explain the need for Siegfried's death
Heil! Heil! Willkommen! ('Hail! Hail and welcome!'): the Gibichung vassals greet Gunther and Brünnhilde

ACT II
Alberich appears to his son in his sleep and encourages him in his malevolent scheming. He explains that Siegfried alone is untouched by the curse on the Ring and must therefore be destroyed in order that Alberich and Hagen may enjoy its power undisturbed.

Siegfried returns and tell Hagen how he won Brünnhilde for Gunther. He claims Gutrune as his bride. All prepare for the ceremonial welcome of Gunther and Gutrune, and Hagen organizes a feast.

Brünnhilde, led into the hall by Gunther, is astonished to find Siegfried there. When she is told that he is Gutrune's husband and sees that he is wearing the Ring taken from her, she claims in bewilderment that it was stolen from her by Gunther. He denies giving it to Siegfried, who says that he acquired it when he killed the dragon. She cries out that she has been betrayed, that it is Siegfried to whom she is married. The guests are stunned by the accusation. Siegfried, all memory destroyed by Hagen's potion, denies any guilt and willingly swears on Hagen's spear, inviting death from its point if what he says is not true.

Helle Wehr! ('On this bright blade!'): Siegfried's oath that he has never dishonoured Brünnhilde

Enraged, Brünnhilde seizes the spear, invoking its vengeance against the man who has so deceitfully broken his vow. Siegfried scornfully advises Gunther to let his new wife sleep off her madness. While he and Gutrune lead the way to the feast, Brünnhilde is left miserably confused.

Welche Unholds List ('What evil deception'): Brünnhilde cannot understand Siegfried's treachery

Hagen offers himself as her avenger but, sneering at his inadequacy, she bitterly reflects that Siegfried is protected against attack. Since, however, he would never turn his back on an enemy, there alone is he unprotected, Hagen, with Gunther's agreement, plans to murder him the next day, claiming the Ring as his price.

On the banks of the Rhine

ACT III
As the three Rhinemaidens play in the water, dreaming of the return of their gold, they see Siegfried on the river bank. He has lost track of the bear he was pursuing and they offer to help him in return for the Ring. They flirt with him and as they swim away he suddenly feels inclined to give it to them. In a moment they are back. They warn him of the curse and of his approaching death if he does not quickly surrender it. But now his courage

flares up at their threats and he insists he is a match for any danger.

Horns announce the arrival of Hagen and Gunther. Siegfried entertains them by how he forged Nothung, slew the dragon and was helped by a bird to outwit Mime. Encouraged by his audience, he continues with his story up to and including the moment when he found himself in Brünnhilde's arms. As Gunther jumps to his feet in horror, two ravens despatched by Wotan to bring news of the end flutter into the sky, flying down the Rhine. As Hagen points to them, Siegfried turns to watch them and Hagen plunges his spear into Siegfried's back. He walks away as Siegfried calls out a last impassioned greeting to Brünnhilde before dying. The huntsmen lift his body on to his shield. An orchestral interlude accompanies their procession back to the castle.

Mime heiss ein mürrischer Zwerg ('Mime was the name of the ill-natured Dwarf'): Siegfried reminisces about his past

Brünnhilde! Heilige Braut! ('Brünnhilde my sacred bride!'): Siegfried's dying image of his lost wife
The Funeral March

The Hall of the Gibichungs

Gutrune's sleep has been disturbed by fears for Siegfried. There is no sign of Brünnhilde. Then the funeral procession appears. Gutrune flings herself across Siegfried's body and Gunther, who has turned against Hagen, curses him for his cowardly attack. Hagen now claims the Ring and, when Gunther tries to stop him, Hagen cuts him down. With a triumphant cry he runs to take it from Siegfried's finger, but to his horror the corpse's hand begins to rise. As Hagen backs away, Brünnhilde enters.

Assuming command, Brünnhilde orders the building of a colossal funeral pyre. She sings the praises of the dead hero and calls out to the ravens, sending them home to tell Wotan that all is at an end. Putting the Ring on her finger, she flings a flaming torch on to the pyre and mounts her horse. Together they leap into the flames. With a great surge, the Rhine overflows its banks bringing with it the Rhinemaidens, who now regain the Ring. Hagen with a last angry cry tries to take it back, and the Rhinemaidens pull him under the water. In the sky the fire has taken hold of the wood piled up against Valhalla. The curse on the Ring is purged by Brünnhilde's sacrifice of herself and, as the orchestra for the last time plays the majestic Valhalla motif, the power of the Gods passes away in the inferno. The orchestra announces, in the closing bars, the beginning of a new era: that of redemption through love.

Starke Scheite schichtet mir dort ('Your strongest wood'): Brünnhilde commands the building of Siegfried's funeral pyre

Zurück vom Ring! ('Give back the Ring!'): Hagen's last attempt to reclaim the Ring

PARSIFAL

Amfortas, leader of the knights of the Grail	baritone
Gurnemanz, an elderly knight of the Grail	bass
Kundry, a wild woman	soprano
Klingsor, a magician, enemy of the knights	bass
Parsifal	tenor

Montsalvat, Spain, 10th century: Amfortas lost the sacred Spear to Klingsor and sustained a wound that can be healed only by a holy fool. This is Parsifal. As Amfortas is about to perform the ceremony of the Holy Grail for the last time, Parsifal appears.

This, Wagner's last opera is a deeply religious work, blending Christian and pagan mythology. The composer's libretto is based principally on Wolfram von Eschenbach's poem *Parzival*. The first performance took the form of the dedication of the Bayreuth Festspielhaus in 1882. Wagner forbade the production of the opera outside Bayreuth even to Ludwig of Bavaria, who had provided so much support for it.

The domain of the Grail

Durch Mitleid wissend ('Understanding through compassion'): Amfortas reveals that the wound inflicted by Klingsor can be healed only by a holy fool

ACT I

Gurnemanz and his companions offer a morning prayer. Amfortas is to bathe in the lake to soothe his wound. Kundry, in wild disarray, brings a balsam from Arabia as a cure for Amfortas, who is carried in on a litter.

Gurnemanz now reveals that Amfortas was entrusted by his father, King Titurel, with the Holy Grail and the sacred Spear, used to pierce Christ's side at the Crucifixion. Klingsor, prevented by his wrongdoings from becoming a knight of the Grail, arranged for Amfortas to be seduced by a beautiful girl in a magic garden. He stole the Spear and with it wounded Amfortas. Only a holy fool (*der reine Tor*) can heal the wound and recover the Spear, he repeats.

A wounded swan flies across the lake, to the horror of those assembled. It was shot by a young man (Parsifal). Penitent, he knows little about himself: not even his name. He is shocked by Kundry's disclosure that his mother, who brought him up apart from the world, is dead. Gurnemanz wonders whether he might be the chosen one.

Hall of the Knights
Mein Sohn Amfortas ('Amfortas, my son'): the voice of Titurel, father of Amfortas, at the beginning of the ceremony at which the Grail is revealed

At Holy Communion, at which Amfortas has to be persuaded to perform his sacred office, the Grail is revealed to the bewildered young man. Gurnemanz, who is angered by his passivity, sends him on his way, slamming the door angrily behind him.

Klingsor's magic castle

ACT II

Klingsor orders Kundry, who is in his power, to exercise her charms on the approaching Parsifal as she once did on Amfortas.

The magic garden
Ihr schönen Kinder ('You beautiful children'): Parsifal, leaping into the garden, flatters the flower maidens

Klingsor vanishes and the garden is filled with flower maidens. They try to ensnare Parsifal, but he stands aloof. Kundry appears, now a voluptuous beauty, and she surprises him by calling him by his name, of which he was ignorant. She instructs him further on his origins, telling him that his mother died of grief when he strayed from her. Weakened by remorse, Parsifal begins to yield to her, and she kisses him on the lips. Then he reminds himself of Amfortas' plight and draws back. He learns that Kundry's present state is a punishment for laughing at Christ on the Cross. As Parsifal finally rejects Kundry, she calls for Klingsor, for though Parsifal may save her, she is obliged to try to entrap him.

Klingsor hurls the Spear at Parsifal. He catches it and makes with it the sign of the Cross. The castle falls in ruins. As he leaves, Parsifal calls to Kundry that she knows where to find him again.

A meadow in the domain of the Grail

ACT III

Gurnemanz, now an old man, discovers the unconsious Kundry and revives her. She pledges herself to serving him. Parsifal appears. Clad in black armour, he is at first unrecognized. He kneels in prayer before the Spear, which he has thrust into the ground. As they recognize each other, Parsifal tells Gurnemanz of his years of wandering and that he has now been directed to bring home the holy relic. Amfortas, he learns, yearns for death as an end to his torture and believes that this may be achieved by refusing to unveil the Grail. Parsifal blames himself for all this misery. Gurnemanz and Kundry anoint him with water and with balsam from a golden phial. His first act as king is to forgive and to baptize Kundry.

Hall of the Knights

Nur eine Waffe taugt ('This one weapon'): Parsifal, understanding Amfortas' suffering, heals his wound with the sacred Spear

Together they proceed to the Knights' Hall. This is the day of Titurel's funeral and Amfortas has sworn to reveal the Grail for the last time, but he is demanding to be slain. As the knights cry for him to perform his duty to his father, Parsifal appears. With the Spear he touches Amfortas' wound and it miraculously heals. Ascending to the altar, Parsifal takes the Grail, which glows bright. From above comes a white dove. Kundry sinks lifeless to the ground. With the Grail, Parsifal blesses the kneeling knights.

CARL MARIA VON WEBER

Born Eutin 1786, died London 1826. Studying for a time with Haydn's brother, Weber published his first piece of music at the age of 12; his first opera *Das Waldmädchen* (1800) was performed when he was 14. A piano virtuoso, influential music critic and talented conductor, he held a series of posts as director of music. In the latter role he revolutionized opera production, supervising every detail himself and reorganizing the structure of the opera orchestra. *Der Freischütz* (1821), which appeared at a time when German nationalism was an emerging force, is a harbinger of German Romantic opera. His portrayal of familiar, everyday aspects of German life, combined with supernatural elements, was to influence Wagner. Its success brought commissions from Vienna for *Euryanthe* (1823) and from Covent Garden for *Oberon* (1826).

DER FREISCHUTZ

(THE FREESHOOTER)

Max, a forester	tenor
Kuno, the chief forester	bass
Agathe, his daughter	soprano
Kaspar, a forester	bass
Samiel, the black huntsman	speaking part
Prince Ottokar	tenor

Bohemia, mid-18th century: to win the hand of Agathe, Max must prove himself as a marksman. To this end, he submits to the evil influence of Kaspar, but is in the end victorious.

The libretto is by Johann Friedrich Kind and the opera was first performed in Berlin in 1821. *Der Freischütz* can be seen as the bridge between Mozart and Wagner in the development of specifically German opera. Wagner saw it in Dresden aged nine, conducted by Weber, and it was his favourite opera.

Outside a woodland tavern

Durch die Wälder ('Through the forests'): Max's memories of a happier time, when he and Agathe together enjoyed the triumphs of his marksmanship

ACT I

Max, a forester, is in love with Agathe, daughter of Kuno, whose hereditary job as chief forester will pass to whoever becomes his son-in-law. Max, perhaps because of the evil influence of the demonic Samiel, seems to have lost his skill with the gun and has been defeated in a contest by a local peasant. Kuno tells him that he may not marry Agathe if he fails again, by order of the Prince.

Kaspar has learned of the legend of the 'free' bullets (six always hit their mark, but the seventh is directed by the Devil). Max, in despair, listens to Kaspar's story of the

Schweig, schweig ('Softly, softly'): Kaspar's sinister aria in which he gloats on his impending revenge for the loss of Agathe

A room in the forester's house
Kommt ein schlanker Bursch gegangen ('When a pretty boy approaches'): Agathe's friend describes the pleasures of flirting
Leise, leise, fromme Weise! ('Gently, lightly, lift my song'): Agathe's prayer that she and Max may find happiness together

The Wolf's Glen, lit by the moon with thunderstorms approaching

The forest

Agathe's room

Und ob die Wolke ('Behind the clouds the sun continues, everlasting in the sky'): Agathe's cavatina, trusting in God's continuing protection
Einst träumte meiner sel'gen Base ('My cousin dreamed before she died'): the friend's ironical counter to Agathe's forebodings

'free' shot. He aims with Kaspar's gun at an eagle high in the sky and, thanks to Samiel's intervention, it falls to the ground. Max is convinced. Kaspar reveals that this was his last bullet, and they agree to meet in a forbidden place to make a new set.

ACT II
Agathe and her friend, rehanging a family portrait, sing about the pleasure of courting. Agathe goes out into the moonlight. She hears Max approaching through the trees and sings a beautiful song of welcome which becomes more passionate as he gets nearer. He is in a confused state and lies to her about the shooting contest which he has lost. He has brought her the eagle and says that he must go quickly to the Wolf's Glen to collect a stag he has shot leaving Agathe worried and afraid.

To a background of ghostly voices, Kaspar, who has sold his soul to Samiel, bargains with Samiel to extend his time on earth. He, for his part, will deliver Max as his new victim and suggests that the seventh bullet be guided by Samiel to strike down Agathe. Samiel's voice grants him a further three years.

Max arrives and is disturbed by the appearance of his mother's ghost warning him. Kaspar calls on Samiel to drive away this phantom and that of Agathe, who seems ready to throw herself into the waterfall. Together they cast the bullets and Kaspar chants a spell over them, his voice echoing through the growing storm. Max calls out the name of Samiel, who disappears as Max makes the sign of the Cross.

ACT III
Kaspar and Max have divided the bullets between them, Max taking four. Max has used three and has greatly impressed Prince Ottokar. Kaspar has shot two at magpies. Kaspar refuses to give his last bullet to Max, who also has only one left, and he shoots it into the air.

Agathe, already dressed for the wedding, tells her friend of her terrible dream concerning a white dove. Her friend answers with a ridiculous tale of a nightmare in which a ghost turns out to be dog. This displeases Agathe. The chorus of bridesmaids arrives. Another ill omen is seen by Agathe in the delivery of a box containing a silver funeral wreath instead of a wedding bouquet. The chorus is taken up again but in a more subdued manner.

A romantic landscape

For the final contest, the Prince, who has already approved Max's marriage to Agathe and eventual succession to Kuno's post, orders Max to fire his last 'free' shot at a white dove. Agathe appears and, as he fires, calls out to him not to shoot. The dove flies away but both she and Kaspar (who was watching from a tree) fall. In the confusion, a mysterious Hermit goes to the help of Agathe. As she revives, it is seen to be Kaspar who is dying from the shot. He appears to have recognized in the Hermit heavenly intervention. Seeing Samiel approaching to claim him, he gives a final curse and dies. The Prince angrily sentences Max to exile, but the Hermit intervenes to ask that Max should serve a year of atonement instead. This the Prince grants, and all give thanks for God's mercy.

Du, Samiel, schon hier? ('Is that you, Samiel?'): the dying Kaspar's recognition that the price of his bargain must be paid

OBERON

In three acts, with text (in English) by James Robertson Planché, after Christopher Wieland's play based on the 13th-century ballad *Huon de Bordeaux*. Premiere: Covent Garden, London, 1826. Weber died only six weeks after conducting the premiere of this opera, in which lengthy dialogue, in old pantomime style, interrupts much beautiful fairy-tale music.

France, Baghdad and Tunis, 9th century: after the famous overture, Oberon (t), King of the Fairies, who has quarrelled with his wife Titania (sp), vows not to see her again until he has found a pair of constant lovers. With magical assistance from Puck (s) and to expiate his murder of Charlemagne's son, Sir Huon (t) travels to claim the Caliph of Baghdad's daughter Reiza (s); his squire Sherasmin (bar) rescues her attendant Fatima (ms). The four are shipwrecked: Reiza, alone, sings her great *scena*: 'Ocean, thou mighty monster'. After capture by pirates and slavery in Tunis, they are pardoned by Charlemagne (sp). Oberon acclaims the lovers' constancy.

KURT WEILL

Born Dessau 1900, died New York 1950. He studied with Humperdinck in Berlin before working in opera as répétiteur. From then on, apart from study with Busoni, the stage was always his main concern. He experimented with new forms of music theatre, collaborating particularly with Brecht. In 1943 he became a US citizen and turned to musical comedy. His first opera was *Der Protagonist* (1925). Apart from *Aufstieg und Fall der Stadt Mahagonny* (1930), *Die Dreigroschenoper (The Threepenny Opera*, 1928) is regularly performed; less often *Happy End* (1929), *Die Sieben Todsünden (The Seven Deadly Sins*, 1933) and *Street Scene* (1946).

AUFSTIEG UND FALL DER STADT MAHAGONNY
(RISE AND FALL OF THE CITY OF MAHAGONNY)

In three acts, with text by Bertolt Brecht. Premiere: Neues Theater, Leipzig, 1930. Weill's most purely operatic work blends elements of grand opera, neo-classicism and the popular, especially jazz and cabaret.

Gangster-land America. Three escaped convicts, Leocadia Begbick (**ms**), Fatty the book-keeper (**t**) and Trinity Moses (**bar**) set up a city of material pleasure, Mahagonny. They are joined by Jenny (**s**), a Cuban mulatto, and six prostitutes, and later by Jim Mahoney (**t**) and fellow Alaskan lumber-jacks. Jenny and Jim begin an affair. The city narrowly escapes a hurricane, after which all adopt the motto 'Nothing barred' (the name of the tavern) and indulge in turn in food, sex, prize-fights and drink to excess, Jimmy runs out of cash – the only thing that is forbidden – and goes to the electric chair after trial and a tender farewell with Jenny. Disillusion and inflation bring the city to its knees.

INDEX

e, F.M.

The international
opera guide

AUG 9 1

For Reference

Not to be taken from this room